AF699561

Marxism, Central Planning, and the Soviet Economy

Alexander Erlich
1982

Marxism, Central Planning, and the Soviet Economy

Economic Essays in Honor of Alexander Erlich

edited by
Padma Desai

The MIT Press
Cambridge, Massachusetts
London, England

© 1983 by
The Massachusetts Institute of Technology

All rights reserved. No part of this book may be reproduced in any form or by any means, electronic or mechanical, including photocopying, recording, or by any information storage and retrieval system, without permission in writing from the publisher.

This book was set in Baskerville by Asco Trade Typesetting Ltd., Hong Kong and printed and bound by Murray Printing Company in the United States of America.

Library of Congress Cataloging in Publication Data
Main entry under title:

Marxism, central planning, and the Soviet economy.

Includes bibliographies and index.
1. Soviet Union—Economic policy—1917– —Addresses, essays, lectures.
2. Soviet Union—Economic conditions—1918– —Addresses, essays, lectures.
3. Marxian economics—Addresses, essays, lectures. 4. Erlich, Alexander—Addresses, essays, lectures. I. Erlich, Alexander. II. Desai, Padma.
HC335.M368 1983 330.947 83-7962
ISBN 0-262-04071-9

HC
335
.M1368
1983

Contents

List of Contributors

Kenneth J. Arrow
Stanford University

Abram Bergson
Harvard University

Joseph S. Berliner
Brandeis University

Robert W. Campbell
Indiana University

Padma Desai
Columbia University

Richard E. Ericson
Harvard University

Duncan K. Foley
Columbia University

Gregory Grossman
University of California, Berkeley

Franklyn D. Holzman
Tufts University

Holland Hunter
Haverford College

Ricardo Martin
World Bank

Richard Portes
University of London

John E. Roemer
University of California, Davis

Paul A. Samuelson
Massachusetts Institute of Technology

Martin L. Weitzman
Massachusetts Institute of Technology

Introduction

This festschrift in honor of Alexander Erlich includes contributions by leading theorists and experts on the theory and policy of centrally planned economies (CPEs) and the Soviet economy. The first part on Marxism has essays on different aspects of Marxist economic theory by Paul Samuelson, Duncan Foley, and John Roemer. The second part is on resource allocation and international comparisons in CPEs. The chapters by Kenneth Arrow, Padma Desai and Ricardo Martin, and Richard Ericson address the problem of efficient resource allocation: Arrow discusses decentralized resource allocation from a team theory viewpoint, Desai and Martin analyze the conceptual problems of measuring resource allocational efficiency in a CPE, and Ericson explores the role of second-economy markets in achieving an equilibrium allocation in the institutional framework of a Soviet-type economy. The two contributions by Abram Bergson and Martin Weitzman deal with the complex conceptual issues raised by the need to compare CPE economic performance with that of a market economy, whereas Franklyn Holzman discusses the interaction between CPEs and market economies with a case study of dumping of Polish golf carts. The chapter by Richard Portes is on the monetary economics of central planning. The four essays in the final part are on the Soviet economy. Holland Hunter and Gregory Grossman explore the theme of early Soviet industrialization with emphasis on its goal and performance, whereas Joseph Berliner and Robert Campbell deal respectively with subjects of recent interest such as social structure and fertility and energy policies in the Soviet Union.

I would like to thank William Baumol, Joseph Berliner, Jagdish Bhagwati, Susan Cochrane, Gregory Grossman, Edward Hewett, Franklyn Holzman, Charles Kindelberger, Jacob Mincer, Don Patinkin, Paul Samuelson, and Martin Weitzman for helping me edit several of the essays. My special thanks are due to Jonathan Sanders who took the attractive photograph of Alexander Erlich for the volume.

The task of putting together the collection has extended over many months. It was eased beyond measure by the promptness of the contributors in submitting their pieces and their readiness in carrying out revisions. Indeed it was an altogether pleasurable activity. I extend my appreciation to all of them.

Alexander Erlich: Biographical Sketch

Alexander Erlich was born on December 6, 1912, in St. Petersburg. His father, Henryk Erlich, was a lawyer by profession but spent most of his time in political activities of the Jewish Socialist Bund. His mother, Sophie Dubnov, had studied literature and philosophy at St. Petersburg University and wrote poetry. His grandfather, Simon Dubnov, the eminent Jewish historian was a liberal and an ardent admirer of John Stuart Mill.

Alex graduated from Warsaw High School in June 1930. He spent his undergraduate years at Berlin University. In 1934 he enrolled as a student of the Free Polish University, studied economics, and participated in the youth organization of the Bund. That same year he married Rachel Fligiel, herself a leading activist of the Bundist youth movement. Alex and Rachel have only one child, Miriam.

In April 1941 the Erlich family migrated to the United States. A few years later Alex resumed his graduate studies at the New School for Social Research. He wrote his doctoral dissertation under the guidance of Eduard Heimann, Adolph Lowe, and Hans Neisser and in close contact with Abba Lerner. It was published under the title of *The Soviet Industrialization Debate: 1924–1928* by Harvard University Press in 1960. In 1955 Alex began a long teaching career at Columbia University offering courses on the History of Economic Thought, Marxism, and the Soviet and Eastern European Economies. From 1966 till his retirement in 1981, he was Professor of Economics at the University. He is now Professor Emeritus of Economics and is working on a book on the *Economics of Socialism* for Pantheon Books.

These are the biographical details and dates in Alex's life. They suggest only tangentially the rich texture of his life, its turbulence and its pain, and they do not convey his concern with Marxism and socialism as economic doctrines culminating in his decision to interpret the Soviet industrialization debates to western scholars. Indeed Alex matured as a scholar and a socialist in the midst of unprecedented social and political upheaval. Perhaps, as a result he has become part of the European tradition of socialist thinkers who have also actively participated in socialist and liberal causes. What distinguishes Alex is his profound humanism so that, while he has supported radical causes, he has also fought against authoritarian tactics to promote them. And while he has struggled with personal misfortunes and professional problems, he has managed to retain his mellowness, kindness, and above all his sense of humor.

The Turbulent Years of Childhood and Youth

Alex's childhood memories begin at the age of five with the fateful events of 1917. Throughout the year, the pace of life in the Erlich household was hectic. Henryk Erlich spent days and nights away from home in the meetings of the Petrograd Soviet where he represented the Bund and worked closely with the Menshevik majority. Alex also recalls the May Day of 1917: the Petrograd workers were exuberant at the collapse of the oppressive tsarist regime and the Bolshevik stranglehold of political activity had not yet begun. Then there was the night of November 6 during which the family was awake listening to the thunder of heavy artillery from the battleship Aurora. The Bolshevik revolution had begun.

In the summer of 1918 the family moved to Lublin in Central Poland which was at that time under Austrian-German occupation. Lublin was Henryk Erlich's birthplace, and the move was intended to last out the unsettled condition in St. Petersburg. Soon after, Poland's political fortunes changed dramatically. Germany and Austria capitulated in the war, and Poland regained its independence. The Socialist Bund which was most active in the Polish part of the tsarist empire emerged in the open as a political force, and Henryk Erlich as one of its acknowledged leaders remained in Poland and immersed himself in the activities of the Bund lasting throughout the interwar period.

Alex was enrolled as a student in a Warsaw school. In November 1927, while in high school, he joined the youth organization of the Bund. His first act of protest came within a year. At that time Marshal Pilsudski ruled Poland with an iron hand. He had no doubt come to power in May 1926 after a military coup supported by the entire left. However, he had revealed antidemocratic tendencies right from the start. As was to be expected, Alex refused to sign the address of homage to the marshal on the tenth anniversary of Polish independence and was suspended from school. His first act of protest was thus aimed at the authoritarian rule of the marshal who governed Poland. It was perhaps a foolhardy act for a teenager, but it set the tone of many more protests that followed. The suspension was revoked by the principal who sent a letter to that effect, but Alex's father deemed its contents insolent. Alex was transferred to another school with a more liberal principal.

Having graduated from high school in June 1930, Alex moved to Berlin with a firm resolve to study economics. Immediately upon arriving, he joined the socialist student union. Over time this was followed by participation in the activities of the Social Democratic Party (SPD). While Hitler waited in the wings, the conservative Bruening government pursued its deflationary policies with disastrous consequences. In January 1933 Hitler came to power. Alex lived through the first twenty-five days of his takeover and went back to Warsaw as he always did for the long Easter recess. A couple of days after his departure, the Reichstag was set on fire, and Nazi purges were unleashed in full force. Alex still contemplated returning to Berlin in the spring. However, the new president of Berlin University, a Nazi appointee, made the decision for him by sending him an official letter of expulsion.

Alex stayed back in Warsaw, enrolled at the Free Polish University and became a member of the Bundist student group. In Polish universities, antisemitic violence was rising. At the same time the working class was getting restive and militant, and the intellectuals were increasingly concerned about the profascist tendencies of the Pilsudski regime and of his successors. The atmosphere of the Free University, however, was less oppressive. Being a private school, it was exempted from the ministerial regulation that had introduced "Ghetto Benches" for Jewish students. However, the privileged position did not deter Alex from protesting acts of antisemitic violence, in particular the infamous regulation, and supporting the striking workers. He was officially reprimanded for asking his class to rise in memory of the striking workers of Cracow and Lwow who were killed by the police.

By the spring of 1938 Alex had started working on his Master's thesis on the theme of the Russian serf-labor manofactories in the eighteenth century. He was ill, and the work got off to a slow start. It came to an end with the German invasion of Poland in September 1939. The Polish government had initially decided that Warsaw would not be defended. Subsequently, the decision was reversed, but by that time the mass exodus had begun. In the meantime, the Soviet army had moved into Eastern Poland on the basis of a secret addendum to the Stalin-Hitler pact.

On the night of September 6, 1939, the Erlich family left Warsaw for Eastern Poland. Little did they anticipate the tragic events that were to stalk them along the way. While they were escaping Hitler's atrocities, they were walking into Stalin's expanding conquests of Polish territories and his annexation, in 1940, of the free Baltic republics. As part of the mass exodus from Warsaw, Alex and Rachel traveled in one group, his parents and younger brother, Victor, with another. They were reunited for several days in Pinsk which was already under Soviet control. Later Henryk Erlich left for Brest-Litovsk on a party errand. The plan of the family was to get together again in Vilno. They never saw him again.

They stayed in Vilno for eight months. Victor Erlich's future wife who had escaped from German-occupied Warsaw joined them later. At that time Vilno belonged to Lithuania. Now its fate, like that of the family, was at the mercy of Stalin's ruthless designs. The city was occupied by the Soviet army in September 1939, turned over to Lithuania in early October, and again occupied by the Soviet army in June 1940. Indeed, the three Baltic states of Lithuania, Latvia, and Estonia were annexed with Soviet territories in 1940.

The family went into hiding and struggled to get an exit visa. As luck would have it, the NKVD agents in Lithuania, new to their jobs, failed to identify them as Henryk Erlich's family. Alex, Rachel, and their newborn daughter, Miriam, traveled across the Soviet Union and reached the United States by way of Japan in April 1941.

The war years were heartbreaking: Alex worried about his father's fate and followed news of mass deportations of Polish Jews to Hitler's death camps. In December 1941 he learned about his father's second arrest by the Soviet police. As a matter of fact, Henryk Erlich who had left Pinsk for Brest-Litovsk on that fateful day in September 1939 was arrested by the Soviet secret police at the Brest-Litovsk railway station. Victor Alter, his close friend and associate in the Bund, had been arrested a week earlier. They were interned in Moscow's Butyrki prison on the absurd charges of being Polish spies. However, on June 22, 1941, Hitler suddenly attacked the Soviet Union. In the initial months of military setbacks and disarray, Stalin was desperate for support, even from old adversaries. Erlich and Alter were freed in September 1941 as part of a general amnesty for Polish citizens and were asked to form an international committee to mobilize Jewish public opinion and financial resources in the West to support the war effort. However, it is believed that, as the danger of an imminent military defeat was averted, Stalin decided to dispense with Erlich and Alter. After all, they were acknowledged to be influential Polish leaders who would fight for an independent Poland after the war. They were moved from Moscow in mid-October to Kuibyshev which was then the temporary Soviet capital. At midnight on December 4, they were rearrested. It was news of this second arrest that Alex received in New York. A frantic but largely unpublicized campaign to secure their release proved futile. In February 1943 Maxim Litvinov, the Soviet Ambassador to the United States, informed several eminent signatories of a telegram demanding their release that Henryk Erlich and Victor Alter were tried and executed in December 1941. Around the same time Simon Dubnov was executed by the Nazis in Riga.

One must need a resilient temperament and a sturdy psyche to survive tragedies of such dimensions. Alex Erlich has more than survived them: he has retained his humanity and balance. He could have been self-righteous: instead he is tolerant of disagreements with his opponents while firmly wedded to his beliefs and values. He could have been cynical: instead he has continued supporting causes and remained loving and loyal.

The Study of Socialism and Soviet Industrialization Debate

Alex's interest in socialist doctrine and Marxist theory dates back to his high school years. It is clear that it arose out of concern with social and political issues of the day and was nurtured by the family environment. As a result Alex pursued Marxist-Socialist writings as ardently as he fought for causes. The dual drive implied that he could not have been an armchair Marxist scholar: he had to match his scholarship with a deep commitment to actual causes.

In high school he began pursuing Marxist literature with Karl Kautsky's popularization in German, continued with Bazarov's rendering of Marx's *Das Kapital* in Russian, finally ending with the original Marx. His command of Russian and German were invaluable for the purpose. He was influenced also by the Austrian variation of Marxism rendered by Otto Bauer. After his graduation from high school, Alex found it difficult to study socialist economic theory in the ill-defined program of economics in Polish universities where economics was taught in the faculty of law. Alex had little inclination and hardly any talent for the legal profession. He therefore went to Berlin and enrolled himself in the department of State and Social Sciences. There was an added attraction of going to Berlin: his grandparents had moved to Berlin, and Alex looked forward to the opportunity of staying with them.

Alex remembers a rather disappointing first year of studies in economics at Berlin. Economic theory was not Germany's forte at the time, and Berlin was not an exception. Instead he found participation in the informal study groups of the socialist student union stimulating, in particular because they were led by a gifted young economist Mark Mitnitzsky who had been a junior colleague of Jacob Marschak at Heidelberg. Mitnitzsky accepted substantial elements of Marxian economics but emphatically rejected the labor theory of value. At eighteen, Alex was steeped in Marxist orthodoxy and put up a strong resistance. Alas, he felt ill-equipped for the task and dug deeper in the debates between Böhm-Bawerk and his Marxist opponents. The academic environment at Berlin improved considerably when Emil Lederer, the eminent German economist and a rare socialist academic of his generation moved to Berlin from Heidelberg. While Alex held on to his youthful orthodoxy, he found Lederer's lectures and writings in which he synthesized Marxian and post-Marxian economics stimulating: even more inspiring were Lederer's personal charm and the courage of his convictions. Lederer was forced to go into hiding after Hitler's rise to power, finally reaching the United States where he was one of the cofounders of the Graduate Faculty of the New School for Social Research. Two of the many books Alex read during his Berlin period stand out in his memory. They were both brilliant and iconoclastic from different perspectives: Gyorgy Lukacs's *History and Class Consciousness* and Joseph Schumpeter's *Wesen und Hauptinhalt der theoretischen Nationalökonomie*. The latter, Schumpeter's first major and sparkling work, was never translated into English.

In Berlin, Alex maintained interest in Soviet economic development too. The first Five Year Plan was in full swing and was vigorously debated by socialists, Russian and non-Russian alike. There was no consensus among the participants: some of them characterized it as an economic and political disaster while others, like Otto Bauer, viewed it as a cruel but historically inevitable way of laying the foundations of socialism in a backward country. They were hoping that, after strengthening its economic basis, the system would finally evolve into a genuine socialist democracy. Alex felt that the truth was somewhere in between. Many years later he provided a definitive opinion on the subject.

Having left Hitler's Germany, Alex was back in Warsaw at the Free Polish University. It was the Polish equivalent of the New School for Social Research. In contrast to other Polish universities, it had a separate department of social sciences with only a minimum of courses in law. However, the teaching of economic theory was dismal, sociology was only slightly better, and Alex, by a process of elimination, pursued his interest in economic history under the guidance of a first-rate economic historian, Natalie Gąsiorowska. His interest in Marxism, in the economic theory and strategy of socialism, and in Soviet economic development continued unabated. He acquainted himself with Soviet planning debates of the late twenties from original sources, read De Man's *Plan du travail* and ploughed diligently through the early writings of Oskar Lange and Michal Kalecki. Kalecki's *The Theory of Business Cycle* and the first essay of Lange's *On the Economic Theory of Socialism* had appeared recently and made quite an impact on the economic scene. Several years later Alex was to read them again and get the full measure of their contribution.

Years in America

It was not until mid-1944 that Alex managed to recover from the trauma of the painful circumstances immediately following his exile in the New World. He revived his academic interests with a series of articles in the Yiddish Monthly *Unser Tsait* evaluating the semiofficial restatement of Stalin's economic views which had appeared the previous year in the Soviet periodical *Pod Znamenem Marksizma*. It created quite a stir in American academic and nonacademic publications. In essence, as Alex argued, it was a limited and guarded rehabilitation of the Marxian law of value and its relevance for a socialist economy.

Early in 1945 Alex resumed his academic career by enrolling in the New School for Social Research. The major attraction was Abba Lerner who lectured on Marx and Keynes at the school. For a long time Lerner was the greatest single influence on Alex's economic *Weltanschauung*. He finally managed to discard the labor theory of value and also accept the Lange-Lerner concept of market socialism. It was also rewarding to read and savor Keynes's *General Theory* in the original under Lerner's guidance, for Alex had struggled with it earlier in the German translation during his Vilno exile. In the later years of his life, though continuing to admire Lerner as a scholar and a human being, Alex has moved closer to the position of the Cambridge (England) School, in particular that of Joan Robinson.

Gradually the idea of a dissertation began to take shape. At first Alex thought he would evaluate the Soviet economy in the context of the Lange-Lerner framework. Later, following a decisive meeting with Abram Bergson in the fall of 1946, he settled on the Soviet industrialization debate of the late twenties. The research was financed by a fellowship from the Russian Research Center at Harvard University where Alex spent five happy years. While his research progressed in stimulating interaction with Abram Bergson and Alexander Gerschenkron, Alex formed precious friendships which continue flourishing to this day.

What investment strategy should be pursued to bring about the socialist reconstruction and transformation of the Soviet Union? The participants in the industrialization debate sought to answer this question. Their arguments fell into two broad groups. The group led by Bukharin and Rykov emphasized balanced growth: "The greatest sustained speed is achieved when industry develops on the basis provided by the rapidly growing agriculture." By contrast, the left-wing opposition of Trotsky and Preobrazhenski argued that, in the prevailing Russian conditions, substantial growth of the economy could take place only if industry expanded at the expense of the peasantry. Alex's contribution was to lift the debates out of this broad dichotomy, to trace not only the contrasts but also the overlaps, to lay bare not only the underlying analytical and policy frameworks but also their details and nuances. He argued that the economic position of the two groups was much closer at the end of the debate than at its beginning. He illuminated the discussion with his insights into Russian history and by reference to the history of economic thought. He traced its relevance to Marxist economic doctrine and to the growth and planning literature that was to follow the Soviet industrialization performance. *The Soviet Industrialization Debate: 1924–1928* is indeed a classic.

While unfolding the drama of the debate, Alex brought out the dilemma of the participants at various levels. They were all Marxists caught in the predicament of providing solutions for a non-Marxist situation: the Soviet Union was not a developed capitalist economy, and Marxist doctrine did not provide a solution of the "paradox of socialist victory in a nonindustrialized country." The dilemma was acute also because Soviet political and economic isolation in a hostile world was protracted. External resources were not available to finance the transformation. As a result they had to reshape the Marxist building blocks and conceptual schemes.

More pressing was the problem of suggesting policies and institutional arrangements corresponding to any proposed course of action. Preobrazhenski favored price markups of industrial goods as a way of raising savings whereas his critics preferred direct taxation. However, the ultimate dilemma was: "Could Preobrazhenski's investment program be enforced, no matter what economic devices were used for this purpose?" Ultimately, the investment program with emphasis on heavy industry was implemented under Stalin with a speed and ruthlessness that exceeded all formulations.

Most of the participants, including Bukharin and Preobrazhenski, perished in the terror of the thirties. According to Alex, their fate points to another aspect of the dilemma. Their purpose was to grapple with complex realities and provide solutions that would "stand up against criticism." True, they all belonged to the Bolshevik old-guard which represented the authoritarian wing of Russian Marxism. However, they were ready to accept diversity in thought and action and were not prepared to use ruthless means to stamp it out. "It was the failure of Bukharin, Preobrazhenski, and others to live up to this totalitarian code that sealed their fate."

Did Stalin, on the other hand, manage to have his cake and eat it too? Not really. The ultimate dilemma of Soviet industrialization continues. The investment drive was unprecendented and has propelled the Soviet Union into a superpower. However, "lags in low priority areas have resulted every now and then in major bottlenecks; convulsive shakings and persistent all-pervading stresses and strains have cut into the efficiency of the huge investment efforts and have weakened the stability of the economy." Bukharin repeatedly stressed the problems of unbalanced growth. The Soviet rulers continue to be "confronted with Bukharin's problem in a new guise."

Alex has returned to some of these themes, especially the Stalinist growth model, in a series of articles that followed *The Soviet Industrialization Debate: 1924–1928.*

At the same time his involvement in various issues has continued unabated. The civil rights movement of the early sixties and the demonstrations against the war in Vietnam engaged much of his time. It was not long ago that Alex marched to protest the declaration of Martial Law in Poland.

Alexander Erlich is a humanist and a scholar of immense stature. The festschrift is intended to be a warm and, I trust, adequate tribute to him.

Padma Desai

I Marxism

1

Marx without Matrices: Understanding the Rate of Profit

Paul A. Samuelson

Karl Marx proposed in *Capital* (1867, Vol. I) a new paradigm: *the rate of surplus value*, reckoned as a percentage markup on direct-wage payments alone; its purpose to provide deep understanding and explanation of the competitive *rate of profit*, reckoned as a percentage return or markup on all capitalists' outlays, whether on wages or on raw materials and durable equipment.

The new paradigm shocked mainstream economists, who realized that the competitive arbitrage that equalized the rates of profit in two industries would make unequal Marx's rates of surplus value (save in the singular case where the two industries happened to display the same fractional importance of wage costs to total outlays). This gave rise to criticism and rejection, to confusion and debate, to the attempt by Marx (published by his editor Friedrich Engels) of a defense and reconciliation in *Capital* (1894, Vol. III) under the heading of what has been called "the transformation problem" (between Marxian *values* and bourgeois *prices*). Since the 1907 emendation of Marx by Ladislaus von Bortkiewicz, there has been a thriving intellectual industry dealing with the vectors, matrices, and eigenvalues of input-output systems.

Here I propose to sidestep all the purely *logical* complexities of the transformation problem. I want to clear the decks so we can bear down on the *substantive* problem: What does Marx's innovative paradigm of the rate of surplus value tell us about the laws of motion of competitive capitalism? What new understanding does it give us of labor exploitation, of the distribution of income between wages and property, of the inequality of wealth and incomes? The final verdict turns out to be, No new understanding.

1.1 The One-Department Simplification

Logical simplication can be bought at the price of neglecting inessential microeconomic detail. If corn were the only industry, no mainstream economist would have to be offended by the monstrosity of differing rates of profit between industries. By definition there could arise no transformation-problem difficulty or complication and no need for matrix algebra. We are provided with a crystal-clear test case.

If Marx's new paradigm triumphantly handles this test case, *if* concentrating on his *rate of surplus value* (his *coefficient of labor exploitation*) imparts in the one-department case understanding of why capitalism's wage rates are so low and have a tendency to fall lower still and why the law of the declining rate of profit does apply—*if* this vindication of Marx is the consequence of the simple arithmetic of the one-department case—then fair-minded economists of any ideology will be prepared to pay the price of some distortion in microeconomic detail from use of Marx's paradigm in return for the strong light it throws on the macroeconomic big picture. If, if, and if. . . . Here I put the matter to the test.

1.2 Case of Direct Labor Only

First, to produce 1 unit of corn at the end of the period, C_{t+1}, you need $\mathbf{a_0}$ of direct labor at the beginning of this period. Your primitive production function is

$$\mathbf{a_0}C_{t+1} = L_t. \qquad (1)$$

Second, suppose labor power has a subsistence real wage rate needed to keep it available and being reproduced. Measured in corn, let the specified subsistence real wage be $\mathbf{m}$. Then steady-state equilibrium requires equality of the real wage to the subsistence level

$$\text{wage}/P_{\text{corn}} = \mathbf{m}. \qquad (2)$$

For the system to be viable in the steady state, what labor needs to consume, $\mathbf{m}L$, must not exceed what labor can produce, $a_0{}^{-1}L$.

So the condition for viability, for the existence of a positive profit rate and exploitation, is that we must have a *surplus economy* as guaranteed by $\mathbf{I} - \mathbf{a_0 m} > 0$, where $\mathbf{I}$ stands for one, as in $\mathbf{I} + 2 = 3$.

A good way to see this is to realize that, in effect, corn now is produced out of last period's corn: to produce 1 unit of corn now you need $\mathbf{a_0 m}$ of corn 1 period back (just enough to pay your needed labor its needed subsistence):

$$\text{corn}_{t+1} = (a_0 m)^{-1}\text{corn}_t. \qquad (3)$$

Unless $(a_0 m)^{-1}$ exceeds unity, the system is not a *surplus* economy that can produce consumption and pay a positive rate of profit, written as $R > 0$.

Under competition, where entry is free and knowledge universal, arbitrage ensures that all capitalists earn the same steady-state equilibrium rate of profit, R^*:

$$P_{\text{corn}} = \text{wage } \mathbf{a_0}(1 + \text{R}^*). \tag{4}$$

Combining (2) and (4), we have for the equilibrium profit rate in a subsistence-wage economy

$$1 + R^* = (a_0 m)^{-1}. \tag{5}$$

This profit rate is seen from (3) also to be the *own-corn marginal productivity*:

$$\frac{\partial \text{corn}_{t+1}}{\partial \text{corn}_t} = 1 + R^*. \tag{6}$$

So much for the pre-1867 bourgeois treatment of this simplest model. What is Marx's new 1867 paradigm?

Marx calls this department's outlays for wages, *variable capital*, v. If there had been outlays on raw materials—on corn for seed—Marx would call that *constant capital*, c. The residual markup garnered by the capitalists, Marx calls surplus, s. In all he has for this case

$$c + v + s = c + v + rv = 0 + \mathbf{a_0 w} + r(\mathbf{a_0 w}), \tag{7}$$

where r is the markup solely on wages, Marx's new rate-of-surplus-value concept.

Since there is no nonlabor outlay or constant capital to be marked up in this first case, Marx's rate of surplus value, r^*, is here exactly the same as the R^* profit rate of Adam Smith and David Ricardo. The lower-case accounting regime of Marx in this first case of direct-labor-only exactly parallels the pre-Marx paradigm, adding nothing and subtracting nothing.

Thus, if 1 corn requires 4 hours of labor and each labor requires 1 of corn for a 12-hour day's subsistence, the equilibrium rates of profit and surplus value are the same, both being 200 percent. Here are the two parallel regimes, in capital letters for mainstream economists and in small letters for Marx:

$$\begin{aligned} C + V + S &= C + V + R^*(C + V) \\ &= 0 + \mathbf{a_0}W + R^*(0 + \mathbf{a_0}W) \\ &= 0 + (\tfrac{1}{3}\text{day})W + 2.00(0 + \tfrac{1}{3}\text{day})W \\ &= W; \end{aligned}$$

$$\begin{aligned} c + v + s &= c + v + r^*v \\ &= 0 + \mathbf{a_0}w + r^*(\mathbf{a_0}w) \\ &= 0 + (\tfrac{1}{3}\text{day})w + 2.00(\tfrac{1}{3}\text{day})w \\ &= w. \end{aligned} \tag{8}$$

The verdict is that Marx's paradigm equals Smith's, being no better and no worse in this simplest case where there is direct labor only.

1.3 Capital-Good Input and Labor

Now suppose it takes both direct *labor* and *corn* raw material to make corn. For example, to get 1 unit of corn it takes **1/3** day of direct labor and **2/3** of corn as seed. Again the subsistence requirement to reproduce labor power is **1** corn per (12-hour) day.

Ricardo would perceive that this system could no longer *permanently* pay a positive profit rate. We can see this in two equivalent ways. First is the technocrats' spproach of von Neumann (1931). How much corn at time t is needed to produce 1 unit of corn at $t + 1$? It takes **2/3** corn for seed and also enough subsistence corn to reproduce **1/3** of a day's labor, which is **1/3** of corn more. In all it takes 1 unit of corn_t to produce 1 unit of corn_{t+1}. The system cannot grow, and also the system cannot pay a surplus to a capitalist class.

The competitive market approach arrives at the same result:

$$W/P_{\text{corn}} = \mathbf{m} = 1, \tag{9}$$

$$P_{\text{corn}} = (W\mathbf{a_0} + P_{\text{corn}}\mathbf{a})(1 + R), \tag{10}$$

$$\begin{aligned} P_{\text{corn}} &= \mathbf{a_0}(1 + R)[\mathbf{I} - \mathbf{a}(1 + R)]^{-1} \\ &= \frac{1}{3}(1 + R)\left[\mathbf{I} - \frac{\mathbf{2}}{\mathbf{3}}\left(1 + R\right)\right]^{-1}, \end{aligned} \tag{10'}$$

where $\mathbf{a}$ is the input of corn needed to produce 1 unit of itself as output.

Combining (9) and (10′) gives for the equilibrium rate of profit

$$1 + R^* = [a + ma_0]^{-1} = \left[\frac{2}{3} + 1\left(\frac{1}{3}\right)\right]^{-1} = 1 + 0. \tag{11}$$

Only if some input requirement were reduced, as when an invention lowers $\mathbf{a_0}$ or $\mathbf{a}$, or both, can there be room for capitalists' exploitative return. Thus lower $\mathbf{a}$ to **1/2**, leaving $\mathbf{a_0}$ at **1/3** and $\mathbf{m}$ at 1. Then Smith and Ricardo deduce from equations (9) through (11) an equilibrium profit rate of 20 percent:

$$1 + R^* = [a + ma_0]^{-1} = \left[\frac{1}{2} + \frac{1}{3}\right]^{-1} = \frac{6}{5} = 1 + 0.20. \tag{12}$$

This conventional paradigm, which is equivalent to

$$\begin{aligned} C + V + S &= C + V + R^*(C + V) \\ &= \left(\frac{1}{2} + \frac{1}{3}\right) + 0.2\left(\frac{1}{2} + \frac{1}{3}\right) = \frac{6}{5}\left(\frac{5}{6}\right) = 1, \end{aligned} \tag{13}$$

Marx proposes to replace by his rate-of-surplus-value paradigm

$$\begin{aligned} c + v + s &= c + v + r^*v \\ &= \frac{1}{2} + \frac{1}{3} + 0.5\left(\frac{1}{3}\right) = 1. \end{aligned} \tag{14}$$

The Marxian paradigm proposes an alternative accounting regime to (9) and (10). I use lower-case symbols to write out his proposed paradigm's accounting regime: in terms of Marx's *rate of surplus value*, r, his marked-up value for corn, $p/w = p$, expressed in wage units or days of labor, is as follows:

$$\begin{aligned} P_{\text{corn}} &= P_{\text{corn}}\mathbf{a} + \mathbf{a_0} + r\mathbf{a_0} \\ &= P_{\text{corn}}\tfrac{1}{2} + \tfrac{1}{3} + r\tfrac{1}{3}, \end{aligned} \tag{15}$$

or

$$\frac{P_{\text{corn}}}{w} = \mathbf{a_0}[\mathbf{I} - \mathbf{a}]^{-1}(1 + r), \tag{15'}$$

$$\frac{w}{P_{\text{corn}}} = \mathbf{m} = 1. \tag{16}$$

Combining (15′) and (16) enables us to solve for the rate of surplus value of 50 percent:

$$1 + r^* = \frac{1}{\mathbf{a_0}[\mathbf{I} - \mathbf{a}]^{-1}\mathbf{m}} = \frac{1 - \mathbf{(1/2)}}{\mathbf{1/3}(1)} = 1 + 0.50. \tag{17}$$

Note that R and r always have the same sign, R being between r and 0 for every surplus economy. (The explanation is that, if the total markup is to be the same, the markup rate on wages-only must exceed that on both wages and raw materials. See Morishima (1973) for elaboration that deals with the n-good model.)

1.4 Trial Balance with Negative Results

$$\frac{P_{\text{corn}}}{W} = \frac{p_{\text{corn}}}{w} = 1 \text{ corn per day.} \tag{18}$$

First, has Marx reached the same substantive equilibrium as his predecessors? Yes. In the two paradigms workers get the same real wage rates; capitalists get the same income:

$$\begin{aligned} &\text{Total capitalists' income in corn} \\ &= r^*\text{wages} = r^*v = r^*mL = 0.5L \\ &= R^*(C + V) = 0.20(C + V) \\ &= R^*[\text{m} + aa_0^{-1}]L = R^*[1 + (0.5)(3)]L \\ &= 0.20[2.5]L = 0.5L. \end{aligned} \tag{19}$$

Second, has some new insight into exploitation—of prediction, explanation, understanding, positivist causation, or normative policy—been imparted by the new 1867 paradigm? Review the analysis, and you will see that the answer is negative on any new insight into the facts or likelihoods.

The ethical proposition that laborers should receive all of the steady-state product neither gains nor loses from the insistence that direct labor is indispensable to production. If direct labor can produce its product only when it has raw materials to work with, that is a solid fact basic to the understanding of how laborers are able to be exploited under competition. (Thus, as in the case where direct labor was the sole input needed for production, no worker who is able and willing to wait to be paid until the end of the production period can be deprived of his full steady-state productivity regardless of how avaricious the capitalists are.)

Since R^* and r^* lead to the same wage/nonwage result, the 1867 insistence on the latter adds nothing macroeconomically, microeconomically, or ethically to our understanding of the present one-technique case. Alas, as soon as other techniques are invented, the new 1867 paradigm *subtracts* from our understanding. The next section shows why.

1.5 Viable Inventions

Along with the option of producing 1 unit of corn with 1/3 of direct labor and 1/2 of corn seed, let a new option be discovered by which 1 unit of corn can be produced with 1/2 of direct labor and 3/10 of corn. If the subsistence real

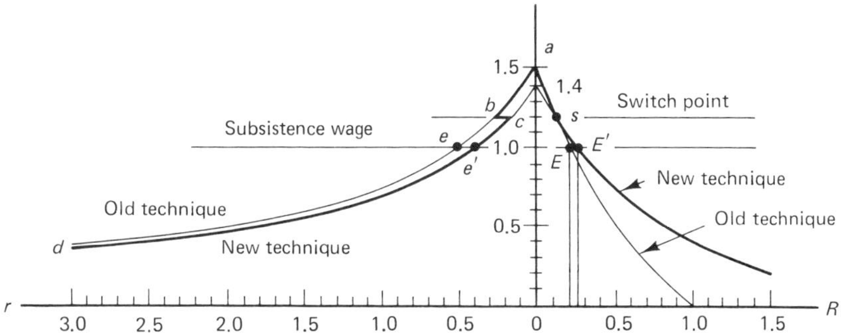

Figure 1.1
On the right, the mainstream economics trade-off between rates of real wage and profit; on the left, the new Marx paradigm involving a rate-of-surplus value. The old paradigm correctly predicts the adoption of new invention even though it lowers the rate-of-surplus value. A Marxian finds the right answer only by returning to the concept of maximized profit rate and disregarding zigzag *bc* at the switchpoint profit rate.

wage is still specified at $\mathbf{m} = 1$ corn per labor-day, which technique will now be used?

If the new technique were used, the rate-of-surplus value would fall—from the old $r^* = 0.50$ to the new $r^* = 0.40$. But the new profit rate would *rise*—from the old $R^* = 0.20$ to the new $R^* = 0.25$! (Recalculating equations (9) through (19) will confirm this.)

The two paradigms seem to tell different stories. Which is the relevant story, the correct one for the case of competitive capitalism? There can be no doubt as to the answer. The bourgeois paradigm of Smith, Ricardo, Pierro Sraffa, and Léon Walras correctly predicts that the new invention will displace the old technique under ruthless competition. Figure 1.1 tells the story. On the left is Marx's *rate-of-surplus value*; on the right is the *rate of profit*. The old equilibrium point E gives way to the higher profit-rate equilibrium point E'. The ASE envelope is well behaved (although it does have a corner at the switchpoint S where the old and new techniques are indifferent).

By contrast, the left-hand diagram has a zigzag *bc* at the switch profit rate of 11.1 percent. Users of the new paradigm, to resolve ambiguity and avoid error, have to peek at the old paradigm and learn that the rate of surplus value *drops* from old *e* to new *e′*.

The participants in the competitive market and the adherents to the competitive-profit-prices paradigm are indifferent to the new Marxian paradigm and are rewarded for their indifference.

1.6 Must the Profit Rate Fall?

One claim for the 1867 Marxian paradigm of the rate of surplus value is that, by means of it and only with it, could Marx prove conclusively his law of the falling rate of profit. Our present model can audit this claim and show why it is not valid.

But first note that Simon Kuznets, Frederick Macaulay, Ralph Hawtrey, Sidney Homer, and others who have seriously studied the statistical trends of profit and interest rates in the centuries before and after Marx do not find a downward trend in the profit rate. Instead, in real terms the actual path is a meandering one. (So trendless is the actual path that economists like Frank Taussig and Gustav Cassel exaggerated the constancy of the interest rate and each fabricated special esoteric theories to explain the law of *constancy* of the interest rate.) So it is a doubtful feather in a theorist's hat if he claims to demonstrate why the profit rate *must* fall.

Non-Marxians as well as Marxians were impressed in the nineteenth century with the complexity and proliferation of capital goods: locomotives, turbines, canal locks and docks, and so forth. Marx found a syllogism that purported to derive, from this apparent increase in the ratio of cost outlays other than labor to direct wage payments, a strong presumption that the rate of profit would fall. At the same time that workers were immiserized—as the pace and length of the working day deteriorated and as child labor became ever more necessary—capitalism's own laws of motion would allegedly propel the profit rate downward.

The facts on real wage rates and profits read otherwise in the chronicles of Kuznets et al. But let us audit the Marxian deductive logic.

I begin with some tautologies:

$$\frac{\text{total profits}}{\text{total wealth}} = \frac{\text{total profits}}{\text{total wages}} \times \frac{\text{total wages}}{\text{total wealth}}. \tag{20}$$

The first of these three ratios is what we mean by the rate of profit, R: it is what invested capital (or wealth) earns divided by that amount of invested capital. The second ratio, at least when applied to our corn-the-only-industry model, is precisely what Marx's *rate of surplus value*, r, is defined as. The third ratio, as we will see, is something that goes down when what Marx calls "the organic composition of capital" goes up.

More precisely, stay with the present model of corn-only. And to keep out logical complexities, stay with the assumption that all nonlabor inputs lack durability: in such a circulating-capital model corn seed is used up completely in the one period. So the rate of turnover is unity.

Under these stark simplifications the total invested wealth is Marx's $c + v$, which is identically the same as bourgeois $C + V$. My earlier tautology now becomes

$$R = r \times \frac{v}{c+v} \equiv r\frac{V}{C+V}$$
$$= r[1 - \gamma], \tag{21}$$

where the organic composition of capital, γ, is by definition the ratio

$$\gamma = \frac{C}{C+V} \tag{22}$$

The growing plenitude and complexity of nineteenth-century capital—recall those locomotives and other such evidences of "increasing roundaboutness" of modes of production—both Marxians and non-Marxians would hope to identify with a trend toward increasing organic composition of capital, a trend of rising γ.[1]

Tautologically, if r can be supposed to be constant, and if the organic composition of capital rises, then the rate of profit, R, must fall. This constitutes the Marxian purported proof of the alleged downward trend in the profit rate:

$$\frac{\partial R}{\partial \gamma} = \frac{\partial[r(1-\gamma)]}{\partial \gamma} = -r < 0. \tag{23}$$

I find it strange that such a thin syllogism has been taken so seriously for so long a period of time. The Achilles heel of the argument is located in the arbitrariness of the airy presumption that the rate of surplus value is a *constant* through the dramatic changes of the industrial revolution.[2] To name a concept (in this case the rate of surplus value) is to reify it and give it constancy in the presence of ignorance. But, as students of subjective probability had to learn the bitter way, out of ignorance can come only ignorance. If we don't know whether there are either men or women on Mars, it is gratuitous to opine that their numbers are probably equal since there is insufficient reason to expect the one to exceed the other.

Marx's empty tautology distracts attention from the one thing that can be said about the present version of his model.

THEOREM So long as the steady-state real wage does not rise, the equilibrium rate of profit *cannot fall*. A substantive invention that bludgeons its way into competitive use *must* raise the real wage rate or the profit rate or both.

My numerical example of an invention, shown in figure 1.1, illustrates how misleading the tautology in equation (20) can be. Let's see why.

My new invention happened to be a clearcut case where the organic composition of capital was reduced. There is no empirical law against that occurring in the industrial revolution. "No wonder your profit rate rose," a Marxian may say, "our tautology is useful because that is what it predicts when you reverse our hypothesis about the direction of change for the organic composition of capital."

Not so. The tautology does not apply, either directly or in reverse. As γ changed, it was impossible in the example that r stay the same: r is an endogenous variable, not one given by some exogenous power of bargaining by the capitalist class; technologically, r had to fall—from 50 to 40 percent, as we saw in figure 1.1. Deprived of the pre-Marx paradigm, the Marxian has no way of knowing in which direction and by how much the rate of surplus value will change, and so has no assurance that the change in r will not more than wipe out the postulated change in organic composition of capital.

But this impotence is purely of Marx's own making. The actual answer is a definite one and already known to pre-1867 economists such as Ricardo: the real wage rate and profit rate are in a trade-off relation; with the former set by the subsistence wage, the latter can only rise. In the tautology r cannot move perversely so as to wipe out quantitatively the viable change in $1 - \gamma$—a truth lost in the 1867 purported innovation!

1.7 Concluding Remarks

A subsistence-wage model, in fact, is a poor key to nineteenth-century reality. So much the worse for large parts of classical and Marxist economics. But that is no reason to mishandle the logic of such models.

The notion of exploitation is a complicated one. Relating profits to the denominator of wages rather than to the denominator of wealth solves none of the problems presented by exploitation. Nor can insight into exploitation come from calculating the ratio of the actual competitive real wage to what it could be with the same techniques were profits zero—which is what calculating r means to an a-Marxian agnostic.

Emotive language aside, the Ricardo-Marx model of this chapter could well be formulated for an egalitarian society. Each person could live in retirement on the interest and principal of the assets accumulated from scratch during adult working life. Each person's real income could be determined in equilibrium at precisely that critical level at which population numbers are stationary. If no one is exploiting, no one is being exploited. A determinate positive interest rate is then merely the result of finite human lives, with what that implies for Modigliani-Turgot life cycle consuming.

Supply-demand economics permits the scientist to handle and understand special and general patterns of behavior. Alas, to understand the fortunes of Andrew Carnegie, J. P. Morgan, Albert Hearst, Baron Rothschild, J. D. Rockefeller—to say nothing of the economic circumstances of David Copperfield and Becky Sharp, and of their great-nephews and great-nieces—the $c + v + s$ tableaux, even in their modernized von Neumann formulations, are mostly a digression. Theory, too often, is the opiate of the theorists. That does not have to be.

Elsewhere I have fair-mindedly examined how the Marxian and conventional paradigms fare in handling a variety of test cases. As with the present case of technical change, the Samuelson (1982) verdict is a damning one for the 1867 innovation.

With the full matrix complications, or under all admissible simplifications, the Marxian paradigm of surplus value fails to deliver the goods of description, understanding, prediction, and prescription. It is not that the Emperor has no clothes; rather it is the case that the garments are confining and deceptive, disguising structure and displaying nonexistent bulges and hollows.

1.8 Mathematical Appendix

A 1-good model needs no matrices. However, using boldface type to represent the technological and subsistence-requirements data of the problem, I will hint at how the full matrix study would go.

Thus in the one-technique case the equilibrium that was defined by (10′) will still apply when I add to corn any number of other goods. In matrix terms the equilibrium profit rate is given by the single relation

$$\mathbf{a_0}(1 + R)[\mathbf{I} - \mathbf{a}(1 + R)]^{-1}\mathbf{m} = 1, \tag{A.1}$$

where now $\mathbf{a_0}$ is a row vector, $\mathbf{a}$ is a square matrix, and $\mathbf{m}$ is a column vector.

Always, R^*, the competitive rate of profit, can be interpreted as the highest own-marginal-productivity of a vector of all the goods in producing itself. That is, $1 + R^*$ is defined by the Seton (1957) eigenvector property

$$[\mathbf{a} + \mathbf{ma_0}]\mathbf{Q}^*(1 + R^*) = \mathbf{Q}^*. \tag{A.2}$$

where $\mathbf{ma_0} = [m_i a_{0j}]$ represents the subsistence-wage requirements that must be added to the $[a_{ij}]$ technical requirements in the Seton fashion.

Also

$$1 + R^* = \operatorname*{Max}_{\mathbf{Q}} \lambda \tag{A.3}$$

subject to

$$[Q_i] = \mathbf{Q}(t) \geqq \lambda\mathbf{Q}(t + 1) \tag{A.4}$$

and where all the stipulated constraints on production and subsistence are obeyed.

Joint Products: Durable Goods

Smith and Ricardo recognized that cost would not suffice to determine prices of joint products like wool and mutton; intensity of demand would affect their real prices. The complications of joint products can be ignored in the standard case where each department produces solely one product, and does so with raw material inputs that are used up completely in one use (have a turnover rate of unity per period).

Modern students of Leontief-Sraffa single-produce systems realize that one kind of durability of inputs can be admitted without losing the simplicity of Leontief-Sraffa systems and their nonsubstitution theorem linearities. This is the case of *exponential* depreciation, where the force of mortality and depreciation is the same percentage for each period regardless of the input's age. As suggested in Samuelson (1971, p. 425, n. 37; 1982), the formula for nondurable models

$$\begin{aligned}\mathbf{P} &= [W\mathbf{a_0} + \mathbf{Pa}]\,(1 + R) \\ &= W\mathbf{a_0}(1 + R)\,[\mathbf{I} - \mathbf{a}(1 + R)]^{-1}\end{aligned} \tag{A.5}$$

need only be replaced by

$$\begin{aligned}\mathbf{P} &= [W\mathbf{a_0} + \mathbf{Pa}]\,(1 + R) - \mathbf{P}[a_{ij}(1 - d_{ij})] \\ &= W\mathbf{a_0}(1 + R) + \mathbf{P}[a_{ij}(d_{ij} + R)] \\ &= W\mathbf{a_0}(1 + R)\,[I - a_{ij}(d_{ij} + R)]^{-1},\end{aligned} \tag{A.6}$$

where d_{ij} is the fraction of the ijth intermediate input that is used up in one period's use. When $d_{ij} \equiv 1$, (A.6) becomes (A.5).

With exponential depreciation, we see how Marx's $C + V + S$ formulations should have been handled by his editor.

For the jth industry (A.6) suggests we write

$$\sum_{i=1}^{n} P_i a_{ij} d_{ij} Q_j + W a_{0j} Q_j + R\left(\sum_{i=1}^{n} P_i a_{ij} Q_j + W a_{0j} Q_j\right)$$
$$= \sum_{i=1}^{n} C_{ij} + V_j + R\left(V_j + \sum_{i=1}^{n} C_{ij} d_{ij}^{-1}\right) \tag{A.7}$$
$$= C_j + V_j + R(V_j + C_j \bar{d}_j^{-1}), \quad j = 1, \ldots, n$$

it being understood that $\bar{d}_j^{-1}$ is the weighted mean length of life of the industry's various input items

$$\bar{d}_j^{-1} = \frac{\sum_i C_{ij} d_{ij}^{-1}}{\sum_i C_{ij}}. \tag{A.8}$$

Of course changes in R will alter $\bar{d}_j^{-1}$, as it will V_j/C_j ratios.

Presumably, in terms of the rate of surplus value, Marx would write

$$c_j + v_j + s_j = \sum_{i=1}^{n} p_i a_{ij} d_{ij} Q_j + w a_{0j} Q_j (1 + r), \tag{A. 9}$$

where

$$\begin{bmatrix} \frac{p_j}{w} \end{bmatrix} = [a_{0j}]\,[I - a_{ij} d_{ij}]^{-1}\,(1 + r). \tag{A.10}$$

Reswitching in a One-Department Model

Reswitching is the phenomenon that occurs when a particular set of techniques is competitively viable in two different ranges of the profit rate, but not inbetween. A corn-only model, involving no durable capital good but only corn as a raw material used up in the single period of production, cannot exhibit reswitching. This impossibility follows from the linearity of the (real wage, profit rate) trade-off, when $n = 1$ and the real wage is paid *post factum* (at the end rather than the beginning of the period). Also with exponential depreciation, as in (A.6), linearity precludes reswitching.

However, if I admit a durable good into my corn-only model, I can easily specify examples of reswitching. Here is an example with two such options:

1. This involves no durability. To produce 1 unit of corn, we need 1/4 of direct labor and 0.52 of corn seed.

2. Now suppose we can also produce 1 unit of corn by 1 unit of direct labor combined with 1 unit of corn input congealed into a durable tool. Then, along with our output of corn, we get as a joint product one used durable tool: we may suppose that this used tool can produce 2 units of corn without requiring any direct labor.

Which option will be competitively viable? That depends on the profit rate. The durable option can be shown to pay at low interest rates and at high interest rates, but at intermediate interest rates the nondurable technique of option 1 will win out competitively.

Here are the steady-state unit cost relations for corn price, P, as in Samuelson (1959, eq. 22):

Option 1

$$P = (W\bar{a}_0 + P\bar{a}) = \frac{W\bar{a}_0(1 + R)}{1 - \bar{a}(1 + R)}; \tag{A.11}$$

$$\frac{W}{P} = f_1(R) = \frac{1 - 0.52(1 + R)}{0.25(1 + R)}. \tag{A.12}$$

Option 2

$$\begin{aligned} P &= (Wa_0 + Pa)(1 + R) - P_{\text{used}}a \\ &= (W + P)(1 + R) - P_{\text{used}}, \end{aligned} \tag{A.13}$$

$$P = P_{\text{used}}\hat{a}(1 + R) = P_{\text{used}}\frac{1}{2}(1 + R). \tag{A.14}$$

This can be solved to give

$$\frac{W}{P} = \frac{1 - a(1 + R) + a\hat{a}^{-1}(1 + R)^{-1}}{a_0(1 + R)} \tag{A.15}$$

$$= \frac{1 - (1 + R) + 2(1 + R)^{-1}}{1 + R} = f_2(R). \tag{A.16}$$

Under ruthless competition, for each R the option that yields the higher real wage will win out:

$$W/P = \max\,[f_1(R), f_2(R)] = f^*(R). \tag{A.17}$$

Equating $f_1(R)$ to $f_2(R)$ and solving the quadratic equation that is thereby implied, we find

$$\begin{aligned} f^*(R) &= f_2(R), \quad 0 \le \mathrm{R} \le \frac{1}{9}, \\ &= f_1(R), \quad \frac{1}{9} \le \mathrm{R} \le \frac{2}{3}, \\ &= f_2(R), \quad \frac{2}{3} \le \mathrm{R} \le 1, \end{aligned} \tag{A.18}$$

where 1/9 and 2/3 are the roots of the quadratic

$$1.08(1 + R)^2 - 3(1 + R) + 2$$
$$= 1.08\left[(1 + R) - \left(1 + \frac{1}{9}\right)\right]\left[(1 + R) - 1 + \frac{2}{3}\right]. \quad (A.19)$$

This numerical example of reswitching has a point of interest in the present connection. Reswitching reminds us how ambiguous it is to judge that (1) one technique has a higher or lower organic composition of capital, (2) is more roundabout and time intensive, or (3) is more mechanized than the other. When the system is moved by an invention from option 1 to option 2 and to higher profit rates, is that definitely a decrease in the organic composition of capital? If the same change occurs, but to a lower profit rate, what then? If the reverse occurs, from option 2 to option 1, what definite can be said? To ask these questions is to realize that they admit of no definite answers. What is new here is the demonstration that even a one-department model can display all the complications of the n-department case, complications that the 1867 paradigm cannot handle.

Notes

I owe thanks to the National Science Foundation for aid, and thanks to Kate Crowley and Aase Huggins for editorial assistance.

1. Sraffa and Joan Robinson have alerted scholars to the ambiguity involved in the notion of the organic composition of capital, or in kindred notions of increasing degrees of mechanization or of roundaboutness of modes of production. Seeing a locomotive doesn't tell you whether the capital/output ratio rose on the average between 1800 and 1850. In figure 1.1 I could have given the mathematical appendix example of *reswitching*—of a durable-good alternative that would be commercially superior to my original circulating-capital technique at very high and low interest rates! Which is more mechanized—the machine case or the corn seed case?

2. P. M. Sweezy (1942, ch. 4) provides a useful exposition of the $R/r = 1 - \gamma$ tautology. See H. D. Dickinson (1956–7) for a commendable reexamination of this tautology. In particular, see his p. 127, n. 1 and n. 2, for quotations from Marx and Bortkiewicz that recognize that what changes γ may not leave r constant. Dickinson's own researches point out that certain processes associated with accumulation (non-consuming now so that future output may more nearly attain golden-rule levels) can often be expected to cause the profit rate to fall at the same time that such measures of capital intensity as the organic composition of capital are rising. It is a pity that no modern treatment of the whole matter appears in the literature to show how slight is the insight forthcoming from the rate of surplus value for the (real wage, profit rate) relationships. See the useful Roemer (1977) analysis of Marxian reasonings. In Samuelson (1982) I show how misleading is Roemer's taxonomy of "socially desirable" inventions that competition allegedly will not adopt: in fact, normatively,

competition avoids deadweight loss in the sense of intertemporal Pareto non-optimality; a planned society can rationally eschew inventions that Roemer calls socially desirable.

References

Bortkiewicz, L. von, 1907. On the correction of Marx's fundamental theoretical construction in the third volume of *Capital*. *Jahrbuch Nationalökonomie Statistik* 34: 370–385.

Dickinson H. D., 1957. The falling rate of profit in Marxian economies. *Review of Economic Studies* 24: 120–130.

Marx, Karl. *Capital*. Vol. I, 1867; Vol. II, 1885; Vol. III, 1894.

Morishima, M., 1973. *Marx's Economies: A Dual Theory of Value and Growth*. Cambridge: Cambridge University Press.

Roemer, J., 1977. Technical change and the tendency of the rate of profit to fall. *Journal of Economic Theory* (December): 403–424.

Samuelson, P. A. *Collected Scientific Papers*. Vol. I, 1965; Vol. II, 1965; Vol. III, 1972; Vol. IV, 1977. Cambridge, Mass.: The MIT Press, chs. 29–32, pp. 113, 117, 152–155, 225–231.

Samuelson, P. A., 1982. The normative and positivistic inferiority of Marx's values paradigm. *Southern Economic Journal* (July): 11–18.

Seton, F., 1957. The transformation problem. *Review of Economic Studies* 24: 149–160.

Sweezy, P. M., 1942. *The Theory of Capitalist Development*. New York: Oxford University Press.

von Neumann, J., 1946. A model of general economic equilibrium (transl. by G. Morgenstern). *Review of Economic Studies* 13: 1–9.

2 Money and Effective Demand in Marx's Scheme of Expanded Reproduction

Duncan K. Foley

In several interesting papers Alexander Erlich has shown how Marx's schemes of reproduction can throw light on the vicissitudes of socialist accumulation in the Soviet Union (Erlich 1977, 1978). In these papers Erlich emphasizes the link between proportionality (what fraction of total resources must be devoted to capital formation to sustain a program of rapid accumulation) and gestation times (how long it takes for investment projects to be finished and available as working capacity) in judging the feasibility of a program of accumulation.

In this chapter I take up the theme of time lags in production in an analysis of the problems of capitalist accumulation. Marx initially intended his reproduction schemes as tools for examining in detail two problems in capitalist accumulation: the proportions in which social capital must be allocated between production of means of production and means of subsistence on an accumulation path, and the problem of the source of effective demand to realize produced commodities in an expanding capitalist system. Marx's discussion in *Capital* (Vol. II, ch. 21), however, leaves these questions well posed but the answers to them somewhat obscure.

The second problem, the source of aggregate effective demand, has been the subject of a great debate in later Marxist literature, after the appearance of Rosa Luxemburg's critique of Marx's analysis (Luxemburg 1951, Luxemburg and Bukharin 1972), and is the focus of this chapter.

2.1 A Model of the Circuit of Capital

To focus attention clearly on the issue of money aggregate demand and expanded reproduction, I will present a mathematical model of the circuit of capital, a concept Marx analyzed exhaustively in the early pages of *Capital* (Vol. II). This model allows us to see more clearly the time sequence of events in the circuit of capital. As a model of *aggregate* capital, it does not exhibit the division of production into departments I and II which Marx employs in his analysis of simple and expanded reproduction. This division is not necessary to study the problem of effective demand, useful as it is in unraveling the question of strategies of investment and the problem of proportionality.

Marx represents the circuit of individual capital in the diagram

$$M - C(LP, MP) \ldots (P) \ldots C' - M' = M + \Delta M.$$

A capitalist begins the circuit of capital with value in the form of money, M. The capitalist buys commodities, namely, labor power, LP, and means of production, MP, on the market with this money. The workers hired process the means of production (including raw materials, tools, and facilities) into the finished product, another commodity, C'. This produced commodity is sold on the market for money, M', in general for more money than the capitalist originally advanced, since it includes the surplus value ΔM.

This diagram corresponds to the income, or profit and loss, statement of a capitalist firm. The income statement records the flows of value through the productive circuit. Marx's M' is the sales of the capital during the period. The values of means of production, including an allowance for depreciation of long-lived means of production, and of wages are the direct costs of producing the commodities sold. The gross margin or gross profit, the difference between sales and direct costs, is Marx's surplus value.

Each of these phases of production takes time. Thus if we look at a capitalist firm, we see at any moment a certain amount of value tied up in productive capital—the value of tools and facilities, inventories of raw materials and of partly finished commodities (valued to include the labor costs already expended on them). We will also see a certain amount of value tied up in commercial or commodity capital—finished commodities awaiting sale. Finally, some value will be found in the form of money (some money-denominated financial asset)—value realized in the past by sale but not yet recommitted to production. The balance sheet of the capitalist firm measures (perhaps imperfectly) these stocks of value which arise because of time lags in the various phases of the circuit of capital.

There is a strict correspondence then between the circuit of capital as analyzed by Marx and the income statements and balance sheets of capitalist firms. This correspondence holds at any level of aggregation, since we can simply add up the corresponding items for all the capitals we want to aggregate. We can think of the circuit of *social* capital, the aggregation of all the individual capitals in the society. This social circuit will be the center of our analysis.

To keep things mathematically simple let us restrict our modeling of time lags in different phases of the circuit of capital to simple *time delays*, where value that enters a phase of the circuit at time t all emerges again at time $t + T$, having waited, or delayed, T time units in that phase of the circuit. Then we can write down equations to represent the circuit of capital as follows:

$$Q(t) = C(t - T_n), \tag{1}$$

$$S(t) = S'(t) + S''(t) = Q(t - T_m) + qQ(t - T_m), \tag{2}$$

$$C(t) = S'(t - T_f) + pS''(t - T_f), \tag{3}$$

where $C(t)$ is the flow of value committed as costs at time t, including gross investment in long-lived means of production; $Q(t)$ is the flow of value of finished product valued at cost at time t; T_n is the time lag for production; $S(t)$ is the flow of value of sales at time t, comprised of $S'(t)$, the recovery of costs, and $S''(t)$, the realization of surplus value; q is the markup of final sales price over costs, the ratio of surplus value to costs in the commodities sold; T_m is the time delay between production and sales; p is the fraction of the surplus value recommitted to production; and T_f is the time lag between sales and the recommitting of value to production. Throughout we assume that the value of money, the labor time represented by a unit of money, is constant.

The stocks of value tied up in each of these phases are productive capital, N, which includes the value of inventories of raw materials and partly finished commodities, and the as yet undepreciated value of long-lived means of production; commercial (or commodity) capital, M, which is the value of inventories of finished commodities awaiting sale (valued in this paper at cost), and money capital, F, the stock of money denominated financial assets held by capitalist firms. These stocks are related to the flows by the laws:

$$\frac{dN(t)}{dt} = C(t) - Q(t) \tag{4}$$

$$\frac{dM(t)}{dt} = \frac{Q(t) - S(t)}{(1 + q)} \tag{5}$$

$$\frac{dF(t)}{dt} = S'(t) + pS''(t) - C(t) \tag{6}$$

where we assume in (6) that the fraction $(1 - p)$ of surplus value which leaves the circuit of capital in the form of capitalist consumption, wages of unproductive labor, or taxes is paid directly out of realized surplus value without time delay.

The labor theory of value in Marx's analysis appears as the key to understanding the determinants of the markup, q, in the circuit. The markup is the ratio of the flow of surplus value to the flow of total costs:

$$q = \frac{s}{(c + v)} = \frac{S''}{C} = \left(\frac{s}{v}\right)\left(\frac{v}{(v + c)}\right) = ek, \tag{7}$$

where, following the labor theory of value, the markup is decomposed into the product of the rate of surplus value ($e = s/v$) and the composition of costs ($k = v/(v + c)$), which represents the same division of total costs between variable and constant capital as Marx's organic composition of capital, c/v. Here c, v, and s are used in their usual Marxist sense, standing for constant capital (nonwage costs of production), variable capital (wages), and surplus value. The labor theory of value suggests this decomposition in arguing that only labor adds value to commodities, so that the fundamental determinant of surplus value is the division of value added between surplus value and variable capital. We do not, however, need these results from the labor theory of value for our investigation of the problem of aggregate effective demand in the circuit of capital, except insofar as they authorize our taking the markup as determined outside the relations analyzed in the circuit of capital itself.

If we assume, in order to understand the logic of this system, that the time lags, markup, and rate of capitalization remain constant over time, we can analyze the paths of accumulation in this system. In reality of course capital accumulation involves qualitative changes in the social and technical relations of production, changes that would be reflected in systematic movements of the rate of surplus value and the composition of costs.

With the artificial assumption of an unchanging rate of surplus value and composition of costs, the circuit of capital is capable of a steady balanced accumulation path in which all flows and stocks of value are growing at a common exponential rate. We can in fact see that this growth rate, call it g, depends in a simple way on the parameters of the system: the markup, q, the rate of capitalization, p, and the time lags, T_n, T_m, and T_f.

Suppose that $C(t) = C(0) \exp(gt)$, where g is the still unknown growth rate and $C(0)$ the flow of money value in costs at time 0. Then successive substitution of (1), (2), and (3) yield the relation:

$$\begin{aligned} C(t) &= C(0) \exp(gt) = (1 + pq)C(t - (T_n + T_m + T_f)) \\ &= (1 + pq)C(0) \exp(gt) \exp(-g(T_n + T_m + T_f)) \end{aligned} \tag{8}$$

or, dividing through by $C(0) \exp(gt)$,

$$1 = (1 + pq) \exp(-g(T_n + T_m + T_f)), \tag{9}$$

which simplifies to

$$g = \frac{\ln(1 + pq)}{(T_n + T_m + T_f)}. \tag{10}$$

This result shows that the rate of accumulation rises with the markup and capitalization rate and falls with longer turnover times for capital in any of the phases of the circuit.

On a steady-state path of this kind we can also calculate the stocks of value tied up in the various phases of the circuit—the aggregate assets of the firms—by solving equations (4) through (6):

$$\frac{N(t)}{C(t)} = 1 - \exp(-gT_n)/g, \tag{11}$$

$$\frac{M(t)}{C(t)} = \exp(-gT_n)(1 - \exp(-gT_m))/g, \tag{12}$$

$$\frac{F(t)}{C(t)} = (1 + pq)\exp(-g(T_n + T_m))(1 - \exp(-gT_f))/g. \tag{13}$$

In the case of simple reproduction, where no surplus value is accumulated, so that $p = 0$ and $g = 0$, these ratios become

$$\frac{N(t)}{C(t)} = T_n, \tag{11'}$$

$$\frac{M(t)}{C(t)} = T_m, \tag{12'}$$

$$\frac{F(t)}{C(t)} = T_f. \tag{13'}$$

These results correspond to our intuition that in simple reproduction stocks are proportional to the time delay in each phase of the circuit. The simple reproduction equations are also the limits of the expanded reproduction equations as p and g go to 0.

The circuit of capital thus provides a framework in which the labor theory of value analysis of capitalist production and accumulation can be linked to the observed flows of money value in a system of capitalist firms.

2.2 Money and Aggregate Demand in Simple Reproduction

So far I have abstracted from the problem of realization, or, in Keynesian language, aggregate effective demand. In assuming that the realization lag, T_m, is a constant parameter of the accumulation process, we implicitly suppose that all a capitalist need do to sell a commodity is to produce it and wait the requisite time for it to be taken off the shelf. The money demand for the commodity is simply posited as appearing on the market at the proper time.

But, as Marx points out, this is true neither for the individual capital nor for social capital. Realization is the ultimate necessity for the commodity; a failure to make it means losses for a capitalist firm, and a crisis of realization for social capital. Let us then consider where effective demand comes from, first in the case of simple reproduction.

The Pure Commodity Money Case

Marx insists (*Capital*, Vol. II, pp. 500ff) on the importance of analyzing reproduction first on the hypothesis of a pure commodity money system, with no credit. We will follow this procedure here. The money commodity I will call gold, though it could be any produced commodity serving as the general equivalent. Gold is produced in the circuit of capital like any other commodity. I will assume that gold production requires the same composition of capital and has the same rates of turnover as the social average, so that gold exchanges against other commodities at its labor value and that this labor value is unchanging through the accumulation process. Gold differs from other commodities only in that it is self-realizing; once produced, it is already in the form of money. Gold does not have to make the leap of realization on the market.

In this model gold is the only form of monetary asset. A commodity is realized by being exchanged for gold, which stays in the firm's possession until it is paid out as interest or dividends, or spent by the firm to hire workers and buy means of production to initiate a new cycle of production.

Since we are analyzing simple reproduction, we assume that the whole surplus value is paid as soon as it is realized to capitalist households which hold it for a time, T_c, in gold and then spend it all on consumption. (It would make no difference if some of the surplus value were paid as wages to unproductive labor or as taxes to the state, as long as the spending lags were the same.)

What are the sources of aggregate demand in this system? First, when a firm advances a dollar in the flow of costs, C, a portion $(1 - k)$ takes the form of purchases of raw materials and means of production. These purchases constitute a direct money demand for produced commodities. The other part of the outlay for costs, kC, is paid to workers as wages. This money value enters the circuit of workers' consumption (in Marx's terms, a *C-M-C* circuit, in which one commodity, labor power, is sold for money, which is used to buy other commodities, namely, means of subsistence). This part of the costs is indirectly a source of effective demand, since workers will sooner or later spend their wages on means of subsistence—"sooner or later" because workers may accumulate temporary reserves of money value to tide them over spells of unemployment or to provide for their retirement. We model this by assuming that workers also delay for a time, T_c, the same delay as capitalist households, in spending their revenue.

The third source of demand is the surplus value being spent by capitalist households, after the lag T_c. If we write D for current effective aggregate demand,

$$D(t) = (1 - k)C(t) + kC(t - T_c) + S''(t - T_c). \tag{14}$$

A moment's thought will show that this is indeed demand enough to realize the total of commodities currently being offered for sale. This value is

$$S(t) = (1 + q)Q(t - T_m) = C(t - (T_n + T_m)) + qC(t - (T_n + T_m)). \tag{15}$$

In simple reproduction $C(t) = C(t - T_c) = C(t - (T_n + T_m))$, that is, the flow of costs is constant through time, and $S''(t - T_c) = qC(t - (T_n + T_m))$ as well, so that $D(t) = S(t)$.

To sustain this process, a certain amount of gold is tied up at any moment in stocks. The capitalist firms hold $C(t)\,T_f$ in gold; workers' households hold $kC(t)\,T_c$; and capitalist households hold $qC(t)\,T_c$. If this gold were completely imperishable, there would be no need to mine any more. The gold-producing sector would employ no labor or capital and would produce no output.

Marx (*Capital*, Vol. II, pp. 469ff) considers the case where gold coins wear out in circulation. The problem here is to find a way to model this phenomenon within the circuit of capital. When gold coins are circulating and wearing out, each agent in the system finds that the coins it receives are on average slightly lighter than those it pays out. (In reality there is considerable unevenness in this process. Agents with a large cash flow may find it profitable to cull their coins so as to pay out the lightest ones, as English tavernkeepers did in the nineteenth century.) To make up for this loss, the agents must pay out fewer coins (though the same weight of gold) than they receive. This will create a shortfall in money demand.

Suppose, for instance, that d is the fraction of their weight that coins lose in each transaction, so that coins received on average weigh $(1 - d)$ times the weight of coins paid out. Each agent must restrict its spending in coins to the fraction $(1 - d)$ of the coins it receives. The total flow of value to be realized then is still

$$S(t) = (1 + q)C(t - (T_n + T_m)). \tag{15'}$$

The demand *in coins* available to realize this value is

$$\begin{aligned} D(t) &= (1 - d)(1 - k)S'(t - T_f) + (1 - d)(1 - d)kS'(t - (T_f + T_c)) \\ &\quad + (1 - d)S''(t - T_c) \qquad (14') \\ &= (1 - d)(1 + q)C(t) - d(1 - d)dkC(t), \end{aligned}$$

using (1) through (3) and the fact that $C(t)$ is constant in simple reproduction. There is thus a shortfall of $d(1 + q)C(t) + d(1 - d)dkC(t)$ in effective demand in coins. This must be exactly the size of the gold-producing sector, whose product does not need to be realized by being exchanged for coin. This flow of new gold into the system is just sufficient to maintain the real value of gold due to wear and tear in circulation.

The exact mechanism through which this replacement occurs will depend on the details of institutional management of the coinage. Perhaps the simplest situation to conceptualize would be one where each agent recoins the light coins it receives into full-weight coins before spending them. The new gold would thus enter the system when it is spent by gold producers and would become light coin in that first transaction.

Whether or not we take account of the wear on coinage, it is possible to solve the problem of realization in simple reproduction. Notice that this solution requires capitalist households to hold a reserve of money to realize the surplus value, in addition to the money capital held by firms. This is the method Marx uses to explain the realization of surplus value in simple reproduction (*Capital*, Vol. II, p. 400).

Credit

In a loan transaction a holder of gold lends the gold to another agent. The original holder retains a claim on money value in the amount of the loan and may be able to bargain for a further money payment (interest) as an inducement to make the loan. From the lender's point of view the loan is functionally like holding gold; it is a reserve of money value that can be drawn on later to finance spending. From the borrower's point of view borrowing is a substitute for drawing down balances of gold. It allows the borrower to spend in the present value it expects to receive in the future.

In simple reproduction borrowing simply eliminates the need for a certain portion of the stocks of gold. For example, a capitalist firm may lend some of its idle money to another firm. The lending firm continues to hold a stock of money value for the time T_f, but some of it is in the form of a loan to another firm. Since the borrowing firm spends the gold at once, the total gold holding of the two firms taken together is smaller. The balance sheet of the typical firm changes from

Assets	**Liabilities**
Money Gold CT_f	
Productive Capital CT_n	
Commodity Capital CT_m	Net Worth $C(T_n + T_m + T_f)$

to

Assets	**Liabilities**
Money Gold aCT_f Loan $(1 - a)CT_f$	Loans $(1 - a)CT_f$
Productive Capital CT_n	
Commodity Capital CT_m	Net Worth $C(T_n + T_m + aT_f)$

where $(1 - a)$ is the proportion of money capital lent out and held in the form of the loan. If a goes to 0, the system can operate without any physical gold holdings. Gold would still play a virtual role in the system, since loans would be repayable in gold in principle, even if they were never repaid in gold in fact.

The same analysis could be applied to household-household borrowing. If there were household-firm lending, some part of wages or surplus value would be accumulated, contrary to the assumption of simple reproduction.

Thus the introduction of lending in the model of simple reproduction does not alter the original commodity money analysis in any substantive way. It merely reduces the amount of physical gold required to maintain the system on the path of simple reproduction.

2.3 Expanded Reproduction

The analysis of simple reproduction clarifies certain issues but is inadequate even as a first approximation to a study of real capitalist production. Capital exists as expanding value, and accumulation is its natural mode. Real accumulation involves a qualitative change in the underlying relations of production, which will be reflected in the parameters of the accumulation process, especially the rate of surplus value and the composition of costs.

In general, accumulation has four sources. First, capitalist firms may retain a certain proportion of the surplus value they realize and spend this money to expand the scale of their production. Second, some of the surplus value paid to households as interest, dividends, or the salaries of unproductive workers may be lent back to capitalist firms through financial intermediaries or financial markets. Third, some part of workers' saving may be lent to capitalist firms and contribute to accumulation. Finally, the state may lend to capitalist firms out of its tax revenues. To simplify the exposition of this section, I will abstract from workers' and capitalists' household savings, and from the state, and assume that all accumulation is financed directly by retention of some part of the surplus value. This amounts analytically to assuming that the consumption lag, T_c, is zero, so that no stocks of value accumulate in households.

As in section 2.2 I will consider first the situation where a commodity money system operates without credit (something of a fiction, since credit relations tend to develop step by step with accumulation itself) and then the situation where borrowing between capitalist firms occurs.

The Pure Commodity Money Case

For this analysis I will ignore the complications introduced by taking account of the wear and tear on coins in circulation. The sources of aggregate effective demand in an expanding circuit of capital are the same as those in simple reproduction and are expressed by equation (14), which with $T_c = 0$ becomes

$$D(t) = C(t) + (1 - p)S''(t). \tag{16}$$

Since wages are assumed to be spent instantaneously by workers, the whole of current costs appear as effective demand, together with the proportion $(1 - p)$ of currently realized surplus value which is paid to capitalist households and spent instantaneously by them.

Current cost outlays, $C(t)$, are financed from value realized in sale in the past. In fact under the assumptions of this section

$$C(t) = S'(t - T_f) + pS''(t - T_f). \tag{17}$$

Suppose now that the system is on a steady accumulation path growing exponentially at rate g. Then

$$S'(t - T_f) + pS''(t - T_f) = (S'(t) + pS''(t)) \exp(-gT_f). \tag{18}$$

If we combine this with (16), we get

$$D(t) = (S'(t) + pS''(t)) \exp(-gT_f) + (1 - p)S''(t). \tag{19}$$

If $gT_f > 0$, this will clearly be smaller than $S(t) = S'(t) + S''(t)$. The reason is intuitively clear: on a path of positive accumulation current costs correspond to lagged sales, which must be smaller than current sales if the system is growing uniformly. The difference must be the value produced by the gold-producing sector.

We can see the same point in another way. On a path of steady accumulation capitalist firms are increasing their holdings of gold due to the lag between sales and spending. This increase in gold holdings, by equation (6), is just $S'(t) + pS''(t) - C(t)$, which is just equal to the difference between $S(t)$ and $D(t)$ as calculated here. A gold-producing sector just large enough to fill the gap between effective demand and the total value being realized will also produce just the amount of gold necessary to maintain the relative size of stocks of money capital.

Thus even in the absence of wear and tear on gold coinage there will be positive gold production on a path of steady accumulation. The general expansion of the circuit of capital requires new sources of gold to maintain the money balances of the capitalist firms.

We can also see that there is a close connection between the scale of gold production and the realized rate of accumulation. The faster the rate of accumulation, the larger will be the gap between $D(t)$ and $S(t)$, and the larger will be the gold-producing sector. A faster rate of accumulation could be achieved with p, q, T_n, and T_f constant by a shortening of T_m, the realization lag, as equation (10) shows. It would be well to be cautious, however, in deciding which way causation runs between gold production and accumulation.

Marx, in his discussion of expanded reproduction, eventually arrived at this solution to the problem of effective demand in expanded reproduction (*Capital*, Vol. II, pp. 522–523). But earlier in that chapter he grappled with the problem of realization and gold production in these terms:

> If we were to conceive the process of circulation between the various parts of the annual reproduction as taking place in a straight line—which would be wrong as it always consists with a few exceptions of mutually opposite movements—then we should have to start from the producer of gold (or silver) who buys without selling, and to assume that all others sell to him. In that case the entire yearly social surplus-product (the bearer of the entire surplus-value) would pass into his hands, and all the other capitalists would distribute among themselves *pro rata* his surplus product, which naturally exists in the form of money, ... The surplus value of the gold producer ... would then be the sole fund from which all other capitalists would draw the material for the conversion of their annual surplus-product into money.... Absurd as these assumptions would be, they would do nothing more than explain the possibility of a universal simultaneous formation of a hoard, and would not get reproduction itself one step further, except on the part of the gold producer. (*Capital*, Vol. II, p. 491)

This paragraph is correct up to its last sentence but as a whole is misleading. First, as Marx himself says, annual reproduction does not take place in a straight line, with one sector buying first, then the next, and so forth. As a result gold producers are not the sole fund out of which other capitalists can realize surplus value. Each capitalist is spending out of his own reserve of money capital, so that the gold producers need only realize the *excess* surplus value (exactly the difference between $D(t)$ and $S(t)$ calculated here). The last sentence seems wrong because realizing all other capitalists' surplus values through newly produced gold *would* get reproduction one step further, namely, past the obstacle of realization itself.

Rosa Luxemburg (1951, p. 141) was misled by this paragraph and rejected too quickly the formal possibility of gold production resolving the aggregate demand problem. But perhaps the present analysis suggests why Luxemburg saw a problem in Marx's treatment of expanded reproduction. Bukharin (Luxemburg and Bukharin 1972, pp. 200ff) criticizes Luxemburg very sharply for her neglect of gold production as a solution to the realization problem, though he does not work out this solution in any detail.

Credit

Once again, as in simple reproduction, credit relations can substitute for gold in resolving the problem of realization and the money holdings of capitalist firms.

Consider now the case where there is no active gold production (though the production cost of gold remains the determinant of the value of money), but there is borrowing between capitalist firms. In this case some part of current cost $C(t)$ will be financed out of value realized in the past, but some will be financed by new or expanded borrowing $B(t)$, by anticipating future sales revenues. Thus we must alter equation (3) to

$$C(t) = S'(t - T_f) + pS''(t - T_f) + B(t). \tag{20}$$

If we apply the same reasoning we used to derive equation (19), we find:

$$D(t) = (S'(t) + pS''(t)) \exp(-gT_f) + B(t) + (1 - p)S''(t). \tag{21}$$

If $B(t)$ grows exponentially, this system is capable of consistent expansion. We must have

$$D(t) = S(t) = S'(t) + S''(t), \tag{22}$$

which, with (21) yields

$$(1 - \exp(-gT_f) = \frac{B(t)}{S'(t) + pS''(t)}, \tag{23}$$

or, using equations (1) or (2)

$$\frac{B(t)}{C(t)} = (1 - \exp(-gT_f))(1 + pq) \exp(-g(T_n + T_m)). \tag{24}$$

This equation shows the relation between new borrowing as a proportion of the costs advanced by capitalist firms and the realized rate of accumulation, g. The larger the new borrowing relative to the flow of value in the circuit of capital, the more rapidly can the system expand.(The realizable growth rate, g, is of course limited by the fact that the realization lag in equation (10) cannot become negative. See Foley 1982 for a fuller discussion of this relation.)

On these paths the capitalist firms are holding all their money capital in the form of loans to other firms. Although each firm delays the time T_f in respending value, from an aggregate point of view all realized value is spent instantaneously. The new borrowing just suffices to borrow back the value firms are adding to their stocks of money capital or, equivalently, provides just the amount of financial assets firms want to hold as money capital.

Thus, when new borrowing provides the effective demand to solve the realization problem, the scale of new borrowing is related to the realized rate of accumulation in the same way the scale of gold production is in the commodity money case.

2.4 Concluding Remarks

In Marx's *Capital* (Vol. II) we encounter two separate attempts to conceptualize the capitalist economic system as a whole: the circuit of capital, and the schemes of reproduction. Marx uses the schemes of reproduction to attack two different problems, the question of the allocation of social capital between departments, on the one hand, and the problem of aggregate effective demand, on the other. The analysis of simple reproduction goes smoothly on both fronts, in part because the aggregate demand issue can be resolved simply by positing a large enough reserve of money in the hands of capitalist households to allow them to realize their own surplus value. Time lags in spending, which Marx conceives in virtual terms by asking where the money comes from which is spent to realize surplus value, give rise in simple reproduction only to mediating stocks of money value. Gold production and credit appear in simple reproduction as nonessential additions to the system of production itself.

Expanded reproduction raises new questions. Time lags in spending interact with a positive rate of accumulation to produce a discrepancy between aggregate demand and the flow of sales of finished commodities, a discrepancy that becomes larger the more rapidly accumulation proceeds. As a result gold production and credit, which fill this gap, become linked in an essential way to the realized rate of accumulation.

The schemes of reproduction, with the division of production into separate departments, help us to grasp the issue of proportionality in accumulation. But they seem to be ill-designed to tackle the problem of money and aggregate effective demand, which the circuit of capital analysis reveals is at its heart a problem of the timing of flows of value through the circuit of capital. There would appear to be no technical obstacle at present to joining the two department structure of the schemes of reproduction with the circuit of capital model and thereby unifying Marx's two conceptions of capitalist economic relations as a whole.

Notes

I would like to thank Arnold Collery for conversations that stimulated my interest in the problems examined here.

References

Erlich, Alexander, 1977. Stalinism and Marxian growth models. In Robert C. Tucker, ed. *Stalinism: Essays in Historical Interpretation*. Norton, New York.

Erlich, Alexander, 1978. Dobb and the Marx-Fel'dman model: a problem in Soviet economic strategy. *Cambridge Journal of Economics* 2, 203–214.

Foley, D., 1982. Accumulation and realization in a Marxian model of the circuit of capital. *Journal of Economic Theory*, forthcoming.

Luxemburg, Rosa, 1951. *The Accumulation of Capital*. Transl. by A. Schwarzschild. Monthly Review, New York.

Luxemburg, R., and N. Bukharin, 1972. *The Accumulation of Capital—An Anti-Critique* and *Imperialism and the Accumulation of Capital*. Ed. by Kenneth J. Tarbuck, transl. by R. Wichmann. Monthly Review, New York.

Marx, Karl, 1967. *Capital*, Vol. II. International Publishers, New York.

3 Unequal Exchange, Labor Migration, and International Capital Flows: A Theoretical Synthesis

John E. Roemer

Unequal exchange between countries, as discussed by radical and Marxian economists after Emmanuel (1972), usually takes place in an international environment where countries differ in a number of attributes: the technologies they face, the subsistence wage which is customary, their factor endowments. The phenomenon, however, can be entirely explained by differential capital-labor ratios across countries. Moreover three issues at the heart of radical analysis of international economic relations can be linked: unequal exchange, international labor migration, and imperialism (narrowly defined as the export of finance capital). Indeed, the direction of labor migration across a nation's borders, or the direction of capital flow across its borders, enables us immediately to deduce its status with regard to the "inequality" of exchange. The models in which this is verified are quite general; they are *n*-sector models, with labor the only primary factor. Although for simplicity I use a Leontief technology, all the results are true when the production set is taken to be a convex cone, with the proper generalization of concepts such as embodied labor time to the conical environment.[1]

The definition offered of unequal exchange depends on the concept of embodied labor time and hence is only applicable if we assume the production set is such as to allow the definition of embodied labor time (in particular we assume labor is the only primary factor).[2] A country will be said to be "suffering" from unequal exchange when its national income is insufficient to purchase goods that embody as much labor as its workers expended in production; a country will be said to be "gaining" from unequal exchange if its national income forces it to purchase, in a certain unambiguous way, commodities embodying more labor than its population expended. In general, both gainers and sufferers from unequal exchange exist at equilibrium, even when all countries have knowledge of the same technology, but capital-labor ratios differ across countries. Indeed this is so even when there is no international labor or capital market but only produced commodities flow across borders. If we allow an international labor market to operate, we can show that countries can be classified according as they maximize national income by exporting labor, importing labor, or doing neither. A main theorem proves a relationship exists between a country's position vis-à-vis unequal exchange, and its class position with respect to the international labor market, to wit: any country that maximizes national income by exporting labor is necessarily suffering from unequal exchange, and any country that maximizes national income by importing guest workers is gaining from unequal exchange. An international credit market is introduced, with or without a labor market, and countries are then classified according as they maximize national income by borrowing capital, lending capital abroad, or doing neither. A country that must borrow capital to maximize national income is necessarily a sufferer from unequal exchange, and a country that maximizes national income by exporting finance capital is necessarily a gainer from unequal exchange. Thus an isomorphism is exhibited between unequal exchange, labor migration, and the international capital flows. Some disagreements between Marxists/radicals and neoclassicals are examined concerning unequal exchange. Unequal exchange does not preempt mutual gains from trade. The ethical presumption underlying the appellation "unequal" is explained, and I indicate how it contrasts with the neoclassical ethical presumption.

3. International Trade in Produced Commodities Only

The Model

Consider a world of N countries all of which have knowledge of the *same* Leontief technology (A, L), where A is an $n \times n$ input matrix and L an n-dimensional (row) vector of direct labor coefficients for operating the n sectors. International trade occurs only in the n-produced goods, not in labor or capital. The only primary input into production is labor. Production takes time, however, and, to operate an activity today, a country must be able to finance its requirement for inputs, which can be paid for only with "capital" produced in the past. That is, to operate an activity vector x (in $\mathbb{R}^n_+$), a country must be able to advance finance capital to pay for inputs Ax, which cost pAx at price p.

There are internal labor and capital markets in each country, but for the moment those will be suppressed, as international trade does not occur in labor or capital. Thus the international price vector is a row vector p in $\mathbb{R}^n_+$, representing the prices of the n-produced and traded commodities. Let ω^ν be the n-dimensional column vector which is the stock of produced commodities possessed by country ν at the beginning of the period. Let l^ν be the labor supply of country ν. Then, if p is the international price vector, we summarize the economic problem for country ν as

$$\textbf{(P1)} \quad \begin{aligned} &\text{choose} \quad x^\nu \geqq 0 \quad \text{to} \\ &\qquad \max \quad p(1 - A)x^\nu, \\ &\qquad \text{s.t.} \quad pAx^\nu \leqq p\omega^\nu, \qquad (1) \\ &\qquad\qquad Lx^\nu \leqq l^\nu. \qquad (2) \end{aligned}$$

Subject to its capital constraint (1) and labor constraint (2), country ν seeks to choose production activities to maximize *net national product*. The capital available in country ν, once prices exist, is the valuation of its stocks $p\omega^\nu$, which we will also call K^ν.

Our concept of an equilibrium price vector will be quite general. Let $\mathscr{A}^\nu(p)$ be the set of optimal solutions to **(P1)** for country ν, at prices p. Call this model $\mathscr{E}(p)$.

DEFINITION A price vector p will be called an equilibrium for $\mathscr{E}(p)$ if[3]
(D1) $\exists x^\nu \in \mathscr{A}^\nu(p)$ for all ν, such that
(D2) $Ax \leqq \omega$, where $x = \Sigma x^\nu$ and $\omega = \Sigma\omega^\nu$,
(D3) $x > 0$.

That is, p is an equilibrium if, when each nation optimizes at prices p, the vector of total inputs required can be supplied by aggregate stocks, condition **(D2)**, and international gross output is a positive vector **(D3)**. Condition **(D2)** guarantees that trades can take place for production inputs so that each country can satisfy its planned input demand, and **(D3)** requires that every activity operate.

The equilibrium concept has been called general because no stipulation is made for final demands of the various countries. One might, alternatively, stipulate that at prices p, country ν will have a demand $f^\nu(p)$ and replace **(D3)** with $x = \Sigma f^\nu(p)$. (Or, if each country wanted to replace its depreciated stocks, we could specify final demand $f^\nu(p)$ net of replacement and stipulate $(1 - A)x = \Sigma f^\nu(p)$.) But our analysis has the merit that it is *independent of tastes of countries* in the sense that we require only **(D3)** and do not put any more structure on demand than that. We could be more specific than **(D3)** and require instead

(D3′) $(1 - A)x \geq 0$.

Condition (**D3′**) states that international net output is a non-negative (non-zero) vector, which is to say, that aggregate stocks do not run down in any component. If A is assumed indecomposable, than $(1 - A)^{-1} > 0$ and **(D3′)** will imply $x > 0$. If we think of a steady state in which each country wishes to replace its depreciated stocks ω^ν at each period, then **(D3′)** becomes a reasonable specification. But for our purposes only **(D3)** is required.

Note that, more properly, time superscripts should be placed on prices, since output x appears later than inputs Ax are paid for. We limit our analysis to a steady state in which prices are unchanging to simplify the analysis. (Such a steady-state solution need not exist for an arbitrary specification of the data, but that is not our concern.) Note also that, although countries can trade their stocks to acquire their input requirements, this does not comprise an international capital market. Trading capital would mean one country could borrow *finance* capital from another, at an interest rate, and that is not allowed here. Each country must finance its production with its own finance capital K^ν.

We do not specify the optimization decisions internal to each country which result in the aggregate optimization program: maximize net national product. The maximization of national income will be the result of the usual sort of agent optimization. The program **(P1)** suppresses the micro behavior that leads to the aggregate result. Inquiring into the micro decisions, we might think of the labor supply l^ν as a function of prices, as workers decide to trade off leisure against other goods. It would do no harm to write $l^\nu(p)$, for in our analysis we shall fix a solution p and carry on from there.

To analyze what happens at an equilibrium p, consider the dual program to **(P1)**. Let π^ν and w^ν be the dual variables associated with the two primal constraints (1) and (2), respectively. Then for country ν the dual to **(P1)** is

(Q1)

$$\begin{aligned} &\text{choose} \quad \pi^\nu \quad \text{and} \quad w^\nu \quad \text{to} \\ &\min \quad \pi^\nu K^\nu + w^\nu l^\nu, \\ &\text{s.t.} \quad \pi^\nu pA + w^\nu L \geqq p(1 - A). \end{aligned} \tag{3}$$

Note the dual constraint (3) can be written:

$$(1 + \pi^\nu)pA + w^\nu L \geqq p$$

and then the interpretation of the dual variables is clear. π^ν is a profit rate on capital, and w^ν a wage rate. By complementary slackness applied to (3), at the optimal solution x^ν, only those sectors will be operated by ν that produce the maximal profit rate, at wage w^ν, on capital invested. Indeed, π^ν and w^ν will be the rate of interest and the wage in the *internal* capital and labor markets in country ν, and since

$$p(1 - A)x^\nu = \pi^\nu K^\nu + w^\nu l^\nu$$

at the optimal solution (the duality theorem), we have the decomposition of the value of net national product into profits and wages. Thus, although the internal labor and capital markets were initially suppressed, they now emerge.[4]

What can we say about the factor prices (π^v, w^v)? There is no reason that profit or interest rates and wage rates should be equalized across countries in this world, as there is no international trade in capital or labor.[5] Notice that a country's factor prices are determined solely by its capital-labor ratio K^v/l^v (we have fixed p at an equilibrium). For the primal program **(P1)** can be equivalently written:

$$\textbf{(P}'\textbf{1)}\qquad \begin{array}{ll} \text{choose} & \bar{x}^v \text{ to} \\ & \max \ p(1 - A)\bar{x}^v, \\ & \text{s.t.} \ p A\bar{x}^v \leqq \dfrac{K^v}{l^v}, \\ & \quad L\bar{x}^v \leqq 1, \\ & \quad \bar{x}^v \geqq 0. \end{array}$$

To solve **(P1)** from **(P′1)**, set $x^v \equiv l^v\bar{x}^v$. The dual to **(P′1)** is

$$\textbf{(Q}'\textbf{1)}\qquad \begin{array}{ll} \min & \pi^v\left(\dfrac{K^v}{l^v}\right) + w^v, \\ \text{s.t.} & (1 + \pi^v)pA + w^vL \geqq p, \end{array}$$

whose solution (π^v, w^v) is obviously identical to the solution of **(Q1)**.

Factor Prices and the International Division of Labor

From now on, fix p at an equilibrium. Let $k^v \equiv K^v/l^v$ be the forthcoming capital-labor ratio in v. We now tell a familiar story: as k^v increases across countries v, the internal profit rate π^v decreases, and the internal wage rate w^v decreases. This is most easily seen by graphing the dual program **(Q′1)** in (w, π) space. For any wage rate w, there is a maximum profit rate achievable among the n sectors at prices p, call it $\pi(w)$, defined by

$$\pi(w) = \max_i \frac{p_i - (pA_i + wL_i)}{pA_i}$$

(i ranges over the n columns of p, A, and L). In figure 3.1, $\pi(w)$ is graphed for a four-sector economy. Typically, there will be as many linear segments in the graph of $\pi(w)$ as there are sectors, although this is not necessarily the case. In the example of figure 3.1 the maximal profit rate for a wage of zero is achieved in sector 3; then, as the wage increases, sector 1 becomes most

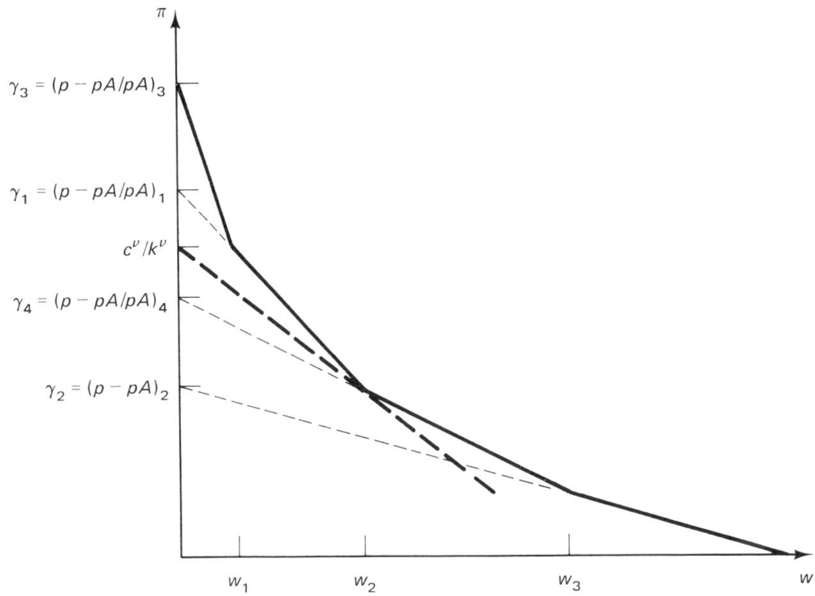

Figure 3.1

profitable, then sector 4, and eventually sector 2. The convex shape of $\pi(w)$ follows from the definition of $\pi(w)$.

The program for country v is to choose (w, π) on or above the curve $\pi(w)$ to minimize c^{v} where $c^{v} = \pi k^{v} + w$. Written as $\pi = \frac{c^{v}}{k^{v}} - \frac{w}{k^{v}}$, we see the graphical problem is to find the line of slope $-\frac{1}{k^{v}}$, with the smallest π-intercept tangent to the curve $\pi(w)$. The line is shown in figure 3.1. At the optimal (w^{v}, π^{v}) this country achieves its profit rate π^{v} by operating only sectors 1 and 4. (Operating any other sector brings a profit rate lower than π^{v} at the wage w^{v}, and hence v will operate only sectors 1 and 4. This is the economic interpretation of the complementary slackness condition of linear programming in **(P′1)** and **(Q′1)**.)

From the fact that $x > 0$ at a solution, we know each sector is operated by some country. It follows that each sector must achieve the maximal profit rate at some wage level: each sector must enjoy at least one point on the frontier $\pi(w)$. It is, however, possible that the profit rate-wage frontier for some sector is tangent to $\pi(w)$ at only one point, and not in a line segment of positive length, which explains the remark above that it is possible for the frontier $\pi(w)$ to have fewer than n linear segments.

It is immediately seen that the factor prices π^{ν} and w^{ν} vary in the appropriate way as k^{ν} changes. As k^{ν} increases, the slope $-\frac{1}{k^{\nu}}$ of the modified dual objective function increases, and the optimal solution therefore travels down the schedule $\pi(w)$, decreasing π^{ν} and increasing w^{ν}. Indeed, countries with a suitably large k^{ν} will have zero internal profit rates, and countries with a suitably small k^{ν} will have zero internal wage rates. We do not impose a further restriction of a subsistence wage (or minimal profit rate), which could prevent this, for the sake of simplicity in exposition.

We observe an *international division of labor*. Typically, each country ν will operate at most two sectors, as illustrated. As k^{ν} increases, the sectors ν will operate increase in their capital intensity, as measured by the ratio pA_i/L_i. To see this, write

$$\pi(w) = \max_i \left(\frac{p_i - pA_i}{pA_i} - w\frac{L_i}{pA_i} \right)$$

and therefore observe that the slope of a segment along the graph of $\pi(w)$ is $= L_i/pA_i$, where sector i is the one achieving the maximal π for given w. Thus, as k^{ν} increases, and we travel down the graph of $\pi(w)$, the numbers pA_i/L_i increase. Typically a country will operate at most two sectors of neighboring capital intensity pA/L, and the capital intensities of the operated sectors increase as the capital-labor ratio k^{ν} increases. From the fact that every sector's profit rate-wage frontier is tangent to the envelope $\pi(w)$, it follows that every sector fits into this spectrum of increasing capital intensities at the wage for which it becomes the maximally profitable sector.

Unequal Exchange

The results above are very neoclassical. We next show how Marxian exploitation between countries, otherwise known as unequal exchange, comes about in this neoclassical world.

The traditional notion of unequal exchange is that some countries export goods embodying a lot of labor and import in return goods embodying little labor. That is, a country may be able to purchase only goods embodying less labor than its population expended in production. Equilibrium prices somehow cause this to happen. The proponents of the term "unequal exchange" generally view the countries that export more embodied labor than they import as being exploited or cheated, or suffering from unequal exchange. This judgment will be evaluated later. For the moment we show those countries with a low capital-labor ratio k^v will "suffer" from unequal exchange at the solution p, and those with a high k^v will "gain."[6] A country is said to "gain" from unequal exchange if it imports goods embodying more labor than its population expends in production.

Recall the vector of embodied labor times for this technology is $\Lambda = L(1 - A)^{-1}$. We propose a definition of *unequal exchange exploitation* which is independent of demand, as follows:

DEFINITION A country will be said to be *unequal exchange* (UE) *exploited* at equilibrium p if, no matter how it spends its national income on goods, it cannot purchase goods embodying as much labor as it supplied. A country is *UE exploiting* if, no matter how it chooses to spend its national income on goods, it always commands more labor than it supplied.

To phrase this definition analytically, observe that the most efficient way for a country to purchase embodied labor per dollar spent is to spend the entire national income on the good with the maximal ratio Λ_i/p_i. Let

$$\left(\frac{\Lambda}{p}\right)_{\max} \equiv \max_i \frac{\Lambda_i}{p_i}.$$

If country v expends all its national income (which is $\pi^v K^v + w^v l^v$) in this way, then it will "purchase" embodied labor in total amount

$$(\pi^v K^v + w^v l^v)\left(\frac{\Lambda}{p}\right)_{\max}.$$

Thus v is UE exploited if, and only if,

$$(\pi^v K^v + w^v l^v)\left(\frac{\Lambda}{p}\right)_{\max} < l^v. \tag{4}$$

Similarly, country v is UE exploiting if, and only if,

$$(\pi^v K^v + w^v l^v)\left(\frac{\Lambda}{p}\right)_{\min} > l^v. \tag{5}$$

There will in general be countries for which neither (4) nor (5) holds: they are *exploitation neutral*.[7]

Dividing (4) and (5) by l^v, the definitions become as follows:

DEFINITION v is *UE exploited* when

$$(\pi^v k^v + w^v)\left(\frac{\Lambda}{p}\right)_{\max} < 1; \tag{4'}$$

v is *UE exploiting* when

$$(\pi^{v}k^{v} + w^{v})\left(\frac{\Lambda}{p}\right)_{\min} > 1. \tag{5'}$$

But $(\pi^{v}k^{v} + w^{v})$ is national income per capita (employed) and increases with k^{v}, because national income per capita (employed) is precisely the value of the objective function of **(P′1)**, which increases with k^{v}, the program's only constraining parameter. Hence only very low k^{v} countries can be UE exploited and only very high k^{v} countries can be UE exploiting, by (4′) and (5′). Exploitation status "improves" monotonically with k^{v}.

This does not show there will actually be any exploited and exploiting countries. That, indeed, cannot be verified in general, as all countries could be exploitation neutral at a solution, because of the very strong condition that has been required for exploitation. We can show at the extremes, however, a definitive answer.

THEOREM 1 Fix p, an equilibrium, and let A be indecomposable.
a. Let v be a country whose dual program **(Q1)** has solutions only with $w^{v} = 0$. Then v is UE exploited.
b. Let v be a country for whom $\pi^{v} = 0$ is an optimal solution. Then v is UE exploiting, except in the singular case when p is proportional to Λ.

Thus countries whose capital-labor ratio k^{v} is such as to give them a labor surplus $(w^{v} = 0)$ are surely UE exploited, and countries with a capital surplus are UE exploiting.

Proof
Part a. Let $w^{v} = 0$ necessarily as hypothesized. With reference to figure 3.1, it follows that the slope of v's dual objective function is greater in absolute value than the slopes of every segment along $\pi(w)$:

$$\frac{1}{k^{v}} > \left(\frac{L}{pA}\right)_{\max}. \tag{6}$$

(To make this statement, it is important to note that every sector is somewhere tangent to the curve $\pi(w)$. This is assured by $x > 0$ at the solution.) It follows that

$$pA > k^{v}L$$

and

$$\pi^{v}pA > \pi^{v}k^{v}L. \tag{6'}$$

Since $w^v = 0$, we have from inequality (3):

$$p \geqq (1 + \pi^v)pA \tag{7}$$

or

$$p(1 - A) \geqq \pi^v pA. \tag{7'}$$

From (6′) and (7′)

$$p(1 - A) > \pi^v k^v L. \tag{8}$$

Postmultiplying (8) by the positive matrix $(1 - A)^{-1}$ gives

$$p > \pi^v k^v \Lambda$$

or

$$1 > \pi^v k^v \left(\frac{\Lambda}{p}\right)_{max}. \tag{9}$$

But (9) is equivalent to (4′) since $w^v = 0$ and v is shown to be UE exploited.

Part b. If $\pi^v = 0$, then, by definition of (w^v, π^v),

$$pA + w^v L \geqq p. \tag{10}$$

If vector equality holds in (10), then

$$p = w^v \Lambda, \tag{11}$$

which contradicts the assumption that p is not proportional to Λ. Thus (10) must be

$$pA + w^v L \geq p$$

or

$$w^v L \geq p(1 - A). \tag{10'}$$

Postmultiplying (10′) by the positive matrix $(1 - A)^{-1}$ yields

$$w^v \Lambda > p$$

or

$$w^v \left(\frac{\Lambda}{p}\right)_{min} > 1, \tag{12}$$

which is equivalent to (5′) since $\pi^v = 0$.[8] ∎

To review, at a solution p, a country with a high capital-labor ratio is gaining from unequal exchange in the sense that its national income unambiguously commands more embodied labor, through the goods it can purchase than the labor that is expended by its population in production. Similarly, a country with a low capital-labor ratio is exploited in the sense that its national income cannot possibly command as much embodied labor, in the purchase of goods, as its population expended in production. We observe as well an international division of labor, although each country has knowledge of all the production processes.

It is worthwhile to reiterate that this result is independent of the pattern of demand. We do not ask what package of goods a country actually consumes, but rather what it could afford to purchase. If we endow agents within countries with preferences over goods and make final demand specific in the definition of an equilibrium solution, then we easily see that, although some countries are UE exploited at a solution, they also gain from trade. (This is a familiar argument.) Thus, gains from trade and unequal exchange are not mutually exclusive events.

The model of this section is unusual in the unequal exchange literature in that there is no international trade in either capital or labor. Traditionally, an international capital market is assumed to exist. In the next two sections we modify our model to allow for this. With the introduction of the international capital market, the division of labor will be lost. Capital in this first model, as a factor that cannot be traded, is playing a role more akin to land in classical models, although in our case it is a produced commodity.

3.2 Unequal Exchange with Labor Migration

We could at this juncture introduce either labor migration (an international labor market) or capital migration in the model. It will turn out the two resulting stories are equivalent. As the international capital market is the one usually introduced in the unequal exchange discussions, I introduce instead an international labor market.

The Model

We assume then that labor can migrate freely across borders, and does so, to find the highest wage. Thus no equilibrium concept can allow differential wages across countries. International capital flows, however, are not allowed. The international price vector is now (p, w), where $p \in \mathbb{R}^n_+$ as before is the vector of commodity prices and $w \in R_+$ is the wage. The program for country ν is

$$\textbf{(P2)}\quad \begin{array}{ll} \text{choose} & x^{\nu} \in R^n_+, \quad y^{\nu} \in R^n_+, \quad x^{\nu}_0 \in R_+ \quad \text{to} \\ & \max \quad p(I - A)x^{\nu} + (p - (pA + wL))y^{\nu} + wx^{\nu}_0, \\ & \text{s.t.} \quad pAx^{\nu} + pAy^{\nu} \leqq p\omega^{\nu}, \qquad (13) \\ & \qquad Lx^{\nu} + x^{\nu}_0 \leqq l^{\nu}. \qquad (14) \end{array}$$

x^{ν} is the vector of activities that country ν operates using domestic labor; y^{ν} is the vector of activities ν operates using foreign labor; x^{ν}_0 is the amount of labor country ν exports. The three terms in the objective function are the contributions to national income from production operated by domestic workers, production operated by foreign workers (who repatriate their earnings at the end of the period), and the repatriated incomes of home workers from abroad. Constraint (13) states that capital requirements for aggregate production $(x^{\nu} + y^{\nu})$ must be financed from existing finance capital; (14) is the labor constraint. (As in section 3.1, wages are paid out of revenues and need not be advanced from capital.) For prices (p, w), let $\mathscr{A}^{\nu}(p, w)$ be the set of optimal solutions $(x^{\nu}, y^{\nu}, x^{\nu}_0)$ for country ν. Call this model $\mathscr{E}(p, w)$.

DEFINITION (p, w) is an equilibrium for $\mathscr{E}(p, w)$ when

(D1) $\exists (x^{\nu}, y^{0}, x^{\nu}_0) \in \mathscr{A}^{\nu}(p, w)$ for all ν, such that

(D2a) $A(x + y) \leqq \omega$, where $x + y = \sum_{\nu} (x^{\nu} + y^{\nu})$ and $\omega = \sum_{\nu} \omega^{\nu}$,

(D2b) $Lx + Ly = \sum l^{\nu}$,

(D3) $x + y > 0$.

The motivation is the same as in section 3.1. Each country maximizes national income, and an equilibrium price vector is one that allows this to occur, subject to the requirement that all activities operate. We require an additional input market to clear the international labor market.

The analysis of the equilibrium is somewhat simpler in this model than in the first one, because the existence of the additional market guarantees that equilibrium prices take on a simple form. Define the profit rate in sector i, at given prices (p, w), as

$$\pi_i = \frac{p_i - (pA_i + wL_i)}{pA_i}.$$

LEMMA

a. At prices (p, w) any country can optimize by setting $x^{\nu} = 0$.
b. At an equilibrium profit rates are equalized for all sectors: there is a number π such that $\pi_i = \pi$ for all i and $p = (1 + \pi)pA + wL$.

c. At an equilibrium (p, w) country v's national income is $\pi K^{v} + wl^{v}$.

Proof

Rewrite the objective function of **(P2)** as

$$p(1 - A)(x^{v} + y^{v}) + w(x_0^{v} - Ly^{v}). \tag{15}$$

Let (x^{v}, y^{v}, x_0^{v}) be an optimal solution for v. It is clear $(\mathbf{x}^{v}, \mathbf{y}^{v}, \mathbf{x}_0^{v})$ is also optimal where:

$$\mathbf{x}^{v} + \mathbf{y}^{v} = x^{v} + y^{v} \quad \text{and} \quad \mathbf{x}_0^{v} - L\mathbf{y}^{v} = x_0^{v} - Ly^{v}. \tag{16}$$

Note that, if (16) is satisfied, then both constraints (13) and (14) of **(P2)** continue to hold. From (15) it follows that the values of the objective function at (x^{v}, y^{v}, x_0^{v}) and $(\mathbf{x}^{v}, \mathbf{y}^{v}, \mathbf{x}_0^{v})$ are the same. The claim follows.

For a given solution (x^{v}, y^{v}, x_0^{v}) we construct another solution:

$$\begin{aligned} \mathbf{x}^{v} &= 0, \\ \mathbf{y}^{v} &= x^{v} + y^{v}, \\ \mathbf{x}_0^{v} &= Lx^{v} + x_0^{v}. \end{aligned} \tag{17}$$

By (16), $(\mathbf{x}^{v}, \mathbf{y}^{v}, \mathbf{x}_0^{v})$ is optimal. This says a country can always optimize by exporting all its own workers and operating all domestic production with foreign labor.

Since an optimal solution always exists with $\mathbf{x}^{v} = 0$, without loss of generality the program for v may be rewritten:

$$\textbf{(P'2)} \qquad \begin{aligned} &\text{choose } y^{v} \text{ and } x_0^{v} \text{ to} \\ &\max \quad (p - (pA + wL))y^{v} + wx_0^{v}, \\ &\text{s.t.} \quad pAy^{v} \leqq p\omega^{v} = K^{v}, \\ &\qquad\quad x_0^{v} \leqq l^{v}. \end{aligned}$$

But the nature of the solution to **(P′2)** is clear. Simply set $x_0^{v} = l^{v}$, and hire foreign workers to operate only the sectors that maximize profits $[(p - (pA + wL))y^{v}]$ per dollar invested (pAy^{v})—to operate only the maximal profit rate sectors. The value of the objective function is thus

$$\pi_{\max} K^{v} + wl^{v},$$

where $\pi_{\max} = \max_i \pi_i$.

To prove (b), it suffices to notice that, in any optimal solution (x^{v}, y^{v}, x_0^{v}) to **(P2)**, domestic workers also will only be hired to operate $\pi_{\max}$ sectors. For if not, then the alternate solution $(0, \mathbf{y}^{v}, \mathbf{x}_0^{v})$ constructed in (17) would have foreign workers operating a less-than-maximal profit rate sector, which we know is impossible. Hence, if some sector does not generate the maximal profit rate at prices (p, w), then no country will operate it, using domestic or foreign labor. But then condition **(D3)** of the equilibrium requirements does not hold. Hence all sectors must generate the maximal profit rate, and hence all profit rates are equal. Thus the price vector has the form specified. ∎

Once a labor market exists, equilibrium prices are of the equal-profit-rate variety, a fact not true in the model of section 3.1.

Unequal Exchange

The analysis of unequal exchange is identical to that of the previous section. By part c of lemma 1 it follows that a country ν cannot command with its national income labor embodied equal to labor expended by its population in production if, and only if,

$$(\pi K^{\nu} + wl^{\nu})\left(\frac{\Lambda}{p}\right)_{\max} < l^{\nu}$$

or

$$(\pi k^{\nu} + w)\left(\frac{\Lambda}{p}\right)_{\max} < 1. \tag{18}$$

This is the condition for a country to be UE exploited. Similarly, a country is UE exploiting if, and only if,

$$(\pi k^{\nu} + w)\left(\frac{\Lambda}{p}\right)_{\min} > 1. \tag{19}$$

Since π and w are now equal across countries, it is obvious from (18) and (19) that the gainers from UE exploitation are the countries with high capital-labor ratios, and the losers are the countries with low k^{ν}.

Class Decomposition of Countries

Inequalities (18) and (19) allow us to decompose countries into three groups: the UE exploiters, the UE exploiting, and the exploitation neutral. A second decomposition of countries exists in this model into *classes* of countries. We define a country's class by its relation to the importation or exportation of labor. Suppose country ν possesses an optimal solution to its program **(P2)**, at equilibrium prices (p, w), of the form $(x^{\nu}, 0, x_0^{\nu})$ where $x^{\nu} \neq 0 \neq x_0^{\nu}$. Schematically, we may say it has a solution of the form $(+, 0, +)$. We know, from lemma 1, that all countries possess solutions of the form $(0, +, +)$, except countries with zero capital which possess solutions only of the form $(0, 0, +)$. Is there any interesting decomposition of countries according to the type of optimal solutions they possess, represented schematically in this way? Define four types of country as follows:

$C^1 = \{\nu | \nu$ possesses an optimal solution of form $(+, +, 0)$ but not one of form $(+, 0, 0)\}$,
$C^2 = \{\nu | \nu$ possesses an optimal solution of form $(+, 0, 0)\}$,
$C^3 = \{\nu | \nu$ possesses an optimal solution of form $(+, 0, +)$ but not one of form $(+, 0, 0)\}$,
$C^4 = \{\nu | \nu$ possesses an optimal solution of form $(0, 0, +)\}$.

Schematically,

$$C^1 = (+, +, 0) - (+, 0, 0),$$
$$C^2 = (+, 0, 0),$$
$$C^3 = (+, 0, +) - (+, 0, 0),$$
$$C^4 = (0, 0, +).$$

THEOREM 2 Let (p, w) be an equilibrium, with $\pi > 0$. Then the decomposition of countries into classes C^1, C^2, C^3, C^4 is exhaustive and pairwise disjoint. Furthermore, if countries are arranged in decreasing order of k^ν, then the class ordering falls monotonically in the order C^1, C^2, C^3, C^4. That is, the largest k^ν countries are of class C^1, then come the C^2 countries, and so on.

Countries in C^1 are those who can only optimize by importing labor. Countries in C^4 can only optimize by exporting *all* their labor. Countries in C^3 can only optimize by exporting some labor. Countries in C^2 can optimize without either exporting or importing labor. I call this decomposition one into *classes*, as it characterizes a country with respect to its need to sell or hire labor to or from abroad in order to optimize. A class, in Marxian usage, is a group of agents all of whom relate to the selling or hiring of labor power in the same way. In this case we think of the country as the agent. Thus C^4 are the "proletarian" countries.

Theorem 2 may be proved by verifying the following:

LEMMA 2 Let $\pi > 0$ at the equilibrium (p, w).
a. $\nu \in C^1 \Leftrightarrow \forall$ solutions (x^ν, y^ν, x_0^ν), $Ly^\nu > x_0^\nu$.
b. $\nu \in C^2 \Leftrightarrow \exists$ a solution (x^ν, y^ν, x_0^ν), $Ly^\nu = x_0^\nu$.
c. $\nu \in C^3 \Leftrightarrow \forall$ solutions (x^ν, y^ν, x_0^ν), $Ly^\nu < x_0^\nu$ and $K^\nu \neq 0$.
d. $\nu \in C^4 \Leftrightarrow K^\nu = 0$.

Proof of Theorem 2
From lemma 2 it immediately follows that the four classes are pairwise disjoint. We next verify the classes are ordered according to their capital-

labor ratios, as claimed. Countries in C^4 are those and only those with no capital and hence clearly fall at the bottom of the ordering by k^ν. To verify the ordering of C^1, C^2, and C^3, it suffices to show that, whenever $\nu \in C^1$ and $\mu \in C^2$, then $k^\nu > k^\mu$, and $\mu \in C^2$ and $\rho \in C^3$ implies $k^\mu > k^\rho$. The first of these claims is next shown; the second can be shown in like manner.

Consider $\nu \in C^1$ and $\mu \in C^2$. If ν (or μ) exhausts its capital $p\omega^\nu$ (or $p\omega^\mu$) by hiring workers and placing them arbitrarily in sectors, and then exports all its labor, that will comprise an optimal solution, since the revenue thereby generated is $\pi K^\nu + wl^\nu$, which is optimal by lemma 1. By lemma 1 there are solutions of the form $(0, y^\nu, x_0^\nu)$ and $(0, y^\mu, x_0^\mu)$ for ν and μ. In fact for such solutions $x_0^\nu = l^\nu$ and $x_0^\mu = l^\mu$, and by hypothesis $(0, y^\mu x_0^\mu)$ can be chosen so that $Ly^\mu = x_0^\mu$, hence

$$L\left(\frac{y^\mu}{l^\mu}\right) = 1. \tag{20}$$

By definition of C^1 we must have

$$L\left(\frac{y^\nu}{l^\nu}\right) > 1. \tag{21}$$

But since investment in sectors can be completely arbitrary, because of profit-rate equalization, y^ν can be chosen to be a scalar multiple of y^μ. It then follows from (20) and (21) that there must be more capital per man in ν than in μ.

It remains to prove lemma 2. Part d is obvious, since if $K^\nu > 0$, ν must invest its capital either by hiring domestic or foreign labor to maximize national income, since $\pi > 0$. Parts a through c can be verified by a routine consideration of the canonical solutions of the form $(0, y^\nu, x_0^\nu)$ discussed in lemma 1, which will not be carried out here.

If there is unequal exchange, we know that countries with a high capital-labor ratio are the recipients of more labor embodied than hours worked by their populations. We know also that countries of high capital-labor ratio can only optimize by importing workers, thus are in the class C^1. The next task is to relate the two decompositions of countries—the one according to UE-exploitation status, the other according to class status.

The Correspondence between Unequal Exchange and Labor Migration

We have related the labor migration across the borders of a country to its capital-labor ratio k^ν and also its status as exploiter or exploited vis-à-vis the unequal exchange criterion to its ratio k^ν. Using the capital-labor ratio as a yardstick for both unequal exchange and labor migration allows us to relate these two measured quantities to each other. There is indeed a tidy relationship between unequal exchange and labor migration, summarized in theorem 3.

THEOREM 3 Any country $\nu \in C^1$ is UE exploiting, and any country $\nu \in C^3 \cup C^4$ is UE exploited. That is, a country that can only optimize by importing foreign labor (a member of C^1) must be a gainer from unequal exchange, and a country that can only optimize by exporting domestic labor (a member of C^3 or C^4) must be suffering from unequal exchange.

We require, first, another formulation of the characterization of a country's class by its capital-labor ratio.

LEMMA 3 Let $\pi > 0$ at an equilibrium (p, w).

a. $\nu \in C^1 \Leftrightarrow k^\nu > (pA/L)_{\max}$,

b. $\nu \in C^2 \Leftrightarrow (pA/L)_{\min} \leqq k^\nu \leqq (pA/L)_{\max}$,

c. $\nu \in C^3 \Leftrightarrow 0 < k^\nu < (pA/L)_{\min}$,

d. $\nu \in C^4 \Leftrightarrow 0 = k^\nu$.

Proof

From lemma 2 it suffices to prove b, and the other parts will follow. First, suppose $\nu \in C^2$. Then according to lemma 2 there is an optimal solution $(0, y^\nu, x_0^\nu)$ for ν with $Ly^\nu = l^\nu$. Since π is positive, ν must use all its capital to optimize, and so $pAy^\nu = K^\nu$. These two latest equations imply that

$$\frac{pAy^\nu}{Ly^\nu} = \frac{K^\nu}{l^\nu}, \tag{22}$$

which immediately implies

$$\left(\frac{pA}{L}\right)_{\min} \leqq k^\nu \leqq \left(\frac{pA}{L}\right)_{\max}. \tag{23}$$

Conversely, let (23) hold. Then there exists a semipositive vector, call it y^ν, such that

$$Ly^\nu = l^\nu \quad \text{and} \quad pAy^\nu = K^\nu. \tag{24}$$

Since any way of investing one's capital is profit maximizing, because all sectors make the same profit rate, the vector y^ν of (24) belongs to an optimal solution for ν of the form $(0, y^\nu, x_0^\nu)$, with $x_0^\nu = l^\nu$ and thus $Ly^\nu = x_0^\nu$. If follows from lemma 2 that $\nu \in C^2$.

We now can prove theorem 3. This is done by comparing the characterizations of UE exploitation status, on the one hand, and class position of countries, on the other, in terms of the common yardstick k^ν. From (18) country ν is UE exploited if, and only if,

$$k^\nu < \frac{1 - w\left(\dfrac{\Lambda}{p}\right)_{\max}}{\pi\left(\dfrac{\Lambda}{p}\right)_{\max}}. \tag{25}$$

According to lemma 3, $\nu \in C^3 \cup C^4$ if, and only if,

$$k^\nu < \left(\frac{pA}{L}\right)_{\min}. \tag{26}$$

Thus any country in $C^3 \cup C^4$ will be UE exploited if

$$\left(\frac{pA}{L}\right)_{\min} \leqq \frac{1 - w\left(\dfrac{\Lambda}{p}\right)_{\max}}{\pi\left(\dfrac{\Lambda}{p}\right)_{\max}}. \tag{27}$$

Similar reasoning implies that any country in C^1 will be UE exploiting if

$$\left(\frac{pA}{L}\right)_{\max} \geqq \frac{1 - w\left(\dfrac{\Lambda}{p}\right)_{\min}}{\pi\left(\dfrac{\Lambda}{p}\right)_{\min}}. \tag{28}$$

by virtue of lemma 3 and inequality (19). Thus we need to prove (27) and (28). Following is a proof of (28). The proof of (27) is identical.

Proof

Suppose (28) were false. Then:

$$\left(\frac{pA}{L}\right)_j < \frac{1 - w\left(\dfrac{\Lambda}{p}\right)_{\min}}{\pi\left(\dfrac{\Lambda}{p}\right)_{\min}}, \quad \text{for all } j = 1, n, \tag{29}$$

from which the vector inequality (30) follows:

$$\pi\left(\frac{\Lambda}{p}\right)_{\min} pA < L - w\left(\frac{\Lambda}{p}\right)_{\min} L. \tag{30}$$

By definition of p and π lemma 1b, (15) can be written:

$$[p(1 - A) - wL]\left(\frac{\Lambda}{p}\right)_{\min} < L - w\left(\frac{\Lambda}{p}\right)_{\min} L, \tag{31}$$

from which

$$p(1 - A) < \left(\frac{p}{\Lambda}\right)_{\max} L. \tag{32}$$

Postmultiplying (32) by the positive matrix $(1 - A)^{-1}$ yields

$$p < \left(\frac{p}{\Lambda}\right)_{\max} L(1 - A)^{-1} = \left(\frac{p}{\Lambda}\right)_{\max} \Lambda, \tag{33}$$

which by definition of $\left(\frac{p}{\Lambda}\right)_{\max}$ is an impossibility.

It follows that (28) is true, and the theorem is proved. ■

Discussion

With the advent of international labor migration not only does unequal exchange exploitation exist, but countries become divided into labor-exporting and labor-importing ones. Theorem 3 demonstrates the relationship between unequal exchange and labor migration. Note the theorem does not allow us to conclude that, *if* we see a country exporting labor, then it is UE exploited: only if it *must* export to maximize national income is it UE exploited. (In particular, according to lemma 1, every country possesses an optimal solution wherein it exports labor.) Of course this model is simplistic in that it assumes no disutility is involved for the worker in going abroad. In reality selling one's labor abroad and at home is not a choice of indifference. If this were properly incorporated into the model, we might be able to prove that countries that export labor must export labor, and then the observation of labor exportation could suffice to conclude UE exploitation.

It is worth reiterating the very strong criterion that has been adopted to define UE exploitation. A country is UE exploited only if there is no conceivable way for it to buy goods, with its national income, embodying as much labor as its population worked. We might, alternatively, wish to adopt the following more "actual" criterion: A country is UE exploited if the goods it actually purchases with its national income embody less labor than its citizens work, and similarly for the reformulation of UE exploiting. But note that, according to theorem 3, it remains true that countries in C^1 are UE exploiting (by the reformulated definition) and countries in $C^3 \cup C^4$ are still UE exploited. This holds since we know, no matter what bundle a country in

$C^3 \cup C^4$ purchases, it must embody less labor than its citizens worked, and hence the particular bundle it actually chooses to purchase will have this characteristic. As theorem 3 is formulated to be independent of demand, it holds *regardless of the structure of preferences.*

The converse to theorem 3 is not true. There may be UE-exploited and UE-exploiting countries in class C^3. In fact, if we adopt the preference-dependent (actual) definition of unequal exchange, then almost all countries in C^3 will be exploited or exploiting, and not exploitation neutral. (I believe the preference-independent criterion for UE exploitation is much the better one.)

The criterion for UE exploitation does not distinguish between the goods a country imports and the goods it purchases for final demand from domestic production at international prices. The source of goods is immaterial from the point of view of evaluating unequal exchange, as it should be if all sectors can be operated in every country as a profit-maximizing strategy. This is to be contrasted with the classical description of unequal exchange, in which the labor embodied in imports is compared to the labor embodied in a country's exports. Without loss of generality we may assume that a country's final demand is entirely satisfied from imports, and its home production is entirely exported, but this is a distinction without a difference in our model, because all goods trade at international prices and can be profitably produced anywhere.

3.3 International Capital Flows

Instead of introducing migration of labor, as was done in section 3.2, suppose instead an international capital market is introduced into the model $\mathscr{E}(p)$ of section 3.1. Countries can trade commodities and borrow (lend) capital, but there is no migration of labor. This is a more classical unequal exchange environment. We can write the optimization problem this way: country ν chooses (x^ν, z^ν, y^ν) to

$$\textbf{(P3)}\begin{cases} \max & p(1-A)x^\nu + (p-(1+r)pA)y^\nu + rz^\nu, \\ \text{s.t.} & pAx^\nu + z^\nu \leqq p\omega^\nu = K^\nu, \\ & Lx^\nu + Ly^\nu \leqq l^\nu, \\ & x^\nu, y^\nu, z^\nu \leqq 0, \end{cases}$$

where (p, r) is the international price vector, including interest rate r and

x^ν = vector of activities ν operates with its own finance capital,
y^ν = vector of activities ν operates on borrowed finance capital,
z^ν = amount of finance capital lent abroad.

The three terms in the objective function of **(P3)** are the contributions to national income from production with home capital, production with borrowed capital, and interest from capital lent abroad. All workers are domestic by hypothesis, and so the (domestic) wage is suppressed, as in section 3.1. Call this model $\mathscr{E}(p, r)$.

As in the previous section, (p, r) will be called an equilibrium for $\mathscr{E}(p, r)$ if

(D1) There is an optimal solution (x^ν, z^ν, y^ν) for each ν,

(D2a) $A(x + y) \leqq \omega$, where $x + y = \sum_\nu (x^\nu + y^\nu)$,

(D2b) $z = pAy$, where $z = \sum_\nu z^\nu$,

(D3) $x + y > 0$.

Only **(D2b)** requires comment: it states the international capital market clears and is the counterpart of the labor market clearance condition in $\mathscr{E}(p, w)$.

The analysis of this model is in fact identical to the analysis of $\mathscr{E}(p, w)$ and therefore will not be carried out. First, as in lemma 1, it can be shown that at a solution vector (p, r) there will exist a scalar w such that

$$p = (1 + r)\, pA + wL.$$

Thus an international capital market sets a common wage in all countries. This is the exact analog of lemma 1b, where it was shown that an international labor market in fact sets a uniform profit rate on capital in all countries, despite the lack of an international capital market in that model. As in section 3.2 there are UE-exploited and UE-exploiting countries, in general, at a solution.

Moreover classes of countries can be defined with reference to the use of the credit market. Consider the schematic representation of solutions (x^ν, z^ν, y^ν) as $(+, +, 0)$, etc. Thus define

$C^1 = \{\nu \mid \nu$ possesses a solution $(+, +, 0)$ but none of form $(+, 0, 0)\}$,
$C^2 = \{\nu \mid \nu$ possesses a solution $(+, 0, 0)\}$,
$C^3 = \{\nu \mid \nu$ possesses a solution $(+, 0, +)$ but none of form $(+, 0, 0)\}$,
$C^4 = \{\nu \mid \nu$ possesses a solution $(0, 0, +)\}$.

Countries in C^1 must lend capital abroad to maximize national income; countries in C^2 can maximize national income without lending or borrowing capital; countries in C^3 must borrow capital from abroad to maximize national income; countries in C^4 can only maximize national income by borrowing all their operating capital from abroad.

The design of the class typology is purposefully done to make the classes in $\mathscr{E}(p, r)$ look like the classes in $\mathscr{E}(p, w)$. That indeed is the main theorem: $\mathscr{E}(p, r)$ and $\mathscr{E}(p, w)$ are isomorphic models. Imagine two worlds, in one of which the international capital market operates and in the other the international labor market operates. Each world is a duplicate of the other, in the sense that the countries are identical in the two, each country in one having a twin with the same (ω^ν, l^ν) endowment. Then the two worlds possess identical equilibriums, with isomorphic class and exploitation properties.

THEOREM 4 Let $(\bar{p}, \bar{w})$ be a solution for a model $\mathscr{E}(p, w)$ with countries 1, $\ldots, \mathcal{N}$ possessing capital-labor endowments $\{(\omega^\nu, l^\nu) \mid \nu = 1, \mathcal{N}\}$, using the labor market. Consider the same world operating with credit market model $\mathscr{E}(p, r)$. Then there is an interest rate $\bar{r}$ such that $(\bar{p}, \bar{r})$ is an equilibrium solution for $\mathscr{E}(p, r)$. Moreover each country is the member of the same class C^j in the two solutions, and the national income of each country is the same at the two equilibriums. Thus each country sustains identical characteristics of class and UE exploitation in $\mathscr{E}(p, w)$ and $\mathscr{E}(p, r)$. Conversely, any solution (p', r') in $\mathscr{E}(p, r)$ induces a wage w' for which (p', w') is an isomorphic solution in $\mathscr{E}(p, w)$.

The proof of this theorem is straightforward and will not be reproduced here.[9] The theorem verifies the old adage "It doesn't matter whether capital hires labor or labor hires capital." In $\mathscr{E}(p, w)$ international capital is hiring labor, and in $\mathscr{E}(p, r)$ international labor is hiring capital. Truly, the outcome is the same using either market: those countries with low capital per man are UE exploited no matter how the cat is skinned.

In particular, because of this isomorphism theorm it follows that the correspondence between UE exploitation and class in $\mathscr{E}(p, r)$ holds: *any country that must export capital in $\mathscr{E}(p, r)$ to maximize national income is UE exploiting and any country that must import capital to maximize national income is UE exploited.*

The isomorphism theorem tells us that the international capital market and labor market are functionally equivalent. (In reality this is not so, because there are different costs to labor migration than to capital migration, costs ignored in these frictionless models.) It should not come as a surprise, then, that if both markets exist, one will always be redundant. That is, in a model $\mathscr{E}(p, w, r)$ where countries have the option to import and export both labor and capital, at an equilibrium solution, one market can always be dispensed with, in the sense that an equilibrium arrangement always exists using either of the markets.

THEOREM 5 Let (p, w, r) be an equilibrium solution in $\mathscr{E}(p, w, r)$. Then equilibrium actions can always be assigned to all countries so that only the capital market or the labor market is used, but not both. Equilibrium prices are of the form $p = (1 + r)pA + wL$.

This theorem is not proved here, but it is a simple corrollarly to theorem 4.

3.4 Why Call It Unequal Exchange?

The neoclassical interpretation of this story does not support the contention that the transfer of embodied labor in the phenomenon in question should be viewed as unequal or unfair exchange. What occurs is the exchange of labor today for access to capital produced in the past. A country with low capital per man must trade current labor for access to accumulated dead labor (capital). All countries gain from trade as a result. So long as private property in capital is respected, there is nothing unfair about such trades, and they are unequal only by a misnomer that obscures the fact that labor expended in the past does not have the same value as labor expended today if the rate of interest is positive. If production takes time, and capital is necessary for production, then countries without much capital will pay a price to have use of it.

In many cases the radical or Marxian claim of unequal exchange has not been sufficiently aware of this response. That is, there is nothing more unfair or unequal about "unequal international exchange" (at least in models such as the ones in this chapter) than there is about the exchange of labor power for the wage in capitalism in one country. And Marx, of all people, was at pains to show that the transaction on the labor market was, in some sense, the consequence of an *equal* exchange of labor power for the wage, between worker and capitalist. Nevertheless, Marxists speak of exploitation of the worker by the capitalist, despite the "equality" of the exchange. In like manner, I have spoken of UE exploitation between countries. How, then, can an "equal" exchange give rise to the description of exploitation?

As I discuss at length elsewhere, whether one considers a relationship exploitative depends upon the counterfactual against which one is comparing the present allocation resulting from the relationship.[10] For the moment consider the situation of workers (who own no means of production) and capitalists (who do) in one country. The neoclassical analyst does not consider the capitalist-worker relationship exploitative because the counterfactual, or alternative arrangement, against which he compares the capitalistic allocation is one in which workers do not trade with capitalists. If you will, workers are imagined to withdraw from the economy with their own assets, and we ask: Will they be better off? The answer is, No, that is, the workers *do* gain from trade with capitalists. The Marxian counterfactual is, however, different. It poses the question: How well off could the workers be if everyone had equal access to society's capital? If the workers withdrew with their *proportionate share* of social capital, not their own assets, how well-off would they be? It is shown in the mentioned references that this counterfactual characterizes Marxian exploitation. Workers are not neoclassically exploited, because neoclassical exploitation results from barriers to free trade of one's own assets; workers are, however, Marxian exploited, because Marxian exploitation results from the unequal access of agents to the non-human, alienable means of production. It is beyond my scope here to discuss the philosophical basis of this distinction.

One can now conclude in what sense exchange between countries with different capital-labor ratios can be called "unequal": it is so under the hypothetical alternative of a redistribution of capital among countries in which each country will receive an equal amount of capital per worker. We have shown that the unequal exchange phenomenon can be driven *entirely* by different capital-labor ratios, and the annihilation of the phenomenon requires the annihilation of those differentials. Put this way, it is evident that the ethical basis for calling for such a redistribution must examine arguments similar to the call for redistribution of capital in one country, the traditional Marxist appeal. If some agents (countries or people) accumulated their capital stock by robbery and plunder, for instance, then a redistribution would seem justifiable.

Marxists have developed an elaborate theory for the socialization of capital within advanced capitalist countries, regardless of the way that capital came to be accumulated. It is not immediately clear that the argument applies as well to the socialization of capital among nation-states, which is what must be presupposed in the unequal exchange discussion, according to this analysis. If there is any ethical imperative in the appellation of unequal exchange, it must concern itself with annihilation of differential capital-labor ratios among countries.

3.5 Concluding Remarks

1. The strategy of this paper has been to eliminate all differences between countries save one: the capital-labor ratio. All countries have knowledge of the same technique and have equally skilled workers. Nevertheless, unequal exchange exists in the sense that some countries are unable to command as much labor, embodied in goods purchased with their national income, as the labor expended by their own workers, while some countries always command more labor with their income than their populations worked. Occam's

razor leads us to characterize unequal exchange as resulting, then, from differential capital-labor ratios.

The other conclusions may be briefly reported:

2. In $\mathscr{E}(p)$ although there is no international capital or labor market, unequal exchange, nevertheless, exists. In this world there is an international division of labor, wherein countries with lower k^ν operate more labor-intensive sectors. One might argue, although not within the context of the present model, that the international division of labor that is adopted is to the detriment of the capital-poor countries, for other reasons than unequal exchange.

3. With an international labor market, in the model $\mathscr{E}(p, w)$, the international division of labor disappears, a consequence of the international equalization of the profit rate. A class phenomenon appears, in which some countries must export labor to maximize national income, and some must import it. The main theorem identifies labor exportation with being UE exploited and importation of labor with being an UE exploiter.

4. Likewise, with an international capital market capital-exporting countries are identified as UE exploiters and capital-importing countries as UE exploited.

5. The international capital and labor markets are functionally equivalent in these frictionless models. Labor migration can be isomorphically transformed into capital migration in the opposite direction.

6. The neoclassical and radical positions on unequal exchange are clarified by proposing the implicit and different counterfactuals that underlie their contrasting judgments. The parallel is drawn between unequal exchange between countries and Marxian exploitation of workers by capitalists in one country; the same disagreement between Marxists and neoclassicals exists in the one country case as in the international case.

I must conclude with this caveat: there are many elements of friction or noncompetitiveness or "imperfections" that can also lead, a fortiori, to unequal exchanges. Countries may not all have knowledge of the same technique; subsistence wages may differ across countries; there may exist alternative technologies in the subsistence sector of varying degrees of efficiency in different countries (which can give rise to different subsistence wages); other primary factors may be necessary for production and may be differentially endowed across countries. All of these factors will exacerbate the inequality of exchange. Clearly the present analysis cannot evaluate such models. My strategy has been to show how much one can do even with the minimal assumption of differential capital-labor ratios.

Notes

1. Marxian economics with the production set specified as a general convex set is developed in Roemer (1981, ch. 2). Models bearing a family resemblance to the ones in this paper, but with production specified as a convex cone, are developed in Roemer (1982, ch. 5).

2. However, if labor is the only primary factor, joint production is allowed. It is shown in Morishima (1974) and Roemer (1981) that embodied labor time can be defined for any conical production set in which labor is the unique primary factor.

3. Convention on vector (and matrix) orderings: For vectors x and y, $x > y$ means in all components $x_i > y_i$; $x \geqq y$ means $x_i \geqq y_i$ for all components i; $x \geq y$ means $x \geqq y$ and $x \neq y$.

4. It is assumed that the internal markets in country are competitive, so nothing prevents the wage rate from settling at w^ν. If w^ν were below the subsistence wage, the analysis would be slightly different.

5. The factor price equalization theorem does not apply, as there are more goods than primary factors.

6. "Suffer" and "gain" are put in quotations, as the usage implied is the one of the proponents of unequal exchange with which a neoclassical would disagree.

7. There is a caveat on (4). If a country has a very low k^ν, then its labor constraint (2) will be slack at its optimum. (This happens only when $w^\nu = 0$, which means low k^ν.) For such countries we should replace l^ν in (4) with the amount of labor actually supplied, $\bar{l}^\nu$. This does not alter the argument that follows at all, and for notational simplicity we therefore simply identify l^ν as the amount of labor actually used, which may in some cases be less than the labor supply. (That is, set $l^\nu = \bar{l}^\nu$.)

8. If (11) holds, it can be shown that, although ν is not UE exploiting, every country with a positive profit rate is UE exploited. (In any case the proportionality of p and Λ is a singular event at an equilibrium.)

9. The proof proceeds as follows: Corresponding to a solution (p, w) in $\mathscr{E}(p, w)$, we know there is a uniform profit rate $\bar{\pi}$. Choose $r = \bar{\pi}$. We then show (p, r) is a solution in $\mathscr{E}(p, r)$. Every country that in $\mathscr{E}(p, w)$ was importing labor is assigned in $\mathscr{E}(p, r)$ to export capital to that labor that now stays in its home country. Thus labor importing is transformed into lending capital, and labor exporting into borrowing capital. One checks that this assignment of actions in $\mathscr{E}(p, r)$ at prices (p, r) generates an optimal solution with the identical class and exploitation characteristics as claimed.

10. In Roemer (1982a) and (1982b).

References

Emmanuel, A., 1972. *Unequal Exchange.* New York, Monthly Review Press.

Roemer, J., 1981. *Analytical Foundations of Marxian Economic Theory*, New York, Cambridge University Press.

Roemer, J., 1982a. *A General Theory of Exploitation and Class.* Cambridge, Harvard University Press.

Roemer, J., 1982b. Exploitation, alternatives, and socialism. *Economic Journal* 92 (March): 87–107.

Morishima, M., 1974. Marx in the light of modern economic theory. *Econometrica* 42 (June): 611–632.

II

Central Planning: Resource Allocation and International Comparisons

4 Team Theory and Decentralized Resource Allocation: An Example

Kenneth J. Arrow

The traditional discussion of the price system and alternative forms of decentralized resource allocation in organizations and entire economies has an ambivalent attitude to the ease of transferring information from one locus in the economic system to another. On the one hand, the very need for decentralization is based on the assumption that the transmission of information is costly. If this were not so, there would be no reason not to transfer all information on the availability of resources and the technology of production to one place and compute at one stroke the optimum allocation of resources.[1] On the other hand, the literature has tended to seek algorithms that in some sense minimize the amount of information transferred but at the same time yield in the end the fully optimal allocation of resources.[2] In short, there is no true trade-off between information costs and other resource costs. If there were, one would expect that an optimal allocation of resources, taking account of information costs, would differ from the optimal allocation in the absence of information costs. The standard tradition can be rationalized only by assuming that information costs are infinitesimal but not zero; hence they should be minimized to the extent possible without affecting the overall allocation.[3]

The theory of teams was introduced by Jacob Marschak precisely to bring information costs into the allocation process explicitly; see J. Marschak (1955), J. Marschak and Radner (1972). It does so in a way that is polar to the standard tradition. It assumes a fixed amount of communication in fixed channels. The "costs" of communication are modeled by scarcity.

Team theory differs in other ways from the standard approach. It makes more use of prior information about the economy. In the usual form of the price- or quantity-adjustment iterative process for achieving an optimal allocation of resources, the rule design uses only the broadest qualitative information about the economy. There are no assumptions about the likely shapes of the production functions or the range of possible levels of resource supplies.[4] In team theory some or all of the basic parameters of technology or resources are unknown; otherwise there would be no informational problem at all. But there is prior information in the sense that probabilities are attached to different possible values of the parameters. The decisions made under decentralization can then take advantage of this knowledge and reduce the probability of a bad decision as far as possible.

There is still another difference between the standard approach and team theory, which follows from the fact that there are irreducible differences in information among the members of the team. In the standard approach the decisions are ultimately all made by the central authority, the individual parts being only sources of information. In a sense, since relevant information is eventually equalized, it does not really matter who makes the decisions. In team theory, as in real life, the allocations are ultimately the results of many individual decisions. The decentralization is real.

One implication among others is that the rules must be designed to ensure feasibility without a full exchange of information on resource supplies.

The general form of the team problem then is this: The system has a number of agents, each charged with making certain decisions. The system's operations are governed by a number of parameters, initially unknown to the agents. There is a probability distribution over these parameters, reflecting prior knowledge. Each agent is given some information on some of the parameters. That is, the probability distribution of the parameters is conditioned on the agents' items of information. Each agent then makes a decision within its competence as a function of the information available to it. The team problem is to choose in advance the rules or *decision functions* for all agents. These decision functions are determined jointly to optimize the expected outcome, which is a function of the true values of the parameters and of the decisions made.

I will not try here to repeat in more detail the general formulation of the team problem, which can be found in J. Marschak and Radner (1972). The structure will be sufficiently clear from the specific example to be analyzed. This example is very simple but requires sufficient analysis to indicate the nature of the team theory approach to resource allocation and the problems that need to be solved in applying it.

We assume a known production structure, indeed the simple one of fixed coefficients. Unknown a priori are the resource supplies. Each resource manager knows the supply of his or her own resource and is required to divide it between the general production using all supplies and a specialized alternative use. This chapter is devoted primarily to establishing the decision rules for the resource managers that yield the optimal resource allocation for the given information structure.

A modification of the model would permit the resource managers to transmit incomplete information about resource holdings. In that case the center, having received the information, would then issue decision rules to the resource managers. The extension is in fact very straightforward. The calculation of the benefits from the additional information is straightforward in principle but does not lend itself to simple expression in formulas. These benefits should be compared with the costs of the additional information.

4.1 Formal Statement of the Model

We are assumed to have n resources. These resources can be used jointly to produce a product. The production structure is defined by fixed coefficients: each unit of output requires a fixed amount of each resource. By choosing units properly, we can assume that the fixed coefficients are all 1, that it requires 1 unit of each resource to produce 1 unit of the output. Let

y = output,
x_i = amount of ith resource available,
x'_i = amount of ith resource used in production of output.

Then

$$y = \min (x'_1, \ldots, x'_n) = \min_i x'_i. \qquad (1)$$

Clearly, if the only use of the resources is in the production of this product, there is no interesting resource allocation problem. The entire amounts x_i are delivered to the production unit; no resource manager should be affected by the fact that he or she does not know the amounts of the other resources. Notice that resources other than the ones in least supply are useless in production; but if there are no alternative uses, that does not matter.

To make the allocation interesting therefore, assume that each resource has another use, with a unit value that is constant relative to the joint product. Let

w_i = unit value of resource in alternate use, with joint product as numeraire.

The aim of the team is to achieve as large a value of

$$y + \sum_{i=1}^{n} w_i(x_i - x'_i)$$

as possible.

If the resource availabilities x_i were known, this problem would have an easy solution. It must of course satisfy the feasibility constraints

$$0 \leqq x_i \leqq x'_i \qquad \text{all } i. \tag{2}$$

The problem would have a totally trivial solution if

$$\sum_{i=1}^{n} w_i \geqq 1,$$

for in that case it would always be at least as good to engage only in specialized use of the resources. To see this, consider any feasible allocation. Now consider a new one that simply shuts down the joint production. The value of the specialized uses of the resources increases by $\sum w_i x'_i$, while the amount of the joint produce decreases by $\min_i x'$. Hence the net gain is

$$\sum_{i=1}^{n} w_i x'_i - \min_i x'_i \geq \sum_{i=1}^{n} w_i \min_i x'_i - \min_i x'_i = \left(\sum_{i=1}^{n} w_i - 1\right) \min_i x'_i \geq 0.$$

There is never any loss in shutting down joint production. In this case then the decision rules for the individual resource managers are simple: use all the resources for the specialized use. This rule can be carried out by the resource managers without any knowledge of each other's resources availabilities.

Hence we assume

$$\sum_{i=1}^{n} w_i < 1. \tag{3}$$

If there is complete information, then clearly the optimal policy would be to set, $x'_i = \min_j x_j$ for each i. That is, we would want to invest as much as possible of each resource in the general production process, subject to the nonwastefulness condition that an equal amount of each resource be used. This is because increasing the allocation of each resource to the general process by 1 unit, if feasible, increases output of the community by 1 and decreases the total value in the specialized processes by $\sum w_i$.

This allocation, however, requires that each resource manager know the amounts of all other resources (or at least the minimum of all other resource availabilities). Let us state explicitly our decision and information assumptions. Beforehand, when the rules are to be determined, each of the variables x_i is assumed to be a random variable, with a distribution known to all. For simplicity I will assume that these variables are independent of each other. The resources become available, but for each resource only the manager knows the availability. Because of the independence assumption no manager has any more information about the availability of other resources than he or she did before the realization of the random variables. The manager has then to determine the amount allocated to the general production process in accordance with the rules laid down.

The allocation that finally results depends on the resources actually available; it must in fact satisfy the resource feasibility conditions (2). But it must also satisfy what may be termed the conditions of *informational feasibility*: a decision cannot depend on more information than is available to the decision-maker.

The last condition, stated formally, is that x'_i, the amount of resource i devoted to general production, can depend only on x_i, the amount of resource i available, for this is all the information available to the manager for resource i. The allocation x'_i cannot depend on the availabilities of any resources x_j for $j \neq i$. The team allocation problem then requires the choice of function, $x'_i(x_i)$, satisfying (2).

$$0 \leqq x'_i(x_i) \leqq x_i, \quad \text{for all values of } x_i. \tag{4}$$

Finally, what is the maximand of the team problem? Since we regard the availabilities, x_i, as random variables, we must seek to maximize the expected payoff for each individual realization:

$$y + \sum_{i=1}^{n} w_i(x_i - x'_i) = \min_i x'_i(x_i) + \sum_{i=1}^{n} w_i[x_i - x'_i(x_i)].$$

Therefore we can finally state the team version of the allocation problem as follows:

Choose n function, $x'_i(x_i)$, the ith function depending on the quantity x_i alone, so as to maximize

$$W = E\left\{\min_i x'_i(x_i) + \sum_{i=1}^{n} w_i[x_i - x'_i(x_i)]\right\}, \tag{5}$$

subject to the constraints (4).

It may be useful to remark that the standard price- and quantity-adjustment procedures amount to full information revelation in the present context. Since resource supplies are inelastic, at the very first announcement of prices the full set of supplies is announced in the price-adjustment procedure. As for the quantity-adjustment procedure this depends on the center's knowing how much of each resource is available, and hence this procedure presupposes full information. In the present simple example the standard methods of decentralized resource allocation require full information by the end of the first round of approximations.

4.2 Form of the Optimal Team Policy

Optimizing on functions is intrinsically more difficult than optimizing on variables. The problem is complicated here by the fact that the functions are defined over specified variables, differing from one to another. In general therefore, team theory problems are difficult to solve. But in this case the functions can be shown to have some relatively simple forms, and the problem can be reduced to an optimization over ordinary real-valued variables.

If we have chosen our policy optimally, then it must also be that the decision rule for any one manager must be optimal, given the rules for all other managers. Consider manager 1. The policies, $x_i'(x_i)$ of all managers with $i > 1$ are taken as given. Since x_i is independent of x_1, for $i > 1$ it is also true that $x_i'(x_i)$ is independent of x_1 for $i > 1$. Hence manager 1 may regard the allocations, x_i', of other managers as given random variables independent of the observed variable, x_1.

Observe also that to choose an optimal function or rule, $x_1'(x_1)$ is really the same as choosing an optimal value for x_1' for each given value of x_1, since x_1 is a known magnitude to manager 1.

We will rewrite (5) so as to separate the terms involving x_1' from the others, over which manager 1 has no influence. We use the fact that the expectation of a sum is the sum of the expectations. First, write

$$W = E\left[\min_i x_i' - \sum_{i=1}^{n} w_i x_1'\right] + E\left[\sum_{i=1}^{n} w_i x_i\right]. \tag{6}$$

The last term is independent of any manager's actions; it is just a constant that does not affect the choice of the optimal team decision rules. Therefore write the first terms separately:

$$W_1 = E\left[\min_i x_i' - \sum_{i=1}^{n} w_i x_i'\right]. \tag{7}$$

W_1 is to be maximized by choice of the decision functions, $x_i'(x_i)$.

Now, to consider the optimization problem for manager 1 alone, write

$$x'_{-1} = \min_{i>1} x_i'.$$

Then

$$\min_i x_i' = \min\,(x_1', x'_{-1}).$$

Write (7) as follows:

$$W_1 = E[\min\,(x_1', x'_{-1})] - w_1 x_1' - E\left[\sum_{i=2}^{n} w_i x_i'\right]. \tag{8}$$

From the viewpoint of manager 1 the values of x_i' for $i > 1$ are given random variables. Hence the third term is a constant; in the first term x'_{-1} is taken as a given random variable. Finally, x_1 is known to manager 1. It does not enter explicitly in (8) at all, but it sets an upper bound to the choice of x'_1, through the feasibility constraint (2) for $i = 1$:

$$0 \leqq x'_1 \leqq x_1. \tag{9}$$

The manager's aim is to choose x'_1 to maximize (8) subject to (9). In technical terms (8) is a concave function of the decision variable x'_1, that is, the marginal contribution of x'_1 decreases. We use a well-known general result, recapitulated in the appendix to this chapter: If x is any random variable and x^* a number to be chosen, then

$$\frac{dE[\min(x^*, x)]}{dx^*} = \text{Prob}(x > x^*). \tag{10}$$

Apply this to the differentiation of (8), with x^* replaced by x'_1, x by x'_{-1}:

$$\frac{dW_1}{dx'_1} = \text{Prob}(x'_{-1} > x'_1) - w_1.$$

As x'_1 increases, the probability of exceeding it necessarily decreases. As x'_1 becomes very small, Prob $(x'_{-1} > x'_1)$ tends to 1, so that dW_1/dx'_1 tends to $1 - w_1$; in view of assumption (3) this must be positive. As x'_1 becomes large, Prob $(x'_{-1} > x'_1)$ approaches 0, so that dW_1/dx'_1 approaches $-w_1 < 0$. Hence there is an intermediate point, say, x_1^*, at which the function w_1 achieves a maximum. It is increasing up to x_1^* and decreasing after that.

This gives the unconstrained maximum for W_1. However, we have to take account of the upper-bound constraint (9). Clearly, if $x_1 > x_1^*$, then the manager should choose x_1^*, the unconditional maximum, while, if $x_1 < x_1^*$, the manager wants to choose x_1, since W_1 is increasing up to that point. In summary the optimal decision rule for manager 1 has the form

$$x'_1(x_1) = \min(x_1^*, x_1).$$

That is, there is a fixed number x_1^* independent of x_1 that defines the optimal rule.

Since the same argument holds for any manager, not merely the first, we have established that the optimal decision rules have the form

$$x'_1(x_i) = \min(x_i^*, x_i). \tag{11}$$

These results show that the problem of choosing n functions, $x'_i(x_i)$, has been reduced to that of choosing n numbers, x_i^*.

We will substitute (11) into (10) and then optimize with respect to the parameters x_i^*. Because of (11) the feasibility constraints (4) are automatically satisfied. To simplify the resulting expression, introduce the new notation

$$x^* = \min_i x_i^*,$$

$$x = \min_i x_i.$$

Note that x is a random variable of known distribution, since it is the minimum of n independent random variables whose distributions are known. Then from (11)

$$\min_i x'_i(x_i) = \min_i \min (x_i^*, x_i) = \min (\min_i x_i^*, \min_i x_i) = \min (x^*, x),$$

$$W_1 = E\left[\min (x^*, x) - \sum_{i=1}^{n} w_i \min (x_i^*, x_i)\right].$$

Suppose the x_i^*'s are not all equal, say, $x_1^* > x^*$. By definition of x^* a small decrease in x_1^* will leave x^* unchanged, but it will decrease min (x_1^*, x_1) for at least some values of x_1. The change therefore increases the expression in brackets for some values of the random variables and decreases it for none, so that W_1 is increased. Hence at the optimum, $x_1^* = x^*$, and, in general, $x_i^* = x^*$ for all i.

The optimization problem has now been reduced to the choice of a single number. *Choose x^* to maximize*

$$W_1(x^*) = E\left[\min (x^*, x) - \sum_{i=1}^{n} w_i \min (x^*, x_i)\right] \tag{12}$$

$$= E[\min (x^*, x)] - \sum_{i=1}^{n} w_i E[\min (x^*, x_i)].$$

Then the optimal decision rule for the ith manager is

$$x'_i(x_i) = \min (x^*, x_i). \tag{13}$$

4.3 Determination of the Optimal Decision Rule

It remains then only to determine x^* so as to maximize (12). The procedure is straightforward; the derivative of W_1 with respect to x^* is equated to zero. From (10) we see how to differentiate each of the terms in (12):

$$\frac{dW_1}{dx^*} = \text{Prob } (x > x^*) - \sum_{i=1}^{n} w_i \text{ Prob } (x_i > x^*).$$

For simplicity introduce the following notation:

$$P(y) = \text{Prob}\ (x > y),$$

$$P_i(y) = \text{Prob}\ (x_i > y_i).$$

These functions are like the well-known cumulative distribution functions, except that they are cumulated from above rather than below. Also let

$$W_1'(x^*) = \frac{dW_1}{dx^*}.$$

Then

$$W_1'(y) = P(y) - \sum_{i=1}^{n} w_i P_i(y).$$

We now use the assumption that the random variables x_i are independent to express $P(y)$ in terms of the probabilities $P_i(y)$. Indeed the assertion $x > y$ is by definition equivalent to the assertion $\min x_i \geq y$, and this in turn, by the definition of a minimum, holds if, and only if, $x_i > y$ for all i. But the events $x_i > y$ for any fixed y are independent events, so the probability of their joint occurrence is the product of the probabilities of their individual occurrences. In symbols

$$P(y) = \text{Prob}\ (x > y) = \text{Prob}\ (\min_i x_i > y) = \text{Prob}\ (x_i > y \quad \text{for all } i)$$

$$= \prod_{i=1}^{n} \text{Prob}\ (x_i > y) = \prod_{i=1}^{n} P_i(y),$$

The hypothesis of independence is used only in the fourth equality. We have then

$$W_1'(y) = \prod_{i=1}^{n} P_i(y) - \sum_{i=1}^{n} w_i P_i(y). \tag{14}$$

We know that x^* satisfies the condition $W_i'(x^*) = 0$, but we need to show that such a root exists and in fact gives the maximum. In particular it should be unique, at least in some relevant range; otherwise the equation may have several solutions, only one of which is the true optimum.

Let $\bar{x}$ be the smallest value of y such that $P_i(y) = 0$ for some i. It is obvious that one would never want to set x^* higher than that, for the contribution of the resource for which $P_i(\bar{x}) = 0$ will never be more than $\bar{x}$, and any allocation of any other resource beyond $\bar{x}$ will be certainly wasted. In the appendix the following is demonstrated: *within the range from* 0 *to* $\bar{x}$, *there is in ordinary circumstances precisely one value of* x^* *for which*

$W_1'(x^*) = 0,$

where W_1' *is defined in* (14), *and this value of* x^*, *used in* (13), *defines the optimal team rules for the managers.*

4.4 Remarks on Operating Characteristics and Partial Information Transfer

Given the optimum policy, it is always possible to determine its performance by substituting back into the expected payoff function, W, as given by (5). This can easily be done numerically in any given case, but no simply interpretable general formula seems available.

Within the framework of the problem as formulated, there is no especial need to determine the performance or operating characteristics of the team decision rule. However, it would be very useful if one were to contemplate alternative team descriptions, in particular the introduction of partial or total information transfer. In the latter case one could calculate the operating characteristics for complete information, where the optimal policy is to set

$$x_i' = \min_j x_j,$$

as noted before. Of course this rule will give a higher expected payoff. However, there is presumably a cost to the provision of complete information, and this should be compared with the gain in payoff. It is for this reason that one would want to compute operating characteristics.

We consider briefly the case of partial information transfer. Suppose each resource manager provides the center with a random variable that is a signal for the availability of that resource. By a signal will be meant a random variable whose distribution is conditional on the actual value of the resource but independent of anything else, in particular of the availabilities of other resources. By Bayes's theorem, then, the center can compute a conditional distribution of the resource availability, x_i, for each i, which differs in general from the prior distribution. The Center can compute x^* as before, but using the conditional distributions, and transmit that value as an instruction to each of the resource managers. The new ceiling on allocations to general production, x^*, is now a function of the signals transmitted. In the extreme case where the transmitted signal is x_i itself, we have complete information, and the value of x^* transmitted will be the optimal value under complete information.

An important but difficult optimization problem is the choice of signals, in other words, of the amount of information transfer to the center. Clearly, some signals are more informative than others: they convey knowledge of the resource availabilities more or less accurately.[5] Hence use of a more informative signal will yield a higher expected payoff. Presumably, however, more informative signals will tend to be more expensive. Hence there is a need for comparing the expected gains with the expected additional costs. While the expected gains can be computed in any given case, as already seen, little apparently can be asserted of a general nature.

4.5 Appendix

The proofs of two assertions were left to this appendix.

The first is (10). Let x be any random variable and x^* any fixed number. We seek the derivative of $E[\min(x^*, x)]$ with respect to x^*.

An expectation is essentially an integral. We can differentiate it by differentiating under the integral sign. Now $\min(x^*, x) = x^*$ if $x > x^*$ and x if $x < x^*$. Hence

$$\frac{d \min(x^*, x)}{dx^*} = 1, \quad \text{if } x > x^*,$$

$$= 0, \quad \text{if } x < x^*.$$

The derivative is undefined when $x = x^*$. However, if, as we have been implicitly assuming, x is a continuous random variable, the probability that it takes on any particular value x^* is zero, so the lack of definition of the derivative at one point does not affect the expectation.

We also note that if a function of a random variable is 1 on some range of x-values, say, the set E, and 0 elsewhere, then the expectation of that function is the probability of E. Hence

$$\frac{dE[\min(x^*, x)]}{dx^*} = E\left[\frac{d \min(x^*, x)}{dx^*}\right] = \text{Prob}(x > x^*),$$

as asserted.

The second assertion left for proof in this appendix is that the function, $W_1'(y)$, as defined in (14), has precisely one zero as y varies from 0 to $\bar{x}$, where $\bar{x}$ is the smallest value of y for which $P_i(y) = 0$ for some i. (It is not excluded that $P_i(y) > 0$ for all i and all y, in which case we may take $\bar{x}$ to be infinite.)

For $y < \bar{x}$, $P_i(y) > 0$ for all i, and therefore

$$\prod_{i=1}^{n} P_i(y) > 0. \tag{A.1}$$

Let

$$V(y) = \frac{W_1'(y)}{\prod_{j=1}^{n} P_j(y)} = 1 - \sum_{i=1}^{n} w_i \frac{P_i(y)}{\prod_{j=1}^{n} P_j(y)} = 1 - \sum_{i=1}^{n} \frac{w_i}{\prod_{j \neq i}^{n} P_j(y)}. \quad \text{(A.2)}$$

From the definition of $P_i(y)$, as the probability that a random variable is greater than y, it must be true that P_i is monotone decreasing as y increases. It is also true that P_i is nonnegative and in fact positive so long as $y < \bar{x}$. Clearly then, the product of any number of P_i's is positive and monotone decreasing. In particular for each i the function

$$\prod_{j \neq 1}^{n} P_j(y)$$

is positive and monotone decreasing. Hence $V(y)$ is monotone decreasing. We also observe that $P_j(0) = 1$, from the definition (resource availability is certainly positive), so that $V(0) = 1 - \sum w_i > 0$. As y approaches $\bar{x}$, $P_j(y)$ approaches 0 for one or more values of j, so that, from (A.2), $V(y)$ approaches negative infinity. Therefore $V(y)$ must equal zero at least once in the interval from 0 to $\bar{x}$.

Since $V(y)$ is monotone decreasing, it would ordinarily be true that it has exactly one zero. Strictly speaking, however, it is conceivable that a monotone-decreasing function is zero on a whole interval.

Thus $V(y)$ is positive for y small, 0 at a point or on an interval, and then negative. By construction $W_1'(y)$ has the same sign (positive, zero, or negative) as $V(y)$. Hence W_1 increases for small y, reaches a maximum, which may be at a point or over an interval, and then decreases.

Therefore any solution of the equations, $V(y) = 0$, or $W_1'(y) = 0$, may be taken as the value of the operating parameter, x^*, which determines the optimal team decision policy.

Notes

1. For the present purposes I assimilate computation and its costs to information transfer. The economics of computation has so far not been well integrated with that of information. For an early and interesting essay, see T. Marschak (1959).

2. Actually, there is rarely any explicit measurement of the information costs of alternative algorithms for achieving optimal resource allocation. Most of the work is satisfied with exhibiting a process that manifestly requires a good deal less than complete information transfer. For an explicit comparison of alternative algorithms according to the amount of information transfer needed, see Oniki (1974).

3. What I have called the standard tradition of decentralized achievement of optimal resource allocation goes back to Adam Smith's "invisible hand," and continues through Walras (1954, pp. 84–86, 90–91, 105–106, 169–172, 243–254, and 184–195), Pareto (1927, pp. 233–234), Barone, pp. 245–290 in von Hayek (1935), J. Marschak (1924), Lange, pp. 57–142 in Lippincott (1938), Taylor, pp. 41–54 in Lippincott (1938), and the more modern literature surveyed in Hurwicz, pp. 3–37 in Arrow and Hurwicz (1977). Most of this literature has emphasized the parametric role of prices and the successive adjustment of prices in accordance with excess demands and supplies. A variant strain has emphasized quantity allocations and their revision so as to bring the shadow prices of each resource in different uses into equality; see especially Kornai and Lipták (1965), Marglin (1969), and Arrow (1976). A very good survey of the entire literature is found in Heal (1973).

It should be added that Hurwicz, pp. 393–412 in Arrow and Hurwicz (1977) and other papers has given a more abstract version of the process of successive adjustments which includes the price- and quantity-adjustment types of algorithms as special cases. However, it has in common with the rest of the literature that information costs do not appear explicitly and that the process seeks a fully optimal allocation disregarding such costs.

4. Indirectly, however, knowledge of the economy may be used to determine the starting point of the iterative process. In practice, of course, the length of the iterative process may be very much reduced by a suitable initial condition.

5. The relation between signals, "more informative than," is definable in different ways. In general, it cannot be an ordering; given any two signals, it is not necessarily true that one is more informative than the other. The most general useful definition is that of Blackwell (1953). With this definition it is always true that a more informative signal will yield a higher expected payoff.

References

Arrow, K. J., 1976. Quantity adjustments in resource allocation: A statistical interpretation. In *Public and Urban Economics*. Edited by R. E. Grieson. Lexington, Mass., Lexington Books, pp. 3–12.

Arrow, K. J., and L. Hurwicz, 1977. *Studies in Resource Allocation Processes*. New York, Cambridge University Press.

Blackwell, D., 1953. Comparison of experiments. *Proceedings of the Second Berkeley Symposium on Mathematical Statistics and Probability*. Edited by J. Neyman. Berkeley, University of California Press, pp. 93–102.

von Hayek, F. (ed.), 1935. *Collectivist Economic Planning*. London, Routledge & Kegan Paul.

Heal, G. M., 1973. *The Theory of Economic Planning*. Amsterdam: North Holland.

Kornai, J., and T. Lipták, 1965. Two-level planning. *Econometrica* 33: 141–169.

Lippincott, B. (ed.), 1938. *On the Economic Theory of Socialism*. Minneapolis, University of Minnesota Press.

Marglin, S. A., 1969. Information in price and command systems of planning. *Public Economics*. Edited by J. Margolis and H. Guitton. New York, St. Martin's Press, pp. 54–77.

Marschak, J., 1924. Wirtschaftsrechung und Gemeinwirschaft. *Archiv für Sozialwissenschaft und Sozialpolitik* 51. 501–520.

Marschak, J., 1955. Elements for a theory of teams. *Management Science* 1: 127–137.

Marschak, J., and R. Radner, 1972. *Economic Theory of Teams*. New Haven, Yale University Press.

Marschak, T., 1959. Centralization and decentralization in economic organizations. *Econometrica* 27: 399–430.

Oniki, H., 1974. The cost of communication in economic organization. *Quarterly Journal of Economics* 88: 529–550.

Pareto, V., 1927. *Manuel d'économie politique*. 2d ed. Paris, Marcel Giard.

Walras, L., 1954. *Elements of Pure Economics*. Edited and translated by W. Jaffé. London, George Allen and Unwin.

5 On the Measurement of Soviet Real Defense Outlays

Abram Bergson

This essay focuses on some conceptual issues concerning calculations of Soviet real defense expenditures by the Office of Strategic Research (OSR) of the Central Intelligence Agency (CIA). The resulting measures of real defense expenditures of course take the form of index numbers, and the issues that are to be considered essentially lie within the realm of index number theory. The nature of the relevant principles and their application to Soviet defense outlays, however, may not yet have been sufficiently explored.

Measurement of Soviet real defense outlays is a theme that seems only rarely to be examined from a theoretic standpoint.[1] By providing further analytic perspective on that important matter, this essay will perhaps serve as a fitting tribute to Alexander Erlich, who has done so much to illuminate the Soviet economy generally.

The OSR compiles two sorts of measures of Soviet real defense expenditures, one relating to the variation in such outlays over time, and the other, to their volume compared with that of the corresponding outlays in the United States. I focus primarily on the latter, but the main argument is readily extended to apply to measures of Soviet real outlays over time.

In the intelligence community measurement of comparative real outlays in the U.S.S.R. and the United States has come to be called the "sizing" problem. In addressing that problem, an initial question that the OSR had to deal with concerns the appropriate scope of such expenditures. This matter is also perhaps somewhat more complex than might be supposed, but it is not of primary interest here.[2] Suffice it to say that OSR construes military outlays in a broadly conventional way to include weapons procurement, defense construction, military personnel costs, various operational and maintenance outlays, and R and D outlays that are taken to be defense related.[3]

In whatever way defense expenditures are delineated, a comparison of such outlays in different countries must be made in constant prices. In the present case the calculations might be made in dollar or ruble prices. The OSR has focused especially on the derivation of comparative data in dollar prices.

Obtaining appropriate data on U.S. outlays can pose no problem for the OSR, at least none in principle. As for the corresponding figures for the U.S.S.R., the OSR has elucidated in numerous unclassified reports the general nature of the procedures it employs in deriving such measures.[4] By now the so-called "building-block" method it applies must be broadly familiar. Essentially, the concern is to establish insofar as possible the physical magnitudes of different Soviet defense goods and services and then to value the items directly in dollar prices commanded by comparable defense goods and services in the United States. The OSR also in some instances uses variants of the building-block method, but that is the chief procedure employed.[5]

The building-block method is of course a very usual one in practical work with index numbers. Given data on the quantities of defense goods and services that the Soviet government is procuring, the procedure evidently can be readily applied where dollar prices happen to be quoted in the United States for precisely the same items as are procured in the U.S.S.R. What, however, if, as is often the case, an item in one country is unique and not produced in the other?

The OSR apparently assumes that U.S. and Soviet defense items are often sufficiently similar, and thus dollar prices of the former may still be applied to the latter. Probably the outstanding instances are in the sphere of military manpower, where services of a given rank in the U.S.S.R. are simply valued at the compensation rates, including money pay, allowances and rations, for services in a corresponding rank in the United States.[6]

Whether such a procedure is always warranted is an interesting question that cannot be pursued here. In this chapter I focus predominantly on goods, rather than services, where circumstances are admittedly otherwise: the Soviet defense items have no identical counterpart in the United States, nor even a sufficiently near one to warrant evaluation simply at the dollar prices of U.S. procurements. Such Soviet items must be numerous, especially among relatively fabricated goods such as munitions. Here, according to a statement submitted by the CIA to the Joint Economic Committee, the OSR has proceeded in this way:

> Our dollar concept is the cost of producing the Soviet design in the United States using base year U.S. production technology, input prices, and profit margins. Our ability to reflect the Soviet design depends to a large degree upon our knowledge of the physical and performance characteristics of the

individual weapons. When we have good data, our cost estimates capture the "austerity or complexity" of the Soviet weapon. We have to fall back on U.S. analogs for weapons or components when our knowledge is less complete. In these cases we attempt to adjust the analog results by extrapolating from our general understanding of Soviet design practices.

When we have sufficient information we do engineering cost studies. Most of our costs are derived using cost estimating relationships (CER's) which are based on U.S. weapons costs adjusted to "Sovietize" the weapon. Some weapons—usually lower cost items—are costed on the basis of the nearest equivalent U.S. weapons.[7]

In other words, where there is no U.S. good identical or deemed very close to a Soviet good, an inquiry is made as to what the factor or resource cost (including an appropriate profit margin) might be of replicating the Soviet good in the United States. The Soviet good is valued at that U.S. factor or resource cost. That is the essential principle applied.

On the face of it this principle can be defended theoretically, by extending to the intercountry comparison of real defense outlays the familiar analysis applied when real national income is compared among countries. Theory teaches that in the latter case we obtain an observation on comparative production capacity in the countries in question. I refer to the capacity to produce goods and services with available factor supplies such as labor and capital.[8] In comparing real defense outlays, we must think correspondingly of the capacity represented by factor supplies committed to the production of defense goods and services.

In national income comparisons production capacity may be understood to refer specifically to comparative capacity to produce the same mix of goods and services in the two countries. The mix to be considered as standard in that sense depends on the prices in which output is valued; paradoxically, with valuation in prices of one country the standard mix is the one actually found in the other. Pursuing further the analogy to real national income comparisons, we see that the comparison of real defense outlays may be construed as indicating relative capacities to produce, with resources committed to defense, the mix of military goods and services found in one country, particularly the one other than that whose prices are used in valuing output. With valuation in dollars, then, the standard mix is the one actually produced in the U.S.S.R.

As usually formulated, the theory of real national income comparison relates to circumstances where any good produced in one country is also produced in the other. The analysis may be extended, however, to circumstances where that is not so, and that is true also of the comparison of real defense outlays. In the case now in question the OSR valuation procedure is seen to be an appropriate one. For Soviet defense goods not produced in the United States, valuation at the dollar factor cost of replicating such goods in this country evidently permits us to construe the defense outlay comparison in dollars as before, that is, as providing an observation on the comparative capacity in the two countries to produce the Soviet mix of defense goods, given the respective volumes of resources committed to defense. That applies to the Soviet mix whether or not there are counterparts in the United States.

The OSR procedure is not the only one available, however. An interesting alternative approach may be formulated based on work in a different context by the late Rush Greenslade, the essentials of which were outlined in a brief memorandum he prepared several years ago.[9] I present the approach in somewhat different terms from Greenslade's and with a rather different rationale from the one that he indicated.

As concerns Soviet products not produced in the United States, and on the valuation of those products in dollars, the OSR procedure estimate is the resource or factor cost of replicating the Soviet product in the United States. Reference is apparently to physical replication, but, so far as that is done, the U.S. replica of course will have the same performance characteristics as the Soviet product; if there is complete physical replication, the performance must be the same.

Yet that is not the only way to get the same performance characteristics. In the United States, if we were seeking to replicate the performance characteristics in question, we might choose to produce them with different inputs—materials, labor, and the like—from those used in the Soviet product. Indeed it would be surprising if we should not do so. Given the disparate technologies, labor supplies, materials, and so forth, in the two countries, scarcity relations in the United States differ from those in the U.S.S.R. To achieve certain performance characteristics, we might find it economical to substitute one sort of factor input for another. So there is the possibility that to some degree similar performance characteristics could be achieved at a different and presumably lower dollar cost than would be entailed in replicating physical characteristics.

In the alternative, as in the OSR calculation, one turns to U.S. manufacturers to obtain estimates of cost. The primary stress, however, is on the cost of replicating performance characteristics, although in some cases this might entail replication of physical characteristics as well. More specifically, valuation at a least-cost reproduction of the Soviet performance characteristics would be sought. Ideally, the Soviet defense goods are to be valued in dollars on that basis.

What is the comparative merit of this and the OSR procedure? While there is a conventional, theoretic basis for the OSR calculation, which makes it seem the more obvious one to employ, the proposed alternative merits consideration. Essentially, when defense outlays in the two countries are valued in dollars and the alternative procedure is applied to Soviet goods that lack any near counterpart in the United States, the resulting data would still be indicative of the comparative capacity of the two countries, with the resources committed to defense, to produce the Soviet mix of defense goods. In the case of Soviet goods lacking any counterpart in the United States, however, reference is to U.S. capacity to produce the performance equivalent of the Soviet good rather than the identical physical item.

The result we get by comparing the real defense outlays of the two economies in that way is arguably more significant than the one from the OSR kind of calculation. What we seek to obtain ideally are observations on comparative "military utility." As we need not ponder long to become aware, military utility measurement is a very difficult thing indeed. We hardly have data we can interpret easily from that standpoint.[10] In any event a comparison of production capacity is certainly not the same thing as a comparison of military utility. But as between capacity to produce physical replicas and capacity to produce performance equivalents, the latter would seem closer to the ultimate desideratum.

I have been considering the OSR procedure as it is in principle. In practice OSR must make many compromises, and no doubt they themselves must often take performance characteristics as an indication of physical characteristics. The difference between the two procedures therefore might not be as great as it might seem on paper. But there is an indisputable difference, and the result is that measured U.S. defense capacity tends to be lower relatively to that of the U.S.S.R. than it would be if the alternative stressing performance were employed.[11]

But I have been referring to the comparative magnitudes of index numbers obtained under the alternative procedures. It remains to consider that, as observations on defense production capacity, both sorts of measures are apt to err. In index number theory that is a familiar kind of theme, but we are concerned with it in a rather novel context. It may be well to expatiate on the matter in formal terms.

Whichever of the two approaches is employed, the index number to be obtained is given by this formula:

$$I_{01} = \frac{V^{11}}{V^{01}}. \tag{1}$$

Here V^{11} is U.S. defense outlays in dollar prices, and V^{01}, Soviet defense outlays in dollar prices, which is given by the formula:

$$V^{01} = \sum_{i=1}^{g} p_i^1 q_i^0 + \sum_{j=h}^{w} \bar{p}_j^1 q_j^0. \qquad (2)$$

There are w defense items purchased in the U.S.S.R., of which g have identical or near identical counterparts in the United States, and $(w - g)$ have no such counterparts. In obtaining the total Soviet outlays, the quantities of the former, q_i^0, are valued at actual U.S. prices, p_i^1, and the latter, q_j^0, are valued at U.S. replication costs, $\bar{p}_j^1$. Depending on the approach adopted, reference is to the replication of physical counterparts in one case and performance equivalents in the other.

In formula (1), as implied,

$$V^{11} = \sum_{i=1}^{t} p_i^1 q_i^1, \qquad (3)$$

where t items are produced in the United States, and p_i^1 and q_i^1 are their actual dollar prices and quantities. Formula (3) applies whether items produced only in the U.S.S.R. are valued at physical replication or performance equivalent cost. For clarity, however, we must also consider alternative hypothetical mixes of defense items that the United States could purchase for the same dollar total:

$$V^{11} = \sum_{i=1}^{g} p_i^1 r_i^1 + \sum_{j=h}^{t} \bar{p}_j^1 s_j^1. \qquad (4)$$

Here r_i^1 is a possibly varying quantity of an item procured in the United States that has a near counterpart in the U.S.S.R., while s_j^1 represents a possibly varying amount of the U.S. reproduction of an item produced in the U.S.S.R. that has no near counterpart in the United States. Depending on the approach adopted, reference is either to a physical replica or a performance equivalent, and $\bar{p}_j^1$ is construed correspondingly.

I have referred to resources committed to defense. When a country's overall production capacity is in question, the resources that constrain output are understood correspondingly as those available to the country as a whole. Since our concern is only with the defense sector, one is tempted to try to delineate from the economywide totals the resources committed to that sector alone. That would be conceptually difficult, for the mix of factors employed in defense could be expected to vary with the mix of defense goods and services produced. But we can define at once the country's capacity to produce defense goods and services in a manner appropriate here simply on the understanding that we refer to mixes that can be produced when the

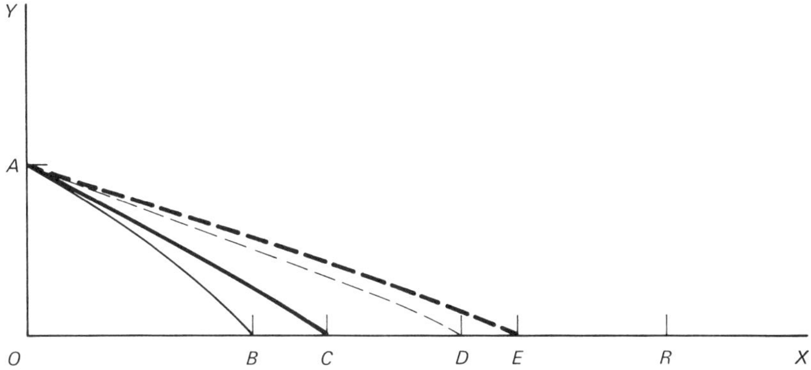

Figure 5.1
Comparative defense production capacity

quantities of all other goods produced are constant. With economywide resources given, that would seem to represent plausibly our desideratum: the capacity corresponding to a given commitment of resources to defense.

Resulting production capacity frontiers for the United States are illustrated (Figure 5.1). While actually producing only a single defense item, say, a type *Y* tank, the U.S. is capable of producing different mixes of that and a corresponding item, say, a type *X* tank, produced by the U.S.S.R. Feasible mixes are represented by *AB*, when for type *X* we refer to physical replicas of that tank, and by *AD*, when the performance equivalent of that tank is in question. Both frontiers are segments of the economywide production capacity surface on the plane corresponding to constant outputs of all nondefense items. Also shown are U.S. defense "budget" lines delineated by (4). Here *AC* is given by that formula when the second term on the right refers to physical replicas and AE, when that term refers to performance equivalents.

Relative to Soviet output of the type *X* tank then, the U.S. capacity to produce its physical replica is given by the ratio

$$C_{01}^{*} = \frac{OB}{OR}, \tag{5}$$

where *OR* stands for the actual Soviet output. With (1) to (4) likewise referring in the case of our single Soviet defense item to its physical replica in the United States, I_{01} has the magnitude:

$$I_{01}^{*} = \frac{OC}{OR}, \tag{6}$$

which should tend to approximate C_{01}^{*} but need not equal it. Similarly, where reference is to U.S. capacity to produce a performance equivalent of the Soviet tank, the relevant capacity ratio becomes

$$C_{01}^{**} = \frac{OD}{OR}, \tag{7}$$

and the corresponding magnitude of I_{01} is

$$I_{01}^{**} = \frac{OE}{OR}, \tag{8}$$

which should approximate C_{01}^{**}.

Since in the case graphed each country produces but a single item, the standard mix consists of only one item: with sizing in dollars, that is, the item produced in the U.S.S.R. With many items produced in each country, however, formulas (1) through (4) still provide alternative observations on U.S. capacity to produce the Soviet mix. The particular observation depends, as before, on the kind of U.S. reproduction in question for Soviet items.

Figure 5.1 shows the production capacity frontiers as concave from below, which is of course the way they usually are drawn. Given that curvature, formula (1) overstates U.S. capacity relative to that of the U.S.S.R. That is so no matter which of the two approaches is adopted. For the simple case illustrated, the overstatement under each approach is evident. Should there be economies of scale, however, the production capacity frontier may or may not be concave from below. The direction of bias in (1) is then uncertain. Many sorts of defense goods are of a highly fabricated kind such that economies of scale often obtain.

The foregoing assumes that the U.S. cost of replicating a Soviet defense item is calculated for a small batch. Should reference instead be to a larger batch that exploits scale economies in greater or less degree, there is perhaps some presumption against understatement of U.S. capacity. What bias, if any, obtains, however, would depend on the degree to which scale economies are allowed for over a relevant range of U.S. output variation. That range might itself be a rather complex matter to gauge.[12]

Costs not only may vary with scale; for highly fabricated products they often vary also with time, through a learning experience. There seems to be no way to rule theoretically between different cost levels that might be experienced in such circumstances. A level some distance out on the learning curve, I suspect, would usually be of primary interest.

We must judge, however, how the OSR deals with cost variation from occasional statements, such as this concerning the valuation of a Soviet ICBM:

> ... the estimated annual dollar costs of this procurement ... is derived by applying the production numbers to an estimate of the cost of the initial unit produced and then bringing the costs down a cost reduction curve which U.S. production experience has led us to believe is appropriate for this kind of hardware.[13]

The production numbers in question apparently refer to the scale of actual Soviet output rather than, as is theoretically indicated, of the hypothetical U.S. output associated with U.S. procurements of a standard, Soviet mix. It is not clear whether the "cost reduction curve" referred to relates only to cost variation with scale or embodies learning experience as well.

So much for the sizing of Soviet defense outlays in dollars. Soviet and U.S. defense outlays can also be compared in ruble prices. U.S. outlays can be translated into rubles in just the same way as the OSR translates Soviet outlays into dollars, with U.S. physical procurement for the most part being valued at ruble prices. So far as U.S. products have no near counterpart in the U.S.S.R., reference might be to the hypothetical factor cost in rubles of replicating those products with respect to their physical characteristics in the U.S.S.R. That evidently would be the mirror image of the procedure used by the OSR to value in dollars Soviet munitions that have no near counterpart in the United States. Or reference might be made to an alternative procedure, such as I have described, where the concern is with replication of performance characteristics. The results again must differ. The procedure stressing physical replication should now result in a measured level of U.S. relative to Soviet defense outlays that is higher, not lower, than the procedure stressing performance. In either case, the measured level then may deviate from comparative defense production capacity in a manner that has been explained.

One may suppose such calculations are possible, but the data would hardly be available in practice. Among other things Soviet manufacturers are not likely to cooperate readily with inquiries into Soviet factor cost of replicating U.S. defense goods. Understandably, the OSR, in comparing defense outlays in ruble prices, must employ rather different methods from those it uses in its dollar comparison. For U.S. products that have no near counterpart in the U.S.S.R., the procedure employed also differs from that emphasizing performance.

Essentially, in calculating Soviet defense outlays in rubles, the OSR values some Soviet defense goods and services directly in ruble prices.[14] For example, military manpower is apparently valued directly in the ruble pay and subsistence of Soviet troops. But for a considerable volume of Soviet defense goods OSR begins with dollar values that have been derived in the manner described earlier. The OSR apparently is also able to refer to ratios of rubles and dollar prices for some defense goods and goods deemed to be similar to defense goods in comparative Soviet and U.S. costs. These ratios provide a basis for translating into rubles the Soviet defense goods initially valued in dollars. As for the calculation of U.S. defense outlays in rubles, the OSR again values some items such as military manpower directly in rubles but begins with dollar procurement values for a large volume of defense goods and translates these into rubles by reference to ruble/dollar price ratios.

This procedure calls for several comments. To begin with, it is fairly obvious that the OSR has to operate with a relatively limited sample of ruble/dollar ratios. Although the sample has grown in time, the ratios themselves must often be inferred from indirect evidence.[15] The calculations in ruble terms therefore must be especially crude. The crudeness is to some extent highlighted by the drastic revision that occurred a few years ago when apparently some additional information became available on ruble/dollar price ratios.[16] The additional information is comforting, but the sensitivity of the results to it is disconcerting.

In fairness, the OSR itself acknowledges the relatively inexact nature of its ruble comparison, and the results have generally been published as a range rather than in single figures. For some time the range for Soviet outlays has been but 11 to 13 percent of the GNP. That allows for a variation of about 20 percent in the defense outlays, but about half of that reflects a difference in concept. One wonders whether the margin of error can be as limited as implied.

However accurate or inaccurate the OSR's calculations in ruble prices may be, as theory teaches and our analysis has clearly implied, production capacity appraisal presupposes that relative commodity prices ideally correspond to "marginal rates of transformation." For well-known reasons one may wonder to what extent dollar prices for defense goods conform to that principle, but the limitations of ruble prices generally are proverbial (see Bergson 1961). Ruble prices of defense goods could not be expected to be an exception to that rule.

Further reference to theoretic principles at this point seems otiose, but a conceptual issue may be worth airing. In compiling ruble/dollar price ratios, suppose that in the case of dollar prices reference for some defense goods must be to the estimated dollar cost of replicating a Soviet product in the United States. Of the two procedures for obtaining such an estimate that I have discussed, which is the more appropriate in determining dollar prices that are to be used in compiling ruble/dollar ratios? For purposes of translating Soviet defense outlays from dollars to rubles, the answer presumably must be that the procedure should be the same as that employed in deriving the dollar values to begin with. For purposes of translating U.S. defense outlays from dollars to rubles, the matter is not so clear, but, the least-cost replication of performance should yield a dollar price that, when compared with a corresponding ruble price, could be more or less indicative of ruble/dollar ratios for defense goods, while a dollar price given by the cost of replicating physical characteristics could easily be off the mark. Actual dollar prices of defense goods should tend to reflect least-cost production of performance characteristics. The market for defense goods, with all of its proverbial limitations, should not sustain for long egregiously uneconomic production of performance characteristics.

In such discussions as have occurred about the rationale behind OSR's methods of sizing Soviet defense outlays, a question frequently raised concerns the treatment of a product of only one country that might be "infinitely" costly to replicate in the other. The main problem here concerns the ruble costs of replicating U.S. high-technology defense goods when sizing is in ruble prices.[17] No satisfactory solution seems to have been found.

Whether there are any products in the United States that would be infinitely costly to replicate in the U.S.S.R. is an interesting issue, but there are doubtless some products whose costs of replication would be so high as to make a literal application of the OSR methodology of doubtful interest. Replication of performance equivalents would to some extent avoid such an outcome.

Recourse is possible, however, to another expedient not yet considered: omit the items in question from the calculation. If one simply excludes from U.S. expenditures the hypothetical ruble outlays on such items, the resulting index would still indicate comparative capacities to produce the U.S. defense mix. I refer, however, to capacities delineated by resources committed to procurement of U.S. items other than those that are infinitely costly to replicate in the U.S.S.R. The U.S. mix that serves as standard must be construed correspondingly. Should any Soviet defense goods be infinitely costly to replicate in the United States, they might be treated similarly in the comparison in dollar terms, with a similarly construed result. In either case the limited coverage must be stressed. With inclusion of the omitted items, comparative outlays of one country or the other become exceedingly large, the country in question being the one whose output is infinitely costly to replicate in the other country.

My discussion of measurement of the comparative volume of Soviet and U.S. defense outlays can be readily extended to the analogous problem of measuring the change in Soviet and U.S. defense outlays over time in constant prices. Usually such a calculation is made in prices of the country concerned, but a choice must be made between early and late prices. Since old products may drop out of and new ones enter the mix of goods produced, here too the problem arises of valuing in one period goods produced in another. At least in principle then we are again confronted with alternative procedures, one stressing physical replication and the other performance. There are also parallel differences in results. With valuation in late prices the procedure emphasizing physical replication should yield a lower measured rate of growth than the one emphasizing performance. With valuation in early prices the relation of the two series of procedures is reversed. Viewed as observations on the change in production capacity over time, both measures are subject to a bias parallel to that obtaining for intercountry comparisons at one time.

The foregoing applies equally to measurements of real defense outlays over time in the U.S.S.R. and the United States. Insofar as the measurements for the U.S.S.R. are in rubles, however, and derived, as in the OSR calculations, through the mediation of dollar values, meaningful application of either of the two procedures must be difficult.

The concept of comparative capacities to produce performance equivalents inevitably calls to mind the so-called "hedonic" approach that lately has come into use in the calculation of the cost of living and real income. While there is an obvious affinity between the two measures, it should be noted that, whether we refer to performance or hedonic equivalents, what is in question is only items within relatively limited commodity categories. As between categories, comparative physical volume is calculated in the one case by use of production cost weights to measure comparative production capacity and, in the other, by use of prices reflecting relative utilities to measure real income changes as they relate to variations in utility.

By considering performance equivalence within categories, I admittedly derive an index of a conceptually mixed character. The result, I believe, is still interesting and meaningful, more so probably than when, as is sometimes done, hedonic equivalents are determined by comparative costs.[18]

Notes

I elaborate here on ideas presented initially in a lecture at the Air Force Academy, Colorado Springs, August 18, 1978. I have benefited from comments of an unidentified reader on an earlier version.

1. An exception, however, is Franklyn D. Holzman, Are the Soviets really outspending the U.S. on defense? *International Security* (Spring 1980). See also Abraham S. Becker, *Military Expenditure Limitations for Arms Control*, Cambridge, Mass.: Ballinger, 1977, ch. 2.

2. Becker, *Military Expenditure*, ch. 2.

3. On the scope of defense outlays as understood by OSR and on the OSR calculations of Soviet defense outlays more generally, see Joint Economic Committee, United States Congress (hereafter, JEC), *Allocation of Resources in the Soviet Union and China—1975*, Washington, D.C., 1975; volumes with corresponding titles for later years that were issued by the JEC in Washington, D.C., in 1976, 1977, 1978 and 1979; Permanent Select Committee on Intelligence, House of Representatives, *CIA Estimates of Soviet Defense Spending*, Washington, D.C., 1980; CIA, *Estimated Soviet Defense Spending in Rubles, 1970–1975*, SR 76-10121 U, May 1976; CIA, *A Dollar Comparison of Soviet and U.S. Defense Activities 1965–1975*, SR 76-10053, February 1976; CIA, *Estimated Soviet Defense Spending: Trends and Prospects*, SR 78-10121, June 1978; CIA, *A Dollar Cost Comparison of Soviet and US Defense Activities, 1966–1976*, SR 77-10001 U, January 1977; and corresponding CIA reports for 1967–1977, 1968–1978, 1970–1979, and 1971–1980 issued, respectively, as SR 78-10002, January 1978; SR 79-10004, January 1979; SR 80-10005, January 1980; SR 81-10005, January 1981. The foregoing CIA reports are cited hereafter by number and date.

4. See note 3.

5. The variants apparently are employed mainly in the case of operation and maintenance and R and D.

6. JEC, *Allocation of Resources in the Soviet Union and China—1975*, pp. 21, 81; Permanent Select Committee on Intelligence, *CIA Estimates*, p. 8.

7. JEC, *Allocation of Resources in the Soviet Union and China—1975*, p. 83. See also Permanent Select Committee on Intelligence, *CIA Estimates*, pp. 2ff, 73ff.

8. For a brief exposition and bibliography, see Abram Bergson, *The Real National Income of Soviet Russia since 1928*, Cambridge, Mass.; Harvard University Press, 1961, ch. 3.

9. Rush V. Greenslade, Resource cost versus performance cost standard in valuing soviet defense (typescript), October 4, 1976.

10. Compare Becker, *Military Expenditure*, ch. 2.

11. Whatever the characteristics considered, the CIA reportedly very often derives the appropriate dollar figure from a regression equation relating dollar costs to those characteristics. Provided the regression equation itself is based on empirical inquiry into U.S. dollar costs, that procedure would seem to be unexceptionable in principle, though as with any such application of regression analysis the result is necessarily subject to error.

Given the nature of the underlying empirical inquiry, however, theory decrees that reference ideally be to dollar costs of the year for which Soviet defense outlays are being sized in relation to those of the United States. Only on that basis can the calculations be read, as theory teaches they might be, as observations on the production capacity frontier. For this reason, Steven S. Rosefielde (in testimony before the Permanent Select Committee on Intelligence, *CIA Estimates*, pp. 10ff) has a point in holding that the CIA's use of 1970 dollar cost relations for other years, would be a further source of error in the agency's calculation's. According to Rosefielde, that has been a usual practice. I for one, though, am unable to grasp why the resulting bias must be as Rosefielde seems to argue in the direction of understating Soviet outlays in post-1970 years. From correspondence with Rosefielde, I have come to wonder whether I have misunderstood him at this point.

12. The shape of the production capacity frontier is affected by U.S. economies of scale not only for Soviet items that lack near counterparts in the U.S. but also for Soviet items that have such counterparts. What is in question for each item is how costs vary over a range defined, on the one hand, by actual U.S. production and, on the other, by the hypothetical output indicated when the U.S. produces a mix conforming to that of the U.S.S.R. To determine that range evidently would require a knowledge of the U.S. production capacity frontier, but it could be approximated so far as formula (4) itself is a near surrogate for that.

To make matters still more complex, where many defense goods are produced, the nature of the least-cost U.S. performance equivalent of any particular Soviet defense good might depend on the mix of defense goods in question. It must be understood therefore that reference is in principle to that U.S. performance equivalent that would be produced at least cost when the United States is producing a mix of defense goods corresponding to the Soviet mix.

13. JEC, *Allocation of Resources in the Soviet Union and China—1975*, p. 23.

14. On the OSR procedures for sizing Soviet defense outlays in rubles, see the items in note 3, especially JEC, *Allocation of Resources in the Soviet Union and China—1975*; the sequels to that volume for 1976 and 1977; CIA, SR 76-10121U, May 1976; Permanent Select Committee on Intelligence, *CIA Estimates*.

15. See Rosefield's testimony in Permanent Select Committee on Intelligence, *CIA Estimates*, p. 14.

16. See CIA, SR 76-10121 U, May 1976.

17. See Holzman, Are the Soviets really outspending, pp. 93–94; Permanent Select Committee on Intelligence, *CIA Estimates*, pp. 9, 45, 76.

18. On hedonic index numbers, see Zvi Griliches, ed., *Price Indexes and Quality Change*, Cambridge, Mass.: Harvard University Press, 1971.

6 Measuring Resource-Allocational Efficiency in Centrally Planned Economies: A Theoretical Analysis

Padma Desai and Ricardo Martin

When in different sectors of a centrally planned economy econometric estimates of production functions and the observed allocation of resources among sectors suggest that resources have been misallocated, how should one measure the implied loss? This chapter is addressed to developing appropriate measures of such misallocational losses. A companion study, Desai and Martin (1983), utilizes one of these measures to calculate resource allocational losses in Soviet industry, using production function estimates for eight industrial branches from Desai (1981).

6.1 Conceptual Issues

Assume that the actual situation is characterized by the absence of equality between marginal rates of substitution (MRS) of factors in different industrial branches. Hence, when MRS are equalized, the reallocation of factors will lead to more output for the same factor use or less factor use for the same output. We can then analyze the measurement issues, first, with reference to the output loss resulting from the suboptimal utilization of given factors and, next, extend the analysis to include measures of factor savings when the same basket of output is produced with less factor utilization.

6.2 Measures of Output Loss

For convenience of geometric exposition we begin our discussion with the symmetric case of two factors, capital (K) and labor (L), and two commodities, X_1 and X_2.

In this 2 × 2 model the observed inefficient allocation is as at $\hat{P}$ in figure 6.1, where AB is the technologically efficient production possibility frontier when $\bar{K}$, $\bar{L}$ are the total endowments of K and L. The corresponding point of factor allocation $\hat{P}$ is evidently off the Edgeworth-Bowley contract curve

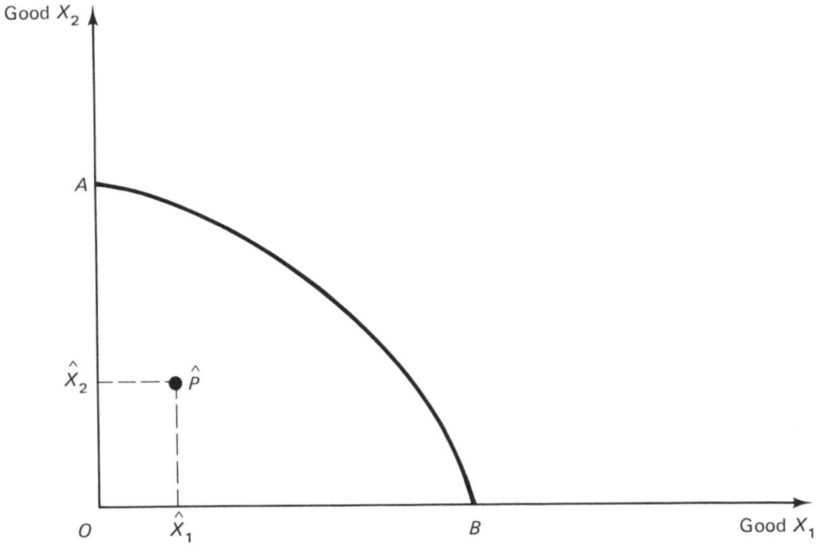

Figure 6.1

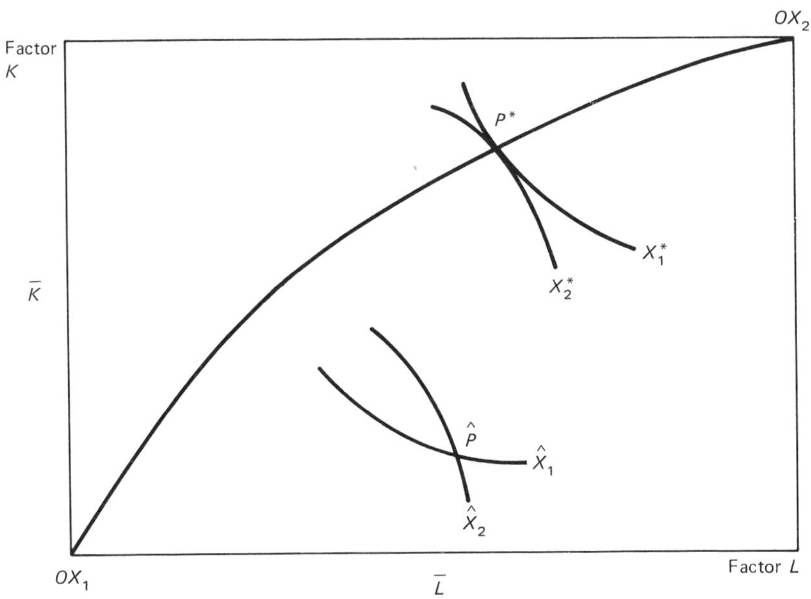

Figure 6.2

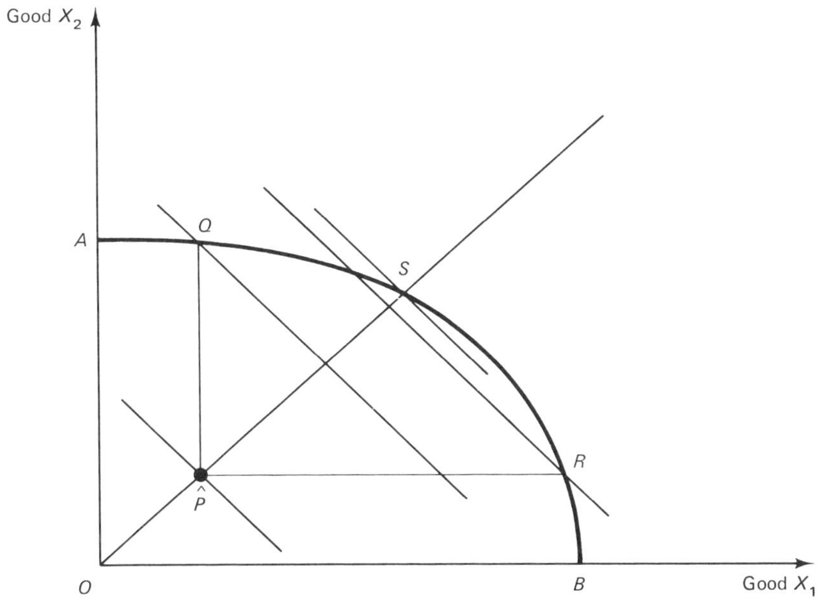

Figure 6.3

OX_1OX_2 in figure 6.2 and is characterized by intersecting $\hat{X}_1$ and $\hat{X}_2$ isoquants. The MRS in the two branches are not equal.[1]

How are we to measure the output loss that the allocation and production at $\hat{P}$ clearly represents? Evidently, numerous alternative procedures may be employed to decide, in figure 6.1, which of the efficient points on AB is to be chosen and which price vector is to be used in turn to evaluate this production point as well as $(\hat{X}_1, \hat{X}_2)$ at $\hat{P}$ to arrive at an inefficiency index.

Among the arbitrary methods that may be used are the following, illustrated in figure 6.3: (1) choose the maximum of one good that can be produced, given the (distorted) observed level of the other, and evaluate at the observed price ratio through $\hat{P}$ using either Q or R; (2) choose the higher of these, R; (3) choose the production point along AB on a ray from the origin through $\hat{P}$, which expands the production of all goods in the same proportion yielding S, and evaluate at the observed price ratio through $\hat{P}$. Note that in the last case the measured *proportionate* loss is independent of the price ratio used.

To be economically meaningful, however, we need to choose in this aggregation the production and price vectors that reflect social utility. Consider in this respect the following alternative possibilities, first, in the context of a closed economy and, then, an open economy:

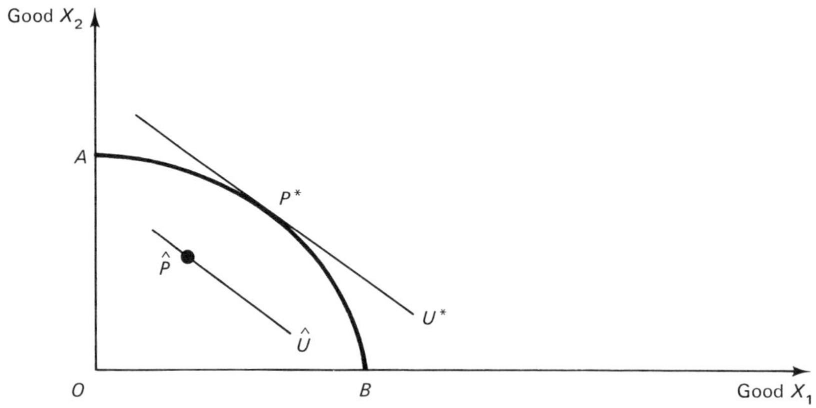

Figure 6.4

1. Closed economy, linear utility function. In figure 6.4 the assumptions of a closed economy and a linear utility function would imply that P^* is the chosen point on AB obtained by putting the indifference curve, that is, the observed price vector at $\hat{P}$, tangent to AB. The valuation would also be at that price vector.

2. Closed economy, nonlinear utility function. Consider the case for a closed economy where the point P^* on AB is chosen optimally by tangency of AB with a convex social indifference curve, as in figure 6.5. The observed price ratio at $\hat{P}$, however, differs from the optimal price ratio that would obtain at P^*.

The fact that two different price ratios would be involved at $\hat{P}$ and P^* implies that we have the familiar problem of choosing between the equivalent-variational and compensating-variational measures of the loss from misallocation at $\hat{P}$.[2]

3. Open, small economy. In figure 6.6 we have the case of a small, open economy with fixed terms of trade $\hat{P}\hat{C} = P^*C^*$. The optimal production point on AB is P^*, and the valuation of $\hat{P}$ and P^*, and hence the measure of inefficiency loss, would be at the international prices.

6.3 Measures of Factor Saving

We now discuss the alternative approach of measuring the inefficiency loss at $\hat{P}$.[3] This approach measures the release or saving of factors that will follow from *efficiently* producing and then achieving social utility $\hat{U}$ with the pro-

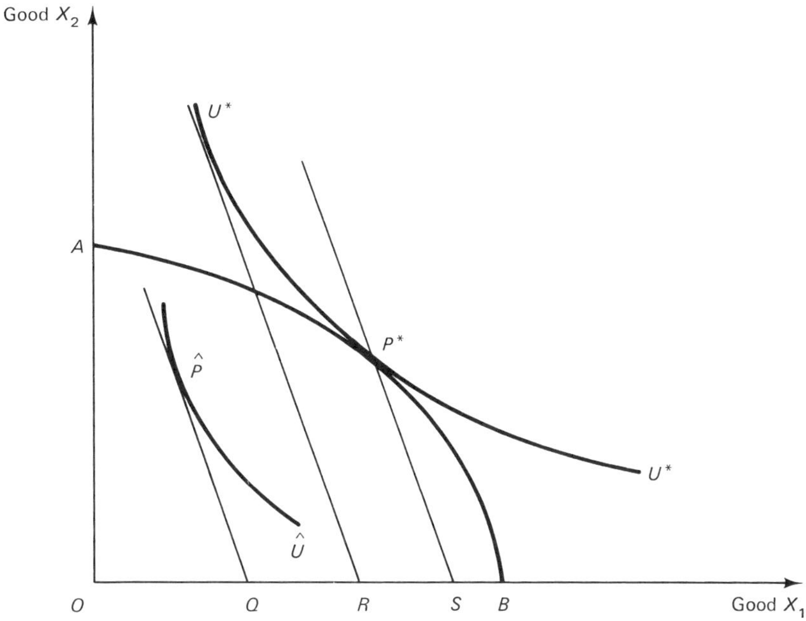

Figure 6.5

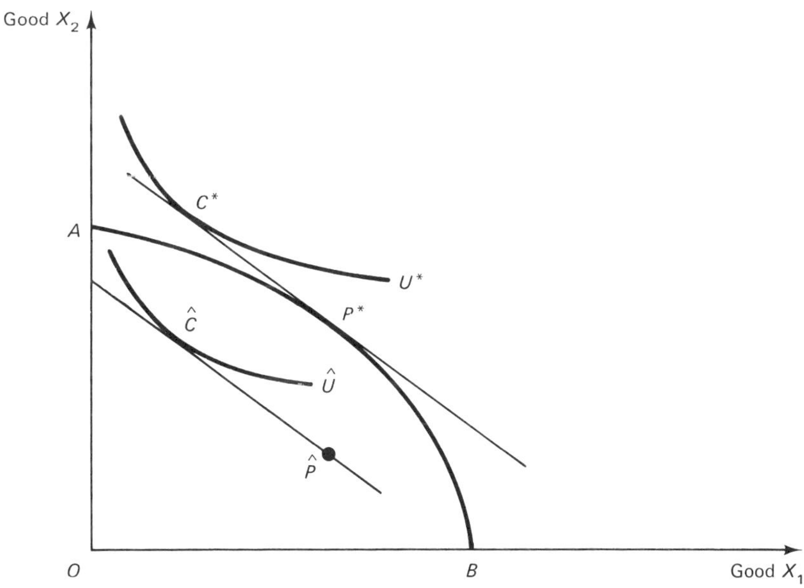

Figure 6.6

duction bundle $(\hat{X}_1, \hat{X}_2)$ at $\hat{P}$. This efficient production naturally must involve equalizing the MRS between the two factors across the two activities.

We now introduce the concept of an efficiency isoquant for producing U. This is done at a general level in the appendix, where its convexity properties are demonstrated. This efficiency isoquant, *QRES* in figure 6.7a, reflects the minimum combinations of factors K and L necessary to achieve a utility level equal to $\hat{U}$. Corresponding to each such (K, L) combination as Q, there is a wage-rental ratio between the two sectors equal and tangent to the efficiency isoquant at the given point (see appendix).

Now the actual factor endowment, as utilized at $\hat{P}$, is G, that is, $(\bar{K}, \bar{L})$. We have again the problem, as in the output loss approach, of deciding which point to pick on the $\hat{U}$ isoquant *QRES* for comparison with G, and which factor prices to use for evaluating the difference between the factor bundles.

As before, we can choose an arbitrary procedure. We may, for example, release only one factor, leaving the other unchanged: this yields Q or S in figure 6.7a. Or we may release both factors in the same proportion, yielding R.[4] The valuation of the factor bundles would be done at the factor-price ratio yielded by the tangent at Q, S, or R, respectively. Yet another procedure is to take a factor price more or less arbitrarily and compare the cost of $(\bar{K}, \bar{L})$ with that of minimum cost on the $\hat{U}$ isoquant.[5]

The different product loss and factor-saving measures can be related by using the well-known Lerner-Samuelson relationship between factor and goods prices in general equilibrium (which holds equally between shadow prices associated with optimum allocations; see the appendix).

To do this, we turn now to figure 6.7b, the goods diagram, and relate it to figure 6.7a, the factor diagram. In figure 6.7b optimal production is at P^* with corresponding optimal goods-price ratio P^*V, whereas actual production is at $\hat{P}$ where the distorted goods price ratio $\hat{P}W$ is tangent to $\hat{U}$. The latter corresponds to figure 6.7a where *QRES* is the (efficient) isoquant for producing $\hat{U}$ and G corresponds to the available factor endowment used in producing $\hat{P}$.

Now, corresponding to the goods price ratio P^*V, we have a factor price ratio *JH*, which can be obtained as the common slope of two isoquants for X_1 and X_2 producing the same *value* of output at prices P^*V. This factor price is also the slope of the U^* isoquant at the endowment point G in figure 6.7a. Inversely, from *JH* in figure 6.7a we can obtain the goods-price ratio P^*V as the ratio of outputs of the isoquants for X_1 and X_2 tangent to a line of slope equal to that of *JH*.

In this simple 2×2 model we can start in the same way with the distorted, observed price $\hat{P}W$ and obtain an associated factor-price ratio *EF*

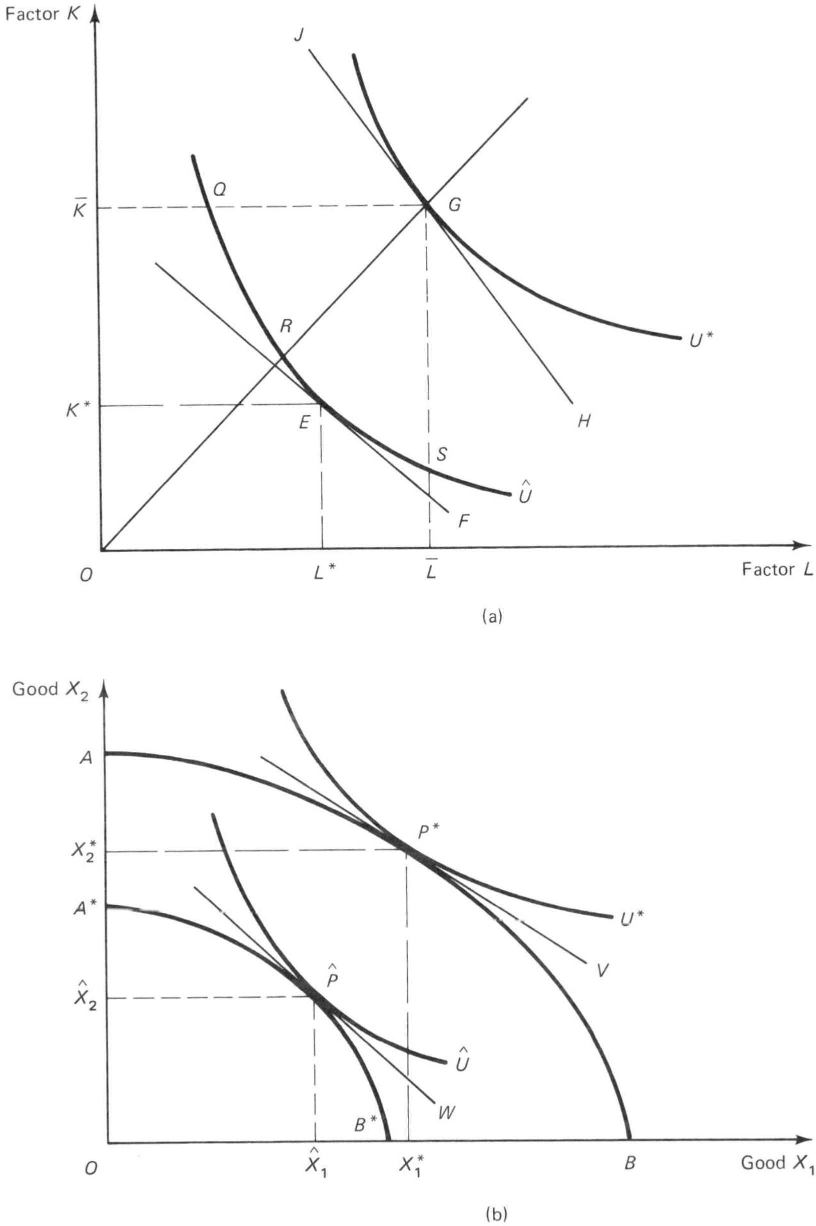

Factor K
J
Q
$\bar{K}$
G
R
U^*
K^*
E
H
S
$\hat{U}$
F
O
L^*
$\bar{L}$
Factor L
(a)
Good X_2
A
X_2^*
P^*
A^*
U^*
V
$\hat{P}$
$\hat{X}_2$
$\hat{U}$
W
B^*
O
$\hat{X}_1$
X_1^*
B
Good X_1
(b)

Figure 6.7

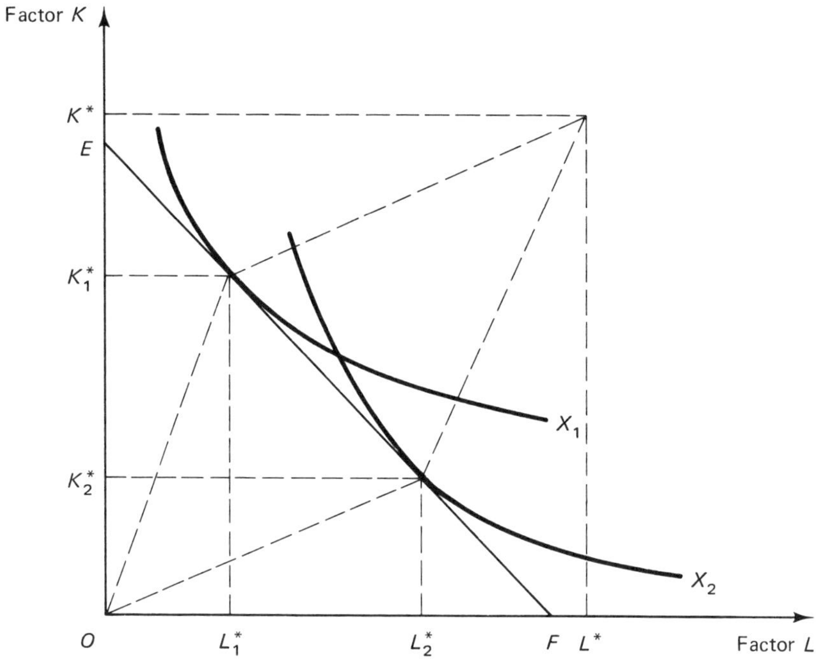

Figure 6.8

(as in figure 6.8 where both isoquants produce the same value at prices $\hat{P}W$) that will be tangent to the $\hat{U}$ isoquant in figure 6.7a.[6] The tangency point (K^*, L^*) is such that the corresponding production possibility set (A^*B^* in figure 6.7b) has a slope given by $\hat{P}W$ at the point $\hat{P}$, that is, $(\hat{X}_1, \hat{X}_2)$.

Therefore we have four alternative sets of measures of inefficiency: the measures of output loss (from P^* to $\hat{P}$ in figure 6.7b at optimal or distorted price ratios P^*V and $\hat{P}W$, respectively) and the associated measures of factor saving (from G to E in figure 6.7a using prices JH or EF). We show in the appendix the general relationship between these four measures.

6.4 Measure of Inefficiency Loss and Compensating, Equivalent Variations

Whether we use the product loss or the factor-saving approach, the measure of inefficiency loss will depend on whether we employ the distorted prices at $\hat{P}$, the compensating variational method, or the optimal prices at P^*, the equivalent variational method, to measure losses. We discuss the inefficiency loss for these two measures in the context of a closed economy.

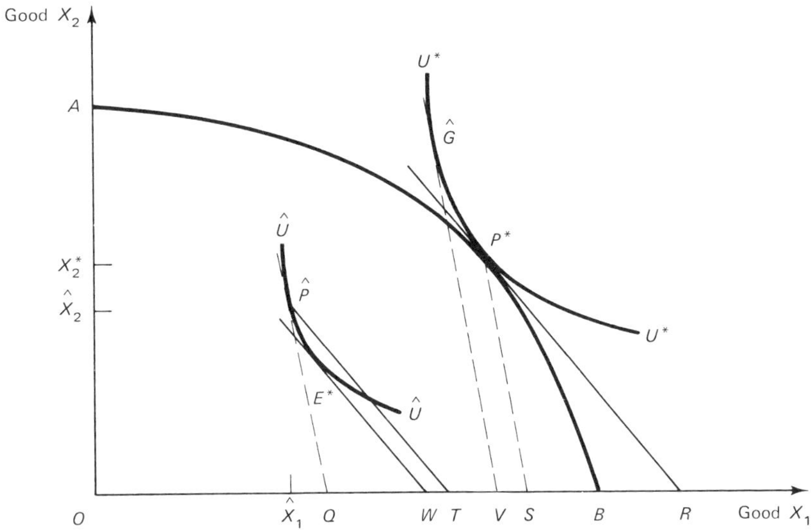

Figure 6.9

First, choose the compensating variational measure of the output loss in moving from P^* to $\hat{P}$ in figure 6.9. How much would the economy have to be compensated when it moves to the $\hat{P}$ equilibrium so as to have it return to the utility level U^* corresponding to P^*? Evidently, this loss amounts to QV, measured in terms of X_1. Note also that, except for the singular case where the distorted goods price ratio at $\hat{P}$ and the optimal price ratio at P^* are identical, the valuation of P^* at the distorted goods price ratio at $\hat{P}$ will overestimate the utility loss. This is evident in figure 6.9 where the overestimate amounts to VS. There is a similar overestimate of factor saving when it is calculated at the distorted factor-price ratio corresponding to $\hat{P}$ in figure 6.10 of amount VS in terms of factor L. We establish in the appendix that the proportional overestimation is larger in this case, that is, VS/QV is larger in figure 6.10 than in figure 6.9.

Consider instead the equivalent variational measure in figure 6.9. Here the loss resulting from a shift from P^* to $\hat{P}$ can be equivalently achieved by retaining the P^* equilibrium prices but removing income from the economy of amount WR in terms of good X_1—for such extraction of income would equivalently take the economy down to $\hat{U}$. Again, except in a singular case, the valuation of the production bundle at $\hat{P}$ in terms of the estimated price ratio at P^* would result in an *underestimate* of the loss—by the amount WT in figure 6.9. Also the alternative estimate of factor saving at the optimal factor-

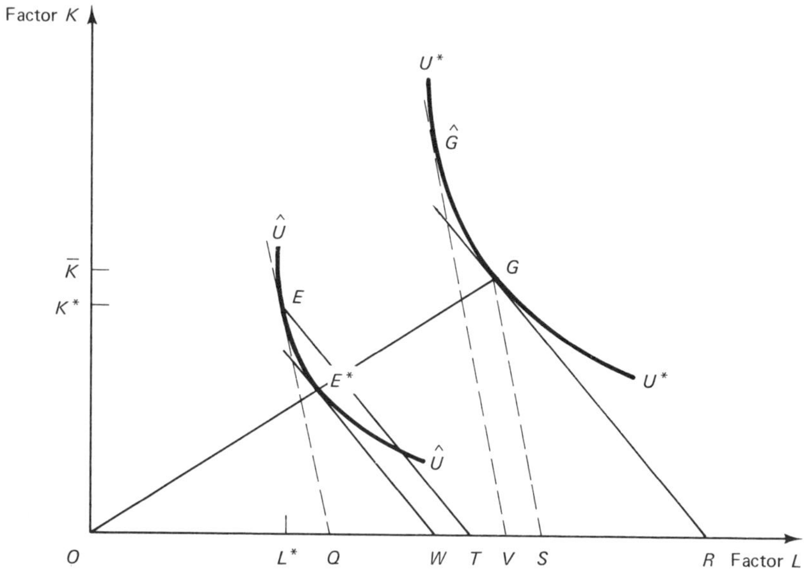

Figure 6.10

price ratio at P^* will result in an underestimate of the true loss—by the amount WT in terms of factor L. Again it can be shown that the error is larger when measured as factor saving.

It is clear that the valuation of the losses at the price ratios at $\hat{P}$—the compensating variation—will *overestimate* the losses whereas the valuation of the losses in terms of the price ratios at P^*—the equivalent variation—will *underestimate* them regardless of whether the output loss or the factor saving approach is used. But there is no reason to limit ourselves to these four measures. In fact points P^* and E in figures 6.9 and 6.10 are not observed; they have to be calculated using information on technology and social objectives. We can thus obtain E^* or $\hat{G}$ as easily and with them an exact measure of the efficiency loss.

There is still some ambiguity, to be sure, if the utility index is not homothetic: the increase in the value of output (or cost of factor) in going from $\hat{U}$ to U^* may depend on the prices used (QV/OQ need not be equal to WR/OW). But this indeterminancy is presumably of little quantitative significance; besides nothing can be done about it unless the utility index is given cardinal significance, in which case $(U^* - \hat{U})$ is the obvious true measure of the efficiency loss.[7] It seems reasonable therefore, as a starting point, to postulate a homothetic utility index so that these ambiguities do not arise. Under the assumption of a homothetic utility index the calculation of potential additional output or factor saving based on exact (as opposed to over) compensation results in comparing two output baskets, or two factor endowments, that are proportional to each other.[8] Thus there is no issue of selecting a price index.

The foregoing discussion assumes knowledge of the utility index $u(x)$. How can it be estimated in practice? Obviously, it can not. But there are two polar cases that can provide useful bounds on the estimated efficiency loss:

1. a linear utility index (for example, with marginal utilities proportional to the prices observed at the initial point $\hat{P}$ or to comparable international prices), or the case where
2. all goods enter the utility index in fixed proportions (for example, those observed at the initial point $\hat{P}$).

The reason for using polar cases is that it is not clear what degree of substitutability should be postulated between goods, such as machinery, electricity, and food. Case 1, the linear utility index, is useful, however, as an upper bound on the estimated loss. Yet it cannot claim much realism, particularly when, as in our empirical exercise in the companion work (Desai and Martin 1983), the number of goods exceeds substantially the number of factors so that with most prices the optimal production basket implies specialization in just a few industries. Case 2, on the other hand, is a conservative estimate, as it does not allow for gains through changes in the composition of production. It seems to be the most relevant when not much is known about the criteria used to determine this composition.

Therefore, in Desai and Martin (1983), we have simply imposed the observed proportions between outputs of different industries (case 2) and calculated measures of the loss using the factor-saving approach, which is also computationally much simpler with only two factors but eight goods (though including some unpublished calculations based on a linear utility index, case 1).

6.5 Computing Inefficiency Loss in Terms of Factor Saving and Selecting the Global Wage-Rental Ratio

Our calculations in terms of factor saving imply the estimation of a global wage-rental ratio ω, to which the marginal rates of substitution in all branches will be equalized while producing efficiently the initial levels of output with less of both factors. How should ω be defined and derived for this purpose?

Obviously, the defining characteristic of ω for the case of homothetic utility indexes is that the implied overall capital-labor ratio $k^* = K^*/L^*$ under reallocation on the efficient isoquant is identical with the initial factor ratio $\bar{k} = \bar{K}/\bar{L}$, which in turn implies that the use of both factors is reduced by the same proportion. That ω, defined as ω^*, has to be calculated iteratively by the condition:[9]

$$\frac{\sum_{i=1}^{8} K_i^*}{\sum_{i=1}^{8} L_i^*} = \frac{\sum_{i=1}^{8} \hat{K}_i}{\sum_{i=1}^{8} \hat{L}_i}. \tag{1}$$

The factor-saving μ^* associated with ω^* is then given by E^*G/OE^* in figure 6.10, with the saving expressed as a proportion of efficient factor use. On the other hand, among all the *arbitrary* factor-price ratios that could be used to calculate factor saving, or to start estimating ω^*, two slightly less arbitrary are

$$\omega_I = \frac{\sum_{i=1}^{8} \hat{L}_i \hat{\omega}_i}{\sum_{i=1}^{8} \hat{L}_i}, \tag{2}$$

$$\omega_{II} = \frac{\sum_{i=1}^{8} \hat{K}_i}{\sum_{i=1}^{8} (\hat{K}_i/\hat{\omega}_i)}, \tag{3}$$

where $\hat{\omega}_i$ is the observed wage-rental ratio in sector i at the initial position, and $\hat{K}_i$ and $\hat{L}_i$ are the actual amounts of each factor used at that position. Each of these factor-price ratios represents a weighted average of the observed, distorted wage-rental ratios in the different sectors, the weights being the share of each sector in initial labor and capital use, respectively. Both at the initial position reproduce the factor shares in total income under the assumption of uniform returns to capital (ω_I) or uniform wages (ω_{II}) in all sectors.[10]

As already discussed, μ^* estimates *exactly* the utility loss in terms of factor saving whereas μ_I and μ_{II} (corresponding to ω_I and ω_{II}, respectively) imply an *overestimate* of the utility loss, both being of the compensating-variational variety. (In some unpublished estimates of μ^*, μ_I, and μ_{II} for soviet industry we find that μ_I and μ_{II} are substantially larger than μ^*.) Note also that, given the assumption of homotheticity of the utility function, μ^* is also equivalently an exact estimate of output loss due to the observed misallocation of given factor endowments. Therefore, if we were to regard the output-loss measure as a more interesting and appropriate measure of inefficient allocation—since the factor endowments are given and we may want to focus on how these *given* endowments ought to be reallocated to advantage—then μ^* is indeed conceptually also a superior estimate to μ_I and μ_{II}.

Notes

Thanks are due to the National Science Foundation, Grant SO677-07254 of the first author, for financial support of the underlying research in this chapter. The appendix was authored exclusively by Ricardo Martin. The comments of Richard Brecher, Robert Feenstra, Tatsuo Hatta, Peter Neary, T. N. Srinivasan, and John Whalley were helpful in improving this chapter.

1. We do not need to make any specific assumption here about why this outcome occurs in a centrally planned economy. Where a *market economy* is characterized by a wage differential between sectors, for example, this outcome is inevitable, with consequences studied at length by trade theorists such as Bhagwati and Srinivasan (1971), Jones (1971), and Neary (1978).

2. For a similar discussion of these alternative measures at a national level, in the context of the problem of gains from trade, see Bhagwati and Johnson (1960, sec. 3).

3. For an earlier, interesting use of this approach, see Thornton (1971). Her valuable paper, however, does not discuss the conceptual issues analyzed here. Also see note 5.

4. T. N. Srinivasan has pointed out that the procedure where R is taken along the ray OG from the origin, corresponds, as it happens, to Debreu's (1951) "coefficient of resource utilization" procedure in a much-neglected paper.

5. This is, in effect, the procedure of Thornton (1971), though she holds production levels, rather than social utility, constant.

6. We must note, however, that, when the number of goods exceeds the number of factors, there is no guarantee that there is a factor endowment point corresponding to any point on the $\hat{U}$ indifference curve in figure 6.7b that makes the given production bundle optimal (that is, a point of simultaneous tangency to the indifference curve and a production possibility set). This corresponds in figure 6.8 to the general impossibility of one line being tangent to three or more arbitrary isoquants. On the other hand, associated with *every* point on the isoquants in factor space, there are goods prices (equal to the minimum cost of production at the given factor prices) that separate (are tangent at the same point to) the production possibility set generated by the given factor bundle and the indifference curve. Even when the number of goods and factors is equal, there may be output combinations that are not optimal for *any* factor endowment.

7. It is interesting that Whalley (1976) in his sensitivity analysis of Thornton's (1971) original exercise for the Soviet economy postulated an explicit utility function (of the CES type) but still did not choose to calculate with it an exact measure of the

efficiency loss and used instead the (approximate) compensating and equivalent variation measures.

8. The implied measure is, as noted earlier, equivalent to Debreu's (1951) coefficient of resource allocation, having in effect the minimax property discussed by him. The equivalence is obtained under our twin assumptions of a homothetic utility index and constant returns to scale in production.

9. For a statement of the exact methodology of estimating ω^*, see Desai and Martin (1982).

10. Thornton (1971) used ω_{II} in her factor-saving calculations.

11. That is, for all $\mathbf{v}^1$, $\mathbf{v}^2$ in R^m and any two non-negative numbers l_1, l_2 we have that $F_i(l_1\mathbf{v}^1 + l_2\mathbf{v}^2) \geq l_1F_i(\mathbf{v}^1) + l_2F_i(\mathbf{v}^2)$, for all i. If $\mathbf{v}^1$ is proportional to $\mathbf{v}^2$, the equality holds. Implicit in (A.1) is the assumption of free disposal of outputs and inputs.

12. If $u(\mathbf{x})$ has only *ordinal* significance, concavity should be understood as quasi concavity (convex indifference curves) and linear homogeneity is relaxed to homotheticity. Obviously, if $u(\mathbf{x})$ is changed by a nondecreasing transformation $g(u(\mathbf{x}))$, $f(\mathbf{v})$ is transformed in the same way.

Appendix

This appendix shows that the efficient isoquants are convex and their slopes measure the factor-price ratios associated with efficient production. It also discusses the connection between the four measures of efficiency loss introduced in the text.

Properties of the Efficient Isoquants

Let $\mathbf{x} \in R^n$ (the n-dimensional real space) indicate the level of outputs of the n sectors, $\mathbf{v} \in R^m$ the factor availability, and $T(\mathbf{v})$ the production possibility set (PPS) associated with $\mathbf{v}$. We assume no joint production so that the PPS can be defined as

$$T(\mathbf{v}) = \left\{ x_1, \ldots, x_n \middle| x_i \leq F_i(\mathbf{z}_i), i = n; \sum_{i=1}^{n} \mathbf{z_i} \leq \mathbf{v} \right\} \tag{A.1}$$

with $F_i(\cdot)$ being the production function for x_i, assumed to be concave and linear homogeneous.[11]

Given a concave utility index $u(\mathbf{x})$, we can define an aggregate production function, $f(\mathbf{v})$, as the maximum value of $u(\mathbf{x})$ that can be obtained with the existing technology and factor endowment:

$$f(\mathbf{v}) = \max u(\mathbf{x}) \quad \text{subject to} \quad \mathbf{x} \in T(\mathbf{v}). \tag{A.2}$$

By definition, if $\mathbf{x}$ can be produced with $\mathbf{v}, f(\mathbf{v}) \geq u(\mathbf{x})$; moreover for all factor endowments there is a vector of outputs for which the equality holds. Note, however, that the converse is not true, as there may be production baskets that are not optimal for any factor endowment. This may happen even when $n = m$, but it will follow when there are more goods than factors, as the PPS has $(n - m)$-dimensional flat frontiers. We can show now that $f(\mathbf{v})$ has the properties of a production function.

PROPOSITION 1 $f(\mathbf{v})$ is a concave function. If $u(\mathbf{x})$ is linear homogeneous, so is $f(\mathbf{v})$.[12]

Proof

Let $f(\mathbf{v}^k) = u(\mathbf{x}^k) = \max u(\mathbf{x})$ s.t. $\mathbf{x} \in T(\mathbf{v}^k)$, $k = 1,2$, and l_1, l_2 be two positive numbers between 0 and 1. Then by concavity of the production functions, $\sum l_k \mathbf{x}^k \in T(\sum l_k \mathbf{v}^k)$ so that $f(\sum l_k \mathbf{v}^k) \geq u(\sum l_k \mathbf{x}^k) \geq \sum l_k u(\mathbf{x}^k)$, with the last inequality following from concavity of $u(\mathbf{x})$. This proves that the efficient isoquants are convex and that $f(\mathbf{v})$ does not show increasing returns to scale.

Assume now that $u(\mathbf{x})$ is a linear homogeneous utility index, that is, for all $l > 0$, $u(l\mathbf{x}) = lu(\mathbf{x})$. Suppose $f(\mathbf{v})$ shows declining returns to scale, so that $f(l_0\mathbf{v}^0) > l_0 f(\mathbf{v}^0)$ for some $\mathbf{v}^0$, $l_0 > 0$. If $\mathbf{x}^0$ is the optimal output level associated to $l_0\mathbf{v}^0$, it is certainly feasible to produce $(1/l_0)\mathbf{x}^0$ when the factor endowment is $\mathbf{v}^0$, so that $f(\mathbf{v}^0) \geq u(\mathbf{x}^0)/l_0 = f(l_0\mathbf{v}^0)/l_0$, which contradicts the assumption of decreasing returns. ∎

Take now $\mathbf{v} = \mathbf{v}^0$, any factor endowment. By applying the Kuhn-Tucker theorem to problem (A.2), we know that associated with the optimal solution $x_i^0 \leq F_i(\mathbf{z}_i^0)$, $i = 1, \ldots, n$, there are non-negative shadow prices $\mathbf{p}^0$, $\mathbf{w}^0$, such that the Lagrangian function

$$L(\mathbf{x}, \mathbf{z}_1, \ldots, \mathbf{z}_n; \mathbf{p}, \mathbf{w}; \mathbf{v}^0) = u(\mathbf{x}) - \sum p_i[x_i - F_i(\mathbf{z}_i)] - w(\sum \mathbf{z}_i - \mathbf{v}^0) \tag{A.3}$$

has a saddle point at the solution values; that is, for all $\mathbf{p} \geq \mathbf{0}, \mathbf{w} \geq \mathbf{0}, \mathbf{x} \geq \mathbf{0}$, and $Z = (\mathbf{z}_1, \ldots, \mathbf{z}_n) \geq 0$, we have

$$L(\mathbf{x}^0, Z^0; \mathbf{p}, \mathbf{w}) \geq L(\mathbf{x}^0, Z^0; \mathbf{p}^0, \mathbf{w}^0) \geq L(\mathbf{x}, Z; \mathbf{p}^0, \mathbf{w}^0). \tag{A.4}$$

As an implication of these inequalities, we have the following revealed preference and profit-maximization inequalities:

PROPOSITION 2

i. $u(\mathbf{x}) \geq u(\mathbf{x}^0)$ implies $\mathbf{p}^0\mathbf{x} \geq \mathbf{p}^0\mathbf{x}^0$,

ii. for all $\mathbf{z}_i$, $p_i^0 F_i(\mathbf{z}_i) - \mathbf{w}^0\mathbf{z}_i \leq p_i^0 F_i(\mathbf{z}_i^0) - \mathbf{w}^0\mathbf{z}_i^0 = 0$,

iii. for all $\mathbf{x} \in T(\mathbf{v})$, $\mathbf{p}^0\mathbf{x} - \mathbf{w}^0\mathbf{v} \leq \mathbf{p}^0\mathbf{x}^0 - \mathbf{w}^0\mathbf{v}^0 = 0$,

iv. $f(\mathbf{v}) \geq f(\mathbf{v}^0)$ implies $\mathbf{w}^0\mathbf{v} \geq \mathbf{w}^0\mathbf{v}^0$.

Proof

The second inequality in (A.4) requires $u(\mathbf{x}) - \mathbf{p}^0\mathbf{x} \leq u(\mathbf{x}^0) - \mathbf{p}^0\mathbf{x}^0$ for all $\mathbf{x}$, and $p_i^0F_i(\mathbf{z}_i) - \mathbf{w}^0\mathbf{z}_i \leq p_i^0F_i(\mathbf{z}_i^0) - \mathbf{w}^0\mathbf{z}_i^0$, for all $\mathbf{z}_i$. This proves (i) and the first part of (ii). To complete the proof of (ii), notice that by the assumption of free disposal, $p_i^0F_i(\mathbf{z}_i^0) - \mathbf{w}^0\mathbf{z}_i^0 \geq 0$. On the other hand, with constant returns to scale the inequality cannot hold since, for example doubling inputs would double output and profits, contradicting the inequality just proved.

If $\mathbf{x} \in T(\mathbf{v})$, by definition of the PPS, $x_i \leq F_i(\mathbf{z}_i)$ with $\sum \mathbf{z}_i \leq \mathbf{v}$. As the prices $\mathbf{p}^0$ and $\mathbf{w}^0$ are non-negative we must have thus $\mathbf{p}^0\mathbf{x} - \mathbf{w}^0\mathbf{v} \leq \sum(p_i^0F_i(\mathbf{z}_i) - \mathbf{w}^0\mathbf{z}_i)$, which is nonpositive by (ii). The first inequality in (A.4), on the other hand, implies that free goods or factors have zero prices, that is, for i and j, $p_i^0(x_i^0 - F_i(\mathbf{z}_i^0)) = 0 = w_j^0(\sum z_{ij}^0 - v_j^0)$. This shows that $\mathbf{p}^0\mathbf{x}^0 - \mathbf{w}^0\mathbf{v}^0 = 0$.

Finally, from (iii) and (1) we have $u(\mathbf{x}) \leq u(\mathbf{x}^0) + \mathbf{w}^0(\mathbf{v} - \mathbf{v}^0)$, whenever $\mathbf{x} \in T(\mathbf{v})$. Thus implies (iv) when we take $\mathbf{x}$ to be the optimal output associated to the factor endowment $\mathbf{v}$, so that $f(\mathbf{v}) = u(\mathbf{x})$. ∎

The last part of proposition 2 shows that, at factor prices $\mathbf{w}^0$, $\mathbf{v}^0$ is the factor endowment that achieves a utility level of at least $u^0 = u(\mathbf{x}^0)$ with the lower cost. Part (ii) means that all industries also minimize production costs at the same factor prices: the marginal rate of transformation between any pair of factors is equal in all industries and on the efficient isoquant, as noted in the text. Part (iii) shows that in any optimal allocation aggregate profits are maximized. This result will be useful in comparing the different measures of efficiency loss.

Comparison of Measures of Efficiency Loss

Consider now the relationship among the different measures of efficiency loss defined in the text. For that, let $\mathbf{x}^0$ be the initial (inefficiently produced) output and $\mathbf{v}^0$ the actual factor endowment. The inefficiency is indicated by the fact that $u(\mathbf{x}^0) = \bar{U} < U^* = u(\mathbf{x}^*) = f(\mathbf{v}^0)$. With a cardinal utility index the proportional loss would be given by

$$\mu = \frac{(\bar{U}^* - \bar{U})}{\bar{U}}. \tag{A.5}$$

It is useful to measure the loss in terms of national aggregates such as GNP. For that we need to consider measures based on price indexes. By concavity of the utility index we can always find an output price vector, $\mathbf{p}^0$, tangent to $u(\mathbf{x})$ at $\mathbf{x}^0$. Those prices give the social marginal rate of substitution between goods at the existing situation, but, they generally differ from the *observed* prices at $\mathbf{x}^0$ or the *marginal costs* of producing $\mathbf{x}^0$ efficiently.

Associated with $\bar{U}$, and for *any arbitrary* factor price vector, $\bar{\mathbf{w}}$, we can define the least-cost way of producing that level of social utility. For that we must solve

$$\min_{\mathbf{v}} \bar{\mathbf{w}}\,\mathbf{v} \quad \text{subject to} \quad f(\mathbf{v}) \geq U. \tag{A.6}$$

Let $\mathbf{v} = \bar{\mathbf{v}}$ be the factor endowment that solves (A.6), so that $f(\bar{\mathbf{v}}) = \bar{U}$. The prices $\bar{\mathbf{w}}$ and the corresponding output prices, $\bar{\mathbf{p}}$, satisfy all the properties specified in proposition 2. Finally, let $\mathbf{w}^*$ and $\mathbf{p}^*$ be the prices obtained when solving (A.2) with the *existing* factor endowment, $\mathbf{v}^* = \mathbf{v}^0$, and let $\mathbf{x}^*$ be the corresponding optimal production point.

The four measures of efficiency loss, the compensating and equivalent variation in output and factor spaces, are

$$\begin{aligned}
\mu_1 &= \frac{\mathbf{p}^*(\mathbf{x}^* - \bar{\mathbf{x}})}{\mathbf{p}^*\bar{\mathbf{x}}},\\
\mu_2 &= \frac{\bar{\mathbf{p}}(\mathbf{x}^* - \bar{\mathbf{x}})}{\bar{\mathbf{p}}\bar{\mathbf{x}}},\\
\mu_3 &= \frac{\mathbf{w}^*(\mathbf{v}^* - \bar{\mathbf{v}})}{\mathbf{w}^*\bar{\mathbf{v}}},\\
\mu_4 &= \frac{\bar{\mathbf{w}}(\mathbf{v}^* - \bar{\mathbf{v}})}{\bar{\mathbf{w}}\bar{\mathbf{v}}}.
\end{aligned} \tag{A.7}$$

Indexes μ_2 and μ_4 are overcompensating measures of the efficiency loss. We can define also a measure based on exact compensation: for that we need to calculate what is the minimal additional income needed, at prices $\bar{\mathbf{p}}$, to achieve the potential real income level of U^*. We obtain then an index $\bar{\mu}$ defined by

$$\begin{aligned}
\bar{\mu} &= \frac{\bar{\mathbf{p}}(\mathbf{x}^{**} - \bar{\mathbf{x}})}{\bar{\mathbf{p}}\bar{\mathbf{x}}}, \quad \text{with}\\
\bar{\mathbf{p}}\mathbf{x}^{**} &= \min \bar{\mathbf{p}}\mathbf{x} \quad \text{subject to} \quad u(\mathbf{x}) \geq U^*.
\end{aligned} \tag{A.8}$$

In a similar way an exact measure based on the equivalent variation concept would compare $\mathbf{p}^*\mathbf{x}^*$ with the minimum level of income capable of keeping society on the $u(\mathbf{x}) = \bar{U}$ frontier, valued at prices $\mathbf{p}^*$. This index is

$$\mu^* = \frac{\mathbf{p}^*(\mathbf{x}^* - \bar{\bar{\mathbf{x}}})}{\mathbf{p}^*\bar{\bar{\mathbf{x}}}}, \quad \text{with} \tag{A.9}$$

$$\mathbf{p}^*\bar{\bar{\mathbf{x}}} = \min \mathbf{p}^*\mathbf{x} \quad \text{subject to} \quad u(\mathbf{x}) \geq \bar{U}.$$

If the utility index is homothetic, clearly $\mu^* = \bar{\mu}$. If it is cardinally defined and linear homogeneous, $\mu^* = \bar{\mu} = \mu$.

PROPOSITION 3 $\mu_4 \geq \mu_2 \geq \bar{\mu}$ and $\mu^* \geq \mu_1 \geq \mu_3$.

Proof

From proposition 3(iii), $\mathbf{p}^*\bar{\mathbf{x}} \geq \mathbf{w}^*\bar{\mathbf{v}}$ and $\bar{\mathbf{p}}\mathbf{x}^* \geq \bar{\mathbf{w}}\mathbf{v}^*$, while $\mathbf{p}^*\mathbf{x}^* = \mathbf{w}^*\mathbf{v}^*$ and $\bar{\mathbf{p}}\bar{\mathbf{x}} = \bar{\mathbf{w}}\bar{\mathbf{v}}$. Thus $\mu_4 \geq \mu_2$ and $\mu_1 \geq \mu_3$. The other two inequalities are obvious from the definition of $\bar{\mu}$ and μ^*. ∎

This proposition shows that, if we calculate the efficiency loss as factor savings at arbitrary factor prices (to obtain μ_4), the true loss $\bar{\mu}$ is overestimated. A better approximation, namely, μ_2, would be obtained using the associated efficient prices to evaluate the additional output that could be obtained with the existing factor endowment. We calculate correctly the loss only if the potential savings in factor use is evaluated using factor prices that measure the true (potential) value of factors is the economy, those associated with the optimal allocation. Then $\bar{\mathbf{w}} = \mathbf{w}^*$, and $\mu_4 = \mu$.

Note that if the utility index is homothetic, then $\bar{\mathbf{w}} = \mathbf{w}^*$ and $\bar{\mathbf{v}}$ and $\mathbf{v}^*$ are proportional to each other. This forms the basis for the iterative procedure for calculating $\mathbf{w}^*$, described in the text.

It may be useful to repeat that proposition 3 refers only to mutually consistent factor and output prices. In particular, the measure based on observed output prices may be larger than the one obtained from arbitrary factor prices.

References

Bhagwati, J., and H. G. Johnson, 1960. Notes on some controversies in the theory of international trade. *Economic Journal* 70 (March): 74–93.

Bhagwati, J., and T. N. Srinivasan, 1971. The theory of wage differentials: production response and factor-price equalization. *Journal of International Economics* 1 (February): 19–35.

Debreu, Gerard, 1951. The coefficient of resource utilization. *Econometrica* 19 (July): 273–292.

Desai, Padma, 1981. The rate and pattern of technical change in Soviet industrial branches: 1950–1975. *Mimeographed.* Working Paper Series, Department of Economics, Columbia University.

Desai, Padma, and Ricardo Martin, 1983. Efficiency loss from resource misallocation in Soviet industry. *Quarterly Journal of Economics*, in press.

Jones, R., 1971. Distortions in factor markets and the general equilibrium model of production. *Journal of Political Economy* 79 (May/June): 437–439.

Neary, J. P., 1978. Dynamic stability and the theory of factor-market distortions. *American Economic Review* 68 (September): 671–682.

Thornton, J., 1971. Differential capital charges and resource allocation in Soviet industry. *Journal of Political Economy* 79 (May/June): 545–561.

Whalley, J., 1976. Thornton's estimates of efficiency losses in Soviet industry: some fixed-point-method recalculations. *Journal of Political Economy* 84 (February): 153–159.

7 On an Allocative Role of the Soviet Second Economy

Richard E. Ericson

The attention of scholars studying the Soviet Union has recently been attracted to a large, and apparently growing, set of phenomena generally known as the "second economy." While its precise definition and scope are still areas of active debate, the starting point of any discussion is the characterization of the second economy as consisting of "all production and exchange that fulfills at least one of the two following tests: (a) being directly for private gain; and (b) being in some significant respect in contravention of existing law" (Grossman 1977, p. 25). The term embraces all private economic activity, whether legal or not, and a vast range of informal, semilegal, and illegal actions of official institutions and organizations. Some of the more significant activities in the vast area encompassed by the second economy are

1. agricultural production on private plots and sale on farmers' markets,
2. private provision of consumer and professional services,
3. private construction of housing and agricultural objects,
4. open private trade in secondhand and used items,
5. theft of socialist property for personal use or resale,
6. black markets of producer and consumer products and foreign currency,
7. evasion of tax, licensing, and production prohibition,
8. theft of socialist property for inputs into production activity,
9. private production with or without the facade of a Socialist organization,
10. "speculation," commercial intermediation, and information brokerage,
11. bribery and corruption,
12. use of official position for personal gain and extortion,
13. violation or subversion of the plan,

14. illegal trade or barter between socialist organizations, in particular enterprises.

The areas of second economy activity that have to date received the most attention deal with its impact on individual incomes and consumption possibilities. In particular emphasis has been placed on official corruption, the derivation of entrepreneurial and supplementary income and the acquisition of both consumption necessities and luxuries.[1] This is in part due to the wealth of information that has just recently become available through the emigration of large numbers of people who have intimate knowledge of these areas. Further these activities include many that would also be illegal in a western market economy, thus inviting comparative study and providing independent grounds for evaluating their significance. Finally, the bias in western economics toward evaluation on the basis of individual welfare adds to this emphasis. One consequence of such emphasis has been to reduce the attention paid to an aspect of the second economy brought to our professional attention over twenty years ago: the area of interenterprise relations.

In the late 1950s both Berliner (1959) and Granick (1959) pointed out numerous illegal, semilegal, and/or simply informal/unauthorized practices prevalent within Soviet industrial enterprises and in their interaction. These were implicit in Berliner's three guiding principles of Soviet managerial behavior: (1) *strakhovka* ("safety factor"), (2) *ochkovtiratel'stvo* ("simulation"), (3) *blat* ("pull/influence") whose implementation included or required what is now known as second-economy activity. At that time particular importance was laid to the use of influence, connections, expeditors (*tolkachi*), bribery, and illegal trade in the procurement of production inputs needed for the enterprise to have a chance at fulfilling the plan. While still recognized as important by all students of the Soviet second economy, the area of intermediate product procurement seems to have aroused less excitement recently than other aspects of corruption and the private economy under central planning. Yet this type of activity seems to play a very important role in facilitating plan fulfillment and the normal functioning of the socialist (first) planned economy. It is this role of the second economy that I investigate in this chapter.

Intermediate product and materials allocation in industry is undoubtably the most thoroughly controlled process in centrally planned economies (CPE's). Indeed it is the heart of coordinative planning so necessary in the absence of an extensive system of highly developed intermediate product markets to achieve that "prime imperative of a social economy . . . *microbal-*

ance" (Grossman 1963, p. 101). The continual functioning of the economy requires that detailed coordination in the production sector not break down, that very specific material inputs be available in just the correct quantities and just when needed. Attempting to achieve this comprises by far the largest part of planning in the Soviet Union, with the resulting plans and their implementing orders carrying the force of law.[2] Yet it is in the production sector where the greatest number of problems arise in the functioning of the economy, as the Soviet press continually reminds both us and their citizenry. Plans are necessarily incomplete and less than fully consistent (never mind, optimal) and hence must be supplemented by "extra-plan" mechanisms for a tolerable micro balance to be achieved. Numerous critical decisions must be left in the unobserved hands of managers and low-level administrators who are responsible for implementing the less than fully operational plan and hence are often forced to resort to extra-plan maneuvers.[3] The legal force of the plans, as well as the logic of planning, however, implies that any extra-plan allocation must also be extra-legal, that is, be perforce a part of the second economy. The use of *blat*, *tolkachi*, illegal barter, and bribery, described by Berliner (1959), Granick (1959), Katsenelinboigen (1978), Grossman (1977, 1979), and numerous others, to induce allocations of intermediate products and materials thus appears as a natural response to the need for microbalance. These activities in effect generate the ability to "purchase" an allocation, item by item, through the second economy. Hence planned allocations and resource flow plans might be interpreted as providing only a set of initial conditions (endowments or property rights) from which actual final allocations are realized. In addition to the commanded allocation a series of markets seem to have arisen to generate that prerequisite for the existence of a complex social economy—a rough, tolerable balance of sources and needs.[4]

This line of argument immediately raises the question as to how reasonable it is to suppose that something resembling a set of second-economy markets could achieve an equilibrium allocation within the institutional framework of a CPE or command economy such as that of the Soviet Union. I will answer that question in the affirmative by proposing an equilibrium model of second-economy markets for intermediate production inputs and demonstrating that a well-defined equilibrium allocation (a "bribes equilibrium") exists and is Pareto superior, in terms of output achievable in the production sector, to the initial commanded plan allocation.[5] Hence there is a direct individual incentive for those responsible for meeting a production plan to take part in these second-economy markets to preserve their privileged positions. The model also allows for "skimming" by low-level administrators of materials stocks and flows (such as *skladovshchiki* and *snabzhentsy* ["warehouse and procurement personnel"], *tolkachi*) thus allowing a direct private gain as incentive for their willing cooperation in second-economy activity. Finally, the model and its results depend crucially on two important institutional characteristics of the Soviet (or any other CPE) economy: (1) the rigidity and nonmarket-clearing nature of industrial prices; (2) the duality of the monetary system, with enterprise money and consumer money circulating in almost totally isolated realms.[6] Thus it provides a framework in which we can explain and analyze the appearance of second-economy allocative mechanisms that supplement planned allocations of intermediate products. In so doing, it clarifies what I believe to be one of the most important roles of the Soviet second economy.

7.1 The Model of Second-Economy Intermediate Product Markets

Before modeling the relevant aspect of the second economy as a set of markets for intermediate products, we first must model the essential (basic) institutional framework of the first economy.

We will concentrate on the production side of the economy, which consists of n producers (enterprises, production associations, or sectors), indexed $i = 1, \ldots, n$, each facing a detailed supply/production plan $(\bar{x}^i, \bar{y}^i)$, fixed official prices, p, and each subject to evaluation by superior authorities according to the criterion/reward function, $\hat{u}^i$. Thus the formulation incorporates these three important institutional features of the first (socialist) economy in the Soviet Union: (1) the planned nature of all productive activity; (2) the rigidity of prices, formally fixed for long periods between major price reforms by the State Committee on Prices; (3) the hierarchical/centralized evaluation of performance. There are m products/materials in the economy, indexed $j = 1, \ldots, m$, which are used as inputs into production and are centrally allocated according to the supply plan, $\hat{x} = (\hat{x}^1, \ldots, \hat{x}^n)$. In addition, there is an $m + 1$ good ($j = 0$), official funds, used to pay for the allocations of productive inputs at the monitored fixed official prices; it provides a simple monitor of the flow of production materials in the system. These arise from the "market form" used to implement planned allocations in the Soviet Union: the actual document of implementation is the contract (*dogovor*), specifying the precise nomenclature and timing and the accompanying formal payments, which carry out the sales (*raznariadki*) and purchase (*nariady*) commands subsequent to general allocation orders (*fondy*).[7] This market form is crucial to the model in providing a framework within which the market essence of the second economy can arise.

This also incorporates a further crucial institutional characteristic of the Soviet economy: the existence of a dual monetary system with enterprise money (official funds) and consumer money (cash) circulating in almost totally isolated realms.[8] Purchases of producers and intermediate goods can only be made using official funds at official prices, with the transfer of funds taking place entirely within the books of the State Bank and thus subject to extremely close monitoring. These funds do not exist in physical form, cannot be bought for cash (rubles), and cannot be turned into cash. They are a pure unit of account, the main use of which is for planning and control of industrial/economic activity (*koltrol' rublëm*). Further these funds are worthless for the direct purchase of consumer goods and services and in any kind of private transaction. Similarly cash, with which wage payments and payments for consumer goods and and services are made, is of no direct use in the purchase of intermediate goods and materials. It cannot enhance an enterprise's holdings of official funds and thus loosen the official budget constraint. The full supply plan is then an $m + 1$ vector of planned allocations of official funds and material inputs, $\bar{x}^i = (\bar{x}_0^i, \hat{\bar{x}}^i)$, fixed transfer prices which form an $m + 1$ vector, $p = (1, p_1, \ldots, p_m)$, and the output plan, $\bar{y}^i$, which will for notational simplicity be assumed to be a scalar.[9]

The most important criterion for reward of a Soviet enterprise (for its managers) is its performance with regard to the output plan, whether in physical (*val*) or value (*realizatsiia*) terms. In generating output, each producer, i, is constrained by his production function, $f^i : \hat{X}^i \to R_+$, where $\hat{X}^i$ is the set of all feasible input combinations. Hence $X^i = R_+ \times \hat{X}^i \subset R_+^{m+1}$ can be taken as the set over which the criterion functional u^i representing the preferences of the problem is defined:

$$u^i : X^i \to R, \quad u^i(x_0^i, \hat{x}^i) \triangleq \hat{u}^i(x_0^i, f^i(\hat{x}^i)) \equiv \hat{u}^i(x_0^i, y^i), \tag{1}$$

where $\hat{x}^i = (x_1^i, \ldots, x_m^i)$ are the material inputs used, x_0^i the final official funds holdings in the State Bank, and y^i the realized output. Of course $u^i(\cdot)$ also depends on plan parameters $(\bar{x}^i, \bar{y}^i)$ which have been suppressed in the notation and have no necessary relation to the final realized (x, y). Further we assume that the enterprise has at its disposal in any plan period an endowment, $w^i = (w_0^i, \ldots, w_m^i)$, which is the amounts of funds and material inputs actually received for production purposes in that period.

Although we should expect w^i to have some relationship to the planned allocation $\bar{x}^i$, the experience of the Soviet Union shows that that relationship need not be very close. Indeed the inconsistency of plans is one of the best-documented characteristics of Soviet planning, so we shouldn't expect $w^i = \bar{x}^i$. Yet even if $w^i = \bar{x}^i$, the nature of central plans is such that $f^i(\bar{x}^i) \geq$

$\bar{y}^i$ will generally not be the case due to taut planning and the general pressure characteristic of Soviet planning.[10] Managers are under constant pressure from superiors to "make do," "uncover hidden reserves," as the plan can't be changed. Further, supply problems are not an acceptable excuse in the Soviet Union for nonfulfillment of the plan. Thus if enterprises merely make do with what they have, managers will suffer from the inconsistencies in, and general infeasibility of, the detailed central plans. To protect themselves—to insure adequate, if not outstanding, performance in the eyes of their superiors—managers must scramble for inputs, must attempt purchases or trades that will improve their performance indicator, u^i, by increasing their output.

The model outlined here thus generates a pure exchange economy in intermediate products (inputs) as enterprises attempt to alter their initial allocations through exchange to improve their (observed) performance. In other words, each faces the problem:

$$\max_{z^i} u^i(x^i) \quad \text{subject to} \quad pz^i = 0 \quad \text{or} \quad \hat{p}z^i = w_0^i - x_0^i = -z_0^i, \tag{2}$$

where $z^i = x^i - w^i$ and the caret over a variable indicates its last m components. As prices are arbitrarily fixed from the point of view of relative scarcities, the total demand generated by each enterprise solving (2) will in general be inconsistent with total material availability in the economy: $\sum z^{i*} \neq 0$, where x^{i*} solves (2) for i (the enterprise's Walrasian demand for inputs). Official prices, monitored by the State Bank, inadequately ration scarce inputs and inadequately encourage the use of surpluses. This implies that the scrambling for inputs will be truly in earnest, particularly if, as is wont to happen, plans are infeasible either due to inconsistency or excessive tautness. The value of inputs to enterprises will be markedly different from the prices that can be legally paid. Yet enterprises cannot change the price they offer, or will accept, as payment must be made in official funds that are under direct control of the State Bank. So some other inducement, in addition to payment at official prices and the presentation of necessary documentation (*nariady*, *fondy*), must be offered in order to realize a desired transaction.

In the Soviet Union some of the common forms of inducement are (1) monetary sidepayments/bribes, (2) aid as an intermediary in procurement or dumping, (3) tied sales, (4) direct barter of materials at rates unrelated to official prices, (5) the offering of consumption services and goods. The use of these types of inducements seems increasingly widespread and systematized, yielding an apparently increasing ability to purchase an allocation item by item through the second economy at known going market rates (in money or kind).[11] This generates very real *implicit prices* that ration enterprise participation in some scarce transaction (as buyer or seller). Taking advantage of the duality of the monetary system, we will concentrate on the first type of inducement for modeling purposes: inducements will be modeled as sidepayments/bribes paid in cash (rubles). This loose cash arises in practice (largely) from the manipulation of the various enterprise Funds, and perhaps from second-economy activity (trading, in this model) in the preceding period.[12] Its disposal is at the discretion of the enterprise managers and their agents (*tolkachi*), and its existence is beyond the ken of the central authorities and enterprise superiors.[13]

The amount of this loose cash that each enterprise, i, has at its disposal is denoted $c^i \geq 0$. For any given intermediate product inducement may have to be offered for procurement or sale (but not both). The per-unit sidepayment for product j is denoted a_j and is negative for sale inducement and positive for purchase inducement. The vector $a = (0, a_1, \ldots, a_m)$ thus represents second-economy prices, payable in cash, which will be referred to as "c-prices." Note that $a_0 \equiv 0$ operationalizes the duality of the monetary system: no amount of official funds will buy cash, and official funds are never constrained by the need for financial inducements.[14] Letting $a_+ = \max(0, a)$ and $a_- = \max(0, -a)$, we see that $a_{+j} \neq 0$ only for those goods that require a financial inducement to consummate a purchase, and $a_{-j} \neq 0$ only for those goods which require a sidepayment to consummate a sale. It is through the flexibility of these second-economy prices—their responsiveness to market pressure (excess demands)—that the appropriate rationing takes place, rendering consistent the demands of the various enterprises using the same materials. So in solving the optimizating problem (2), each enterprise must also take into account a second-economy budget constraint determined by the c-prices, a, and its loose cash holdings, c^i. Notice that the functioning of this c-price mechanism is covered by the market form of the existing command allocation mechanism, as discussed earlier.

In formulating the second-economy budget constraint, we must take account of the fact that no enterprise has full control over the moneys it receives in illicit and/or semilicit transactions. The immediate recipient of cash is always some specific individual rather than the enterprise for which he works. Although the transaction may be undertaken to further the purposes of the enterprise, at least some portion of the cash involved is appropriated by the individuals handling it as a reward for their efforts.[15] This results from the direct utility of cash in the consumption and service sectors (state, private legal, private illegal) which provides a temptation that generally cannot be resisted. Hence some portion of any amount of cash used in transactions "leaks" out of the grasp of the enterprise (top management) during the course of trading to an equilibrium. In addition a portion of this leak can be considered a transactions cost or business expense necessitated by the illegality of the transaction, payments to officials (legal, Party, and plan administration) to "look the other way" or themselves provide support for the transaction. Of course that amount of cash that remains at the disposal of the enterprise ultimately accrues to those most directly responsible for the enterprise's performance, the top management.

For ease of exposition we will assume in this model that the portion of cash receipts lost due to leakage into private pockets is the same for all enterprises and all types of transactions. This rate of leakage will be denoted $\alpha \in (0, 1)$. Thus only $(1 - \alpha)$ of the cash receipts of any transaction can be reused by the enterprise to facilitate further purchases. Under this assumption the second-economy contraint of the enterprise becomes

$$az^i \equiv a\hat{z}^i \leq c^i - \alpha[a_+z^i_- + a_-z^i_+], \tag{3}$$

where the term in brackets shows cash receipts from all transactions, $z_- = \max(0, -z)$, and $z_+ = \max(0, z)$.

This formalization of the model of enterprise second-economy activity in the realm of input procurement has the structure of a pure exchange equilibrium model where agent behavior is given by (2) subject to the additional constraint of equation (3). To complete the structure of the model, I make four largely technical assumptions, *not* the most general that could be used, regarding the components of this model. They are sufficient assumptions facilitating ease of exposition.

ASSUMPTIONS

(A1) $X^i \subset R^{m+1}_+$ is a closed convex set, $\forall i$.

(A2) $w^i \in \text{int } X^i$, $\forall i$.

(A3) u^i is a C^2 strictly quasi-concave function, $\forall i$.

(A4) $\dfrac{\partial u^i}{\partial x_0} > 0, \forall i$.

In the next section we will define an equilibrium concept for this model and demonstrate its existence and optimality properties. But, before doing so, some further comment on agent/enterprise motivation is needed. Evidently accepting inducements to alter (or implement) planned allocations is illegal and thus carries certain risks. Why then should anyone get involved in these second-economy undertakings? Why run the risks of organizational corruption (Montias and Rose-Ackerman 1981)? Why not just follow the plan and do the best with what you've got? An obvious answer is that to do so may be every bit as risky as performance-augmenting participation in the second economy, particularly if others are so doing. In the Soviet economy the lack of necessary inputs is not an acceptable excuse for failure to meet the plan. Failure to meet the plan is a failure in the eyes of superiors that can lead to the loss of a highly lucrative managerial and social position.[16] On the other side of the coin, repeated success in plan fulfillment (in the eyes of superiors) definitely furthers personal career advancement, which generally yields consumption returns far in excess of the accompanying increment in monetary income. Further, participation in the second economy can provide direct lucrative pecuniary gains for those who receive direct payments (bribes) and/or consumption goods and services as inducements. Necessity has its rewards. Finally, one should not discount such factors as pride in job performance, "strengthening the motherland," "building socialism." Thus as long as participation in the second economy can be shown to work, to successfully ration inputs and to be performance enhancing in the eyes of superiors (u^i increasing), there seems to be quite sufficient motivation for a manager's participation.

7.2 Bribes Equilibrium

In the second-economy interpretation of the mechanism by which it is achieved, a performance enhancing equilibrium is called a "bribes equilibrium." A bribes equilibrium is performance enhancing in that it results in a Pareto improvement on the initially realized central allocation, $(w^1, \ldots, w^n)$, in terms of the vector of centrally perceived performance indexes, $(u^1, \ldots, u^n)$. It, however, does not result in a constrained Pareto-optimal allocation since there still remains some room for mutually beneficial exchanges of materials that cannot be generated in the second economy. Also, though productive, this second-economy equilibrium may not be productive in desirable directions from the point of view of the central authorities.

To understand these points we need to be more precise about definitions.

DEFINITION A *bribes equilibrium* of second-economy intermediate product markets is a set of net trades $\{z^i\}_{i=1}^n$ and a c-price vector $a \in \{q \in R^{m+1} \mid q_0 \equiv 0\}$, such that

$$\sum_{i=1}^{n} z^i = 0; \quad z^i \quad x^i - w^i, \quad \forall i; \tag{4}$$

$$x^i \in B^i(a), \quad \forall i; \tag{5}$$

$$B^i(a) \cap \{x \mid u^i(x) > u^i(x^i)\} = \phi, \quad \forall i; \tag{6}$$

where $B^i(a)$ is the budget set determined by the constraints in (2) and (3),

$$B^i(a) = \{x \in X^i | pz^i = 0, \quad az^i \leq c^i - \alpha[a_+ z^i_- + a_- z^i_+]\}, \quad \forall i. \tag{7}$$

The conditions (4) through (6) are, respectively, market clearing, individual feasibility, and individual optimality within the budget set. A bribes equilibrium hence represents the case where the need to offer financial inducements to complete some set of transactions successfully rations intermediate products: each enterprise is doing the best it can, and all input demands so generated are consistent.

DEFINITION An input allocation, $(x^1, \ldots, x^n)$, and/or the net trades generating it, $(z^1, \ldots, z^n)$, will be called a *Pareto improvement* over the initial allocation $(w^1, \ldots, w^n)$ if $u^i(x^i) \geq u^i(w^i)$ for all i and there exists i' such that $u^{i'}(x^{i'}) > u^{i'}(w^{i'})$; see equation (1). Such an allocation is a *constrained Pareto optimum* (CPO) if it is an element of

$$Z = \{(x^1, \ldots, x^n) \in R^{n(m+1)} | x^i \in X^i, pz^i = 0, \forall i; \sum_{i=1}^{n} z^i = 0\}$$

and there exists no $(\tilde{x}^1, \ldots, \tilde{x}^n) \in Z$ such that $(\tilde{x}^1, \ldots, \tilde{x}^n)$ is a Pareto improvement over $(x^1, \ldots, x^n)$.

A Pareto improvement is obviously a situation in which the central authorities perceive performance of some enterprises as better than it would have been given only the initial allocation. This provides a positive incentive for those enterprises to participate in the second economy. Further no enterprise will be perceived as doing worse, though they may not do strictly better. Thus participation is individually rational (there are no disincentives), and the prospect of private pecuniary gain then indeed provides a positive incentive for participation. Were the equilibrium CPO, the same participation incentives would hold as well as the assurance that no further opportunities for mutually beneficial trade exist, given the fixity of official prices. These criteria thus formalize an important condition for a bribes equilibrium to be meaningful.

The first important condition for a bribes equilibrium to be meaningful is that it exists. We will demonstrate such existence under a rather weak assumption on the "imperfection" of the initial allocation, $(w^1, \ldots, w^n)$, and official prices, p. The assumption is that of tradeability.

DEFINITION The assumption of *tradeability* is said to hold if there exists a good l and enterprises i, j, such that

$$(u^i_l(w^i) - \lambda^i p_l) \cdot (u^j_l(w^j) - \lambda^j p_l) < 0, \tag{8}$$

where λ^i is the shadow price of the official budget constraint in enterprise i's optimization problem (2).

What this asserts is that there exists at least one input material such that there are two different enterprises, one of which wants to acquire and the other of which is willing to dispose of that material at the given fixed official price. It is only slightly stronger than the assertion that the realized command allocation and prices, $(w^1, \ldots, w^n, p)$ do not form a Walrasian equilibrium.[17] Thus it would seem hardly a bold assumption in the context of the Soviet Union: certainly most enterprises are willing to trade many materials at existing producer prices. Given this assumption, the major result of this chapter can be given as follows:

THEOREM 1 Under the assumption of tradeability and **(A1)** to **(A4)**, there exists a bribes equilibrium for any $\alpha \in (0, 1)$ and all cash profiles $(c^1, \ldots, c^n)$, $c^i \geq 0, \forall i$, and $c^{i'} > 0$ for some i'.

Proof

The proof consists of three stages. First, we convert the exchange economy of section 7.1 into an abstract economy Γ with $n + 1$ players (Shafer and Sonnenschein 1975). The next stage, lemma 1, shows that it has an equilibrium. Then lemma 2 demonstrates that an equilibrium for Γ defines a bribes equilibrium for our intermediate products exchange economy, with well-defined bribe rates, a.

i. Define an abstract economy: $\Gamma = (\tilde{X}^i, B^i, P^i)_{i=0}^n$, where

$$\tilde{X}^i \triangleq X^i \cap [-\gamma, \gamma]^{m+1}, \quad \gamma \text{ sufficiently large}, i = 1, \ldots, n, \tag{9}$$

$$\tilde{X}^0 \triangleq \{a \in R^{m+1} | a_0 \equiv 0, \sum_{j=1}^m |a_j| \leq 1\};$$

$$B^i\,(a) \triangleq \{x^i \in \tilde{X}^i | pz^i = 0, (a + \alpha a_-)z^i_+ - (a - \alpha a_+)z^i_- \leq \lambda\,(a)c^i\};$$
$$B^0(a) \triangleq \tilde{X}^0; \tag{10}$$

$$\lambda\,(a) \triangleq 1 - \sum_{j=1}^m |a_j|;$$

$$P^i(x, a) \triangleq \{\tilde{x}^i \in \tilde{X}^i | u^i(\tilde{x}^i) > u^i(x^i)\}, x = (x^1, \ldots, x^n), i = 1, \ldots, n, \tag{11}$$

$$P^0(x, a) \triangleq \{\tilde{a} \in \tilde{X}^0 | \tilde{a}z > az\}, z = \sum_{i=1}^n z^i, z^i = x^i - w^i.$$

ii. *Lemma 1* Γ has an equilibrium $(a^0, x^0) \in \tilde{X}^0 \times \tilde{X}^1 \times \ldots \times \tilde{X}^n$, that is,

$$(a^0, x^0) \in B^0(a^0) \times B^1(a^0) \times \ldots \times B^n(a^0), \tag{12}$$

$$B^i(a^0) \cap P^i(x^0, a^0) = \phi, \text{ for } i = 0, 1, \ldots, n. \tag{13}$$

Proof of lemma 1: The proof involves verifying the conditions of the Shafer-Sonnenschein Theorem (1975). First note that $\tilde{X}^i$ and $B^i(a)$ are nonempty, compact, convex subsets of R^{m+1} for a. Further $P^i(x, a)$ has an open graph by **(A3)**. So we need only verify that $B^i(a)$ is continuous for all i. Upper hemicontinuity is immediate as $B^i(a)$ has a closed graph in a compact space. Lower hemicontinuity (l.h.c.) is a consequence of **(A2)**. If $\sum_{j=1}^{m} |\tilde{a}_j| < 1$, then l.h.c. follows at $\tilde{a}$ by the standard argument (Debreu 1959, p. 64–65). If $\sum_{j=1}^{m} |\tilde{a}_j| = 1$, then $w^i \in B^i(\tilde{a})$, $w^i \in \text{int } X^i$, and the linear independence of p and a imply that there exists an $\tilde{x}^i \in \text{int } B^i(\tilde{a})$. Again l.h.c. follows from the standard argument, so $B^i(a)$ is continuous. ■

iii. *Lemma 2*: (a, x) is a bribes equilibrium of the intermediate product exchange economy, where $a \triangleq a^0/(1 - \sum_{j=1}^{m} |a_j^0|)$.

Proof of lemma 2: To show equilibrium, we need to demonstrate that conditions (4), (5), and (6) hold. Clearly, (5) and (6) hold by virtue of (9), (10), and (12) if $\sum_{j=1}^{m} |a_j^0| < 1$. So we need only show that $\sum_{i=1}^{n} z^{0i} = 0$, and that bribe rates a can be unambiguously defined from a^0, that is, $\sum_{j=1}^{m} |a_j^0| < 1$.

Assume $z^0 \triangleq \sum_{i=1}^{n} z_i^0 \neq 0$. Define $|z_r^0| = \max_l |z_l^0|$. Then

$$a^0 z^0 \leq \left(\sum_{j=1}^{m} |a_m^0| \right) \cdot |z_r^0|$$

which by (13) implies that $\sum_{j=1}^{m} |a_j^0| = 1$. Hence from (10) we get $\lambda\,(a^0) = 0$.

Summing individual budget constraints yields

$$0 = \lambda\,(a^0) \sum_{i=1}^{n} c^i \geq a^0 z^0 + \alpha[a_+^0 z_-^0 + a_-^0 z_+^0] \tag{14}$$

while $\alpha[a_+^0 z_-^0 + a_-^0 z_+^0] \geq 0$ by definition. Hence $0 \geq a^0 z^0 \geq a z^0$ for all $a \in \tilde{X}^0$ by (13). Letting $\tilde{a}_r = \text{sgn } z_r^0$, $\tilde{a}_j = 0, j \neq r$, we see that $\tilde{a} z^0 > 0$ implying $0 \geq a^0 z^0 \geq \tilde{a} z^0 > 0$, a contradiction showing $z_l^0 = 0$, $\forall l \neq 0$. Then Walras's law and **(A4)** imply $z_0^0 = 0$, so that $z^0 = 0$.

All that now needs to be shown to complete the proof of lemma 2, and hence of the theorem, is that $\sum_{j=1}^{m} |a_j^0| < 1$ so that $\boldsymbol{a}$ is well defined. From the assumption of tradeability it is immediate that an orderly equilibrium (only one side of the market constrained; see Hahn 1978) must involve some trade (be nontrivial). This is because at equilibrium $u_l^i - \lambda^i p_l$ must have the same sign for all i and every l. Clearly, as min $(a_{j+}, a_{j-}) \equiv 0$ for all j and any a, every bribes equilibrium must be orderly and hence nontrivial: there exists some amount $\Delta > 0$ of some good either bought or sold by an agent who did not have to pay to take part in that transaction. By summing budget constraints,

$$\begin{aligned}\lambda(a^0)\sum_{j=1}^{n} c^i &\geq a^0 z^0 + \alpha[a^0_+ z^0_- + a^0_- z^0_+] \\ &= \alpha[a^0_+ z^0_- + a^0_- z^0_+] \geq \alpha \cdot \Delta \cdot \sum_{j=1}^{m} |a_j^0|. \end{aligned} \tag{15}$$

Using the definition of $\lambda(a^0)$ in equation (10), we see that

$$\sum_{j=1}^{m} |a_j^0| \leq \frac{\sum_{i=1}^{n} c^i}{\left(\sum_{i=1}^{n} c^i + \alpha\Delta\right)} < 1, \tag{16}$$

as $\alpha > 0$, $\Delta > 0$. Therefore c prices, a, are well defined. ∎

We see that, quite generally, a bribes equilibrium exists: the use of loose cash and bribery in second-economy markets can successfully reallocate input materials and ration excess demands at the officially fixed prices. In a sense they fine-tune the initial commanded allocation, $(w^1, \ldots, w^n)$. This naturally raises the question, Is it in anyone's interest to do so? The next proposition answers emphatically, Yes, as indicated in the preceding discussion.

PROPOSITION 1 Every bribes equilibrium is a Pareto improvement.

Proof

First note that the equilibrium is orderly: never more than one side of the market is constrained, forced to pay bribes. This follows from max $(a_{j+}, a_{j-}) \equiv 0$. Next note that there is no forced trading: $c^i \geq 0$ implies the initial/endowed position is always feasible. Thus all trading is voluntary and can only result in a performance improvement. Finally note that by tradeability some positive trade always takes place. ∎

This proposition shows that, under the very weak assumption on official prices and initial plan allocations, essentially that they do not form an equilibrium, there is a positive incentive for enterprises (managers) to participate in the second economy: such participation yields positive performance returns. Aside from this incentive for institutional corruption, the leakage of cash into private hands adds the dimension of individual corruption: even low-level functionaries are motivated to generate second-economy markets, as they are immediately rewarded with a piece of the action, while overseeing organs are induced to look the other way. The only thing more we could ask, while remaining within the constraints of central planning and price fixity is that the resulting allocations be not only Pareto improving but CPO. However, this is not the case.

PROPOSITION 2 A bribes equilibrium is not in general CPO.

Proof
Let $(a, z) \in S \times \mathcal{Z}$ be a bribes equilibrium with partial cash leakage, α. I show there exists $\tilde{z} \in \mathcal{Z}$, $\tilde{x}^i = w^i + \tilde{z}^i$, $\forall i$, such that $u^i(\tilde{x}^i) \geq u^i(x^i)$, $\forall i$, and there exists an i' such that $u^{i'}(\tilde{x}^{i'}) > u^{i'}(x^{i'})$.

The first-order conditions that must hold for every agent at equilibrium are as follows:

$$\begin{aligned} u_j^i(x^i) &= \lambda^i p_j + \mu^i a_j \quad \text{if } i \text{ is constrained on market } j, \\ u_j^i(x^i) &= \lambda^i p_j + (1-\alpha)\mu^i a_j \quad \text{if } i \text{ not constrained on market } j, \end{aligned} \tag{17}$$

where $u_j^i \triangleq \partial u^i / \partial x_j$ and an agent i is said to be constrained on market j if $(\operatorname{sgn} z_j^i)(\operatorname{sgn} a_j) > 0$. It is a simple exercise in linear algebra to show that the first-order conditions for the projection of i's preferences onto the hyperplane $\{x \in R^{m+1} | pz = 0\}$ are the following:

$$\begin{aligned} \hat{u}_j^i &= \mu^i[a_j - \Pi_j a] \quad \text{if } i \text{ constrained on market } j, \\ \hat{u}_j^i &= (1-\alpha)\mu^i[a_j - \Pi_j a] \quad \text{if } i \text{ not constrained on market } j, \end{aligned}$$

where $\Pi = (I - p(p^T p)^{-1} p^T)$ and Π_j is the jth row of Π. Since we have a nontrivial bribes equilibrium, there must be a good, $k \neq 0$, which is traded and for which one side of the market is constrained. Comparing the MRS between that good (k) and official funds $(j=0)$, we see that for enterprises on opposite sides of the kth market these MRS cannot be equal unless $\alpha = 0$:

$$\mathrm{MRS}_{k_0}^i \triangleq (\pi_0 a)^{-1}(a_k - \pi_k a) \neq (1-\alpha)(\pi_0 a)^{-1}(a_i - \pi_k a) \triangleq \mathrm{MRS}_{k_0}^{i'},$$

where i and i' are on opposite sides of the kth market. Hence there must exist Pareto-improving trades $\tilde{z}^i$, $\tilde{z}^{i'}$ such that $\tilde{z}^i + \tilde{z}^{i'} = 0$, $\tilde{z}^h = z^h$, $\forall h \neq i, i'$, $(\tilde{z}^1, \ldots, \tilde{z}^n) \in \mathcal{Z}$, with $u^h(\tilde{x}) = u^h(x)$, $\forall h \neq i, i'$, and $u^i(\tilde{x}) \geq u^i(x)$, $u^{i'}(\tilde{x}) > u^{i'}(x)$. ∎

Proposition 2 shows that, due to leakage of cash from the system, trading will be cut off before a full constrained Pareto optimum is reached. The need to reward subordinates and mollify superiors places a deadweight burden on each illegally induced transaction that prevents some transactions, which are productive from the viewpoint of increasing output of the system, from being consummated. Thus the failure to achieve a CPO allocation can be considered the cost of using the second-economy mechanism, though the fact that its allocations are a Pareto improvement indicates that the net system benefits are positive.

A question raised by these results is, What if second-economy transactions were costless in the sense of $\alpha = 0$? While this question is studied in another paper (Ericson 1981), its answer is outlined here for comparative purposes. First, if a bribes equilibrium exists, then it is CPO. However, existence cannot be assured for an arbitrary cash profile, $(c^1, \ldots, c^n) \in R^n_+$, as long as p remains fixed and cash is not tradeable against official funds.[18] In the cases of nonexistence cash loses its ability to influence allocations; only materials can "purchase" other materials. This leads to the introduction of a closely related, but different, equilibrium concept, the barter equilibrium, which can be shown always to exist and yield CPO allocations. In this equilibrium cash plays no allocative role, information is perfect, and transactions are frictionless (absolutely costless) in spite of a lack of medium of exchange. The result is a purely Walrasian exchange subeconomy, which to me lacks the empirical appeal of the model of this chapter.

A final observation with regard to this model is that there is nothing essential about the uniformity of the rate of leakage. A brief study of the proof of theorem 1 will convince one that it would remain unchanged if α were replaced by $\{\alpha^i\}_{i=1}^n$, $\alpha^i > 0\ \forall i$, as long as $\alpha[a^0_- z^0_+ + a^0_+ z^0_-]$ were replaced by $\sum_{i=1}^{n} \alpha^i [a^0_- z^{i0}_+ + a^0_+ z^{i0}_-]$ in equations (14) and (15). It might also be possible to allow differentiation of rates of leakage by material, though I haven't worked that case out yet.[19] It seems that all we need is some cash leakage in each receiving enterprise (some venial low-level managers or corrupt inspectors) for a bribes equilibrium to exist and yield a Pareto improvement over the initial plan allocation. This is, arguably, what we observe as the outcome of a class of second-economy mechanisms in the Soviet Union.

7.3 Concluding Remarks

This chapter has provided a model that might explain the appearance and continued functioning of a whole set of second-economy ("colored,"

Katsenelinboigen 1978) markets within the rather rigid institutional framework of a command economy. For such a model a well-defined equilibrium concept was presented and shown viable. A Bribes equilibrium provides both individual and institutional incentives for participation in the second economy because it involves leakage and is performance enhancing. It provides a consistent solution to the allocation problem in the face of fixed official prices, one that is a feasible alternative to the rationing command mechanism. Finally, the model is roughly consistent with institutional and anecdotal evidence available from the U.S.S.R.

The logic of the argument behind this model, as it relates to the Soviet Union, is quite simple. In the Soviet socialist context legal access to the material benefits of life depends largely on official position in the hierarchy and proximity to the touchstone of power, the Party.[20] Thus one's utility depends on one's position, which in turn hangs on the evaluation of one's performance by superiors in the hierarchy (state and/or Party). For a manager this evaluation depends, to a significant degree, on one's (perceived) success in plan fulfillment. Plan fulfillment in turn rests crucially on the ability to procure needed inputs. Hence, if such inputs are not forthcoming through official channels, there is a strong incentive to resort to unorthodox methods of procurement.

On the other hand, it is well-known that production and allocation plans are generally inconsistent, particularly on the detailed level, and infeasible. Even when consistent and feasible, input allocations are generally far from efficient. This problem is aggravated by the practice of implementation through contract at fixed official prices and by the fact that supply problems are not an accepted excuse for failure to fulfill the plan. This resort to market form, but not its essence, enhances the discretion of suppliers, already disruptively large due to the general sellers' market and *defitsitnost'* of critical materials. Thus supply realization is rendered highly arbitrary and the need to resort to unorthodox methods even more urgent.

This strong demand for procurement markets is met in the Soviet Union by some highly favorable institutional circumstances for their appearance. Of all the multiple factors fostering the appearance of a second economy under socialism, let me mention only a couple most relevant for any model.[21] The fact that supplies are formally bought and sold at official prices through contractual relations provides an extremely convenient framework in which to embed second-economy markets: it merely involves the addition of market substance to the official form. That there are those willing to supply this substance from both sides of the market follows from the market power implied by general scarcity and the discretionary latitude of suppliers and from the need to assure procurement, to make allocations less arbitrary. Finally, the appearance of true markets is facilitated by the existence of a readily available, always acceptable, value stable means of exchange: cash rubles (*nalichnye den'gi*). This provides a "second" money that always has value in the consumption sectors (of both the first and second economies) and has the inestimable advantage for illegal transactions of being anonymous.[22] This anonymity is particularly important in keeping the extra transactions costs of illegal exchanges at a minimum, and thus more or less successfully monetizing this aspect.

To the extent that the second economy with respect to intermediate product markets is monetized and bartered materials are resalable, all inducements and transactions can be reduced to cash values, evaluated at stable prices as if money had exchanged hands. This effectively monetizes the difference between the marginal benefit from impressing superiors through the use of various inputs and the official prices of those inputs (their user-faced opportunity cost). In doing so, the second economy generates classical gains to trade, though they are limited by the transactions costs of leakage, by the need to induce others to participate or look the other way. That this story is a consistent one, that second-economy intermediate product markets can effectively ration the sellers' market, is the principle theoretical conclusion of this chapter.

So far we have justified the appearance and functioning of second-economy markets in terms of opportunities and incentives for participation in them. We have only incidentally commented on the attitude and reaction of the central authorities to this phenomenon. Clearly, to the extent that they are interested in process, in preserving the tightly controlled, planned nature of the system, the central authorities must find this functioning of the second economy highly disturbing: nonregime goals are being pursued by anti-systemic methods. The changes in the patterns of allocation and production induced by second-economy markets may be wildly at variance with the wishes of the planners. Although they have significant influence in determining the initial allocation, that allocation, as actually realized, may be far from implying centrally desired output patterns, and it is not clear that local initiative does not aggravate that situation. What's more, if a realized allocation should be close to yielding centrally desired output patterns, then the functioning of these second-economy markets is sure to distort it in undesirable directions. Hence there would seem to be strong practical and ideological reasons for the central authorities to seriously attempt to shut down this type of second-economy activity.

Yet we do not seem to see any such effort seriously undertaken in the Soviet

Union. I would argue that this is because the central authorities find the functional aspects of this type of activity outweigh the dysfunctional aspects. The reason lies in the inherent impossibility of ever drawing up a fully consistent economic plan that is sufficiently detailed to be operational. As this is not the place to argue the point in depth, I will just refer to five crucial factors: (1) the bounded rationality (Radner 1975) of both planners and subordinates, (2) the inherent uncertainty in the outcome of any real-time action, (3) the fact that any plan must be in aggregate terms at some level, (4) the wide dispersion of continually changing detailed information needed to make allocation decisions, (5) the ultimately self-interested behavior of all economic agents. Hence no detailed plan can be implemented as written, and some sort of extra-plan mechanism is necessary to specify, adjust, and thus correct the plan decisions, so as to maintain the rough microbalance needed for the continued functioning of the economic system.

Second-economy intermediate product markets appear as just such a mechanism and so, in essence, further the maintenance of the planned structure of the economy. They allow central planners to pick broad directions and proportions and issue detailed instructions to implement those decisions without having to worry overly about the disruptive consequences of those instructions. In this respect, as the results of this model indicate the second economy "fine-tunes" the central allocations, insuring consistency (existence of equilibrium) and generating greater efficiency and output (Pareto improving). Although the increase in output achieved by the second-economy allocation may be in sectors the center finds distasteful, it is also assured that no enterprise is producing less than it would have with the initial allocation. In a sense the second economy contravenes central wishes in this model only on the margin, as the pattern of the bulk of output is determined by the initial allocation. The economy as a whole gains from the increase in output achievable from the efficient allocation of the same amount of inputs, a result that is hard to imagine as displeasing to the central planners.

Further one might even imagine a reform in which the central authorities attempt to manipulate the second economy, using it explicitly as a decentralized mechanism to "fine-tune" the centralized resource allocation process. The usefulness of such a mechanism is evident just from consideration of informational requirements of centralized allocation.[23] While it is conceivable that the center can correctly determine the main proportions and directions of an optimal (according to some criteria) allocation, it is far less reasonable to suppose that the fine details of such an allocation can be centrally commanded. At the detailed level, all the unknown individual aspects and unforeseen perturbations of economic activity become crucial to determining a proper allocation. Thus, once the center has determined the general structure of production through its initial allocation, it may find it advantageous to allow such a decentralized mechanism to fill in the particulars.

Of course none of these observations should be construed as a claim that the Soviet second economy is in all aspects desirable from some social welfare point of view, or even that it always results in increased efficiency in production. Its socially and economically undesirable aspects have been noted by many writers.[24] I have rather tried to draw attention to, and analyze, one socially functional aspect of the Soviet second-economy that I feel has not received the attention it deserves. The central economic point is the well-known assertion that pure reallocation can be productive and does not merely imply a redistribution of losses and gains. Precisely such a reallocation can be generated by markets with flexible prices operating in the face of officially fixed prices and inalterable official budget constraints. Thus the second economy does more than redistribute access to goods and services to the daring and/or corrupt and the politically and economically powerful. Also to a certain extent it raises the efficiency of the socialist (centrally planned) economy and thus contributes to the general welfare. On a deeper level it, arguably, plays a role in maintaining the normal functioning of the socialist economy, in avoiding or minimizing socially disruptive shortages and breakdowns. These factors need to be weighed against the various costs in any evaluation of the role and meaning of the second economy in the Soviet Union.

Notes

Research support of the National Science Foundation, grant SES-804296, is gratefully acknowledged.

1. The listing of areas is my own, somewhat subjective, outline of those covered in the now voluminous, though largely unpublished, literature on the second economy. A major portion of this literature was presented at the Research Conference on the Second Economy of the U.S.S.R. held at the Kennan Institute for Advanced Russian Studies in Washington, D.C., January 24–26, 1980. There the noted emphasis was quite evident. Also see Grossman (1979) for perhaps the most thorough published discusion.

2. This is clear from any of the standard Soviet handbooks/reference works on planning. See, for example, *Tipovaia Metodika Razrabotki Piatiletnego Plana*, *Metodicheskie Ukazaniia k Razrabotke Gosudarstvennykh Planov*, and *Spravochnoe Posobie Direktoru* published in 1975, 1974, and 1977, respectively, the first two by GOSPLAN and the last by Ekonomika Publishers, all in Moscow.

3. This is necessarily the case in any complex social/economic system: reality is far more detailed than can ever be comprehended by any decision-maker. This only becomes a problem, however, when a decision-maker attempts to enforce a plan affecting the behavior of others. A canonical example is the case of ball bearings in the Soviet Union: 14 planned types disaggregate into approximately 72,000 different varieties (Karpov 1972). Ball bearings are crucial to any mechanical production process, and different types (of the 72,000) are nonsubstitutable. Yet the decision as to precisely which types to produce is made operationally at the lowest levels, despite the devastating repercussions that an incorrect decision may have for plan fulfillment.

4. On the more established of these markets see Katsenelinboigen (1978) and Katsenelinboigen and Levine (1976). There a nice color classification (from red and white through grey and brown to black) is given of their relative legality and the degree to which they are tolerated in the Soviet Union.

5. This does not mean that it is necessarily desirable from the point of view of the central planners.

6. On prices, see any of the standard texts on the Soviet Economy, such as Bergson (1964), Gregory and Stuart (1981), Nove (1977). This assertion is of course an exaggeration, as enterprises can apply for price changes (invariably increases) based on objective factors such as cost increases or quality improvements. The process is, however, slow, and the resulting prices are, except by pure coincidence, unrelated to relative scarcities. On the monetary system, also see, for example, Garvy (1966) and Portes (1977).

7. See any Soviet work on material and equipment supply, for example, *Spravochnik po Material'no-tekhnicheskomu Snabzheniiu i Sbytu*, Moscow Ekonomika Publishers, 1976. Also Ericson (1979).

8. See note 6.

9. In principle there seems little difficulty in generalizing the plan to multiple outputs, though it may be harder then to justify the quasi concavity of the criterion functional. Such a generalization would allow the investigation of the assortment choice decision and the possible distortions resulting from second-economy activities.

10. See, for example, Ellman (1971, 1973) on inconsistency. On tautness and pressure, see Hunter (1961), Keren (1972), and Levine (1966), as well as any standard text on the Soviet economy such as Gregory and Stuart (1981).

11. This point has arisen in conversations with Soviet émigrés and was raised at the Research Conference on the Second Economy (note 1). It was first brought to my attention by Gregory Grossman.

12. Among the funds available to the enterprise are Fund for Material Stimulation/Incentive, Directors Fund, Enterprise Development Fund, Housing and Culture Fund, Wage Fund. There are numerous ways to manipulate the books of these accounts so as to generate excess cash. See *Spravochnoe Posobie Direktoru* (note 2).

13. In practice this case is assured by appropriate bribery. See, for example, Simes (1975) and Simis (1977).

14. This is of course an overstatement; it seems possible, though much more difficult, to bribe one's way to an increased allocation of official funds. Further one can effect the same thing with simulated transactions, for example, the delivery of pipe is recorded as completion of an entire construction project, which loosens the official budget constraint. These, however, do not seem to be nearly as common as legitimate transactions induced by sidepayments, whether in cash or kind.

15. This is particularly the case with low-level functionaries who have some control over materials flows, such as the warehouse/inventory manager and workers (*sklad-ovshchiki*), though *tolkachi* also take their share. Some of this skimming should also be considered part of their regular compensation for the job they do, as has been noted by Grossman (1979).

16. Raymond Powell (1977, p. 58), among others, notes this point. It should be mentioned that high managerial positions in socialist societies are far more lucrative than relative monetary incomes indicate. This is due to the vast assortment of privileges and the access to goods and services money can't buy associated with positions of power in these societies. See, for example, Matthews (1978).

17. Tradability is essentially a condition for trade to take place given in Arrow and Hahn (1971, ch. 13) and in the appendix of Hahn (1978). That a situation without tradeability need not be a Walrasian equilibrium is also shown in the former reference.

18. Changing either of the latter conditions reduces the model to a purely Walrasian one.

19. One might be able to allow some $\alpha^i = 0$, though that case has also yet to be worked out. There would seem to be a problem in showing existence if those engaged in unconstrained trade were to have $\alpha^i = 0$.

20. See note 16. This is a point that has not received the attention in Soviet studies literature that it deserves. In particular it would seem to be important for modeling economic processes in the Soviet Union as both opportunity sets (available actions and possible outcomes) and preferences seem to depend strongly on formal position.

21. These factors were discussed from historical, political, sociological, and economic perspectives at the Research Conference on the Second Economy (note 1). The closest to a written summary of economic factors, of which I know, is Montias and Rose-Ackerman (1981).

22. The role of anonymity has been stressed by a number of Soviet economists, notably, Shatalin. This is an aspect of moneyness that has also failed to receive the attention it deserves in western economic literature.

23. The classic statement is in Hayek (1945). More concretely, one need only think of the allocation problem for a nomenclature of over 15 million items among several hundred thousand producers and industrial users in a situation that is continually changing in unpredictable ways.

24. In particular at the Research Conference on the Second Economy (note 1). A clear economic argument is presented in Montias and Rose-Ackerman (1981).

References

Arrow, K., and F. Hahn, 1971. *General Competitive Analysis*. San Francisco, Ca.: Holden-Day.

Bergson, A., 1964. *The Economics of Soviet Planning*. New Haven, Ct.: Yale University Press.

Berliner, J., 1959. *Factory and Manager in the USSR*. Cambridge, Ma.: Harvard University Press.

Debreu, G., 1959. *Theory of Value*. New Haven, Ct.: Yale University Press.

Ellman, M., 1971. *Soviet Planning today*. Cambridge, England: Cambridge University Press.

Ellman, M., 1973. *Planning Problems in the USSR*. Cambridge, England: Cambridge University Press.

Ericson, R., 1979. A theoretical and institutional analysis of industrial supply in the U.S.S.R.: A study of resource allocation under uncertainty. CRMS Working Paper IP-276, March, Berkeley, Ca.

Ericson, R., 1981. The "second economy" and resource allocation under central planning. Discussion Paper 835. Harvard Institute of Economic Research, Cambridge, Ma.

Garvy, G., 1966. *Money, Banking and Credit in Eastern Europe*. New York: Federal Reserve Bank.

Granick, D., 1959. *Management of the Industrial Firm in the USSR*. New York: Columbia University Press.

Gregory, P., and R. Stuart, 1981. *Soviet Economic Structure and Performance*. 2d ed. New York: Harper and Row.

Grossman, G., 1963. Notes for a theory of the command economy. *Soviet Studies* 15: 101–123.

Grossman, G., 1977. The "second economy" of the USSR. *Problems of Communism* (September–October): 25–40.

Grossman, G., 1979. Notes on the illegal private economy and corruption. In JEC Compendium, *Soviet Economy in a Time of Change*. Washington, D.C.: Government Printing Office, pp. 834–855.

Hahn, F., 1978. On non-Walrasian equilibria, *Review of Economic Studies* 45: 1–17.

Hayek, F., 1945. The use of knowledge in society. *American Economic Review* 35: 519–530.

Hunter, H., 1961. Optimal tautness in development planning. *Economic Development and Cultural Change* 9: 561–572.

Karpov, P. P., 1972. *The Allocation of the Means of Production in the New Economic Conditions*. *Ekonomika*, Moscow (in Russian).

Katsenelinboigen, A., 1978. *Studies in Soviet Economic Planning*. New York: M. E. Sharpe.

Katsenelinboigen, A., and H. Levine, 1976. Some observations on the plan-market relationship in centrally planned economies. Discussion Paper 395, University of Pennsylvania, Philadelphia.

Keren, M., 1972. On the tautness of plans. *Review of Economic Studies* 39: 469–486.

Levine, H., 1966. Pressure and planning in the Soviet economy. In H. Rosovsky *Industrialization in Two Systems*. New York: Wiley, pp. 266–286.

Matthews, M., 1978. *Privilege in the Soviet Union*. London: George Allen & Unwin.

Montias, J. M., and S. Rose-Ackerman, 1981. Corruption in a Soviet-type economy: Theoretical considerations. In S. Rosefielde, *Economic Welfare and the Economics of Soviet Socialism*. Cambridge, England: Cambridge University Press, pp. 53–84.

Nove, A., 1977. *The Soviet Economic System*. London: George Allen & Unwin.

Portes, R., 1977. The control of inflation. *Economica* 44: 109–130.

Powell, R., 1977. Plan execution and the workability of Soviet planning. *Journal of Comparative Economics* 1: 51–76.

Radner, R., 1975. Satisficing. *Journal of Mathematical Economics* 2: 253–262.

Shafer, W., and H. Sonnenschein, 1975. Equilibrium in abstract economies without ordered preferences. *Journal of Mathematical Economics* 2: 345–348.

Simes, D. K., 1975. The Soviet parallel market. *Survey* 21: 42–52.

Simis, K., 1977. The machinery of corruption in the Soviet Union. *Survey* 23: 35–55.

8 Dumping by Centrally Planned Economies: The Polish Golf Cart Case

Franklyn D. Holzman

Alex Erlich did not learn to play golf when he was growing up in Poland before World War II. This was not necessarily due to lack of aptitude. In fact until this day no Polish youngster, nor adult for that matter, has had the opportunity to learn golf because in Poland there are no golf courses—none with the exception of a two-hole course in Warsaw set up within the past few years to demonstrate to potential foreign buyers the electrical golf cart that the Poles have been producing and exporting to the United States since 1971.[1] Had the Polish golf cart not been of such superior quality and exported at a relatively low price, this story would be over. With both of these conditions present, however, U.S. producers were moved to resist the Polish competition by invoking various categories of foreign trade and antitrust legislation, particularly the antidumping laws. The Poles have fought back, and the case has become something of a cause célèbre, the notoriety of which has been limited only by the fact that the market for golf carts is so modest. The importance of the case goes far beyond golf carts, however. First, a new method was devised to assess dumping charges against centrally planned economies (CPEs). Second, the CPEs have serious balance-of-payments problems with the West. They need hard currency badly. The success with which Poland resists dumping (and other) charges has significance for the future of eastern attempts to compete in U.S. markets for manufactured products.

8.1 Dumping Defined

Dumping is usually defined as exporting in a foreign market at below the exporter's domestic price for the same product. This is the most common basis of complaint under the U.S. Antidumping Act of 1921 and under GATT's Article VI. In cases where the exporter has no domestic sales, Article VI further defines dumping as the export price that is either less than cost of production (plus selling costs and profits) in the country of origin or less than the export price to a third country. The cost of production test was introduced into U.S. law in 1974. Exporting at discriminatorily low prices or at below cost of production is viewed as selling at "less than fair value" and therefore as unfair competition. If import-competing enterprises are distressed by the dumping and can prove "material damage," the government is obliged to levy antidumping duties which bring the prices of the imports in question up to "fair value."

Dumping is generally viewed as an exercise in price discrimination by private enterprises. Related to this, most nations, including the United States, and the GATT prohibit government subsidies by other nations designed to promote exports and provide for countervailing duties to remove the advantages of the subsidies when such subsidies cause material injury to importing nations' industries.[2] One would have expected that legislation relating to government subsidies and countervailing duties rather than to dumping would have been applied to presumed "less than fair value" sales in the United States by communist foreign trade organizations since these are nationalized enterprises, but this has not been the case. Several possible explanations come to mind. First, it is difficult to verify dumping by centrally planned economies and even more difficult to establish the existence of subsidies since data of this sort have been unavailable. Second, since the U.S. countervailing duty code did not require injury until the Tokyo Round a few years ago, it might have been viewed by the administration as opening the way to a more restrictive import policy than even the most hidebound protectionists would desire. Third, for reasons which are not at all clear, low-priced Soviet sales in the West, especially in the United States, during the 1930s and 1950s, were always discussed primarily as possible cases of dumping even though it was often recognized that, if dumping was being practiced, it might well have been due to government subsidies (Feller 1967, p. 134). This tradition may well be the major reason for the use in recent years of dumping rather than countervailing duty statutes against low-priced CPE exports.

8.2 The Systemic Gap

Products entering the country from CPEs at below the market price are viewed with more than the usual amount of suspicion by import-competing enterprises for nontrivial reasons. CPE-exporting enterprises are virtually all state enterprises with potentially the full power of the state purse behind them. Further it is well known that very commonly in the CPE world enterprises operate for long periods of time at losses covered by state subsidies. Hence it would not be at all surprising to find that enterprises having difficulty selling in western markets are being subsidized to facilitate price competition.

Further suspicion is aroused by the fact that CPE domestic markets are largely insulated from world markets, and domestic prices are not organically related to world prices. In the words of three Polish economists (speaking of price and cost comparisons between the CPE nations): "... because of the autonomous system of domestic prices in each country and the automatic and purely internal character of the monetary system and arbitrary official rates of exchange which do not reflect relative values of currencies, it is impossible to compare prices and costs of particular commodities in different countries."[3] Domestic prices in the CPEs do not reflect market forces, either supply or demand, to any great extent. Prices in the U.S.S.R., for example, have been largely frozen since 1967 despite the enormous changes in basic economic conditions since that time. Relative prices cannot help but be irrational. Obviously, under such conditions, an exchange rate has little meaning as a monetary price through which actual internal commodity prices may be compared with external commodity prices. In fact Soviet foreign trade planners have used some 250 commodity group price adjustment coefficients to compare internal and external prices.

The exchange rate also fails to serve any role in the balance of payments. Changes in the exchange rate do not affect the supply of exports or demand for imports through market forces.[4] The exchange rate is only a unit of account and not a very accurate one at that.[5] If the exchange rates of the CPEs were real prices, they would of course be significantly overvalued vis-à-vis western currencies as indicated by the serious hard currency deficits and large external debts of each CPE nation.

While western business men typically are not aware of the full complexity of these differences, they know that internal CPE prices (or costs) are not relevant to trade, that they are generally unavailable, and that converting them into western currencies via official exchange rates is, in any event, not a meaningful procedure. A western enterprise, when threatened by imports from CPEs (or from other western enterprises), does not need a valid excuse to call for antidumping relief. The U.S. Treasury, which must determine whether the alleged dumping has taken place, is faced, however, with the fact that the usual methods of evaluating dumping charges do not work with nations that have nonmarket costs and prices, nonfunctioning exchange rates, and, in any case, have usually not been willing to disclose industrial accounting information to outsiders.

Evaluation of dumping charges is not the only issue raised by systemic differences. Motives behind dumping may also be different. A western enterprise may dump for several reasons: to eliminate competition, to get rid of a temporary oversupply, or to use price discrimination as a way of increasing one's market in order to achieve economies of scale. The U.S.S.R. was first accused of dumping raw materials and grain on world markets during the Great Depression. Its purpose was to earn hard currency to buy the machinery and equipment required to achieve the industrialization targets of the First five-year plan. While it might appear to others that they were exporting at a loss, from the standpoint of the planners, the gains from the imported machinery paid for by their exports were adequate compensation. That is to say, in the final analysis the planners viewed the exchange of grain and raw materials for machinery and equipment in barter terms rather than as independent transactions.[6] Their motive was not that of a classic dumper even though their impact on the markets where they dumped was no different from that of a classic dumper—and should therefore have been subject to the antidumping laws. This was the period of beggar-thy-neighbor policies, but even in normal times many transactions are undoubtedly rationalized in barter terms.

Dumping charges were levied against the U.S.S.R. again in the 1950s particularly in connection with sales of petroleum. Again the motivation was not that of a classical dumper. Before World War II (and also before World War I) the Russians had a substantial share of the world petroleum market. They simply wanted that share back again. They had no interest in selling at below the market price, but they had no other way of gaining entry. It is significant that just a few years later, a huge field of industrial diamonds was discovered in Siberia. Shortly thereafter it was announced that Soviet diamonds would be marketed by De Beers. Clearly, the capitalists and communists had both learned a lesson and were benefiting from it.[7]

8.3 Exchange Rate Overvaluation and the Inability to Devalue

In theory a proper evaluation of dumping charges should—but never does—take account of over- or undervaluation of exchange rates. An undervalued exchange rate implicitly subsidizes all exports and levies a sales tax on all imports, while an overvalued exchange rate subsidizes imports and levies a sales tax on exports. Such implicit sales taxes and subsidies lead the market to distort true comparative advantage and thus to surpluses in the case of undervaluation and deficits in the case of overvaluation. In figure 8.1, at an overvalued exchange rate, P_0, the nation would export OA and import OB

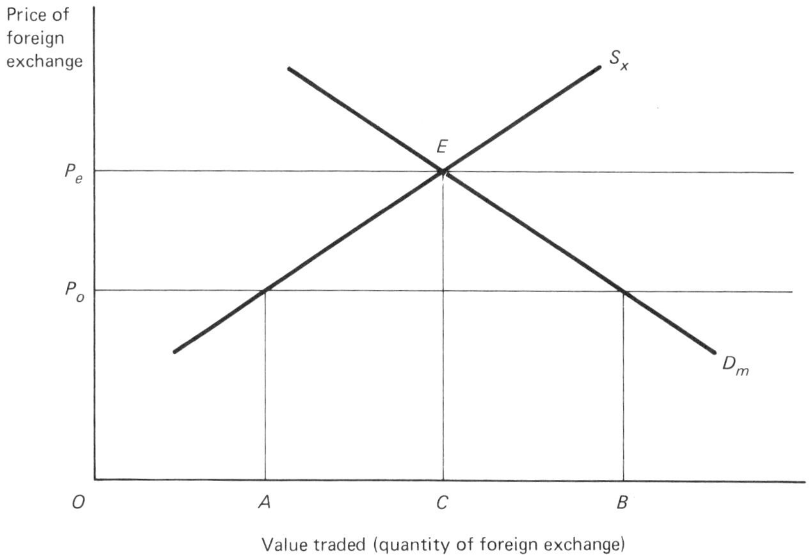

Figure 8.1

for a deficit of *AB*. Devaluation to an equilibrium exchange rate, P_e, would decrease imports and increase exports both to *OC*, thereby balancing trade. True comparative advantage is revealed at P_e. At P_o, *AC* of exports are priced out of the market by the hidden sales tax of a macrodisequilibrium. In fact at P_e all of *AC* but the marginal sale could be made at below the world price without a loss.

Most market economies do not boast of exchange rates that are in equilibrium. Nevertheless, most have the option of changing their exchange rates to approach equilibrium. The CPEs have no such option. As noted earlier, their official exchange rates are not real prices and have little or no effect on foreign trade decision making (Hungary excepted). They simply trade in world currencies at world prices. At world prices they have been experiencing large trade deficits with the West for about a decade.[8] Now a market economy experiencing such deficits would have an overvalued exchange rate and would be suffering from a terms-of-trade illusion due to the implicit subsidies to imports and implicit sales taxes on exports. Devaluation eliminates this illusion. The large trade deficits persistently experienced by the CPEs suggest that they experience something of a terms-of-trade illusion in trading without a real exchange rate at world prices (Holzman 1979, pp. 307–311).[9] In any event, faced with a desire to import more than can be financed by exports or by prudent borrowing, it would not be surprising if they showed an inclination to sell at below world prices to expand exports. They know that, since the value of additional imports (beyond OA) is sufficiently great, it would be worth lowering the price of, say, AC of exports, to finance them. This would not be true dumping although it might appear to be so.[10]

8.4 Polish Golf Carts and the Antidumping Statutes

Approximately a dozen companies in the United States produce some 40 to 50 thousand golf carts annually. Most of these are electrically powered like those imported from Poland. The possibility of producing and exporting golf carts to the United States was suggested to the Poles around 1970 by an American distributor who was dissatisfied with the domestically produced versions he was handling in the United States. A Polish light aircraft enterprise, which exports crop dusters to the United States and other western nations on a fairly large scale felt, after some investigation, that it could compete successfully in the U.S. golf cart market. Exports to the United States were begun in 1971 and since 1972 have amounted to 5 to 10 thousand units annually.

The first of several dumping charges were brought against Pezetel, the Polish foreign trade organization, by Outboard Marine Corporation, a company that went out of the golf cart business because, they claimed, Pezetel was selling its carts at less than fair value. This led to several attempts to find a satisfactory way of determining whether or not Pezetel was dumping to get around the price-cost exchange rate problems:

1. The statutes on dumping provide that, if an exporting nation does not sell its product in its home market, then the price of its export in third nations can be used to assess dumping charges. This alternative could not be used in the present case because all of Polish exports were directed at the U.S. market. In any case this approach has been rejected for CPEs because of the judgment that costs of production in the usual sense are not a controlling factor in the prices charged in third nations, and those prices are therefore not reliable for the purpose at hand.

2. The Antidumping Act of 1921 was amended in 1974 so that the fair value of CPE export prices could be determined from the prices charged by non-CPE producers in other countries, including the United States. At this time the main non-CPE producers were Marathon in Canada and some small companies in Brazil, Mexico, and Japan. The companies in the latter three countries sold their carts at very high prices in protected domestic markets

and were not competitive in foreign markets. Marathon's carts sold in both Canada and the United States, and its price was used as a basis for determining the fair value of Polish carts. Adjustments were made for differences between the Polish and Canadian carts as well as for the fact that the relatively much larger number of carts annually produced by the former (10,000 versus 250) entitled them to economies of scale. Marathon went out of business shortly thereafter forcing all parties to seek a new measure of fair value.

3. An attempt was made at this point to use the prices charged by U.S. golf cart producers as a basis for determining the fair value of Polish carts. It was argued that U.S. producers were, after all, non-CPE producers and their prices were relevant. Under this interpretation Polish carts would have been priced out of the U.S. market because fair value, as determined by this method, was based on full costs of production by U.S. producers not including transport costs to the market. Since Polish transport costs to the U.S. market are so much higher than those of U.S. producers, their selling prices in the United States would necessarily be correspondingly higher. The Polish representatives raised this objection. This method was withdrawn in treasury regulations dated September 8, 1978 (Soltysinski 1980, p. 3).

Objections were raised to attempts 2 and 3 on the grounds that it was unfair to use the costs of production of advanced capitalist countries (Canada, United States) to determine the fair value of a similar product produced by a less-developed nation. Because of differences in factor proportions and factor prices, one could not assess Poland's comparative advantage—in this case fair price—by looking at prices in advanced capitalist nations. In the golf cart case, unfortunately, no nation at a comparable level of development produced a competitive product. In 1979 Poland was accused also of dumping carbon steel plate. Spain was taken as a nation at approximately the same level of development and the price of carbon steel plate at the one Spanish plant that produced it was taken as a measure of fair value.[11] This price was converted from pesetas to dollars at the going Spanish exchange rate, and by this measure it appeared that the Poles were dumping. However, the International Trade Commission determined that the domestic U.S. industry did not suffer material injury, and the case was dropped.

4. As a last resort, if a product is not made or sold in other countries, the law provides for an estimate of the cost of production in a comparable (level of development) third country to be determined. This is the so-called "constructed value" approach. The Polish golf cart case was the first in which this

approach was used for a CPE. Implementation involved the following steps. The specific physical components required to produce the golf cart were estimated. These included hours of labor, quantities of raw materials, amounts of energy, among other factors. These were then valued in prices of a "comparable" market economy, in this case Spain. To the total direct value so obtained were added markups for general expenses (notably, overhead, profits, packaging.) The overall total was then converted into dollars through the surrogate nation's exchange rate.[12] The dollar price thus obtained was not above the price at which the golf carts were being sold in the United States; hence by this measure a charge of dumping could not be sustained.[13]

8.5 Evaluation of Comparable Nation and Constructed Value Approaches

The U.S. Treasury and the Polish Government both appear to be satisfied with the methods used in both the carbon steel plate and golf cart cases. Here are methods which appear to have bridged the systemic gap, providing proxy costs (prices) and proxy exchange rates by which dumping charges can be assessed. The question is, How good are these proxies?

Use of proxy costs from nations of comparable levels of development are based implicitly on a simple Heckscher-Ohlin static comparative advantage model (H-O) with the dynamic properties of Ray Vernon's product cycle model (Vernon 1966). That is to say, nations at different levels of development are likely to have different factor proportions (capital and labor) and different factor prices; at similar levels of development, similar factor proportions and factor prices. Therefore an accurate representation of CPEs product price is more likely, but not necessarily, to be obtained by using either the constructed value (in golf cart case) or actual price of the same product produced in a third nation of similar level of development (in the carbon steel plate case) than in third nations at different levels of development. Nevertheless, there is no special reason to believe that such an H-O approach will always lead to a favorable result (low price) since, with different factor proportions and factor prices, different methods of production may be used which may or may not be more efficient in some comparative advantage sense. The likelihood of a more favorable result is no doubt based intuitively on the Vernon conception that, after new manufactured products have been around a while, less-developed nations with their lower-wage costs gradually begin to outcompete the higher-wage cost advanced nation innovators. This theory assumes that wages are the major cost of production—for most not-too-advanced products, a good assumption.

Using a proxy nation like Spain which is at a similar level of development probably makes more sense than judging Polish costs or prices by data obtained from more (or less) advanced nations. Nevertheless, this approach has serious limitations. In the first place it is subject to all of the well-known criticisms of the oversimple H-O factor proportions theory. Literally hundreds of articles have been written since Leontief's classic study to demonstrate that other considerations than pure factor proportions and prices play a role in determining which nations and enterprises have a comparative advantage. Two nations could be identical by these and other macroindicators and still produce the same product at widely different costs and by different methods. Even within a nation many industries are characterized by large differences in costs between the more and less efficient producers of the same product. How often are firms outcompeted (pricewise) and either bought out or forced into bankruptcy? How often does one hear references to high- as opposed to low-cost producers? Such differences exist for many reasons including those relating to differences of scale, technology, management efficiency, position on the learning curve. Further, between nations with widely different factor proportions and factor prices the most unpredictable product price relationships are found to exist. For example, Abram Becker of Rand Corporation compared ruble/dollar ratios of prices of some 500 producer durables produced in both the U.S.S.R. and United States in 1955. The variations were striking. The overall weighted average ruble/dollar ratio was 0.69 with a low of 0.15 for steam engines and turbines to a high of 1.81 in communication and X-ray equipment. The differences within categories were even more striking: motor vehicles, 0.34 to 2.28; internal combustion engines, 0.42 to 2.09; metal working machinery, 0.42 to 2.09; and so forth.[14]

A final bit of evidence against putting too much faith in the comparable level of development approach is contained in table 8.1, where sixteen nations are ranked by level of per capita GDP and then their prices compared for two products that might be viewed as industrially comparable to golf carts, tractors and metal-working machinery. The prices are selling prices and may not always reflect domestic production costs—but probably in most cases, they do. The striking fact revealed by the estimates in table 8.1 is that there appear to be virtually no linear relationships between relative price and level of development. Regressing price on per capita GDP resulted in r^2 coefficients of 0 and 0.0168 for tractors and machinery, respectively. Eliminating the seven poorest nations from the regressions raised r^2 insignificantly to 0.0394 and 0.0172, respectively. One might argue that these figures are distorted by the fact that different nations support different degrees of disequilibrium in their exchange rates, thereby distorting relative

Table 8.1
Purchasing-power parity comparisons for tractors and metal work machinery, 1970 (U.S. prices = 1.00)

	Per capita GDP (U.S. = 100)	Tractors	Metal work machinery
Kenya	6.33	0.96	0.63
India	6.92	0.70	0.67
Philippines	12.0	1.30	0.77
Republic of Korea	12.1	1.10	0.35
Colombia	18.1	1.06	0.75
Malaysia	19.1	0.85	1.70
Iran	20.3	0.58	0.58
Hungary	42.7	1.02	0.97
Italy	49.2	0.89	0.48
Japan	59.2	0.87	1.14
United Kingdom	63.5	0.77	0.71
Netherlands	68.7	1.01	0.94
Belgium	72.0	1.01	0.89
France	73.2	0.88	0.51
West Germany	78.2	0.95	0.74
United States	100.0	1.00	1.00

Source: Irving Kravis, Alan Heston, and Robert Summers, *International Comparisons of Real Product and Purchasing Power* (Baltimore, Md.: Johns Hopkins University Press, 1978). Prices in local currencies were taken from appendix table 4.3. These were converted into dollar relatives by dividing by dollar exchange rates from table 1.1. Per capita GDP figures taken from table 1.2. It should be noted that the price relatives listed here represent domestic selling prices and some nations may not produce either or both products.

prices. The reply to this argument is that in practice the dumping laws do not distinguish between equilibrium and disequilibrium in exchange rates.

Clearly, there is a lack of what might be called uniform cost hierarchies within and among products between different nations, whether these nations are at the same or different levels of development. Poland relied on the price of carbon steel plate produced by a Spanish company and on the constructed value of a golf cart estimated from Polish factor proportions and priced by Spanish engineers. Had there been several Spanish companies producing carbon steel plate, there might have been as many estimates as companies, and estimates might have varied significantly. Had France or India been chosen as surrogates instead of Spain, the results might have been even more or less favorable to Poland. It would be difficult to guess which nation's costs would be lower or higher than Poland's. Different factor proportions are likely to be offset in unpredictable ways by different relative factor prices. So, for example, higher wage costs in France may be more than offset by labor-saving production techniques.

Had there been more than one set of Spanish engineers estimating the cost of producing Polish golf carts, there might also have been several widely differing proxy prices, for most of the same reasons mentioned in the case of carbon steel plate. In the golf cart case, however, it is methodologically relevant to use a nation that is at a comparable level of development, certainly not one at a higher level of development. This is because the lower-income CPE is likely to use more labor and less capital than an advanced proxy nation. Valuing the CPEs physical mix of labor and capital at the higher-wage levels and lower-capital costs of the more advanced nation would result in an inappropriately higher-cost estimate.

We have argued that the connection between levels of development and costs of production or prices of specific products is very weak. There would also appear to be no necessary relationship between levels of development and exchange rates of any two nations. This could be either because (1) the equilibrium exchange rates differ or (2) because the two nations maintain exchange rates with different degrees of disequilibrium.

Suppose a CPE (*Y*) and a capitalist nation (*Z*) have identical monetary units, factors of production, structures of demand, and so forth. Then, if the two nations had similar organizations of production, the equilibrium exchange rates (notional rate in the case of the CPE) of the two nations should be unit equivalents and should bear identical relationships to other currencies. Suppose now that, with all other things still equal, there is a large autonomous capital inflow into *Z*.[15] The currency of *Z* would immediately appreciate relative to that of Y and other western currencies as well. Under these circumstances, *Z*'s exchange rate would not serve as an accurate surrogate for *Y*'s but would be overvalued. Because two nations are never identical in the ways assumed, and in addition differ with regard to goals, management, distribution of income, and so forth, there are many potential differences, given identical levels of development, that could affect their relative equilibrium exchange rates.

Suppose now that *Y* and *Z* have unit equivalent exchange rates (notional in the case of *Y*) in balance-of-payments equilibrium, but macro policies (or lack of same) dictate that one or both are in disequilibrium. In fact it would be an improbable coincidence for two countries to have the same degree of balance-of-payments disequilibrium at the same time, and therefore it is unlikely that the exchange rate of *Z* would ever precisely represent that of *Y*.

It would also probably be impossible to say when the degrees of disequilibrium in the two nations are approximately the same for many reasons, including the fact that the CPEs repress balance-of-payments disequilibriums by methods invisible to the outside world. A CPE, seeking a surrogate exchange rate, should try to select a nation that is in approximate balance-of-payments equilibrium. Such an exchange rate would in theory provide it with (1) a lens through which it could view its trade without the terms of trade illusion discussed earlier and (2) a relatively low export price. From this standpoint the selection of any surrogate nation with less overvaluation than the CPE exporter would improve its chances of avoiding a determination of dumping. Should the surrogate nation have a more overvalued exchange rate than the CPE (an unlikely possibility), then the latter would find itself handicapped in exporting and forced to charge higher prices than are warranted to avoid a dumping determination. However, regardless of whether the surrogate nation's currency is more or less overvalued than the CPEs, its state of disequilibrium would undoubtedly be totally unrelated to its level of development.

Before leaving this discussion, it is important to mention an important empirical barrier in the identification of dumping, namely, that manufactured products are not usually homogeneous and prices therefore cannot be expected for this reason alone to be identical. Under ordinary circumstances, one might expect in two-market economies a reasonably even distribution of high- and low-"quality" products.[16] As is well-known, however, manufactured products sold by the socialist countries tend to be of lower quality and must be sold in the West at lower prices than comparable western products. Examples of Soviet discount pricing in 1974 to 1975 are transformers, 30 percent; resistors, 30 percent; tractors, 20 to 40 percent; machine tools, 40 to 50 percent; turbines and compressors, 40 to 50 percent; and so forth (Ericson 1976, p. 723). How can one tell whether these lower prices reflect quality or are evidence of dumping? It is almost impossible to make such a judgment from the cost side (How to price such things as servicing convenience and frequency of breakdown). If the value of quality differentials can only be determined by the market, then in these cases differential prices cannot be taken as evidence of dumping (within reasonable limits of course).

8.6 Concluding Remarks

The third-country and constructed-value approaches are clever attempts to bridge the systemic gaps that impede the application of antidumping laws to

CPEs. They are based implicitly on H-O model mechanisms, and this leads to the selection of nations at comparable levels of development to provide proxy costs or prices and proxy exchange rates. The H-O model is too weak to do a reliable job on costs and prices and has no mechanisms through which an appropriate surrogate exchange rate might be generated. So far the results from these approaches have been mixed: the third-country approach provided evidence that Poland was dumping carbon steel plate; the constructed value approach, on the other hand, exonerated Poland from the dumping charge. Polish representatives appear satisfied with these approaches, particularly the constructed value approach. That the third country approach sustained a dumping charge indicates, in my opinion, the weakness of the general framework, for it seems highly unlikely that Poland or other CPEs are engaged in dumping. Apparent dumping by CPEs is unlikely to be true dumping because (1) CPE foreign trade behavior typically reflects notional exchange rate overvaluation (2) most CPE manufactured products are of lower quality than similar western products, and (3) because of overfull employment planning CPEs tend to generate shortages rather than surpluses of goods, so they are unlikely to be seeking temporary external markets. If third-country and constructed-value approaches continue to result in "satisfactory" dumping decisions, then it might be worth staying with them since in a technical sense they bridge the systemic gap. I would be surprised, however, if other future applications of these techniques didn't indicate dumping whether or not true dumping was taking place.

Two possible substitutes to these procedures come to mind. First, there is Richard Cunningham's proposal that imports from CPEs be exempted from dumping charges so long as they are not priced below all other imports.[17] This would take care of most imports from CPEs, and would probably be more than fair to U.S. producers because of the CPE bias against dumping. It would not take care of those instances, like the Polish golf carts where for several years there were no imports from other nations. The third country and constructed value approaches could as a last resort be reserved for such special circumstances. A second possible approach is to discontinue using the antidumping (or countervailing duty) statutes against CPEs and handle all cases of injury to domestic producers under the antimarket disruption clause, Article 406, of the Trade Act of 1974. This has the disadvantage to the CPEs that, if injury is determined, they cannot clear themselves by proving that they are not dumping. On the other hand, (1) domestic industries have access to Article 406 and (2) the techniques developed to determine whether a CPE is dumping, while ingenious, must be recognized as relatively inadequate expedients.

Addenda

1. In May 1980 the U.S. International Trade Commission determined that Polish golf carts were not causing distress to the U.S. industry, thereby removing another basis for the dumping charges.

2. Polish golf cart competition in the United States is still clouded by antitrust action which has been taken against the Poles by the American producers under both the Clayton Act and the almost forgotten Antidumping Act of 1916 which allows treble damages if dumping can be shown to have been motivated by an attempt to destroy competition. Most of the charges by the American companies have been, at present writing (June 1980) refuted, and Pezetel has instituted a countersuit against these companies. Since the purpose of our antitrust laws is to foster domestic competition, it is a little paradoxical to find them being used to prevent foreign competition. Apparently, this is the first time they have been so applied (Schwartz 1980).

3. It is unfortunate that, just as Poland seems to be winning its long fight against its U.S. competitors, it must now face new competition from the Japanese firm, Yamaha.

Notes

1. As my good friend, Dr. James Finkelstein, has noted, "This may be putting the cart before the course!"

2. GATT's Article VI requires material injury for the levy of a countervailing duty. The basic U.S. legislation the Tariff Act of 1930, does not require material injury. However, at the Tokyo Round the United States agreed to require injury also.

3. Cited by Fallenbuchl (1974, p. 104) from a 1971 Polish source. Polish prices have been moving toward greater rationality but, in my opinion, still have considerable way to go.

4. This statement, and other such statements in this paragraph, are less true of Hungary than of the other CPE nations. Also in the few years before August 1980, it was claimed that Polish planners had largely relied on a single notional exchange rate and actual industrial prices to make many of their foreign trade decisions. This notional rate was not published and was unknown to foreigners. It is also not clear how many exceptions to this procedure there were and how reliable the procedure was. Further the rate used must be suspect in light of the large Polish hard currency deficits.

5. The exchange rate in used to convert trade in world prices (dollars, pounds, etc.) into so-called foreign trade valuta (rubles, zlotys, etc.). For integrating the trade accounts with the GNP accounts in internal prices, further conversion coefficients are required.

6. This can be rationalized as a case of exchange rate overvaluation, as discussed in the following section.

7. In the late fifties the U.S.S.R. allegedly dumped aluminum and tin on the world markets. In both of these cases they were getting rid of temporary surpluses and, according to the philosophy behind the antidumping laws, should have been subjected to sanctions.

8. Actually, the basic disequilibriums of the CPEs are probably sharply understated by the sizes of their external debts and hard currency deficits. It is my opinion that imports are repressed and, if the desire to import were given free rein, would be much larger than has been the case.

9. The evidence is also consistent, for some CPEs, with a decision to borrow to expand imports.

10. To some extent the CPEs use foreign trade efficiency indexes to guide their external trade decisions. In their simplest form these consist of a fraction, in which the numerator is the cost of producing an export or import substitute in domestic currency (adjusted for estimated price irrationalities) and the denominator is the hard-currency price at which the export is sold or import purchased. High-ratio products should be imported; low-rate products exported. Such indexes would suggest how much world prices might be undercut, if necessary, to finance desired imports.

11. This approach was initiated by the U.S. Treasury in 1960.

12. This approach was devised and accepted by the U.S. Treasury in fall 1978. The constructed value approach has been used for some time for capitalist countries where neither exporter's domestic nor export to third country prices were available. In these cases, however, the values are constructed directly from the domestic costs of the local producer-exporter.

13. Implementation of this method of evaluating dumping charges requires that the exporting country be willing to allow U.S. customs officials on site access to its factories to determine the physical quantities of inputs. The Polish government granted permission in this case. There is some question as to whether all other CPEs would grant such permission.

14. Although these ruble/dollar ratios are based on Soviet 1955 reform prices, the irrationality of Soviet prices certainly contributes to the scatter of ratios.

15. Alternatively, we could have supposed that like Great Britain Z suddenly discovered and exploited North Sea petroleum reserves.

16. We use the term here to include many dimensions such as durability, servicing, and packaging.

17. A bill (S.958) introduced in February 1981 by Senator Heinz would accomplish this by levying a countervailing tariff on CPE products priced below all other imports. This bill unfortunately does not provide for an injury test. It also abolishes the antimarket disruption clause (Article 406) of the Trade Act of 1974.

References

Abram Becker, 1959. *Prices of Producers' Durables in the United States and the USSR in 1955*. RM-2432, Rand Corporation, August.

Richard Cunningham, 1980. The need for "rules of conduct" approach to the regulation of U.S. trade with non-market economies—orderly expansion versus unpredictable shifts in policy. Paper presented to *Interface Two* Conference in Poznan, Poland, June.

Paul Ericson, 1976. Soviet efforts to increase exports of manufactured products to the West. In JEC, U.S. Congress, *Soviet Economy in a New Perspective*, Washington. D. C.

Z. Fallenbuchl, 1974. East European integration: Comecon. In JEC, U.S. Congress, *Reorientation and Commercial Relations of the Economics of Eastern Europe*, Washington, D. C.

Feller, Peter, 1967. The antidumping act and the future of East–West trade. *Michigan Law Review* (November), 115–133.

Franklyn D. Holzman, 1979. Some theories of the hard-currency shortages of centrally planned economies. In JEC, U.S. Congress, *Soviet Economy in Time of Change, II*, Washington, D. C.

Louis B. Schwartz, 1980. American antitrust and trading with State-Controlled economies. Paper presented to *Interface Two* Conference in Poznan, Poland, June.

Stanislaw Soltysinski, 1980. The Application of U.S. antidumping and other foreign trade competition laws to the so-called state-controlled economy enterprises. Paper presented to *Interface Two* Conference in Poznan, Poland, June.

Raymond Vernon, 1966. International investment and international trade in the product cycle. *Quar. Jl. of Econ.* (May), 190–207.

U.S. International Trade Commission, 1980. *Electric Golf Cars from Poland.* Publication 1089, June.

Background References on Polish Golf Cart Case

Robert Hudec, 1980. Interface revisited: "unfair trade" policy after the Tokyo Round. Paper presented to *Interface Two* Conference in Poznan, Poland, June.

Subcommittee on Trade, House Committee on Ways and Means, 1977. *Hearings: Oversight of the Antidumping Act of 1921*, November 8, pp. 106–123.

Donald Wallace, George Spina, et al. (eds.), 1979. *Interface One.* Georgetown Institute for International and Foreign Trade Law, Washington, D. C.

9 Central Planning and Monetarism: Fellow Travelers?

Richard Portes

The essential characteristic of central planning, or of a centrally planned economy (CPE), is the detailed allocation by a centralized hierarchy of goods and services among producing and distributing organizations. This entails that the allocating bureaucracy also issues binding targets (plans) to each separate organization for its production of individual outputs and use of the inputs needed to make them. By contrast, in a market economy these decisions are taken in a decentralized way, at least partly in response to signals of demands, supplies, and prices communicated between independent agents.

The economic institutions of central planning are unfamiliar to many in the West, but we all have more or less immediate experience with monetarism. To say that it shall be known by its works might be too harsh, but lengthy definition is unnecessary. Indeed, any attempt at precise characterization would have to be very lengthy. The controversies over monetarist theory and policy have been so extensive and its current influence so ubiquitous that numerous variants have been specified. There is no single monetarist model, however. We may therefore take monetarism as a general body of thought stressing the pervasive importance of the aggregate stock of money in macroeconomic relationships, especially those determining quantities denominated in money terms, such as money income.[1]

I have no intention to *judge* either central planning or monetarism in its potential or actual application to Britain, the United States, or anywhere else, either as theory or as policy. Nor is the title meant to tar monetarism with the brush of association with central planning, or indeed the converse. By "fellow traveler" I understand one who does not explicitly adopt a given doctrine nor even openly identify with it but acts as those who do. Here the metaphor suggests common analytical premises, methods and conclusions, albeit usually applied to very different environments.

The title's query, then, is: Along what road might central planners and monetarists travel together, and how far? Are monetarist principles applicable under central planning? Are there similarities between the macroeconomics of central planners and that of market economy monetarists, between their attitudes and intellectual predispositions?

A final disclaimer: when discussing the macroeconomics or monetary economics of central planning, I am not in general referring to Marxist monetary theory, whether applied to a CPE or a market economy. I am certainly not asking whether Marx's monetary theory is monetarist, although this too is by no means an absurd question.

Until quite recently, there was very little macroeconomics for CPEs, and virtually all of this centered on the supply side (aggregate production functions), ignoring aggregate demand and its components.[2] A striking example is the best-known theory of investment "cycles" in CPEs, in which these fluctuations are entirely determined by supply-side forces (Goldmann 1964).

Resistance to a theoretical and applied macroeconomics of CPEs arises from several distinct arguments, none of which I find convincing. First is the belief that if all quantities are planned and determined at the disaggregated, microeconomic level; macroeconomics simply cannot matter. But the planners themselves do not accept this, and they rightly carry out macroeconomic and financial planning, because at least some macroeconomic aggregates, like households' money balances, play a role that cannot be planned centrally at the micro level.

A second reason for ignoring macroeconomics, or at least monetary economics, in CPEs is the widespread, long-standing belief that demand always exceeds supply under central planning, so supply must determine everything. For the household sector, I have challenged the factual premise on a wide variety of empirical grounds (1974, 1977) and, with David Winter, on econometric evidence (1980). Those who start from this assumption often find it hard to implement consistently (Green and Higgins 1977, reviewed in Portes 1979a).

It has also been contended that it is strictly impossible to deal with macroeconomic aggregates in CPEs, because relative prices are so distorted, and that in practice the aggregates are meaningless, because any total of expenditures will include many items bought only because the buyers could not find what they really wanted. Such "forced substitution" is a consequence of both excess aggregate demand and distorted relative prices (Kornai 1981). We find, however, that there will still be a natural correspondence between what is happening at the microeconomic level and what is measured by macroeconomic aggregates (Portes and Winter 1980). Aggregation over quantity-constrained micro markets, some in excess demand and others in excess supply, can yield smooth behavior and well-defined macro variables (Muellbauer 1978).

Finally, there is a general scepticism about theoretical and econometric modeling of CPEs, applied most forcefully to macroeconomics. Thus a leading expert on Soviet money and banking says, "Standard western analytical models for testing monetary aspects of economic processes are not applicable to Soviet reality" (Garvy 1977, p. 8). He believes that the data are inadequate and that we cannot properly specify the rules of economic behavior in CPEs. I reject both propositions. The analysis that follows presupposes that CPE households, enterprises, and planners do exhibit stable behavior that can be modeled and that macroeconomic data in these economies are adequate to describe events to the planners and to western observers. Our empirical work fully justifies this maintained hypothesis.[3]

A brief description of CPE macroeconomic institutions is necessary. This refers to the "standard system," as it has applied for many years in the U.S.S.R. and the six CPEs of Eastern Europe, ignoring economic "reforms" that have in any case made little change, except in Hungary.

The main difference from our own macroeconomic structure is that theirs is much simpler. We have a diverse and complex set of financial institutions, from the central bank to a range of separate commercial deposit banks, building societies, investment banks, and so forth, all performing different roles in the process of financial intermediation between lenders and borrowers, savers and investors. The CPE has a single, combined central and commercial bank with many branches. This monobank facilitates central control over enterprises and monitoring of households' financial behavior. It also enforces a separation of the types of money used by these two sectors: transactions between enterprises are conducted entirely with deposit money—entries on the monobank's books—while those between enterprises and households, and within the household sector, are conducted in cash. Household financial assets are cash and savings deposits.

Therefore in the state productive sector, where resources are allocated centrally in physical terms, money is "passive." Although there is generalized excess monetary demand here (resulting from excess real demand or overfull employment planning), this has little effect or relevance. For producing enterprises, liquidity is offered by stocks of goods, which may be hard to get, rather than the passive money, which is all too easy to obtain. Producers do face a "soft" budget constraint (Kornai 1981). But only if the bank permits can passive money finance wage payments and thereby "leak" into active money, that which circulates in the household sector.

Here money is active because wage labor and material incentives have been maintained in these CPEs. Thus, although the planners set centrally the demand for labor and wage rates, there is a labor market where workers are (relatively) free to offer their services; and while the supplies of consumer goods and their prices are also fixed centrally, there is a market where households are free to use their money to purchase from among what is offered.

I have argued for some time that since the mid-1950s, there has been no clear evidence that generalized, long-term macro-level excess demand or repressed inflation has prevailed for the consumer goods market in CPEs (Portes 1977; Portes and Winter 1977, 1978, 1980). This is contrary to conventional wisdom, but many phenomena usually attributed to monetary disequilibrium, such as shortages and the "second economy" (unofficial, often unrecorded markets and production of various kinds), are in good part due to distorted relative prices and deficiencies of the distributive network. This distinction is important because monetary control cannot be used effectively to deal with relative price problems, and the planners' monetary and macroeconomic policies may still be adequate despite the observed microeconomic disequilibria. To judge these issues, we need macroeconomic analysis and evidence.

Prices are fixed by the planners for long periods. They can keep them that way while enterprise costs vary, by altering the turnover taxes (or subsidies) set at different rates for each good or by altering their deductions from (subsidies to) enterprise profits. Thus a rise in wage costs, say, need not affect prices at all; just as a rise in prices can be met by a reduction in turnover taxes and need not affect enterprise or household incomes and hence their expenditure. Moreover, if there were excess demand for goods, the planners' direct control over supply means that there might be no consequent effect on the demand for labor. All this makes macroeconomic control simpler by cutting the links and feedbacks along which disturbances propagate in the inflationary spirals of market economies. Except in Poland, recent consumer price rises in Eastern Europe are not primarily due to aggregate excess demand or the effects of world inflation (Portes 1980), and their repercussions have been contained.

Monetary control in CPEs is also much easier because of the structure of financial institutions and the very restricted range of financial assets. There are no equity shares or debentures, no stock or bond markets, and little consumer credit; trade credit from a supplier enterprise to its customer is in principle excluded as well. Thus the planners need not worry about the prices and yields of financial assets (interest rates), their effects on expenditure, nor open-market operations. Since there are no independent commercial banks, the planners need not control their lending behavior with reserve or liquidity ratios or interest rates, and there is no such thing as a secondary expansion of credit generated by an expansion of the monetary base.

Finally, the domestic monetary system is completely insulated from and unaffected by foreign-sector transactions, whether on current or capital account. Transactions with nonresidents are centralized in the foreign trade bank (another branch of the monobank), and there are no problems of control over the operations of international banks and multinational corporations.

It should already be evident that a basic empirical prerequisite for monetarism is met more clearly in CPEs than in market economies. The monetary authorities can indeed control and monitor the money supply quite precisely (see Rudcenko 1978, on how they do so operationally). That this control may not be fully effective when its consequences conflict with other objectives, policies, and pressures does not invalidate this proposition, which emerges clearly from the comparison of monetary institutions outlined earlier.

We can now consider how monetarist thought might apply to the macroeconomics of central planning. We may start conveniently with the general monetarist proposition for market economies that money is *neutral*. One form of this is familiarly expressed by the notion "Money is a veil": in the long run real variables like production and employment are independent of monetary phenomena.[5] In a CPE, however, no *macroeconomic* full-employment policy is necessary because full employment is assured at the microeconomic planning level (Ellman 1979). Detailed manpower planning, the desire of planners (and enterprises) to maximize output by using all the labor that is supplied, and the difficulty that any enterprise with some temporarily excess workers would encounter in trying to sack them, all guarantee that anyone desiring a job at the going wage is employed. The objective of monetary policy in CPEs is the control of inflationary pressures.

Likewise in a properly functioning market economy macroeconomic policy for full employment is strictly superfluous, on a monetarist view. Hahn (1980) attributes to monetarism the belief that the economy will not be very often or very far out of a "rational expectations equilibrium," which for our purposes can be taken to imply no involuntary unemployment. Thus output stays around the level given by full employment of labor (unemployment at the "natural rate"). In these circumstances monetary policy should not seek to *affect* real variables but rather to adjust to them, in a CPE, or to avoid perturbing them from their long-run paths, in a market economy. In both cases, provided these fundamental criteria are met, monetary policy has a legitimate independent role in pursuing the authorities' objectives for nominal variables, notably, the price level. With a vertical Phillips curve macroeconomic policy should be concerned with inflation, leaving the reduction of the natural rate of unemployment to microeconomic measures.

All this is a straightforward coincidence of views. Note, however, that in the market economies this aspect of monetarism is based on the belief that markets work, that decentralized allocation can ensure coherence and even efficiency, while in the CPEs based on the belief that planning and centralized signals work, so monetary regulation need not be used to adjust for any mistakes. Regrettably, perfect administration is as rare as perfect markets.

Closely associated with monetarism in the public as well as the professional mind is the quantity equation, $MV = Y = Py$: the nominal stock of money outstanding times the velocity with which it circulates equals the value of national income, or the price level times real national income. As it stands, this is of course a tautology, but there are at least two monetarist interpretations which share the title of the Quantity Theory of Money. One is that V is stable, at least in the medium to long run, so that changes in M will be the principal causes of changes in Y, subject perhaps to long and variable lags. A second is the strict version of the neutrality property: if V and y are determined by real (nonmonetary) forces, then changes in M will determine changes in the price level. Again the causal processes through which this impulse is transmitted are complex, so that lags may be long and variable. Both versions ignore the problem of effective demand, essentially excluding it from the center of macroeconomic concerns, and central planners would certainly go along with that. But we can say more.

Milton Friedman once set up a model which, he argued, was common to monetarists and Keynesians but was missing one equation to make it complete, or determinate. He then maintained that the difference between monetarists and Keynesians was that for the missing equation monetarists chose to fix y at its full-employment (natural-rate) level while Keynesians chose to fix P at a level determined exogenously. In a CPE *both* are fixed "exogenously," *by the planners*. What does that leave for the quantity equation? With velocity again taken as constant, it now gives us the stock of money required to finance transactions. (Here we are coming close to the law of circulation of Marx's monetary theory, according to which P, V, and y determine the quantity of money that will be drawn into circulation from hoards.)

The obvious relation between the two cases, then, is that in the market economy the quantity theory becomes a theory of open inflation while in the

CPE it is a theory of repressed inflation; or alternatively, in both, a guide to noninflationary monetary policy. Whether as theory or policy the causal mechanism is likely to be quicker and more reliable in the CPE—or velocity more stable—given the much simpler institutional and asset structures.[6]

A strong similarity in analytical method emerges from the observation that monetarists center attention on stocks of assets more than on flows of expenditures or receipts. Central planners also emphasize in their analyses the stocks of currency and savings deposits held by the public, as well as inventories held by distributive trade enterprises and ratios of these stocks to retail trade turnover, but not any marginal propensities.

It has often regarded as a basic tenet of monetarism that the stock demand for money function is more stable than the Keynesian flow consumption expenditure function. In a CPE, if we take household money to include both currency and savings deposits, then the absence of other financial assets and debts means that the two functions are virtually equivalent: savings equals the increment to money stocks.

Nevertheless, it might be argued that in a CPE the demand for money is more fundamental, or more stable, for at least two reasons: the rate of interest paid on savings deposits does not vary in the short run, and prices are quite stable, so price expectations are not volatile. Nor are quantity expectations, either of employment or of aggregate consumption goods supplies. Thus, although the planners are concerned about "monetary overhang" and the possibility that in some crisis households may suddenly and massively seek to convert their money savings into goods, this does not appear to happen.[7] Their concern may perhaps be traced to another residual influence of Marxist monetary theory, Marx's emphasis on *hoarding* and his view that paper money will not be hoarded, so that amounts of paper money outstanding in excess of the needs of circulation cause paper money to depreciate relative to gold (commodities).

Both central planners and monetarists of course tend to attribute special significance to one type of asset, money. This is perhaps more understandable for the planners, since money is the only financial asset in CPEs. But its distribution among currency, demand deposits, and time deposits would appear important, because only currency can be used for payment in the shops and between households (in particular in the second economy), while time deposits are often tied to accumulation of the purchase price of specific durable goods.

In fact, in those CPEs for which we have data the ratios of currency to total household money have followed remarkably stable, secular trends downward since the mid-1950s.[8] Nevertheless, since the 1960s households have been able to purchase substantial quantities of durable goods, and it is surprising that the planners seem to be uninterested in household portfolio allocation between money and durables.

The stress on money by market economy monetarists and their attempt to draw somewhere a sharp line between it and other household assets is even less comprehensible, insofar as their view of the mechanism transmitting impulses from money rests on substitutability across a wide range of financial and real assets. But monetarists do often act as if there were only one condition for stock equilibrium, that of equality between the demand for and supply of money.

Despite the mutual analytical and policy emphasis on stocks, there is a major difference in styles of economic policy and monetary control. Whereas market economy monetarists keep stocks at the forefront by making their policy targets the level of monetary aggregates, the central planners' actual monetary control is exercised on the *flow* of *income*.

This observation reveals a common misconception about monetary planning and control in CPEs. It is often said that although the main function of monetary planning in CPEs is to maintain macroeconomic equilibrium (in the household sector), this is *implemented* with controls that operate at the *micro*economic level. These controls are applied directly by the bank, regulating credit to each enterprise on the basis of its plan.

In this view the planning process starts with aggregate macroeconomic quantities (plans for real macro variables), which are then "broken down" (disaggregated) through the planning hierarchy down to the enterprise level. The resulting microeconomic quantities, targets for inputs and outputs for each enterprise, then imply microeconomic financial plans, which are summed to give the macroeconomic or aggregate monetary plan. There is in this scheme *no* aggregate-level control over monetary variables, not even a direct control over total currency emission.

If this were so, monetary policy in CPEs would be much less effective than it actually is. In implementation, the micro-level control over each enterprise's credit is unrelated to the aggregate monetary targets, and it would always be frustrated by the priority of production goals, the impossibility of suppressing trade credit (Podolski 1972), and so forth. But the story so far omits a central character, *incomes policy*, which in CPEs plays a leading role opposite and in harmony with monetary policy.

The primary tool of monetary control is the planning and precribing of wage rates and wage fund targets. These too are "broken down" to enterprises from initial aggregates, just like output plans, and the aggregate wage and output targets are intended to be consistent in both production and consumption. That is, the wage rates set are intended to draw a labor supply equal to the planned demand for labor; the wage fund plan corresponds to the total remuneration, at those rates, of the planned volume of employment; the production plan is related to an aggregate target for consumption goods supply; and at the given consumer prices the aggregate value of this supply is planned to equal the demand which households will express, given their initial assets and the planned wage payments.

This then gives a much more direct relation between wages and the money supply than in any view of a market economy, monetarist or nonmonetarist—but explicitly the other way round: wages determine the supply of money to the household sector. This relation is the key to the monetary economics of CPEs. The cash plan derives from wages, the essential elements of the credit plan derive from the cash plan, and at the center of monetary control is the balance of money incomes and expenditures of the population. Thus the actual control is over the flow of incomes rather than the aggregate stock of household money. The former is the instrument; the latter is the proximate target, with the ultimate targets being consumption demand and labor supply.[9]

Here the planners part company with monetarism on an essential point: in market economy monetarism there appears to be no long-run role whatsoever for incomes policy, because in the long run wages have no independent effect on prices or real output, and in the short run controls are aimed directly at the monetary aggregates. In the CPEs, monetary policy reduces to incomes policy (which in fact is fiscal policy as well, parallel to our income and payroll taxes).

This story of monetary control in CPEs has dealt with the intention and the process, rather than the outcome. The control over wages, and thus over the money supply, can break down. While in a market economy divergence from monetary targets may originate in either the public or the private sector, in the CPE there is only one fundamental source: the relation between the state enterprises and their branches of the monobank. The priority of output among the objectives of planners, enterprise managers, and party secretaries means that the bank will often have to concede finance for above-plan payments, either directly or by extending general credit to enterprises whose costs exceed plans and which consequently find themselves with liquidity problems (Kornai's "soft" budget constraint). Bank managers are understandably reluctant to bankrupt state enterprises, and in any case this would probably be useless. So violators of cost targets are "financed when they overshoot" (Wiles 1977, p. 372). Even Stalin never used the monetary control technique of shooting the bankers when they overfinance, which doubtless would have been quite effective.

This weakness of monetary control in CPEs has its aggregate-level parallel in market economies. Here, an accommodating monetary policy has in the past permitted firms to pass on wage increases in price increases. Where this version of the soft budget constraint has not sufficed, often the state has directly intervened with financial support (for example, Lockheed and Chrysler in the United States). Policy recently changed under the Conservative government in Britain. But as in CPEs the authorities still do not let public sector enterprises go bankrupt, whatever level of wage increases they grant. It remains an open question whether the key weakness of applied monetarism will prove to be a reluctance to permit major, extensive private sector bankruptcies and consequent mass unemployment. Whatever the likelihood that this will lead to a policy "U-turn," it is greater than it would be if, as in the CPEs, there were an incomes policy supporting monetary control.

From a fundamental issue we now turn to a minor but interesting analogy. It was once regarded as a principal tenet of monetarism that the demand for money is relatively insensitive to the rate of interest. Although this is now a less important part of the monetarist story, we should note that it is easily applicable to CPEs. Here the monetary control mechanism has never given any role to the interest rate. Household saving or portfolio allocation behavior might well vary with the interest rate, but this is impossible to establish empirically because since the mid-1950s the planners have seldom altered the interest rate (and, when they have, in discrete steps and practically always upward). They do not use the interest rate as a macroeconomic control variable, in relation to households or to aggregate enterprise investment demand or inventory holdings. The interest rate cannot vary without an explicit planners' decision: it is not a flexible price in any market. Clearly therefore, the central planners would follow market-economy monetarists in regarding the price of money as the inverse of the price level of goods, rather than as the interest rate.

So far I have ignored foreign trade and payments. But all existing CPEs except the U.S.S.R. are now relatively open economies, and even Soviet participation in foreign trade is not negligible. The standard CPE isolates the domestic monetary system and price level from the foreign sector and foreign prices; to do this, it uses the "price-equalization subsidy (tax)."[10] At the macroeconomic level this is the equivalent of a continuously floating exchange rate (see Holzman 1968), the means by which monetarists seek to preserve the autonomy of domestic monetary policy and its effects on the domestic price level. Conversely, a floating exchange rate eliminates the discipline exerted on domestic policy and inflation rates by the balance-of-payments constraint. It appears that for this discipline we must substitute either central planning or a suitably austere and restrictive monetary policy.

The alternative framework is that provided by fixed exchange rates and a gold or gold-exchange standard. This offers an external, autonomous form of control over the domestic money supply and macroeconomic policy (though some monetarists would now agree that even in the medium run, a considerable degree of sterilization of the effects of reserve flows on the domestic money supply is feasible; see Darby 1980). The CPEs have a doctrinal attachment to gold, because of its importance in Marxist monetary theory and, more practically, because the U.S.S.R. is the world's second-largest gold producer. But neither a foreigner nor a resident of any CPE could redeem rubles, zlotys, or lei, however earned, for gold, at either the official or the market rate. Nor could a holder of the domestic currency buy dollars or sterling, except possibly in very limited quantities for authorized tourism.

This is not to say that convertible currencies are valueless in the CPEs. It is quite the contrary, as Mr. Honecker is said to have confirmed on his trip to West Germany, which he found really just like the East: he could buy anything there for Westmarks. Nevertheless, to go to a fixed exchange rate system, with consequent direct relations between domestic and foreign prices and money supplies, would be totally incompatible with central planning. Despite their acknowledgements to David Hume, in practice most monetarists have also favored floating rates.

Central to the debate between monetarists and nonmonetarists in the 1970s was the issue of "crowding out," which supplanted earlier arguments over the relative size and stability of the effects on nominal income of monetary injections and changes in autonomous expenditures. Monetarists assert that government expenditure ultimately crowds out (displaces or substitutes for) an equivalent volume of private expenditure, through some combination of interest rate and price level changes. The consequence is that at least in the long run fiscal policy cannot affect output.

In the centrally planned economy, with full employment and central physical allocation of resources, an increase in the state sector's use of output (say, for investment or military expenditure) must entail an equivalent reduction in the household sector's use (consumption). The only exception could be when the planners adjust net exports, but although there is some evidence they do this in the short run, it is not likely to be a feasible shift of the long-run equilibrium.

Indeed, with prices fixed we have in the CPE a sort of "super crowding out," due to repressed inflation. Starting in full-employment equilibrium with no excess demand, and holding wages constant, a shift in output away from consumption causes excess demand for consumer goods, which discourages labor supply. As workers find they cannot spend as much as they would like, they will react at least partly by working less. The result will be a fall in output, hence in the amount available for consumption and perhaps a further drop in labor supply until this "supply multiplier" process comes to rest (Barro and Grossman 1974, Portes 1981).

If, however, excess demand means that some individuals are now unable to purchase particular goods or services that they find sufficiently important, they may offer (instead of money) goods or services at their disposal which are also in short supply. Thus I may offer to fix your car if you paint my flat, because neither of us can find these services we want offered for money. If this opportunity to barter results in *additional* labor supply (not merely an equal reduction of hours worked for money), we have a paradoxical result: the uselessness of money hoards means that some unsatisfied demands will create or evoke their own corresponding supplies. This is an unfamiliar side of Say's law, which holds that, if there is no hoarding, supply will create its own demand (in the sense that any offer of goods or services must constitute a demand for their equivalent in exchange). If barter were organized properly, and with no transactions costs or uncertainty, there could be no aggregate excess demand.

Paradoxical effects of excess demand extend to CPE foreign trade policy. The macroeconomic problems of CPEs are typically those of excess real demand, not necessarily in the household sector but certainly in the state productive sector, as "overfull-employment planning." The macroeconomic problems of market economies are typically, though not always, excess supply and unemployment. In a market economy one way to combat unemployment is to export it, by running an export surplus. This "beggar-my-neighbor" policy has its CPE counterpart, which is to export excess demand by running an *import* surplus. When the countries of Comecon seek to do this among each other, it is indeed a beggar-my-neighbor policy. When market economies and CPEs are in symmetrical circumstances and trade with each other, however, each will be willing to satisfy the other's policy objectives, provided there is some way of financing the centrally planned economies' deficits with the market economies. This is precisely what has been happening since the early 1970s (Portes 1980).

Neither of these paradoxes is strictly relevant to the relations between central planning and monetarism, but the second does lead directly to an important parallel. It has been suggested (Purvis 1980) that the acid test for a monetarist is the policy recommendation following an increase in the oil price for a major oil importer. The monetarist would argue that this will require a reduction in real income and the real value of money holdings, so that the nominal stock of money should certainly not be increased; a nonmonetarist would argue that the oil price rise will have the deflationary effect of an indirect tax increase, so that monetary policy should be expansionary. On this test the macroeconomics of central planning must be monetarist: the tax effect does not operate and full employment is not threatened (except insofar as the real income loss may induce bottlenecks in production); the only alternative to reducing real incomes and demand is to run an import surplus, exporting the excess demand created by the deterioration of the terms of trade.

Let us return to the roles of fiscal and monetary policies in a closed economy. The monetarist would say that, in view of the relation between money stock and nominal income, the stability of the demand for money relative to consumption behavior, and crowding out, fiscal policy has no independent status and should adjust to monetary targets. In fact fiscal policy is implied by these targets and by the government budget constraint, given a stable private sector demand for money. Thus the monetarist experiment in the United Kingdom has stressed the (empirically weak) relationship between the government deficit, its borrowing requirement, and the monetary aggregates.

In the CPE, with no secondary credit expansion and no possibility for the private sector to create money, fiscal policy is equivalent to monetary policy. The relation is strong and direct. The planners always plan and normally achieve a balanced budget or slight surplus. A surplus would be deflationary, but it is more straightforward to place the responsibility for any inflationary pressures directly on the bank, where it belongs (since an excessive increase in the money supply to households can be identified with an excessive increase in credits to enterprises, net of their deposits with the bank).

Monetarism has long been associated with the case against fine-tuning the economy, using an activist or discretionary monetary policy. Friedman's early arguments rested on the authorities' lack of knowledge about the mechanism of transmission of monetary effects, the lags, and so forth, so that the private sector would be more stable if monetary policy were simply to follow a fixed rule. A more recent justification of a similar conclusion is the argument from the supposed rationality of private sector expectations: that agents use information efficiently in making their forecasts about the economy and taking decisions based on them, and that such information must include knowledge of any systematic policy pursued by the authorities. If so, it is argued, the path of real output is affected only by changes in the money supply that agents *cannot* anticipate and so cannot be part of a systematic policy.

For the CPE we have already seen that the planners do not want or need an active monetary policy, in the sense of one that seeks to influence output or employment. Hence the rule that the state budget should balance, so that any change in household cash will be the mirror image of a change in enterprises' aggregate net liabilities to the monobank. This in turn should be consistent with the material balances and wage plans.

The planners know of course that there will the some overshooting (and hence bank overfinancing of enterprises), and that they must compensate by some conscious underplanning of wages. The hypothesis that expectations are formed rationally is perhaps more plausible in the CPE than in the market economy, because the planners' policy rules are better defined, better known to agents, and their policies change less often.

Thus a wide range of considerations suggest that monetarism as theory and policy might work *better* in CPE circumstances, with Soviet-style financial institutions, than it does in our developed market economies. Our monetary system is excessively intricate, and this makes monetarist regularities less regular than they might be. These complexities appear to come at a high cost with relatively little benefit. Certainly bankers, particularly central bankers, could easily adjust to the changed circumstances. Indeed the two major classes of economic agents whose behavior seems system invariant are central bankers and peasants. Soviet bankers would be quite at home at meetings of the BIS (Bank for International Settlements) in Basle, and Polish bankers identified more with the outlook of the western bankers with whom they dealt than that of their own economic planning, ministry, and party officials.

Successful monetary planning and control in a CPE requires a thoroughgoing, serious incomes policy, coordinated with the monetary targets. In this respect it is ironic that, if the current British experiment (1979 to 1982) should fail, the country might react by going much farther toward central planning than ever before. Such a move might well involve a new structure for the banking system, and it is difficult to imagine the resulting set of policies without a serious policy for incomes, whatever the political opposition. But either consistent monetarism or consistent central planning is so painful a discipline that it may require a degree of political control impossible to realize in a pluralistic society.

The dictionary definition of "fellow-traveler" is one who supports or sympathizes with the program of an organized group without actually joining it, especially a supporter of the Communist party. Thus there is an asymmetry and clearly room for a final paradox: my title left open the question of who follows whom. Perhaps the dictionary definition suggests the wrong leader. Milton Friedman might be alarmed if he looked over his left shoulder.

Notes

I am grateful to John Burkett, Franklyn Holzman, John Muellbauer, Ron Smith, and Dennis Snower for comments and to Stan Rudcenko and David Winter for many discussions in the course of our joint work, and to the SSRC (United Kingdom) for support under its Programme for Quantitative and Comparative Macroeconomics at Birkbeck. The final version of this chapter was completed at the 1981 NBER Summer Institute.

1. Mayer (1978) and Purvis (1980) are excellent general references.

2. Notable exceptions are Robert Campbell (1970), Frank Holzman (1968), and Peter Wiles (1969, 1977). My colleague, Carol Nussey, had also embarked on such work before her untimely death.

3. It does not, however, justify the use for forecasting or policy analysis of any of the existing large-scale macroeconometric models of CPEs. Before one is able to take that activity seriously, much more work on small structural models and hypothesis testing is necessary (for example, Burkett, Portes, and Winter, 1981).

4. How much reduction in household asset and income levels, or rise in the general price level, would be necessary to eliminate excess demand for housing, automobiles, and meat in the eastern European CPEs (given current supplies)? How many other goods would then be in excess supply?

5. This holds in the short run as well if expectations are rational, except for any unsystematic monetary shocks ("surprises").

6. "A planner in an almost totally controlled economy . . . should find the quantity theory more useful than the Keynesian theory" (Mayer 1978, pp. 40–41).

7. Even the breakdown of the consumer goods market in Poland in 1981 was due mainly to wage increases exceeding 20 percent (with fixed consumer prices) and cuts in supplies, rather than massive dishoarding.

8. See Rudcenko (1979) for Czechoslovakia, the GDR, Hungary, and Poland. For the U.S.S.R., Peebles (1981) shows the same picture, except for a temporary jump upward in the mid-1960s.

9. Note that, if they abjure changing the general price level, the planners have only a derivative control (flow) to regulate a stock.

10. See Wolf (1980) for details. This does not mean that domestic monetary policy cannot affect the foreign sector—see Portes (1979b).

References

Barro, R., and H. Grossman, 1974. Suppressed inflation and the supply multiplier. *Review of Economic Studies* 41: 87–104.

Burkett, J., R. Portes, and D. Winter, 1981. Macroeconomic adjustment and foreign trade of centrally planned economies. NBER Working Paper no. 736.

Campbell, R., 1970. Macroeconomic models and central price-setting in the Soviet economy. In Gehrels, F., et al., *Essays in Economic Analysis and Policy*. Bloomington: Indiana University Press, pp. 253–270.

Darby, M., 1980. Sterilization and monetary control under pegged exchange rates: Theory and evidence. National Bureau of Economic Research Working Paper no. 449.

Ellman, M., 1979. Full employment—lessons from state socialism. *De Economist* 127: 489–512.

Garvy, G., 1977. *Money, Financial Flows, and Credit in the Soviet Union*. Cambridge, Mass.: Ballinger.

Goldmann, J., 1964. Fluctuations and trend in the rate of economic growth in some socialist countries. *Economics of Planning* 4: 88–98.

Green, D., and C. Higgins, 1977. *SOVMOD I: A Macroeconomic Model of the Soviet Union*. New York: Academic Press.

Hahn, F., 1980. Monetarism and economic theory. *Economica* 47: 1–17.

Holzman, F., 1968. Soviet central planning and its impact on foreign trade adjustment mechanisms. In Brown, A., and E. Neuberger, eds., *International Trade and Central Planning*. Berkeley: University of California Press.

Kornai, J., 1981. *Economics of Shortage*. Amsterdam: North-Holland.

Mayer, T., et al., 1978. *The Structure of Monetarism*. New York: Norton.

Muellbauer, J., 1978. Macro theory vs. macroeconometrics: The treatment of disequilibrium in macroeconomic models. Birkbeck Discussion Paper in Economics no. 59.

Peebles, G., 1981. Money incomes and expenditures of the population of the Soviet Union: An East European comparison. *Hong Kong Economic Papers*, in press.

Podolski, T., 1972. *Socialist Banking and Monetary Control*. Cambridge: Cambridge University Press.

Portes, R., 1974. Macroeconomic equilibrium under central planning. Institute for International Economic Studies, University of Stockholm, Seminar Paper no. 40.

Portes, R., 1977. The control of inflation: Lessons from East European experience. *Economica* 44: 109–130.

Portes, R., 1979a. Review article: SOVMOD. *Economic Journal* 89: 669–674.

Portes, R., 1979b. Internal and external balance in a centrally planned economy. *Journal of Comparative Economics* 3: 325–345.

Portes, R., 1980. Effects of the world economic crisis on the East European economies. *The World Economy* 3: 13–52.

Portes, R., 1981. Macroeconomic equilibrium and disequilibrium in centrally planned economies. *Economic Inquiry* 19: 559–578.

Portes, R., and D. Winter, 1977. The supply of consumption goods in centrally planned economies. *Journal of Comparative Economics* 1: 351–365.

Portes, R., and D. Winter, 1978. The demand for money and for consumption goods in centrally planned economies. *Review of Economics and Statistics* 60: 8–18.

Portes, R., and D. Winter, 1980. Disequilibrium estimates for consumption goods markets in centrally planned economies. *Review of Economic Studies* 47: 137–159.

Purvis, D., 1980. Monetarism: A review. *Canadian Journal of Economics* 13: 96–122.

Rudcenko, S., 1979. Household money income, expenditure and monetary assets in Czechoslovakia, GDR, Hungary and Poland, 1956–1975. *Jahrbuch der Wirtschaft Osteuropas* 8: 431–450.

Wiles, P., 1969. *Communist International Economics*. Oxford: Blackwell.

Wiles, P., 1977. *Economic Institutions Compared*. Oxford: Blackwell.

Wolf, T., 1980. On the adjustment of centrally planned economies to external economic disturbances. In Marer, P., and J. M. Montias, eds., *East European Integration and East-West Trade*. Bloomington: Indiana University Press.

10 On the Meaning of Comparative Factor Productivity

Martin L. Weitzman

The point of departure for this chapter is a 1975 article by Abram Bergson entitled "Index Numbers and the Computation of Factor Productivity." That essay, which has its immediate origins in previous work of Bergson and Moorsteen, was a wide-ranging analysis of the nature and meaning of index number formulas used in the calculation of factor productivity. What I would like to do here is look closely at one particular aspect of the problem—on the one hand, the relationship between a disaggregated input-output economy having alternative techniques with variable factor proportions and, on the other hand, the standard aggregate production function exercises used in comparing factor productivity.

The basic idea is that even in a quite complicated input-output economy with variable techniques, so long as for each technique capital and labor substitute for each other in fairly similar fashion, the aggregate production function approach can be justified. This idea is not so surprising, but I think a formal statement of it is useful, if only because it may give a clearer picture of what is involved or implied in aggregate production function analysis, and perhaps it may provide some rationale for such conventional practices as aggregating outputs arithmetically and inputs geometrically.

Our scenario is the following. There are two economic situations, α and β. They might represent the same economy at different times, or different economies at the same time, or different economies at different times. Suppose there are two factors of production (the analysis readily generalizes), labor, L, and capital, K. We are interested in the relative total factor productivity of α and β.

The usual approach (at least when it is told as a paradigm) goes something like this. Suppose α is a market economy in equilibrium. Let its national product be Y_α. Let the national product of β, *measured in the prices of* α, be Y_β. Suppose the aggregate production function (more on that —whatever it is —later) for α is of the functional form $f(K, L)$. Economy α's endowments of capital and labor are $\bar{K}_\alpha$ and $\bar{L}_\alpha$, whereas those of β are denoted $\bar{K}_\beta$, $\bar{L}_\beta$.

Total factor productivity is

$$\frac{Y}{f(K, L)}$$

(output, aggregated arithmetically, divided by combined inputs, typically aggregated geometrically corresponding to a Cobb-Douglas production function).

In such a situation *the factor productivity of* α *relative to* β might be defined as

$$\frac{Y_\alpha / f(\bar{K}_\alpha, \bar{L}_\alpha)}{Y_\beta / f(\bar{K}_\beta, \bar{L}_\beta)} \tag{1}$$

(Naturally the definition is entirely from the viewpoint of α, but some asymmetry of that sort is unavoidable; I want to sidestep the issue in this chapter.)

Formula (1) is typically interpreted as some measure of the relative power of the technology of economy α to produce β output mix with β factor endowments. If the technology of α were hypothetically applied to produce β factor endowments, (1) represents how much proportionately more (or less) output could be expected.

We know a fair bit about when such an interpretation of (1) makes sense, at least in simple situations. Indeed, a good part of Bergson's 1975 article is devoted to this issue. What I would like to do here is push the analysis a bit harder to see how far it can be made to go. Nothing revolutionary, or for that matter entirely satisfactory (or even exciting) seems to emerge. But I think it is worthwhile to probe this issue further in a formal theoretical direction because it gives some idea of what we are implicitly assuming when we work with formulas like (1) in a general context.

Any analysis must begin somewhere, and I will start with the following assumptions. Let there be n commodities in α, produced by an input-output technology with variable techniques. If one unit of commodity i is produced by technique j (sometimes denoted j_i when ambiguity must be avoided), it requires a^j_{hi} units of commodity $h (h = 1, \ldots, n)$ and c^j_i units of "composite factor." Composite factor is an amalgam of capital and labor whose substitution possibilities are given by the function $F^j_i(K^j_i, L^j_i)$. In other words, if one unit of commodity i is to be produced by technique j, we must have a combination of capital K and labor L satisfying $F^j_i(K, L) \geq c^j_i$. The equation $F^j_i(K, L) =$ constant merely expresses how capital and labor substitute for each other in producing commodity i with technique j.

We are thus making the special assumption that a technique specifies as fixed coefficients the flow of input materials but leaves some flexibility in the combination of capital and labor required to process the inputs. This is a restriction, though perhaps a fair one. Within each (different) technique for producing a commodity, capital and labor can substitute (differently for each technique) in processing materials, but the materials themselves are relatively fixed in proportions (different for each technique). There are exceptions; however, this formulation seems a fair generalization, and it will give a lot of analytic power.

All production is constant returns to scale (including the functions $F_i^j(\cdot)$).

As postulated, economy α is in market equilibrium with total supplies of capital $\bar{K}_\alpha$ and labor $\bar{L}_\alpha$. Let the equilibrium wage rate be w and the capital rental be r. The competitive price of commodity i is p_i. The following general equilibrium pricing equations must hold:

$$p_i = \min_{j,\, K_i^j,\, L_i^j} \{wL_i^j + rK_i^j + \sum_{h=1}^{n} p_h^j a_{ji}\} \tag{2}$$

$$F_i^j(K_i^j, L_i^j) = c_i^j.$$

The equation states that production is to be done at least cost, and price equals cost. Given w and r, equation (2) will have a solution $j(i)$, $K_i^{j(i)}$, $L_i^{j(i)}$, p_i for each i. Let the corresponding input-output matrix be $A = (a_{hi}^{j(i)})$ with composite factor row vector $c = (c_i^{j(i)})$.

On the demand side, suppose final net output is the column vector D^α. The corresponding vector of gross sectoral output levels is

$$X^\alpha = (I - A)^{-1} D^\alpha. \tag{3}$$

The final equilibrium condition is then

$$\sum X_i^\alpha L_i^{j(i)} = \bar{L}_\alpha, \tag{4}$$

$$\sum X_i^\alpha K_i^{j(i)} = \bar{K}_\alpha. \tag{5}$$

For the purpose of using α data to evaluate β, the only relevant thing about economy β is the net final output vector it produces, D^β, and its endowments of capital $\bar{K}_\beta$ and labor $\bar{L}_\beta$.

Now let us *define* the coefficient of comparative factor productivity as the proportion of β output that could be produced by α technology given β factor endowments. The coefficient of comparative factor productivity μ is then the solution (the maximum value of λ) of the problem:

$$\max \lambda \quad \text{subject to} \quad \sum_{j_i} X_i^{j_i} - \sum_h \sum_{j_h} a_{ih}^{j_h} X_h^{j_h} \geqq \lambda D_i^\beta, \tag{6}$$

$$F_i^j(K_i^j, L_i^j) \geq c_i^j, \tag{7}$$

$$\sum_i \sum_{j_i} K_i^{j_i} X_i^{j_i} \le \bar{K}_\beta, \tag{8}$$

$$\sum_i \sum_{j_i} L_i^{j_i} X_i^{j_i} \le \bar{L}_\beta, \tag{9}$$

$$X_i^{j_i}, K_i^{j_i}, L_i^{j_i} \ge 0. \tag{10}$$

In this problem, $X_i^{j_i}$ is the amount of commodity i produced by technique j_i, and $K_i^{j_i}$ ($L_i^{j_i}$) is the amount of capital (labor) employed per unit output in technique j_i of sector i.

For the most general case it is difficult to characterize the solution of (6) through (10) and state with precision what μ depends upon. Fortunately, it is possible to prove an "approximation theorem." If the sectoral production functions F_i^j are close to being identical to each other (up to a scaling factor), in some sense we are in a situation where an aggregate production function "almost exists." Then it seems reasonable that the standard aggregate factor productivity calculation will be a good approximation to μ.

Suppose, then, there is a production function $f(K, L)$ homogeneous of degree one, such that

$$\| F_i^j(K, L) - f(K, L) \| < \epsilon \tag{11}$$

for some $\epsilon > 0$, all i, j, K, L. As usual, $\| \cdot \|$ denotes any legitimate distance norm. If ϵ is small, f is a good approximation to each of the sectoral production functions.

Let Y_α be the national product of economy α ($Y_\alpha = pD^\alpha$). Let Y_β be the national product of economy β measured in prices of α ($Y_\beta = pD^\beta$). Consider using f as an aggregate production function in the surrogate factor productivity comparison,

$$\hat{\mu} = \frac{Y_\alpha / f(\bar{K}_\alpha, \bar{L}_\alpha)}{Y_\beta / f(\bar{K}_\beta, \bar{L}_\beta)}. \tag{12}$$

The following result is not difficult to show (the proof is omitted).

$$\lim_{\varepsilon \to 0} \hat{\mu}(\epsilon) = \mu. \tag{13}$$

Thus the aggregate approximation of comparative factor productivity (12) becomes the rigorous definition (6) in the limit as the aggregate production function f becomes a perfect approximation to each technique's production function F_i^j. If each technique's production function is close to Cobb-Douglas, with similar capital and labor elasticities, there is a rigorous justification for aggregating price weighted outputs arithmetically and inputs geometrically.

In summary, the economy can have a very complicated input-output structure, but so long as the substitution possibilities between capital and labor are similar for each technique, use of an aggregate production function and price weighted outputs will yield a serviceable approximation to a true measure of comparative factor productivity.

References

Bergson, Abram, 1961. *The Real National Income of Soviet Russia since* 1928. Cambridge, Mass. Harvard University Press.

Bergson, Abram, 1971. Comparative productivity and efficiency in the Soviet Union and the United States. In Alexander Eckstein, ed., *Comparison of Economic System.* Berkeley, Claif.

Bergson, Abram, 1972. The comparative national income of the U.S.S.R. and the United States. Reply. In Conference on Research in Income and Wealth (D. J. Daly, ed.), *International Comparisons of Prices and Output,* New York.

Bergson Abram, 1975. Index numbers and the computation of factor productivity. *The Review of Income and Wealth,* series 21, 2 (June): 259–278.

Domar, E., 1961. On the Measurement of Technological Change. *Economic Journal* 71 (December): 709–729.

Hicks, J. R., 1940. The valuation of social income, *Economica* 7 May: 105–124.

Moorsteen, Richard H., 1961. On measuring productive potential and relative efficiency. *Quarterly Journal of Economics* Vol. LXXV, pp 451–467. (August): 451–467.

Samuelson, P. A. 1950. The evaluation of real national income. *Oxford Economic Paper* 2 (January): 1–30.

Solow, R. M. 1956. The production function and the theory of capital. *The Review of Economic Studies* 23 (Fall): 101–108.

III The Soviet Economy

11 The New Tasks of Soviet Planning in the Thirties

Holland Hunter

Alexander Erlich's economic analysis of the Soviet debate over industrialization in the mid-1920s added theoretic clarity to the doctrinal and institutional arguments of the past.[1] He showed, among other things, how difficult were the tasks confronting Soviet planners. They had to develop operational methods, not only for formulating economywide development plans but also for administering programs for rapid economic growth under new conditions.[2]

With the benefit of half a century's hindsight, it is clear that their problems and achievements deserve the attention of all countries interested in economic development. While detailed evidence is still only partially available, at least to an outsider, the record does permit tentative judgments. Several are summarized herein, with the hope that other countries can learn from this experience.

In reviewing the Soviet record for 1928–1940, I draw on a large project that compares actual Soviet economic expansion with a statistical reconstruction of the economy's potential and that estimates the impact of several major events. The results indicate that the Bolsheviks tried to do too much too fast. Under difficult conditions, their heroic efforts involved very heavy—unnecessarily heavy—costs. In March 1923, V. I. Lenin criticized excessive bureaucracy in an article entitled "Better Fewer, But Better."[3] For application to Soviet economic planning in the thirties, his title could be paraphrased: "Better Slower But Farther."

11.1 Distinctive Features of Soviet Economic Planning

Soviet economic plans are not intended merely to achieve balance. Their goal is not merely static equilibrium. They do not seek to equate supply and demand for every good and service, at levels that thereafter remain constant. In the history of economic thought even this problem (the "millions of equations problem") has in some quarters been thought to be insoluble by a Central Planning Board. In my view it is clearly solvable, under stable conditions, through a process of successive approximation. Be that as it may, Soviet planners have faced a far more complex task.

Soviet economic plans call for growth, but they do not seek *balanced* growth. They have never been drawn up so that every sector grows at the same rate. The eminent mathematician John von Neumann proposed such a balanced-growth model, here at Princeton almost exactly fifty years ago, that could operate in the very long run. Every input and output would eventually grow at the same rate; the population would be growing at the same rate, and it would equal the rate of interest! More recently, a large literature on "turnpikes" (expansion paths) has developed, focusing on maximum rates of growth.[4] To get onto a rapid-growth turnpike, however, an economy starting from a position comparable to that of the U.S.S.R. in 1928 has to go through a period of systematically unbalanced growth, to achieve sectoral proportions that will generate the highest feasible rate of growth. Soviet economic planning after 1928 was directed toward structural transformation, toward unbalanced expansion, in which some economic activities were meant to expand at very high rates, while others were deliberately kept to modest rates of growth. Although in Soviet literature the phrase "planned proportional development" came into widespread use, it was a very misleading term in relation to actual Soviet policy.

The practical necessity for output expansion and structural transformation was perfectly obvious to Lenin. In the summer of 1917 he wrote *State and Revolution*, a substantial effort to spell out operational guidelines for a Bolshevik state. Here he revived a cautionary concept formulated by Marx in 1875—that capitalism would be followed by two stages of political and economic development: first socialism and then communism. Under socialism the state would continue to exist and would enforce the rule "from each according to his ability, to each according to his work." It would only be "In a higher phase of communist society after the enslaving subordination of individuals under division of labor, and therewith also the antithesis between mental and physical labor has vanished ... only then can the narrow horizon of bourgeois right be fully left behind and society inscribe upon its banners: from each according to his ability, to each according to his needs!"[5]

After thus quoting Marx, Lenin explained "that expropriation of the capitalists will inevitably result in the enormous development of the productive forces of human society. But how rapidly this development will proceed ... we do not and cannot know."[6] Nevertheless, the very definition of socialism and communism is here bound up with the "enormous development of productive forces." In mid-September 1917 his pamphlet, *The Impending Catastrophe and How to Combat It*, contained the further admonition:

The result of the revolution has been that the *political* system of Russia has in a few months caught up with that of the advanced countries. But that is not enough. The war is inexorable; it puts the alternatives with ruthless severity: either perish or overtake and outstrip the advanced countries *economically* as well.[7]

Six weeks later the Bolsheviks seized power, and the new regime was launched. It had of course many political, economic, and cultural goals, initially dominated by the sheer need to survive. But central to all of them, and persistently in evidence ever since, has been this basic purpose of catching up with and surpassing the advanced countries of the West, thus confirming the upward progression from capitalism through socialism to communism.

From the spring of 1918 till the end of 1920, however, civil war and foreign intervention made normal development impossible. By early 1921 the Bolsheviks had gained political control of the whole country, but the economy was near collapse. Again Lenin proposed a basic concept that shaped subsequent economic development. In introducing the "new economic policy" (NEP) that prevailed for the next eight years or so, he vividly described a struggle that had both internal and external aspects. Externally, the problem was encirclement by hostile capitalist states. Internally, the problem was a great sea of peasants with the souls of petty capitalists. The Bolsheviks, representing the urban proletariat, held the "commanding heights," that is, industry, the banks, the railroads, and the communications system. The question now was, "Who would beat whom?"[8] Under NEP the regime abandoned its practice of requisitioning and permitted free trade by peasants and retail traders, hoping that revived agriculture would support revived industry, which in turn could supply peasants with consumer goods while simultaneously generating the resources for industrial expansion.

But the Bolsheviks were deeply convinced that individual peasants, farming their own land in small units, were inherently capitalistic. This kind of farming, as Lenin said, "*engenders* capitalism and the bourgeoisie continuously, daily, hourly, spontaneously, and on a mass scale." His most widely quoted statement of the problem, made in December 1920, was the following:

Anyone who has carefully observed life in the countryside, as compared with life in the towns, knows that we have not torn out the roots of capitalism and have not undermined the foundation, the basis of the internal enemy. The latter depends on small-scale production, and there is only one way of undermining it, namely, to place the economy of the country, including agriculture, on a new technical basis of modern large-scale production. And it is only electricity that is such a basis. *Communism is Soviet power plus the electrification of the whole country*. Otherwise, the country will remain a small-peasant country, and we have got to understand that clearly. We are weaker than capitalism, not only on a world scale but also within the country. Everybody knows this. We are conscious of it, and we shall see to it that our economic base is transformed from a small-peasant base into a large-scale industrial base. Only when the country has been electrified, only when our industry, our agriculture, our transport system have been placed upon the technical basis of modern large-scale industry, shall we achieve final victory.[9]

Thus in order to win the internal struggle, the Party would have to organize successful revival and expansion of heavy industry in order to supply agriculture with the modern technology that would gradually convert the peasantry to large-scale, cooperative methods and a socialist outlook.

In stating its goals, the first Soviet Five-Year Plan (hereafter FYP) opens with this statement, building on Lenin's precepts:

The Five-Year Plan for the development of the productive forces of the U.S.S.R., by means of its energetic industrialization and the consequent strengthening of socialist elements, proceeds from the great mission of overtaking and surpassing, in the next historical period, the level of the leading capitalist countries, and thus assuring the triumph of the socialist economic system in its historical competition with the capitalist economic system.[10]

It was in the process of carrying out these tasks that the distinctive features of Soviet economic planning came into being.

11.2 Key Operational Issues

A central issue for Soviet economic policy concerned the maximum feasible speed at which the economy could be transformed. Debates over the issue were clouded in 1927 when the U.S.S.R. and the United Kingdom severed diplomatic relations. A Soviet diplomat had been killed, and the Soviet trade mission in London had been bombed. Moscow feared that war might result. The incident blew over, but thereafter it appeared necessary to hasten Soviet industrialization in order to strengthen Soviet military power.

Rapid expansion and structural transformation were constrained by several political considerations. Building heavy industry required capital accumulation, which meant tightening the belts of Soviet consumers. Current output might be deflected from household consumption into fixed capital formation, but beyond a certain point labor productivity and popular morale would be adversely affected. This was one obvious limitation on the tempo of development. Another lay in the reluctance of the population, especially the peasants, to change their ways. The Party had been experimenting for several years with new institutional arrangements that might attract peasants into cooperative institutions, facilitating introduction of modern agricultural methods, but with little success. Efforts might have been made to elicit greater output and marketings from the Soviet peasantry by offering higher prices, but, as Lenin had so eloquently pointed out, this was the capitalist road, and in addition it seemed unlikely to yield a large volume of resources promptly.

A third political constraint related to the international economic environment. The foreign investment that had bolstered Russian economic development before World War I was no longer either desired or proffered. Bolshevik expectations that revolutions in advanced countries would provide economic support for Soviet development were gradually abandoned, and J. V. Stalin stressed the economic precept that "socialism in one country," that is, self-sufficient economic development, was both necessary and possible. Under conditions of hostile capitalist encirclement, it appeared that the U.S.S.R. would have to win by means of its own unaided efforts.

There were also a variety of technical or structural constraints on the speed with which the economy could be expanded and transformed. Since every sector drew on other sectors for its needs, interindustry flows were organically related in such a way that the expansion of each sector depended on support from its neighbors. Soviet economists had been studying the problem for several years, and research on national balances was uncovering these relationships. The economy's immediate ability to grow was clearly constrained by the existing production capacities in each sector, together with new investments already under way, and these too were receiving detailed attention.

The early Soviet planners were also alert to the fact that it takes time to build new fixed capital and bring it into operation. Gestation periods are sometimes rather brief, but for installations like large, multipurpose hydroelectric dams, they can be as long as eight to ten years. Time is required as well to augment human capital, as in the substantial efforts under way to raise labor skills in industry and develop a new technical intelligentsia. Quantitative and qualitative gains in both physical and human capital take time, and thus the tempo of advance faces upper limits. Nevertheless, the practical question was. How rapidly could expansion proceed, subject to these limits?

Another key operational issue arose around the need for flexible administration of plan priorities. Development experience in the Third World has made everyone familiar with the fact that national economic plans, with their misleadingly exact terminal-year targets, merely provide a framework within which plan administrators respond to emerging events during the plan period, inevitably modifying the plan en route and ending up with achieved levels dispersed above and below the original targets. Soviet plan administrators were the first to grapple with all the resulting problems. Their difficulties can be conveniently illustrated with a simple diagram (see figure 11.1, part a). Imagine that the increases in output called for from major sectors of the economy are displayed in descending order, starting with the sectors whose intended percent increases over the plan period are most ambitious and ending with those whose growth targets are extremely modest. Long horizontal bars extending to the right will mark the former; short bars will identify the latter. The width of the bars can be exactly proportional to the size of each sector's output at the start of the plan period. A set of targets will then display a profile, marked by the right-hand ends of the bars, sloping more and more to the right as the degree of structural change increases. If a plan called for equiproportionate increases in every sector, the plan profile would be vertical.

Now consider how plan administrators can approach the question of adapting to developments during the plan period. Financial appropriations, unskilled labor, and some other resources can be flexibly shifted from one sector to another; several policies are conceivable. In the event that favorable developments add to available resources, they could be assigned evenhandedly to each sector so that the profile of achieved output increases would lie to the right of the initial plan profile, and parallel to it. If difficult conditions required cutbacks, they could be uniformly applied so that the profile of achieved increases would be parallel to the original target profile but lie to the left. These possibilities are illustrated in figure 11.1, part b.

In principle, other approaches could be used. A slow-change approach, for example, would take advantage of favorable developments by letting low-priority sectors exceed their targets without assigning additional resources to high-priority targets. In similar fashion cuts required by unfavorable circumstances could be imposed on high-priority sectors, leaving low-priority activities at their originally intended levels. In each case the effect would be to reduce the speed of structural transformation, lowering the tempo of change, as shown in part c. Conversely, a more Draconian policy would insist on rapid structural change, using unexpected possibilities to raise high-priority outputs, or imposing any necessary cuts on low-priority sectors. The effect would be to make the slope of achieved increases deviate from the vertical even more than the slope of the intended profile, as in part d.

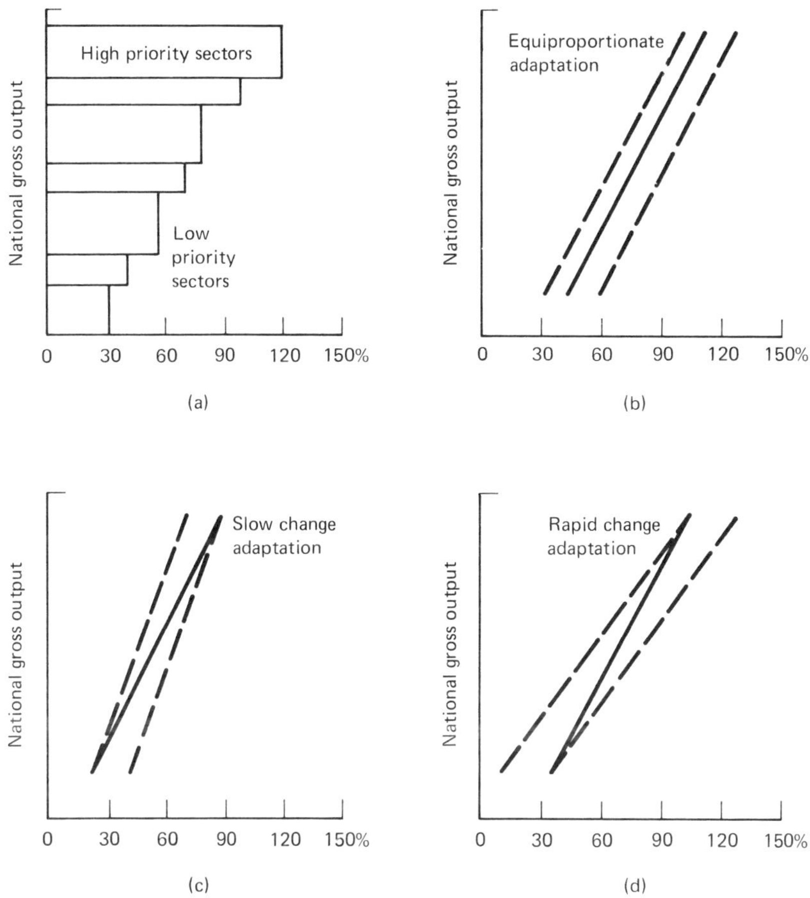

Figure 11.1
Alternative approaches to high- and low-priority sectoral output increases

Table 11.1
Intended and actual gross output by sector in the U.S.S.R., 1928 and 1933 (in billions of rubles at base-period prices)

	1928	Intended 1933	Actual 1933	Percent increases Intended	Percent increases Actual
Electric power	566	2,279	1,848	303	227
Construction	3,888	13,726	10,420	253	168
Trade and distribution	2,825	5,958	2,048	110	−28
Government services	2,954	5,958	4,892	102	66
Consumer goods	7,152	13,405	7,224	87	1
Producer goods industry	14,674	27,117	31,198	85	113
Transport and communication	2,062	3,279	4,586	59	122
Agriculture field crops	11,002	17,065	11,376	55	3
Agriculture livestock products	6,172	9,577	2,926	55	−53
Housing	1,694	2,561	1,913	51	13
Whole economy	52,989	100,925	78,431	90	48

Source: Holland Hunter and Everett J. Rutan, III, *Testing Soviet Economic Policies, 1928–1940* (July 1980 mimeographed report), tables III-2, III-5, and V-9.

These alternative approaches ignore the links among sectors and thus overstate the flexibility available to plan administrators. The focus on sectoral gross outputs also gives inadequate recognition to the complications arising from the fact that policy goals center on final outputs, coupled with the fact that many sectors deliver both to household consumption and fixed capital formation. End uses of a given sector's output might shift toward or away from structural transformation, with no change in that sector's gross output.

Nevertheless, it is instructive to note the intended percentage increases in the first FYP gross output targets for ten basic sectors of the Soviet economy and compare them with estimates of achieved output increases. Table 11.1 contains the numercial estimates, and figure 11.2 shows the contrasting profiles. It will be seen that, while the first FYP called for increases in the output of housing services, agricultural products, and the transport-and-communications services ranging between 50 and 60 percent, the intention was to raise the output of industrial producer goods and consumer goods by some 85 percent. The gross output in the form of government services and trade-and-distribution services was to increase by something over 100 percent, the volume of fixed capital construction was to increase by 250 percent,

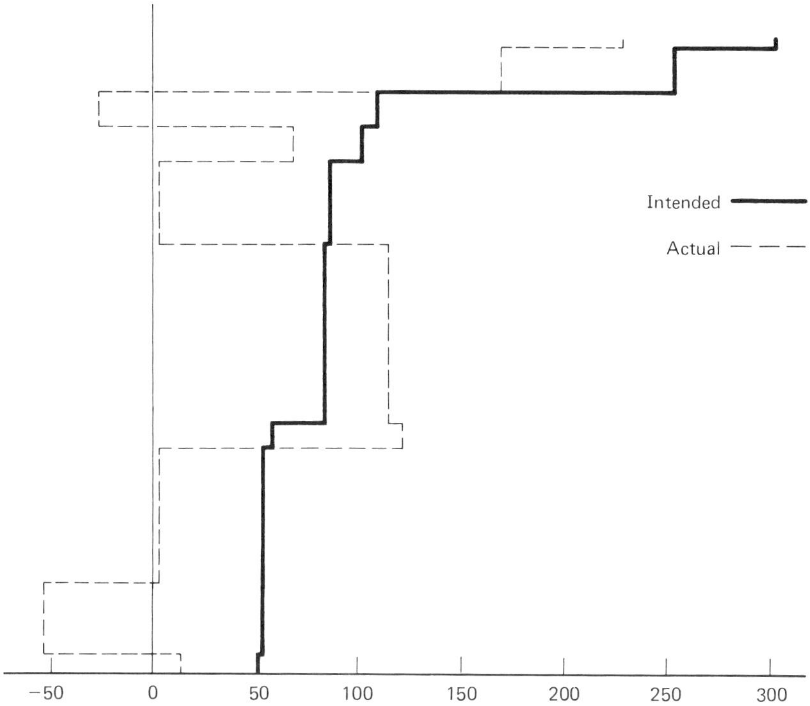

Figure 11.2
Intended and actual sectoral output increases in the U.S.S.R., 1928 to 1933 (in percents)

and electricity output was to be quadrupled, that is, rise by 303 percent. Clearly, this was to be highly disproportionate growth, designed to initiate rapid structural transformation.

Despite very strenuous efforts unfavorable developments during the plan period led to results falling substantially short of these intentions. The economy's total gross output increased by about 48 percent rather than 90 percent. Instead of increasing by about 50 percent, agricultural field crops scarcely rose at all, livestock products fell by more than 50 percent and housing services rose only 13 percent. At the high-priority end of the range, electric power showed a remarkable increase of 227 percent, and the volume of fixed capital construction was 168 percent higher than in 1928, though both these rates of increase fell short of initial hopes. The flow of trade and distribution services, instead of doubling, fell off by 28 percent while the volume of government services rose 66 percent instead of 102 percent.

There was also a sharp contrast in the industrial sector between results for producer goods and consumer goods. Both had been projected to rise about 86 percent; in the event the gross output of producer goods increased by 113 percent while the volume of consumer goods was only 1 percent higher than in 1928. The shortfalls clearly related to activities serving the consumer. The sectors serving investment fared much better, and in fact the output of producer goods was pushed well above originally intended levels. The first FYP also badly underestimated the economy's transport requirements.

The profile of achieved increases did not conform neatly to any of the theoretical patterns sketched here. But if one combines together producer goods, electric power, construction, transportation, and government services, one finds that these five sectors achieved a 119 percent increase, matching their 117 percent intended increase, while the five other sectors (agricultural field crops and livestock products, consumer goods, trade and distribution, and housing) saw an output decline of 12 percent below their starting level, a far cry from the 68 percent increase called for in the first FYP. In this aggregated sense the plan profile was made sharper, pivoting around the high-priority end of the range to impose shortfalls on the population.

Soviet economic planners responded to these operational difficulties in carrying out the first FYP by making a number of practical adjustments in subsequent five-year and annual plans. The rates of output expansion called for were generally lowered, especially by comparison with the incredibly high rates proposed during the 1929–1931 period. Equally important, the number of publicly announced targets was cut back and confined to high-priority activities; in other areas selected data were presented without committing the authorities to comprehensive targets for a given sector. Although presumably the underlying accounting balances covered the whole economy, the published plan left parts of the picture blank. For administrative purposes targets were specified for the output of major Peoples Commissariats (Ministries), rather than aggregate product categories, making it impossible to study the comprehensiveness or consistency of the economywide economic plan. After reviewing the difficulties that led to these responses, and reporting on some tests of the impacts on the overall economy, we should return to the implications of the record.

11.3 Soviet Problems in Developmental Practice

As the first Five-Year Plan noted in introducing its two variants, "construction of the socialized sector in agriculture is projected on almost the same scale for both variants, speeded up as much as possible in the next five years in view of its special significance." The drive for rapid collectivization, under the slogan "liquidation of the kulaks as a class," induced a stubborn response from the peasantry which dealt a heavy blow against the economy. More than half of the working animals supplying draft power for Soviet agriculture were killed or could not be kept alive. The loss of horses forced the regime to supply tractors (initially through imports and then through domestic production) more rapidly than had been intended. This diverted investment away from nonagriculture. The number of working horses fell off so badly that animal draft power during 1934–1938 was only about half of what it had been in 1928; it required several years of substantial deliveries of tractors, trucks, and combines to bring total farm power back to its initial level.

Peasant resistance to "liquidation of the kulaks as a class" also led to a serious lowering of both the quantity and quality of the Soviet diet. There was famine in 1932–33, and throughout the decade meat, milk, and a variety of dairy products were in very short supply. The shrinkage of herds meant, however, that much of the grain and other feed formerly fed to animals was available for human consumption. Calculations based on official data suggest that about a fifth of the population's grain consumption was made available in this way.

A second problem area involved capital construction. While agriculture was being collectivized, a great surge of investment spending and construction activity got underway. Dozens of major construction projects and hundreds of smaller ones were launched all over the country. Outlays on materials and labor quickly exceeded expectations, and projects fell behind schedule, but the regime's response was to pour in more rubles and men. The volume of unfinished construction steadily rose, freezing current output unproductively in sterile form. Eventually, these projects were completed, but the volume of unfinished construction continued to grow throughout the decade.

Because of the difficulties in agriculture and the diversion of current output into capital formation, the situation for consumers deteriorated rapidly after 1928. Ration coupons for food were introduced in major cities in 1929, and pervasive shortages of all consumer goods prevailed until 1935. Although money wages rose rapidly, living costs rose even more rapidly, and real wages plummeted. Special stores for officials and canteens for workers helped maintain living standards for those with access to them, but outside cities, and within cities for the less favored, grim conditions prevailed. Millions of peasants, ejected from their villages, found work on construction projects or in urban jobs. The existing urban housing stock become extremely "productive," as families crowded in. Housing construction was outdistanced by rapidly rising urban population, and the urban living space available per capita fell by 31 percent, from 5.91 square meters in 1928 to 4.09 square meters in 1940.

In another dimension of economic activity, a fourth difficulty developed. The depression that enveloped Western Europe, North America, and the whole world economy made Soviet commodity trade far more difficult. The prices received by the U.S.S.R. for its primary product exports: grain, timber, furs, and so forth, fell much farther below their 1928 levels than did the prices on the machinery and other fabricated commodities the U.S.S.R. was seeking to import. Already saddled with short-term trade debts to Germany in 1929, and unable to obtain appreciable trade credits on feasible terms, the U.S.S.R. was forced to export what it could and import no more than could be financed through exports. The physical volume of Soviet imports and exports rose after 1928 for three years but fell thereafter to very low levels, as shown in table 11.2. The money value of Soviet trade shrank both because quantities were reduced and because prices were lower. Painstaking research by Michael Dohan has shown that, carefully measured, the

Table 11.2
Physical volume and price indexes for Soviet commodity exports and imports, by year, 1928 to 1938 (1928 = 100)

	Exports		Imports	
	Volume	Price	Volume	Price
1928	100.0	100.0	100.0	100.0
1929	129.0	91.6	98.9	94.3
1930	192.9	68.7	121.8	92.0
1931	211.6	49.0	144.5	80.9
1932	165.4	44.4	105.8	70.4
1933	160.8	37.4	56.5	56.3
1934	152.1	35.1	59.1	41.6
1935	136.3	34.4	66.1	38.6
1936	108.0	36.6	67.3	48.4
1937	112.6	42.7	61.5	50.1
1938	100.6	37.2	68.4	48.4

Source: From Michael Dohan and Edward Hewett, *Two Studies in Soviet Terms of Trade, 1918–1970* (Bloomington, Indiana: International Development and Research Center, 1973), table 1, col. 4, p. 24; col. 2 from table 4, col. 6, p. 31; col. 3 from table 2, col. 4, p. 27; col. 4 from table 5, col. 11, p. 33. All series shifted from 1929 = 100 to 1928 = 100.

shrinkage in physical terms was less than indicated by official Soviet records, which fail to maintain constant price weights. The series in table 11.2 show that the physical volume of Soviet exports rose quickly to more than twice the 1928 level in 1931, only to fall back to the starting level by 1938. The physical volume of imports rose by 45 percent to 1931 but then fell quickly to about two-thirds the 1928 level from 1933 to 1938. While the physical volume of Soviet exports was increasing, their selling prices declined precipitously to less than half the 1928 level in 1931 and only 35 percent of the 1928 level in 1934 and 1935. In sharp contrast, the prices paid by the U.S.S.R. for imports had declined only by 19 percent in 1931. Although the import price index continued down to 39 percent of 1928 in 1935, it rose thereafter, and it is clear that by comparison with the optimistic expectations of the first FYP the world depression of the 1930s made Soviet expansion more difficult.

A fifth problem area developed in the transportation sector. For two or three years the railroads responded admirably to burgeoning freight and passenger traffic demands, but for the next three years or so transportation became a bottleneck that interfered seriously with economic effectiveness, hampering the performance of industry, construction, and agriculture. In 1934 and 1935 resources were channeled into transportation, and new operating methods were developed by the railroads, enabling them to work off accumulated backlogs of unshipped freight and cope thereafter with steadily increasing demands. Their successful performance boosted the performance of all the rest of the economy.[11]

The drive for Soviet economic expansion was adversely affected by still another sequence of events: political purges and mass terror. Suspicions of disloyalty and sabotage led to arrests and show trials that decisively influenced the atmosphere under which everyone worked. At first the impact fell mainly on Soviet bourgeois specialists and foreign consultants, but eventually it spread to all Soviet citizens. International publicity was given to the Shakhty trial in 1928 and the Promparty trial of 1933, in which foreign advisors and bourgeois specialists were condemned for sabotaging construction projects. The assassination of S. M. Kirov in December 1934 led to hundreds of arrests of suspected Party members and then to the lurid show trials of former Party leaders in 1935–38. While foreign correspondents were invited to attend these trials, and transcripts of the proceedings were translated into several major languages, the outside world was less aware that mass terror was spreading outside the Party to the general Soviet population. Its impact was most severe during 1937–39.

One can speculate that the impact of purges and terror on economic performance involved two competing forces. On the one hand, it may have spurred managers and workers to greater effort. Conversely, ample evidence indicates that it generated caution in decision making, reluctance to take responsibility, and even paralysis of action. The strain of working under suspicion surely impaired morale and undermined efficiency. Midnight interrogations by the NKVD did not make it easier for economic managers to meet demanding production targets.

The impact of purges and terror appears to have been especially severe in the sectors of greatest concern to the Party leadership. There was wholesale liquidation from the top down in the armed forces, and this had been preceded by extensive arrests in defense-related heavy industry. The transportation sector, especially the railroads, was heavily hit. The mass arrests of economic managers created serious difficulties in finding replacements for experienced executives. A 1970 economic history of Soviet railroads illustrates the point vividly by citing an internal memorandum sent to the new commissar of railroads by his staff. It showed the number of officials at each level of railroad administration who had been at their posts for at least a year, the number with seven to twelve month's experience, and the number with less than eight month's experience, as of November 13, 1938. The implications are shocking. Overall, 43 percent of these officials had occupied their posts for up to eight months and 76 percent for no more than a year. There can be little doubt that similar situations existed in other sectors of the economy.

This list of developments shaping Soviet economic expansion during the 1928–1940 period must also include Soviet efforts to prepare for war. A number of events influenced Soviet policy. In 1931 Japan took control of Manchuria, threatening the Soviet Far East. In 1933 Hitler became Chancellor of Germany, and presumably Moscow was aware of the notions in his *Mein Kampf* (two volumes, 1925 and 1926) concerning German's need for *lebensraum*, the breadbasket of the Ukraine, and the petroleum of the Caucasus. Reviewing the world situation in January 1934, J. V. Stalin said (at the 17th Party Congress): "It is quite clear that things are heading for a new war." In 1936–37 the U.S.S.R. had an opportunity to test its aircraft and other military equipment in the Spanish Civil War. In 1938 and 1939 Soviet forces were involved in fairly extensive skirmishes with Japan near the Soviet-Manchurian frontier. In 1939, after the Soviet-German pact of August, Soviet forces occupied Bessarabia, eastern Poland, and three Baltic nations. In 1939–40 Soviet armed forces gained some painful experience in their war against Finland. All of this was preliminary to the invasion of the U.S.S.R. by Nazi Germany on June 22, 1941.

The Soviet response to the growing threat of war was to concentrate efforts first on building a heavy industrial base. Efforts to equip the armed forces with advanced weapons were modest during the early 1930s. Investment emphasis was placed instead on enlarging the branches of industry producing fuel and raw materials, needed for defense-related manufacturing, and on modernizing and expanding these manufacturing industries. In this fashion the capacity to produce aircraft, tanks, artillery, naval vessels, and ordnance was enlarged.

Clearly, a major timing issue involved the decision to cut back the flow of resources into capacity expansion and shift these resources instead into large-scale production of military material. It was complicated by the fact that weapons technology was improving quite rapidly. The U.S.S.R. evidently learned from its experience in Spain that German weapons were technically

Table 11.3
Budget outlays for defense and the NKVD, 1928 to 1940 (in millions of rubles at current prices), and size of armed forces

	Defense		NKVD		Size of the armed forces (thousands of soldiers)
	Budgeted	Spent	Budgeted	Spent	
1928					586
1929					
1930		1,046			
1931		1,288			562
1932		1,296			638
1933		1,421			885
1934		5,019			940
1935		8,186			1,067
1936		14,883			1,300
1937		17,481		2,995	1,433
1938		23,151		4,244	1,513
1939	40,885	39,181	5,455	5,732	
1940	57,066	56,752	7,045		4,207

Sources: The defense outlay data for 1930–32 are from V. P. Diachenko, *Istoriia finansov SSSR (1917–1950 gg.)* (1978), p. 302; for 1933–37 from *Sotsialisticheskoe nar. khoz. SSSR v 1933–1941 gg.* (1973), pp. 25, 31, and 41. The data for NKVD outlays are from *ibid.*, pp. 25 and 31, and from Eugene Zaleski, *Stalinist Planning for Economic Growth, 1933–1952* (1980), pp. 190 and 194. The armed forces data are from Soviet sources cited in G. Warren Nutter, *The Growth of Industrial Production in the Soviet Union* (1962), p. 327; Richard Moorsteen and Raymond P. Powell, *The Soviet Capital Stock* (1966), p. 629; and Harriet F. and William F. Scott, *The Armed Forces of the USSR* (1979), p. 16.

superior to Soviet weapons, so hasty efforts at upgrading were underway in the late 1930s. Only on the eve of invasion were new models coming into production.

Table 11.3 presents some overall data on annual defense appropriations and the total size of Soviet armed forces. It will be seen that both grew rapidly after 1933. Ample direct and indirect evidence in Soviet sources makes it clear that the appropriations were used to pull resources away from basic industrial capital formation into specific forms of defense-related fixed capital and into military procurement.

11.4 Estimating the Impact of These Developments

In order to obtain rough estimates of the impact of these developments, a quantitative model of the Soviet economy (called KAPROST, for "capital growth" in Russian) was built out of the data available at the end of the 1920s. It uses linear programming in an input-output framework to compute a problem-free reference solution that can be altered in stages to reflect individual events.

Although Soviet official data in current rubles for the 1930s have long been rejected in western scholarly analysis, the data available for the late 1920s need not be similarly scorned. The census of 1926, the control figures for 1927–28, 1928–29 and 1929–30, and the base-period data in the first Five-Year Plan prove to be reasonably reliable for establishing KAPROST's statistical foundation. Especially useful for internal detail was the TsUNKhU document, *Materialy po balansu narodnogo khoziaistva SSSR za 1928, 1929, i 1930 gody*, issued in 1932. The expansion targets embodied in the first Five-Year Plan confirmed in May 1929 were overambitious as regards speed of achievement, but the FYP provides structural parameters that can be unhooked from the terminal year of 1932–33 and used to investigate more feasible expansion paths.[12]

KAPROST divides all output, from each of ten producing sectors, into two flows, one coming from inherited fixed capital and another coming from newly built fixed capital. The old capital embodies pre-1928 technology; this stock steadily depreciates. The newly built fixed capital embodies advanced technology with more productive parameters, and as it comes into being in each sector the labor force switches over to it. The rate of technological progress in each sector therefore is determined by the rate at which its fixed capital stock grows.

We treat the output targets for 1932–33 in the first FYP as the sum of two parts, one coming from old capital in each sector and a residual attributable to newly built capital. The depreciated stock of old capital, multiplied by its known productivity, yields a certain amount of output and requires certain amounts of labor, intermediate goods and imports. Deducting these computed levels of output, capital, labor, intermediate goods, and imports from the 1932–33 FYP targets, we can deduce from the remainders the capital and labor productivities, the intermediate input coefficients, and the required import ratios associated with newly built capital. These properties of advanced-technology, fixed capital are taken to be independent of the year 1932–33.

From the FYP roster of 1,100 industrial installations we derive a pattern for a four-year gestation period required to build new fixed capital in industry. In the absence of detailed evidence this same gestation period is used for all sectors. Existing sectoral differences in the proportions between buildings and structures, on the one hand, and equipment, on the other, are recognized (using FYP evidence), but the probability that equipment had a shorter gestation period than buildings is ignored. Livestock herds have their own pattern.

In setting the stage for our reference solution, we make exogenous assumptions for three important series, extending them forward past 1933 up through 1940. The series for the total labor force is a projection built on the 1926 census. The numbers reaching age sixteen and entering the labor force each year, and the numbers reaching retirement age each year, are used to obtain a potential labor force series, to which is applied a participation rate that rises slowly, as Gosplan expected it to do during 1928–1933.

Gosplan's export projections in the first FYP are extended to 1940, on the assumption of uniform absolute annual growth at the anticipated 1928–1933 rate. The government sector's nondefense final demand purchases are extended to 1940 in the same way. Levels of consumption and investment in each period, along with levels of gross output, are left free as endogenous variables to be maximized subject to the whole set of constraints.

KAPROST delivers output to the rural population (roughly speaking, those who earn incomes in agriculture) and the urban population (those who earn incomes outside agriculture) in patterns that were carefully investigated by Gosplan and TsUNKhU. For peasants and workers separately, we apply the patterns anticipated for 1932–33 in the first FYP, extending it to all periods.

Four of our ten sectors are involved in foreign trade: field crop agriculture (including forestry), livestock products agriculture (including hunting and fishing), producer goods industry, and consumer goods industry. Exogenously specified exports finance imports. Existing short-term trade debits

Table 11.4
Reference solution values for gross output, GNP, and components, by period (absolute data in billions of rubles at base-period prices)

	Twice 1928	1st period	2nd period	3rd period	4th period	5th period	6th period	6th period index[a]
Total gross output	106.0	122.2	149.3	182.1	258.1	331.8	405.8	383
GNP								
Agricultural output	15.0	19.5	21.4	30.3	26.8	27.3	29.7	198
Industry and construction	16.9	26.4	39.6	51.2	89.1	107.4	135.7	803
Services	19.7	19.3	20.1	20.4	29.7	44.0	53.4	271
Total GNP	51.6	65.2	81.1	101.9	145.6	178.7	218.8	424
Consumption	30.6	34.4	33.2	41.0	40.6	66.7	82.4	269
Investment	11.8	20.0	33.7	41.8	79.5	79.4	97.2	824
Government services (exogenous)	5.9	7.7	10.1	12.5	14.9	17.3	19.7	334
Exports (exogenous)	1.2	1.7	2.3	3.0	3.6	4.2	4.8	400
End-of-period stock of fixed capital	65.7	74.6	102.5	122.1	192.5	248.1	327.4	498
Percent increases per period								
Total gross output		15.3	22.2	22.0	41.7	28.6	22.3	
Agricultural output		30.0	9.7	41.6	−11.6	1.9	8.8	
Industry and construction		56.2	50.0	29.3	74.0	20.5	26.4	
Services		−2.0	4.1	1.5	45.6	48.1	21.4	
Total GNP		26.4	24.4	25.6	42.9	22.7	22.4	
Consumption		12.4	−3.5	23.5	−1.0	64.3	23.5	
Investment		69.5	68.5	24.0	90.2	−0.1	22.4	
Percent shares in GNP								
Consumption	59.3	52.8	40.9	40.2	27.9	37.3	37.7	
Investment	22.9	30.7	41.6	41.0	54.6	44.4	44.4	
Absolute increments								
Fixed capital		8.9	27.9	19.6	70.4	55.6	79.3	
GNP (annualized)		6.8	8.0	10.4	21.9	16.6	20.1	
Incremental capital/output ratio		1.30	3.50	1.88	3.22	3.36	3.96	

[a] With the base period (twice 1928) taken as 100.

(chiefly to Germany) are paid off during the first five years; thereafter we assume no credits, loans, or aid. In each importing sector a small fraction of gross output (reflecting the 1929 situation) is required as a supplement to domestic production; beyond this, if export proceeds are available in a given period, KAPROST permits an importing sector to obtain additional imports as well.

With a growing labor force, substantial investment in fixed capital, and structural transformation incorporating technological progress, the Soviet economy as modeled by KAPROST is able to raise output levels quite rapidly after 1928. Table 11.4 shows how the main elements of GNP grow period-by-period in a problem-free reference solution. By the end of the 1930s total gross output is almost four times as large as it was a decade earlier; GNP proper is more than four times as large. Agricultural output doubles, industry and construction produce eight times as much, and services output is 2.7 times as large. This is accomplished, moreover, without any belt tightening; consumption by peasants and workers never falls below 1928 levels and by 1940 is 2.7 times as large.

These are extremely rapid rates of growth, perhaps implausibly high. They reflect optimistic assumptions regarding all the technical parameters governing production and capital formation, though none of the individual parameters lies outside the bounds observable in other times and places. Japan's record a quarter of a century later lends credence to the existence of expansion potentials on this scale. It is surely reasonable, however, to consider this expansion path as indicating the upper bound of those hypothetically achievable.

In adjusting this problem-free solution to incorporate actual developments, we begin by recognizing the impact of world depression. Michael Dohan's reconstructed series for Soviet exports is inserted in place of our initial projection, and imports are constrained as before not to exceed exports. After adjusting other levers of the model to minimize the damage, we obtain a new solution, comparable to the reference solution, showing the impact of world depression on the Soviet economy. Next we insert actual Soviet outlays on rearmament (in current prices), taking account also of data on the size of the armed forces. Again we adjust KAPROST parameters to reflect adaptation to changed circumstances and then compute another solution to reflect this impact alone. In addition we combine these two external events—depression in foreign trade and rearmament—over which the U.S.S.R. had no control, to see the joint impact of exogenous forces on the economy.

Altering KAPROST to reflect the collectivization of agriculture involves two steps. First we insert the actual level of fixed capital stocks in each of the two agricultural sectors. Our second step is to lower capital/output ratios so that in each period KAPROST can produce no more agricultural output than the levels officially reported for this period by the U.S.S.R. (since 1960). Again adjusting various parameters to minimize the damage inflicted by these changes, we obtain a solution showing the impact of collectivization as an isolated event.

Finally, all three of these major developments are combined in a composite reconstruction. If these had been the only economically significant problems detracting from the problem-free solution, we would expect to reproduce the historical record. There were of course other weighty developments not easy to incorporate into KAPROST.

It is reasuring, however, to find that our composite reconstruction does appear to match up fairly closely with the actual record in so far as the record is available. On crucial matters like the level of consumption, period by period, there is as yet no comprehensive evidence against which the estimates generated by KAPROST can be compared. But in two overall dimensions, total gross output and total fixed capital stocks, we find that the most reliable western estimates indicate that our reconstruction has the right dimensions.

In the two sections of table 11.5, line one shows estimates for actual levels of gross output and fixed capital stocks, respectively, while line two reproduces the estimates generated by KAPROST in our composite. It will be seen that KAPROST starts out slightly below the historical level but catches up and surpasses it. This may be because the optimizing algorithm has certain advantages that planners at the time could not employ. One would expect a drawing-board economy to have a higher growth rate, but its linearity also leads to unutilized capacity in some sectors during the first two periods. Unaffected by the inertia that haunts real economic systems, KAPROST does not produce anything it cannot use! Secondly, to the extent that negative developments in the 1930s interfered with expansion but are not adequately captured by KAPROST, one would expect better performance in the model than in real life.

The other lines in table 11.5 make it possible to trace the quantitative impact of the successive adjustments we have been describing. Starting at the bottom with the reference solution, one can move up line by line, noting the impact on output and capital stocks of the world depression, rearmament, these two external forces taken together, collectivization alone, and all three together. In the same format the two sections of table 11.6 show how total household consumption was affected by these developments and what the consequences were for unemployment.

Table 11.5
Comparing solutions by period (in billions of rubles at base-period prices)

	1929–1930	1931–1932	1933–1934	1935–1936	1937–1938	1939–1940	
A. Gross output							
Actual	127	151	169	231	281	307	
Composite	115	139	154	236	307	324	
Agricultural collectivization	117	140	161	244	311	320	
Depression and rearmament	119	148	171	250	331	402	
Rearmament	121	149	167	252	340	419	
World depression	121	149	182	257	330	407	
Reference solution	122	149	182	258	332	406	
B. Total capital stock (start of year)	1929	1931	1933	1935	1937	1939	1941
Actual	67.3	80.5	100.9	123.5	160.2	202.6	265.9
Composite							
Excluding defense capital	67.1	71.8	93.1	125.3	164.6	239.1	229.1
Including defense capital	67.1	71.8	93.1	128.3	184.3	287.9	337.9
Agricultural collectivization	67.1	71.8	95.7	123.9	183.3	273.0	358.1
Depression and rearmament							
Excluding defense capital	65.7	74.6	98.0	125.5	171.1	244.7	262.3
Including defense capital	65.7	74.6	98.0	128.5	190.8	293.5	371.1
Rearmament							
Excluding defense capital	65.7	74.6	96.2	127.0	174.5	250.7	276.4
Including defense capital	65.7	74.6	96.2	130.0	194.2	299.5	385.2
World depression	65.7	74.6	102.4	121.8	191.4	244.9	324.2
Reference solution	65.7	74.6	102.5	122.1	192.5	248.1	327.4

Table 11.6
Comparing solutions, total consumption, and unemployment by period (in billions of rubles at base-period prices) and percent unemployed

	1929–1930	1931–1932	1933–1934	1935–1936	1937–1938	1939–1940
C. Total consumption						
Composite	37.7	31.7	20.9	27.3	32.3	36.3
Agricultural collectivization	36.4	30.0	25.8	29.6	31.7	35.6
Depression and rearmament	36.1	35.6	32.3	31.1	37.8	47.1
Rearmament	36.2	36.2	27.5	30.8	38.4	48.4
World depression	34.7	33.4	40.4	40.6	66.6	82.6
Reference solution	34.4	33.1	41.0	40.6	66.7	82.3
D. Unemployment (percent)						
Composite	13.9	21.5	34.5	26.6	26.8	29.6
Agricultural collectivization	12.4	19.6	28.6	24.3	27.9	31.3
Depression and rearmament	9.3	13.1	14.2	4.9	7.4	0
Rearmament	8.7	12.4	23.2	7.7	7.0	0
World depression	8.5	12.0	0.7	0	0	0
Reference solution	7.8	11.6	0	0	0	0

According to KAPROST the impact of world depression on the Soviet domestic economy was negligible. Rearmament, however, cut sharply into household consumption after the first few years and at the end of the 1930s cut sharply into civilian fixed capital formation as well. If one counts the hardware procured by the military from producer goods industry as capital, on the other hand, total capital stocks are larger under rearmament than in the reference solution.[13]

Agricultural collectivization had a far more drastic impact. According to KAPROST total household consumption over these twelve years came to 298 billion rubles in the reference solution. World depression left this total unchanged. Rearmament lowered consumption by 27 percent, to 218 billion, and the two exogenous factors in combination had the effect of restricting consumption to 220 billion. But collectivization of agriculture by itself reduced total household consumption by 37 percent, to 189 billion, and our composite reconstruction shows a twelve-year total for household consumption of 186 billion rubles. Collectivization reduces gross output, especially toward the end of the 1930s, but does not interfere with fixed capital formation. In fact, because productive possibilities in agriculture are closed off by collectivization, its somewhat perverse effect is to push capital formation off into industry, making the total available by the end of 1940 somewhat larger than under the reference solution.

The drastic fall in household consumption displayed by our composite reconstruction, from a level around 31 or 32 billion rubles at the end of the 1920s (16 billion per year) to something like 21 billion in 1933 and 1934, cannot be checked against official or western estimates, since no continuous estimates are available. J. G. Chapman showed long ago, however, that the nonagricultural real wage in 1937, after substantial recovery from the most difficult years around 1933, was 17 percent below its 1928 level (in terms of the 1928 price structure), or 43 percent below its 1928 level (in terms of the 1937 price structure).[14] For the majority of the population, still in agriculture, the change may well have been worse. If our third-period estimate of 21 billion is compared with the 41 billion attained under the problem-free conditions of the reference solution, the implication is a 49 percent shortfall compared with what might have been!

Another tragic feature of the composite reconstruction in comparison with the reference solution is the massive volume of unemployed labor. The unemployment is organically linked to the shrinkage in real consumption. It is almost as though KAPROST were obeying the principle quoted in Article 12 of the 1936 Soviet Constitution: "He who does not work, neither shall he eat."[15] Since KAPROST has maintained the same physical labor productivities in all the tests from the reference solution on, the successive constrictions on the economy have made more and more labor superfluous. The unemployment section in table 11.3 shows the results. By comparison with the reference solution, which made use of all available labor after the structural shifts of the first two periods were completed, rearmament altered resource use in a way that generated unemployment in periods three, four, and five as well. But the impact of collectivization was far more severe, making between 24 percent and 31 percent of the total labor force unnecessary. Combining collectivization with world depression and rearmament, our composite reconstruction generates unemployment levels running from 14 percent in the first period to 35 percent, 27 percent, 27 percent and 30 percent in the second through sixth periods.

Under the Constitution of 1936 unemployment could not exist in the U.S.S.R., so government policy kept the whole labor force at work: on payrolls in nonagricultural occupations, in *sovkhozy*, as members of *kolkhozy*, or in corrective labor camps. Average labor productivity in physical terms fell far enough below its potential to absorb the extra workers. Massive unemployment was thus camouflaged, in contrast with the explicitly exposed unemployment in the West during the same period.

11.5 Concluding Remarks

The Soviet economic-planning experience in the 1930s suggests a number of important conclusions. First, it is clear that efforts to carry out rapid institutional change can generate highly negative responses from at least part of the population. These negative responses may not only destroy productive resources but also create social and political tensions that spread throughout the economy and harm its transformation. Rapid change may still appear necessary, but careful efforts in advance to weigh costs against benefits, using modern analytic methods, are surely indicated.

A second clear lesson from Soviet experience is that the presence of a large volume of unfinished physical capital construction, tying resources up in sterile form, lowers the productivity of investment and delays the conversion of current output into enlarged future flows. The pressures that give rise to unfinished construction are hard to resist, as Soviet experience continues to demonstrate, but other national planning efforts should at least be on notice concerning the difficulty.

A third lesson from the pre-war Soviet economic-planning experience concerns the damage caused by bottlenecks. An output reduction in one sector will cause problems for sectors using its products, even under placid conditions of static equilibrium. Nevertheless, the problems are magnified if, during a campaign for large-scale structural transformation involving disproportionate growth in the output of individual sectors, specific sectors lag behind. A bottleneck like the Soviet freight transformation bottleneck of the early 1930s gives rise to costly idleness of labor and capital in all sectors making use of freight transportation services. The implication is that planners should make provision for sufficient capacity reserves in each sector to avert any sustained inabilities to meet the needs of other sectors.

These practical implications growing out of the early Soviet planning experience suggest a more general conclusion. An economy's potential for rapid transformation is limited by both political and technical constraints. Efforts to push beyond them can be very costly. The computations obtained with KAPROST suggest that between 1928 and 1940 the U.S.S.R. paid a price for its achievements that was higher than necessary. It follows that latecomers, in charting their economic development, should make systematic efforts to define the point beyond which pressure undermines results.

Notes

1. Alexander Erlich, *The Soviet Industrialization Debate, 1924–1928* (Cambridge, Mass.: Harvard University Press, 1960), esp. chaps. 6 and 9.

2. Cf., "New Conditions—New Tasks in Economic Construction," Stalin's famous speech of June 23, 1931, pp. 448–466, in I. Stalin, *Voprosy leninisma*, 10th ed. (Moscow: Partizdat TsK VKP(B), 1934). English translation in J. V. Stalin, *Works*, Vol. 13 (Moscow: Foreign Languages Publishing House, 1955), pp. 53–82.

3. V. I. Lenin, *Sochineniia*, Vol. 33, 4th ed. (Moscow: GIPL, 1950), pp. 445–460.

4. See the discussion in Robert Dorfman, Paul A. Samuelson, and Robert M. Solow, *Linear Programming and Economic Analysis* (New York: McGraw-Hill, 1958), chap. 11 and 12, esp. pp. 300–308 and 329–335. John von Neumann's lecture was published in Germany in 1937; an English translation appeared in the *Review of Economic Studies 13* (1945–46): 1–9.

5. V. I. Lenin, *Sochineniia* Vol. 25, 4th ed. (Moscow: GIPL, 1949), pp. 439–440. For a convenient English translation, see V. I. Lenin, *Selected Works*, Vol. 7 (New York: International Publishers, 1943), p. 87.

6. Ibid., p. 88.

7. Lenin, *Sochineniia*, Vol. 25, p. 338.

8. Lenin, *Sochineniia*, Vol. 33, pp. 38–56, esp. pp. 43–44. In his *Selected Works*, see Vol. IX, pp. 256–75, esp. pp. 261–62.

9. V. I. Lenin, *Sochineniia*, Vol. 31, 4th ed. (Moscow: GIPL, 1950), pp. 483–484. Cited here from J. V. Stalin's October 19, 1928, speech to a Moscow party group, in his *Works*, Vol. 11 (Moscow: FLPH, 1954), p. 237.

10. Gosplan SSSR, *Piatiletnii plan narodnogo-khoziaistvennogo stroitel'stva SSSR*, Vol. 1, 2nd ed. (Moscow: Izd. Plan. Khoz, 1929), p. 13.

11. See H. Hunter, *Soviet Transportation Policy* (Cambridge: Harvard University Press, 1957), esp. chaps. 3 and 4.

12. See H. Hunter, "The overambitious first Soviet Five-Year Plan, with comments by Robert Campbell, Stephen F, Cohen, and Moshe Lewin, in *Slavic Review* 32 (June 1973): 237–291.

13. Military hardware comes from the producers goods sector alone and has no gestation period, whereas capital goods require construction as well as producers goods industry output and, further, must be built over two periods. This explains the seemingly anomalous result.

14. Cf. Janet G. Chapman, *Real Wages in Soviet Russia Since 1928* (Cambridge: Harvard University Press, 1963), pp. 145–146.

15. *Constitution (Fundamental Law) of the U.S.S.R.* (Moscow: State Publishing House of Political Literature, 1938), p. 15. The quote is from St. Paul's 2nd epistle to the Thessalonians, chap. III, verse 10, and the Moscow translator nicely preserves the formal elegance of the Russian: *Esli kto ne khochet' trudit'sia, tot' i ne esh'*. Cf., *Bibliia: Knigi Sviashchennogo Pisaniia* (London: Britanskago Inostrannago Bibleiskago Obshchestva, 1921). The King James version is: "... if any would not worke, neither should he eate." Cf. *The Holy Bible, Facsimile of the Authorized Version 1611* (Oxford: Oxford University Press, 1911).

12

Economics of Virtuous Haste: A View of Soviet Industrialization and Institutions

Gregory Grossman

12.1

It has been said by an economist that the "crucial dividing line between economic systems seems to lie [not so much between capitalism and socialism, or between plan and market, as] between the systems devoted to single, preconceived, and fixed purposes (maximum growth, 'classlessness,' or the winning of wars), and those giving priority to the diversified, spontaneous, and ever-changing aspirations of individuals."[1] The Soviet Union falls more into the first category than the second. Maximum industrial growth and the rapid amassing of military might (the two have been almost identical for most of Soviet history), while establishing and maintaining a social order committed to a set of distinct ethical values—such has been the overriding national objective of the Soviet Union for the last half century.

The race against time implicit in the military-economic strategy has inevitably imposed its own logic, a kind of logic of haste set against the background of the official vision of the new society. This new society would be morally superior to the old, capitalist, greed-ridden society of unequal wealth, opportunity, and power. It would be—here and now, even before the advent of the classless condition of full communism—a socialist, conflictless, virtuous society. Haste in industrialization, but haste with virtue in sharp contrast to the capitalist variety, is the distinctive Soviet modernization formula, if the official ideology is to be believed.

For a country with an overriding national objective, economic time is not the same as chronological time. As the late Alexander Gerschenkron stressed, the race is not so much against the clock as against someone.[2] *Dognat' i peregnat' Ameriku* ("to catch up with and surpass America") in the industrial realm was the proud goal of the Soviet regime from at least the early years of the Stalin era to nearly the end of Khrushchev's, the first two-thirds of the fifty years here under review.[3] True, since Khrushchev's fall, this goal has not been often proclaimed, but it is not necessarily forgotten. On the other hand, to surpass America in military power seems to continue to be a prime, if prudently veiled, objective of the Kremlin to this day. Yet the race is not only against the historical rival on the outside. It is no less against the hardening of the internal institutional arrangements and the resistant fiber of man's psychology.

The race began in earnest in 1929, the first full year of the first Five-Year Plan (Stalin's plan of course), the year that also saw the fundamental restructuring of Soviet economic institutions for the sake of speedy industrialization and for the "construction of socialism," including the most violent restructuring of all, the collectivization of peasant agriculture. The general outlines of the Soviet economic growth record of the past fifty years are well known. While among its most notable achievements has been the amassing of military might, civilian industrial output and technological capabilities have also increased enormously, an accomplishment that is not greatly diminished by the failure (as yet) to surpass or even to approach the United States in per capita production and consumption. One should also take note of the impressive growth of education and science.

This study is concerned primarily with the interaction between performance, ideology, and the institutional system. Relevant to this standpoint is the persistence of certain seemingly intractable problems that tend to raise questions of the adequacy of the system itself and some of its major institutions at the given historical juncture. Such questions have been openly raised and discussed in the Soviet Union (and in the other countries of Eastern Europe) ever since 1956, when the 20th Party Congress lifted the bars to meaningful discussion of the economy's problems and the possibilities of improving the system. A rather limited, within-system reform of some of the economy's key institutions was attempted by the present (post-Khrushchev) leadership in 1965; it came to naught in practice. Since then the gradually but steadily tightening internal intellectual and political climate, reinforced by external events, such as those in Poland from mid-1980 on, has almost silenced open discussion of yet another try at economic reform, especially since it would have to be much more far-reaching than the 1965 measure to bear any promise of success. But substantial institutional and even systemic reform remains, so to speak, a shadow agenda, the agenda in the minds of economists, managers, and others, which, at this writing, awaits a more auspicious time to emerge into the open.

The logic of haste and the principles of a virtuous social order do not always fit well together, especially as the historical race is hard and the tenets of morality are overly demanding of the individual's powers of resistance to material temptation. Richard Lowenthal's brilliant analysis of this basic clash of principles—"development versus utopia," in his phrase—and of the consequent historical evolution of Soviet society is by now a classic.[5] It is not our purpose to replicate his argument—and certainly not to try to improve on it. Instead we shall attempt to develop a few individual themes that in one way or another illustrate the social tensions and institutional mutations that flow from the inner logic of the economics of "virtuous haste," Soviet-style.

12.2

Paradoxically, the rigidities in the Soviet institutional structure may to some extent derive from the blessings of Mother Nature, that is, the U.S.S.R.'s very rich natural endowment. Excepting some tropical commodities, of which very few had significance for the industrialization drive, and apart from certain serious weaknesses in the natural endowment of agriculture, the Soviet Union is blessed with an exceptionally rich domestic supply of the resources needed to launch and sustain its industrial plans. Thus the rapid growth of industrial output after 1929 rested almost entirely on indigenous natural resources, and in addition these absorbed many of the mistakes of the strategy and management of industrialization. For good systemic reasons Soviet use of its natural resources has been prodigal and continues to be so to this day.

The bulk of the hard currency earned during the past fifty years was generated by raw and semifinished material exports, including gold. The hard currency in turn paid for the purchases of western capital goods and technology, which have played a crucial role in Soviet industrialization (and, one might add, in the military program). In the past decade a substantial portion of the hard currency has had to be diverted to pay for *imports* of raw and semifinished materials, such as rolled steel and materials for the production of aluminum, not to mention very large amounts of grain during years of crop failure, but this is a more recent development.

Yet bountiful natural endowment has not saved the U.S.S.R. from serious balance-of-payments problems (in hard currency). On the contrary, the U.S.S.R. has had them continuously since the day of the Bolshevik revolution in 1917, owing to chronic excess aggregate demand and a generally over-valued exchange rate for the ruble. Foreign exchange has been tightly rationed in a centralized manner. In fact for most of the period the Soviet Union has been dependent on hard-currency imports for its *growth* and not for its day-to-day operating needs. It has hardly ever had to face the relentless discipline of the balance of payments. Moreover, again thanks to the rich natural resource base, such selling as the Soviet Union has been doing in world markets consisted of staple raw and semiprocessed materials, which unlike manufactured goods require little marketing, follow-up service, product innovation, or attention to fashion—in short, little adjustment to changing consumer demand by the Soviet exporter and virtually none by the Soviet domestic producer. They fit in well with the Soviet economic system.

Had it been otherwise—had the U.S.S.R. been from an early date a Hungary, Czechoslovakia, or East Germany, or even Poland, importing most of its raw materials for current operating needs and forced to earn its way through competition in world markets for capital and consumer goods against advanced western countries and (God forbid) Japan—the ineffectiveness of its inflexible, bureaucratic, command economy for such competition would have become evident very soon indeed (as it quickly became evident to the just-named East European countries after the imposition of the Soviet model). In such a case the Soviet economy, lacking another major country to support it economically, would have had to have its economic reform at an early point or go under. With less abundant natural resources it might have had a slower rate of industrial growth initially. But in the long run it might have been better off, not because resource-poverty is an advantage in development but because in the Soviet case resource abundance has been an obstacle to systemic adaptation in good time. Now it may be too late, the institutions may be too rigid and the vested interests too powerful, to reform the system in an orderly, noncataclysmic way.

As already suggested, hard-currency imports have begun to tilt significantly in the direction of current operating and consumer needs and will probably tilt further. At the same time the prospects for continued large exports of raw materials are not sanguine. Petroleum exports, which now account for over half the value of hard-currency merchandise sales (excepting gold), will most likely shrink in quantity (though possibly less in value) in the coming years, owing to domestic production difficulties, though natural gas may partly take their place. Lumber exports, the next largest category, are uncertain, too, for similar reasons. Soviet trade publications speak more and more of a major expansion of machinery exports to take over from raw materials, but this would place quite different demands on exporters, producers, and the whole bureaucratic and planning apparatus. It would require a basic reorganization, a transformation of an administered management of scarcity and physical output targets into a market-oriented, demand-sensitive (albeit socialist) production *and* sales mechanism.

Compromise solutions are not easily reached in this regard. A *partial* liberalization of the hierarchical structure of the domestic (so-called command) economy is not likely to work well, as several East European countries concerned with their balances of payments have learned in the past fifteen years. Planners' directives clash with market signals. The domestic cost-based price structure, on which much of the internal Party and bureaucratic power and privilege ultimately rests, conflicts with world market prices that must define behavior in foreign trade. Nor can the export sector alone be removed from the rest of the economy and turned toward the world economy (unless the bulk of the exports indeed are the traditional Soviet primary commodities). Should something like this be done, the rest of the economy would be a drag on the export sector, preventing speed and flexibility of adaptation to external demand and holding down the quality and modernity of the exportable goods. An economy cannot march at once to the drum beat of the planners' detailed, physical directives and to the siren song of the world market.

In sum, the Soviet economic system became what it is in part thanks to the country's rich resource base, which permitted the planners largely to ignore the day-to-day discipline of the balance of payments and therefore also the imperatives of the market place and the pains of real economic cost. On this basis an elaborate and rigid institutional edifice sprang up. This economic system thrived for two human generations and achieved marked successes by its own criteria. But inevitably it hardened and came to be supported and protected by powerful vested interests. Will it be able to reform itself now, in the face of growing need to respond to the forces of demand, internal as well as external, and to be more sensitive to economic cost?

12.3

The hardening of the economy's institutions and their incrustation with vested interests can be explained in a variety of ways. The sociologists and the political scientists will surely have their own theories. So will the economists who, among other things, will look for peculiarities in the price structure.[6] Soviet prices, wholesale and retail, and wages have been rigidly controlled for over fifty years. It takes little economic sophistication to deduce that the consequences of this policy must have been major, in the economic, social, and perhaps even political spheres.

The partial price control of the later twenties was occasioned by relatively mild inflationary pressure plus social policy favoring the urban working class over the peasantry. Farm prices were deliberately depressed to enhance the purchasing power of urban wages, a policy that significantly contributed to the so-called marketing crisis, the diminution of off-farm sales of foodstuffs, which in turn acted as a stimulus to if not the prime cause of the fateful decision to collectivize agriculture at the end of 1929. So, looking at prices is not just the economist's parochial quirk.

Comprehensive price controls came early in the Five-Year Plan and almost simultaneously with the collectivization drive. The sharp drop in agricultural output (while grain exports were being deliberately pushed to help finance the plan) was certainly a major contributing factor. But no less important was the enormous rise in purchasing power and in demand for consumer goods, producer goods, and labor, as the plan took off—in other words, extremely strong demand pull occasioned by the haste to industrialize, a haste that in those days knew almost no bounds of common prudence, not to say economic reason. The first Five-Year Plan foresaw some government influence on prices but did not provide for anything like comprehensive price control. In other words, the historical and institutional specifics apart, the Soviet Union got into comprehensive price and wage control not so much for reasons of ideology or long-term strategy but in the same way as all countries get into it, by way of emergency response to a sudden inflationary spurt. Of course the ruling ideology was, to put it mildly, conducive to central controls and caused few tears to be shed upon the demise of the market.

The theoretical justifications came a whole decade later, when it became convenient for the dictator and necessary for the political economists to somehow link what was being done with prices to what Marx had said half a century earlier and in a completely different—even opposite—context. But leaving aside the ideological and theoretical aspects of Soviet price control, what *is* important is that in all three sectors—producer goods, consumer goods at retail, and labor—prices have remained controlled, as noted, for the next fifty years. There is no sign of change in this respect.

Yet one must not jump to the conclusion that the controlled prices in all three sectors mentioned are deliberately set with little reference to demand, at levels generally significantly below presumed equilibrium levels. This is in principle true only of producer goods prices, and consequently almost all producer goods of any significance are—as they must be under the circumstances—centrally allocated (rationed) and have been since the early thirties. Here we find one of the origins of the Soviet system of physical planning. Since the allocation of producer goods had to be in physical terms and inevitably grew increasingly detailed, production planning had to conform, rest on physical targets, and become progressively more detailed too. The usual consequences followed: disregard of cost of production, neglect of quality in favor of sheer physical quantity, resistance to innovation, and so forth. Incidentally, there is nothing distinctively Soviet about this list; such are the effects of price control universally, whether under socialism or under capitalism. Equally expected are of course the large bureaucratic establishments that grow and thrive on this soil, leading to the formation of strong vested interests at the levels of the firm itself, the superordinate trust or ministry, and the host of administering and planning agencies. If there are distinctively Soviet touches to this familiar picture they are (1) the fact of almost universal state ownership, the unusually distant separation of ownership and effective control, that does little to minimize the costs and wastes of this system, (2) the presence of the party as a parallel, and indeed paramount, structure of both management and monitoring, and (3) the uncommonly long perdurance of the whole arrangement, causing the institutions in questions and the vested interests resting upon them to be thoroughly entrenched.

Lastly, we should take note of the macroeconomic side of the price-control picture, namely, the maintenance of continuous excess aggregate demand in the production sector. Practically speaking, there is no lid on aggregate demand in the production sector—whatever goods can be obtained one way of another, can be paid for—thanks to an accommodating banking system and virtual disregard of costs of current production by the planners: a perfect engine of inflation, although in this case of the repressed variety. Now the repressed inflation is not entirely unfunctional. First, it makes possible one of the most important Soviet institutions, the virtually complete job security of the individual in a full-employment setting. Only a production system as oblivious of cost and as tolerant of constant excess demand as the Soviet can afford to guarantee nearly every individual's job security. In turn the political imperatives of universal job security help ensure that the repressed inflation in the production sector will continue indefinitely.

12.4

With regard to consumer goods' prices at retail and the remuneration of labor, the situation is somewhat different than with producer goods' prices. While here, too, with certain officially sanctioned exceptions, the state fixes all prices and wages, it generally eschews administrative allocation of scarcity, that is to say, the formal rationing of consumer goods (housing being the major exception) and, to a lesser extent, the administrative allocation of labor. (We may note here in passing the important contrast in this respect between the U.S.S.R. and Maoist China or Fidelist Cuba). In principle the authorities allow freedom of consumer choice and of choice of job, in the technical sense of these concepts. Consequently, the planners must take account of supply-demand relations in individual markets for both consumer goods and labor, must aim for at least a rough macro equilibrium in the household account as a whole, and must seek to set individual retail prices and wages so as to approximate demand-supply balance in specific markets. If they neglect these principles, they run the risk that the distribution of consumer goods and the deployment of labor will be less than orderly. (It must be remembered that "orderliness" is one of the highest virtues in the official value system, perhaps in part because it is more often honored in the breach than in the fact.)

So much for theory. In reality things do not work out quite so neatly. Even with the best of intentions the planners cannot very accurately foresee the demand and supply of every separate consumer good in every locality and at all points in time. In addition the official economic mechanism is inept at distributing goods over time and space. Nor have the planners been able to keep the household sector's total purchasing power under close control, not to speak of its regional and temporal distribution. Both the planners' errors and their priorities tend to combine to bias the outcome on the side of excessive expansion of purchasing power in the hands of the public. In reality therefore the official fixed individual retail prices tend to deviate from their actual equilibrium levels and, more often than not, tend to be too low. Hence shortages of goods abound, though gluts are now also not uncommon so that, at the very least, relative prices tend to be wrong. Considering the official price-fixed sector alone, there seems to be chronic macro disequilibrium in the sense of a persistent repressed inflation; in plain English, persistent shortages of consumer goods in official channels.

This situation has spawned the usual responses, such as black markets, "black production," moonlighting, and bribes of all kinds. These parallel phenomena are widespread and in toto form a large underground economy, which together with the legal private sector constitutes the so-called second economy. The second economy is of course primarily a private-enterprise market economy. Black market prices and bribes (understood in a broad sense) are significant forms of expenditure for nearly everyone, and important sources of income for quite a few. But no less important for the individual is the web of his own personal contacts, the ubiquitous Soviet *blat*, through which favors in terms of access to goods or other benefits can be exchanged, whether for a kilo of meat or for admission to the university. One can perhaps speak of a "*blat* market," which parallels and intertwines with the second economy, the two together paralleling and intertwining with the first economy. The *blat* market is a major one in the Soviet context and even more difficult to estimate in quantitative terms than the second economy. Like any market it requires that the individual trader in *blat* possess some economic resources to trade, unless one can rely on mere family relationships, the Soviet equivalent of the old school tie, or (as the Russians say) one's beautiful eyes.

To acquire and control such resources is then a major objective for the Soviet person, who, as often as not, acquires and exploits them at the expense of the state. A desirable job with the state or a quasi-state organization is one where one can do favors for what we might harshly call bribes. Jobs that cannot be put to personal advantage in this way are poor jobs, and the state may have to pay relatively higher salaries or wages to fill them, other things being equal. Yet let us not forget another important characteristic of good jobs; they afford good possibility to steal from the employer. Possession of resources of this kind is an important, sometimes crucial, form of material advantage to the individual. If most such instances of possession do not have the protection of law, they at least benefit from the strong sanction of custom and the realities of a tight labor market. If not covered by property rights, they at least constitute what might be called crypto-property rights, and these crypto-property rights themselves may be subject to purchase and sale in the black or *blat* market. Indeed one can purchase the crypto-property right to sell crypto-property rights to others, as in the case of a truck dispatcher who buys his job in order to sell illicitly lucrative routes to truck drivers.

There is yet another way, an officially sanctioned one, to overcome the shortage of goods in the normal, official channels of distribution. The state conducts its own parallel economy for the privileged, the so-called closed distributors, a network of retail outlets of limited and strictly controlled access. The closed distributors are themselves differentiated by degree of privilege and the availability (and price) of goods. The best ones are naturally those that serve the top layers of the ruling elite, and judging by the rumors that leak out, they are very good indeed by Soviet and sometimes even capitalist standards. The effect of the closed distributors on national accounts and income distribution is also very difficult to quantify.

As a last resort to try to overcome the goods shortage, there is one's own time to stand in line, if one can spare it, and those who can spare time may have something valuable to sell too.

To recapitulate, in a Soviet-style disequilibrium economy, the poor are not as easily identifiable as they are in a market economy with little price control. The poor in the Soviet case are those who have little cash from legitimate sources, *and* little cash from the second economy or graft, hence little chance to patronize the open and black markets, *and* few resources to trade in the *blat* market, *and* little possibility to steal from the state, *and* no access to privileged forms of goods distribution. The Soviet poor are therefore different from the American poor. Our poor generally lack the purchasing power to afford a minimal basket of goods, period. The Soviet poor often *have* the purchasing power to buy their minimal basket of goods at the *official* prices. Moreover they know that the goods they can afford are there, somewhere, at the prices they can afford. They lack access to goods, as they lack the cash status or other resources to make use of the parallel markets. There may be a difference here in psychological terms, especially in a society formally committed to classlessness and social equality.

The Soviet poor would be very difficult to identify statistically even if the U.S.S.R. published minimally adequate statistics on income distribution, which it does not. The same can be said about those at the opposite tail of the distribution curve. Valiant and imaginative attempts have been made by several able western scholars to arrive at measures of income inequality on the basis of pitifully few Soviet figures. But these figures refer to legal money incomes and nothing else. Hence they may tell us little of the true distribution of the ability to obtain goods and services.

We should also note in passing that in principle there is nothing distinctively Soviet about either the second economy, *blat*, or the other phenomena just described. They are universal. That price control breeds black markets, and corruption is commonplace. There are underground economies harboring tax evaders and drug dealers in all countries, even without the benefit of repressed inflation. The old school tie can be red-white-and-blue, and so on and on. If the Soviet case is different, it is so in two respects. First, by dint of the comprehensive price and wage controls over several human generations, the parallel phenomena must be deeply ingrained in people's minds and affect their perceptions and reactions. The fact of persistent widespread shortages cannot but shape one's perception of one's immediate world. It must shape personal relations: on one hand, everyone for himself, not in earning money as it is with most of us but in the day-to-day struggle for goods (something like a continuous Filene's basement sale); but, on the other hand, one needs many friends and acquaintances for the sake of *blat*. For sheer economic reasons the line between one's friends and the rest would tend to be sharper than in a nondisequilibrium economy. These and other consequences of the economic arrangements, one should think, would color people's assessment of the society they live in, influence their degree of acceptance of deviant economic behavior, and probably affect their notions of the legitimacy of the political regime.

Again the economist has his own explanations to offer. He might point to the disequilibrium economy and the repressed inflation and, beyond that, to the history of Soviet industrialization under extreme pressure and in great haste. It would surely be excessive to argue that the Soviet preference for administrative handling of shortages as against their resolution by a market mechanism—say, for repressed as against open inflation (which in the event has been occurring, nonetheless)—is entirely motivated by the Soviet vision of the good society. Other considerations—power preservationist, pragmatic, self-serving—have played their roles as well. The fact remains that the micro disequilibriums attendant upon the administrative handling of shortages, in conjunction with the ease with which state property is misappropriated, gave an enormous boost to informal and illegal private gain, with numerous unintended effects on the building of the new man and the new society.

The émigré author of a recently published powerful novel about the Soviet economic underground puts it well in the words of one of the story's protagonists:

> Capital! It used to exist in this country (Russia). It has survived. Human nature, forced into marriage with the socialist economy, gave birth to giant enterprises and puny personal income. But from its covert cohabitation with private enterprise there were born tiny enterprises and huge incomes.[7]

Second, in the U.S.S.R., the basis of much of this illicit wealth is private appropriation of state-owned materials, equipment, and time.

12.5

Under Marxism more orthodox than Lenin's and Stalin's there would be no industrialization spurt following a proletarian revolution, in Russia or anywhere. The construction of a socialist society would not proceed simultaneously with the building up of a modern industrial plant. Whatever further accumulation and industrialization might occur after the revolution would hardly qualify as a spurt or a drive. It was of course Lenin's contribution to Marxism to envision the opposite historical sequence, a proletarian revolution under conditions of relative backwardness *preceding* the industrial maturation of the country, and it was Stalin's contribution to Leninism to turn the industrialization spurt under conditions of backwardness into a super-spurt, with correspondingly extreme policies, institutions, and effects.

Nonetheless, a Stalinist industrialization drive after the revolution, a prodigious effort at capital accumulation even while constructing a socialist society, could hardly preserve all the characteristics of its capitalist cousins.

It could scarcely rely on the institutions of private property and private enterprise; it had to be based on state ownership of means of production (or at least quasi-state ownership as in the case of the collective farms). State property was to be sacred, inviolable, untouchable by greedy hands. To be sure, society would employ material incentives to elicit compliance from the as yet not fully socially conscious and committed masses: but did not Marx himself stress in *Critique of the Gotha Program* that under socialism distribution to producers would be "to each according to his labor," according to his contribution to society's total product, and not, as ultimately under communism, "according to need" regardless of one's labor contribution? Other forms of income might be allowed for social reasons, but labor earnings would enjoy the highest honor and security.

Under Soviet socialism, we have been told, there can be no exploitation of man by man, the characteristic mark of all previous societal stages. There are no so-called antagonistic classes, and, although the workers and the peasants are still separate classes, their interests are not irreconcilable and their conflicts are not "antagonistic." In any case the disappearance of the peasantry as a class is to be only a matter of time and from the morrow of the revolution on society moves toward its ultimate classless form under communism. While the resort to material incentives necessarily means some inequality of earnings and personal possessions, the postrevolutionary society will not tolerate undue inequality of material condition. Personal wealth would be no more than accumulated savings from labor earnings, therefore neither unacceptably large in individual cases nor unjustified on moral grounds. The new savings banks were characteristically entitled "labor savings banks." Wealth obtained from income other than labor earnings may be subject to confiscation in some circumstances.

These norms of morality are of course those of man the good socialist producer; they are part of a would-be classless production ethic. The good Soviet producer is disciplined and eagerly productive at work, mindful not only of the pay envelope at the end of the week and the pension at the end of his working life but also of his unique role in advancing the march of history toward the inevitable good society. He stands as a political inspiration, a beacon of hope to the less fortunate workers still unliberated from the shackles of capitalism.

The production ethic extends from the work place to leisure time, dictating socialist realism in literature and art and Victorian prudery in sexual comportment. The Soviet man is to be honest, law abiding, and sober—sober literally as well as figuratively—at work and at play. Naturally, there would be no distinction of status and condition in this society of toilers, except in the case of those few who have mastered the laws of history and have fully committed themselves to their speedy realization, that is to say, the members of the Communist Party who would provide leadership while shouldering especial burdens of responsibility.

Such then has been the vision of the virtuous society in full swing of industrialization and socialist construction, and the policies and institutions of the industrialization drive had to fit within the options permitted by the official norms of morality. It was a tall order. Earlier societies gripped by a production ethic had it easier. Classical capitalism, whatever that was, did not have to combat private acquisitiveness or proscribe nonlabor incomes; it hailed them and harnessed them for its own historic task.

An interesting parallel instance is to be found in American history. The Mormon state in Utah between 1847 and 1890—small in numbers but large in geographic extent and communal aspiration—was an early modern instance of a society committed simultaneously to speedy industrialization (in part for the sake of economic autarky and military security) and total social transformation. It anticipated many of the Soviet economic institutions by nearly a century: a central planning board, development plans, centralization of much of the economy's economic surplus in the hands of the state (or rather the church), an authoritarian policy in a hostile encirclement, and unflinching belief in modern technology and education, church ownership and management of many of the most important means of production, large public investment in infrastructure, central control of external trade, and so forth. The dividing line between the Church and the polity was thin, thinner even than that between Party and government in the Soviet Union. In its organization and functions the Church bears many parallels with the Soviet Party. Mormon society had, as it still has today under very different arrangements, a highly pronounced production ethic. It maintained a *virtuous* social order. It was in many ways successful economically, as its chief economic historian, Leonard J. Arrington, amply documents.[8] If it perished as a territorially based, distinctive, integral economic system, this was by dint of the onward march of the encircling forces, the expanding United States. The strength of its experiment lay, first, in remarkably able leadership with great organizational talent; second, in that its human element, at least in two generations in question, was largely self-chosen and inwardly committed to the system; and, third, in its genius for combining seemingly disparate institutions into a functioning whole. For the system was a mixed one, with a large nationalized ("ecclesiasticized") sector but with full-blown capitalism in the rest of the economy. Material incentive did not stop with labor earnings. Making money was highly approved of by the church, which frequently tapped the privately accumulated fortunes for communal purposes. It is interesting to note that its other major experiment, that of communal farms, failed for lack of labor incentive.

In its own effort to industrialize and build simultaneously a virtuous social order, the U.S.S.R. has been at some disadvantage compared to the Mormons. The Soviet public was, so to speak, drafted and not self-selected for the millenarian experiment. The attempt by the Soviets to harness private interest through deliberately structured material incentives has been less than a full success. To begin with, a fundamental difficulty resides in that the controlled and basically nonfunctional price structure defies attempts to link creatively individual rewards to socially meaningful objectives. Worse still is the use of physical targets. Local success indicators are thus insufficiently congruent with social goals. Every man his own eager and gainful sub-optimizer! The rewards are, as likely as not, paid for antisocial behavior.

12.6

We do not know to what extent the Mormon Church in the last century was successful in protecting its property from grasping private hands. There is little doubt that the Soviet state has had the greatest difficulty in exercizing proper custody over its own. It is on this score that the Soviet moral (not to say criminal) code is most frequently tested and, by all indications, appears to be of little practical effect. In general, the safety of organization's assets from internal pilferage and embezzlement seems to be inversely related to the size of the organization. The Soviet state is a very large organization. What is more, it has to safeguard its assets in an environment of widespread shortages, pervasive cynicism, and a great deal of illegal economic activity in general. In a word, the state is being stolen blind, and not surprisingly the chief thieves are the custodians. Much underground activity, and especially of the large-scale operations of this type, rests on large-scale misappropriation of state property and takes place behind a facade of legitimate state-owned or other socialist entities, a crime that Soviet law qualifies as "private enterprise." (It is curious that in the U.S.S.R. today the official juridicial definition of private enterprise is the use of *state* property to conduct an organized operation for private profit.)

To restore socialist moral norms to their rightful place is not an easy matter in the Soviet Union today. One very traditional Soviet approach is what Leon Lipson, a perceptive student of Soviet law, has called "coercion to virtue."[9] The phrase speaks for itself—and so does the historical record. The other traditional approach, appeals to ideological symbols, exhortation, and the like, are hardly the solution either. If the Chinese and the Cubans have largely failed in this regard, why should the Soviets succeed sixty years after *their* revolution?

There are of course various legal devices to enhance the safety of state-owned property, but their effects are not always predictable.

An illustration can be found in a relatively little-known institution in Soviet law. In Russian it bears the name *material'no otvetstvennoe litso*, which may be translated as "financially liable person" (FLP). Now *any* state employee can be held administratively and sometimes criminally liable for damage to or loss of the physical or monetary assets of his employing organization or enterprise. (Naturally, third parties may be liable under law as well.) But, given the extreme difficulty of safeguarding the state's property, Soviet law provides for a *contractual* agreement between the individual and his employing organization (firm), whereby the individual undertakes full responsibility for the integrity of the organization's (the state's) assets in his custody, and is *personally* liable to the *full* extent and value of any damage or loss. Admittedly, to be so liable the individual must be guilty of wrongdoing, but the burden of proof of lack of guilt is on *him*. There is no presumption of his innocence, no onus of proof of guilt on the state. On this point the law is explicit. Should it come to that, the person must make good to the state out of his *own* pocket; his salary is docked as long as necessary, and his personal property may be confiscated. Such then are the financially liable persons in Soviet law and business practice.[10]

This institution is not without parallel in our own practice. Employees such as bank tellers or cashiers in retail establishments frequently bear a similar kind and measure of liability without the benefit of a presumption of innocence. But it is not unusual in this country for such individuals to be covered by an indemnity bond, and the premium for the bonding may even be paid by the employer. Moreover rules of this degree of strictness apply in this country almost exclusively to handlers of cash. In the Soviet Union the described arrangements may pertain to all those having custody of any kind of state property, and there are no indemnity bonds (another indication of the limited autonomy of the Soviet firm).

Except in certain special cases provided by law, one becomes a financially liable person with reference to a particular set of the state's assets by entering into a written agreement with one's employer, the agreement incorporating an inventory list duly taken for the purpose. Before one can be discharged of the responsibility, or if there is suspicion of loss, another inventory is taken. Should a shortage be revealed in this manner, the financially liable person must make good out of his own pocket, as mentioned. (Incidentally, the mystery of the high proportion of Soviet retail establishments that are at any moment closed for inventory seems to be explainable in these terms.)

One should remember that in the U.S.S.R. state-owned goods of almost any description are close to fair game for anyone able to help himself to them. Consequently, the chance of loss or damage is often great, and hence the financially liable person's own risk is not trifling matter. Yet it should also be noted that at least in ordinary Soviet business practice the individual is not compelled to undertake the risk, he is free to choose whether to assume it. To be sure, refusal to assume the risk may impair one's career in the given organization and possibly even one's immediate earnings; it may also preclude other major benefits, as we shall see. Still, so far as we know, typically the individual is free to choose.

One might ask why anyone *would* choose to serve in this capacity when the risk is so great. Yet there must be millions of people who do. Taking together business (broadly understood in the American sense), agriculture, finance, education, and health care, there are today just about two million establishments. Although many of them may be quite small, each probably has at least one financially liable person, and many have several; the larger establishments may each have many. In addition there must be many more in general government, military units, and so on.

Now a high proportion of the financially liable persons may not in fact incur excessive personal risk, either because the value of property in the individual's custody is modest or because the assets are secure, or for whatever reason.

But many do bear considerable risk, which is of course the state's object. At least in a certain fraction of these cases an interesting psychological transformation seems to have taken place, which helps explain the willingness of individuals to bear the risks. I owe this hypothesis to a number of interviews with recent émigrés who themselves were financially liable persons in the U.S.S.R.

The psychological chain runs as follows. If one is a residual bearer of the unexpected losses of a given state-owned firm, it is not unnatural for one to think of oneself as also the residual beneficiary of the unofficial profits, if any. The next step is to work actively for unplanned, unreported profits, in order to compensate oneself for the risk of personal loss, and the step after that is to work actively for profits, period. A residual bearer of both losses and profits is, after all, the *de facto* owner of the firm in the usufructuary sense. Thus the managers of such firms, who are also the financially liable persons, have come to think of "their" firms as virtually their private possessions, as their crypto property. "The state gets its plan, and everything else goes to me."

The individual may even invest his own money in the firm—the state-owned firm—as in a particular instance in which the manager of a retail store purchased on his own account, at high price on the black market, several cash registers of foreign make ("the Soviet ones are worthless") in order to minimize embezzlement by his cashiers from the store, which now meant from *him*. In a sense the institution of the FLP works as intended; the manager indeed is eager to safeguard the state's money—though in his capacity as residual loss bearer it is really his money, or his profit, he is protecting.

The illicit profit can be very large. Such data as I have so far collected point to gross illicit profits that in some cases are large multiples of the manager's official (legal) income. No wonder that in such cases the individual is prepared to sign the financial liability agreement, indeed eagerly seeks it for it is his status of FLP that delivers the assets—and the profit opportunities—to his charge.

The story does not end here of course. The manager has to share his profits with very many others: his accountant, an indispensable cog in the machine, his hierarchical administrative superiors, and a whole gamut of suppliers (crucial in a seller's market), transporters, and so on. Then there are the inevitable bribes to the innumerable authorities, large and small, from the big local party boss to the fire inspector, any one of whom can stop the money machine. In my interviews the larger operators indicated that 70 to 80 percent of their gross profit went into bribes, though what was left was still more than sunflower seed.

Thus the moral is that a stern device, the institution of FLP, meant to safeguard the state's socialist property has also contributed to the sprouting of thousands of crypto-private operations, large and small but all illegal. Through them it has advanced the corruption of the structure of power and authority. It has indeed helped to strengthen the custodianship of physical and monetary assets, though as the crypto property of the individual residual beneficiaries as well as state property.

12.7

The twentieth century is strewn with social experiments of every ilk and hue, many of them falling into the "virtuous haste" category. The Soviet is not the least of these. Many others are also communist.

In his "Development vs. Utopia" Lowenthal finds, "The existence of a long-term trend toward the victory of modernization over utopianism: as Communist-governed developing societies approach the level of advanced industrial societies, the arbitrary reshaping of their social structure by ideologically guided political power ... becomes increasingly difficult and ultimately impossible." A major reason is the rigidification of the power structure: the "movement regime ... turns into an essentially conservative bureaucracy which is bound to affect its institutional structure as well."[11] The thrust of this chapter is surely in harmony with Lowenthal's conclusion. Specifically, the attempt to combine haste in industrialization with virtue in social arrangements in the course of the Soviet experiment has in a sense succeeded to turn both into their own opposites: haste into waste, leading ultimately to a sharp retardation of growth despite the still very high rate of investment out of GNP, and the virtuous society into one with an inequitable and dysfunctional distribution of material income, private wealth, opportunities, and power.

In evaluating and re-evaluating the Soviet record, and in playing their counterfactual games, historians will long continue to refer to the formative decade of the Soviet Union, for the proper understanding of which Alexander Erlich has made a seminal contribution in his masterful analysis of the *Soviet Industrialization Debate*.

Notes

These observations, humbly offered in personal homage to Alexander Erlich and in deep admiration of his work on the political economy of Soviet history, are a revised version of the Bernard Moses Memorial Lecture (in social science) read on the Berkeley campus of the University of California in May 1980. I am grateful to a number of my Berkeley colleagues for valuable comments.

1. Francis Seton in a comment on Michael Polanyi's Towards a theory of conspicuous production, *Soviet Survey*, no. 34 (October–December. 1960), p. 107; interpolation in square brackets added.

2. See his *Economic Backwardness in Historical Perspective: A Book of Essays* (Cambridge, Mass.: Harvard University Press, 1962), *passim*.

3. The idea actually goes much further back, at least to Dmitrii Ivanovich Mendeleev, the Russian chemist and prolific writer on politico economic subjects, who in 1899 proposed to catch up with American industrial output in twenty to thirty years. D. I. Mendeleev, Zavetnye mysli, *Sochineniia*, vol. 20, p. 280. Here cited from Leon Smolinski, Recent changes in long-range future image of the Soviet economy, processed, June 1977, p. 6.

4. A set of reformlike measures was promulgated in July 1979, which appears to be as unpromising as it is timid and internally inconsistent.

5. Richard Lowenthal, Development vs. utopia in communist policy, in Chalmers Johnson, ed., *Change in Communist Systems* (Stanford, Calif.: Stanford University Press, 1970), pp. 33–116.

6. At times the tendency of different social science disciplines to instinctively look for different causes may border on the humorous. When in 1971 there were street disturbances in Zagreb, ostensibly over the allegedly unfair division of hard-currency proceeds among Yugoslavia's republics, my political science friends were shaking their heads and saying "traditional Croatian nationalism is on the rise again!" But some of my economist friends were patting themselves on the shoulder and saying, "We told you so, the exchange rate of the dinar has been wrong!" The economists were right, too, of course, for, had the external value of the dinar been in equilibrium, the question of the fair division of foreign exchange proceeds could have never even arisen.

7. Nelli Gutina, *Dvoinoe dno* ("*The double bottom*") (Tel Aviv: KANE, 1978), p. 8.

8. Leonard J. Arrington, *The Great Basin Kingdom: An Economic History of the Latter-Day Saints, 1830–1900* (Cambridge, Mass. Harvard University Press, 1958), is the major work in the Mormon theocratic economy.

9. See his Coercion to virtue: First principles and second economy, in Gregory Grossman, ed., *Studies in the Second Economy of Communist Countries*, forthcoming.

10. The Soviet legal literature on this subject is quite voluminous. See, for example, IU. N. Korshunov et al., *Sovetskoe zakonodatel'stvo o trude* ("*Soviet Labor Legislation*") (Moscow: Profiszdat, 1976), Chap. 8.

11. Lowenthal, Development vs. utopia, p. 54.

13 Culture, Social Structure, and Fertility in the U.S.S.R

Joseph S. Berliner

The reproductive behavior of Soviet families is characterized by wide differences among nationalities. In general terms differences in social behavior may be explained by two sets of factors. One set consists of differences that are internal to people. In the language of sociology and anthropology they are called cultural values. In the language of economics they are called tastes or preferences. The other set consists of external circumstances, which may be physical, like climate, or social, like income or class. People may therefore behave differently for one of three reasons; their tastes may be the same but their circumstances may differ; their circumstances may be the same but their tastes may differ; or both their tastes and their circumstances may differ.

Much of the variation in the reproductive behavior of the Soviet nationalities is undoubtedly the consequence of culturally determined differences in tastes. But the various nationality groups also live under different social circumstances, and some portion of the differences in fertility may be explained by the differences in those circumstances. The purpose of this chapter is to assess the extent to which fertility differences may be explained by differences in social circumstances.

The question is important for practical reasons—for evaluating the impact on fertility of governmental social and economic policies, for example. But it also has a certain theoretical interest. Differences in tastes are normally difficult or impossible to observe directly. Hence their influence is usually regarded as part of an unexplained residual. For example, that portion of differences in consumer behavior that cannot be explained by differences in external circumstances (incomes and prices in this case) is normally interpreted as reflecting differences in tastes. There is no independent basis for believing that the tastes of those consumers do in fact differ, other than that differences in their behavior persist even under putatively similar external circumstances. In culture, however, we have a strong

Table 13.1
Fertility by republic and nationality, U.S.S.R., 1972 to 1973

Nationality or republic	Total fertility rate, by republic[a]	Intended fertility, by nationality[b]	Number of children per thousand mothers: Republic average	Low-education rural mothers	High-education urban mothers
	(1)	(2)	(3)	(4)	(5)
Russian	2.02	2.00	1,801	2,269	1,433
Ukrainian	2.08	2.08	1,684	1,887	1,432
Belorussian	2.28	2.31	1,919	2,136	1,554
Uzbek	5.67	6.26	3,300	3,903	1,887
Kazakh	3.32	5.01	2,495	3,125	1,670
Georgian	2.57	2.83	2,177	2,554	1,729
Azerbaidzhani	4.13	4.89	3,271	3,989	2,064
Lithuanian	2.42	2.23	1,838	2,089	1,518
Moldavian	2.63	2.62	2,231	2,656	1,456
Latvian	1.99	1.99	1,546	1,771	1,392
Kirghiz	4.89	6.04	2,851	3,399	1,734
Tadzhik	6.07	5.97	3,381	4,023	1,819
Armenian	3.07	3.42	2,950	3,615	2,124
Turkmen	5.87	5.93	3,289	3,776	1,837
Estonian	2.15	2.18	1,572	1,726	1,461
Mean (unweighted)	3.41	3.71	2,417	2,861.2	1,674
Standard deviation	1.51	1.73	691.3	866.3	236.3

Table 13.1 (continued)

Nationality or republic	Total fertility rate, by republic[a]	Intended fertility, by nationality[b]	Number of children per thousand mothers: Republic average	Low-education rural mothers	High-education urban mothers
Coefficient of variation	0.44	0.47	0.29	0.30	0.14

Sources: Column 1 calculated from *Vestnik Statistiki*, no. 12 (1974), p. 88, table 8; column 2, V. A. Belova et al., *Skol'ko detei budet v sovetskoi sem'e* (Moscow, *Statistika*, 1977), p. 23; columns 3–5, appendix table A13.1.

[a] The total fertility rate is the number of children a woman would bear in her lifetime if her fertility corresponded to the average age-specific fertility rates of women in the years 1972 and 1973.

[b] Intended fertility is the response to the question, How many children do you intend to have?

independent basis for classifying people according to tastes, for one of the central features of culture is the acquisition of values and tastes. Hence in classifying people as Russians or Uzbeks, we can be fairly confident that they have been classified directly by taste difference, and we can be more secure in the judgment that such differences in behavior that remain when external circumstances are the same are a measure of the influence of taste differences. Culture is thus a useful concept for studying the relative influence on behavior of tastes and of external circumstances.

Soviet governmental data are normally published by republic rather than by nationality, as in table 13.1, column 1. Since all the republics are multinational in various degrees, those data are imperfect measures of nationality differences. Special survey research studies do appear from time to time, however, in which the basis of classification is nationality, usually that of the mother. The results of one such large-scale study is presented in column 2 (Belova 1977). The numbers, however, represent intended rather than actual fertility; they are responses to the survey question, How many children do you intend to have?

Both sets of data are deficient as measures of nationality differences in fertility. The republic data employ a good behavioral measure of fertility—the total fertility rate; but the republic is too heterogenous with respect to nationality composition. The nationality data are homogeneous in that respect, but they reflect intentions rather than actual fertility. There is little reason to expect, however, that a better set of data—a behavioral measure based on nationality—would tell a very different story. The rank order of nationalities might be slightly different, but the data would very likely be consistent with the general finding of sharp nationality differences in fertility.

Most of the public discussion of the nationality differences in fertility focuses on differences in cultural values as the primary source of fertility differences; Uzbeks presumably place a higher value on large families than Russians. But Uzbeks differ from Russians in respects other than culture. They differ in levels of income, in levels of education, in extent of urbanization and industrialization, and in other respects. Such differences in what may broadly be called social structure also contribute to differences in fertility. The survey research study reported in Belova (1977), for example, found that in all nationalities rural women expected to have more children than urban, urban women in larger cities expected fewer children than urban women in smaller cities, and so forth (Belova 1977, p. 75). The study examined the effect of a variety of other factors such as women's education and family income, but those results are not analyzed by nationality. Since Soviet published research rarely provides nationality data with two or more variables crossclassified, analysts are usually unable to examine the effect on nationality fertility differentials of more than one variable at a time. Because of that limitation the effect of cultural values on fertility cannot be assessed from nationalitywide data. The difference between Uzbeks with given residence and education characteristics, and Russians or others with the same characteristics, may be larger or smaller than that in columns 1 and 2.

The 1970 Soviet census of population published one tabulation, however, that offers an unusual opportunity to explore the joint effects on reproductive behavior of several variables of social structure. The tabulation presents a measure of fertility crossclassified by three variables: republic, mother's education level, and urban or rural residence. A portion of the data is presented in columns 3 to 5 in table 13.1; the complete data may be found in table 13.2. Unfortunately the measure of fertility is not the same as that in either columns 1 or 2. It is the child/mother ratio, expressed as the number of children per thousand mothers. The limitations of that measure are discussed later. For the present, however, what is of interest is the relation between the republicwide data in column 3 and data for the two subgroups in columns 4 and 5. The mean of the republic data is 2,417 children per thousand mothers. The corresponding figure for low-education rural mothers is substantially higher, 2,861.2; and for high-education urban mothers it is considerably lower, 1,674.

As conjectured earlier, the variation among low-education rural mothers in the several republics is over twice that among high-education urban mothers; the coefficients of variation are 0.30 and 0.14. If we could in addition control for other social characteristics like income and female labor participation, it is conceivable in principle that differences in reproductive behavior among republics and nationalities could be larger than those in table 13.1; or as is more likely, the differences could be very small and possibly disappear.

The 1970 census data are the basis of our effort in this chapter to assess the relative impact of culture and social structure on reproductive behavior. Before proceeding to the analysis, the data will be described and discussed.

13.1 The Data

The data are derived from an enumeration of all Soviet mothers who had children living with them on the census date, January 15, 1970 (*Itogy*, vol. 7, table 27). The groups of mothers are homogeneous with respect to three characteristics: the republic in which they lived, the mother's education level, and urban or rural residence. Since there are fifteen republics, four

Table 13.2
Number of children per thousand mothers in the U.S.S.R., by republic, education of mother, and residence, 1970

	Urban				Rural			
	ED4	ED3	ED2	ED1	ED4	ED3	ED2	ED1
Russia	1,433	1,421	1,654	1,734	1,726	1,784	2,155	2,269
Ukraine	1,432	1,439	1,646	1,617	1,626	1,672	1,911	1,877
Belorussia	1,554	1,542	1,775	1,795	1,821	1,916	2,193	2,136
Uzbekistan	1,887	2,276	2,650	2,972	2,819	3,124	3,983	3,903
Kazakhstan	1,670	1,768	2,088	2,380	2,232	2,633	2,989	3,125
Georgia	1,729	1,862	2,053	2,032	2,044	2,249	2,574	2,554
Azerbaidzhan	2,064	2,334	2,786	3,091	3,141	3,378	4,182	3,989
Lithuania	1,518	1,502	1,675	1,759	1,654	1,759	1,939	2,089
Moldavia	1,456	1,446	1,695	2,074	1,677	1,707	2,159	2,656
Latvia	1,392	1,374	1,490	1,466	1,579	1,586	1,778	1,771
Kirghizia	1,734	1,855	2,232	2,609	2,430	2,730	3,492	3,399
Tadzhikistan	1,819	2,081	2,628	3,224	2,793	2,912	3,960	4,023
Armenia	2,124	2,441	2,777	2,815	2,747	3,009	3,591	3,615
Turkmenistan	1,837	2,264	3,009	3,113	2,949	3,158	4,323	3,776
Estonia	1,461	1,398	1,533	1,514	1,699	1,588	1,889	1,726

Source: TsSU, *Itogy . . . 1970 goda*, vol. 7, table 37, pp. 452–453.

education levels and two residence categories, the number of groups is 120 (that is, 15 × 4 × 2). For each group the mean fertility is recorded; the measure is number of children per thousand mothers. The census does not define the term "children," but from the other publications it may be inferred that it refers to children who have not attained their sixteenth birthday.[1]

The census defines urban residents as those living in localities that are legally defined as cities or urban-type settlements. (TsSU, *Itogy*, vol. 1, p. 5). In the Russian republic a city is defined as a locality with at least 12,000 people and in which at least 85 percent of the population are families of workers or employees. An urban-type settlement is a locality with at least 3,000 people and in which at least 85 percent of the population are families of workers and employees (*Naselenie*, p. 51).

The top of the four education levels is "higher and specialized secondary education" (ED4). It includes (1) those who have graduated from a specialized secondary school like a *tekhnikum*, and (2) those with a partial or complete higher education. The second level, called "general secondary education" (ED3), includes graduates of a nontechnical secondary school with a tenth or eleventh year of instruction. The third level, "incomplete secondary education" (ED2), includes (1) graduates of a middle school, and (2) those who attended one or more years of a secondary school but did not complete it.[2] The lowest level, "primary education or less" (ED1), includes (1) those who have completed the three years of primary school or less, and (2) those who have attended some years of middle school but had not graduated.

The number of mothers in each group is not published, but the census data do permit an estimate of the number of women aged 20 to 54 in each observation group as presented in table 13.3. The summary figures are as follows:

	Urban	Rural
Russia	60.7	47.9
Ukraine	19.4	22.9
Others	19.9	29.2
Total (%)	100.0	100.0
ED4	26.6	15.9
ED3	21.4	8.7
ED2	29.0	27.7
ED1	23.0	47.7
Total (%)	100.0	100.0

Table 13.3
Numbers of women aged 20 to 54 in the U.S.S.R., by republic, education, and residence, 1970 (in thousands and percentages)

	Urban					Rural				
Republic	Total	ED4	ED3	ED2	ED1	Total	ED4	ED3	ED2	ED1
Russia	21,744.6	5,744.1	3,707.6	6,828.6	5,464.5	10,666.1	1,262.3	724.0	2,912.9	5,766.9
	(100)	(26.4)	(17.1)	(31.4)	(25.1)	(100)	(11.8)	(16.8)	(27.3)	(54.1)
Ukraine	6,926.9	1,796.6	1,619.9	1,981.5	1,528.9	5,105.7	444.5	457.3	1,423.7	2,780.2
	(100)	(25.9)	(23.4)	28.6)	(22.1)	(100)	(8.7)	(9.0)	(27.9)	(54.5)
Belorussia	1,064.2	298.8	236.9	298.0	230.5	1,106.4	106.2	77.9	225.7	696.6
	(100)	(28.1)	(22.3)	(28.0)	(21.7)	(100)	(9.6)	(7.0)	(20.4)	(63.0)
Uzbekistan	928.8	237.3	170.2	244.1	277.2	1,143.9	57.8	143.8	381.2	561.1
	(100)	(25.4)	(18.3)	(26.3)	(29.8)	(100)	(5.1)	(12.6)	(33.3)	(49.1)
Kazakhstan	1,559.1	383.7	258.7	475.8	440.9	1,190.9	129.8	119.5	331.5	610.1
	(100)	(24.6)	(16.6)	(30.5)	(28.3)	(100)	(13.9)	(10.0)	(27.8)	(51.2)
Georgia	594.4	196.2	207.7	94.3	96.2	532.3	73.3	118.4	121.6	219.0
	(100)	(33.0)	(34.9)	(15.9)	(16.2)	(100)	(13.8)	(22.2)	(22.8)	(41.1)
Azerbaidzhan	550.1	137.4	121.0	130.1	161.6	400.8	22.5	37.0	118.9	222.4
	(100)	(25.0)	(22.0)	(23.7)	(29.4)	(100)	(5.6)	(9.2)	(29.7)	(55.5)
Lithuania	431.4	111.5	71.6	105.6	142.7	335.6	31.5	14.3	49.7	240.1
	(100)	(25.9)	(16.6)	(24.5)	(33.1)	(100)	(9.4)	(4.3)	(14.8)	(71.5)
Moldavia	300.6	82.9	55.3	74.2	88.2	551.7	38.1	23.7	121.1	368.8
	(100)	(27.6)	(18.4)	(24.7)	(29.3)	(100)	(6.9)	(4.3)	(22.0)	(66.9)
Latvia	413.2	118.2	86.9	112.5	95.6	194.7	27.3	15.6	59.1	92.7
	(100)	(28.6)	(21.0)	(27.3)	(23.1)	(100)	(14.0)	(8.0)	(30.4)	(47.6)
Kirghizia	258.4	69.4	46.3	71.1	71.6	304.2	29.0	33.5	88.4	153.3
	(100)	(26.9)	(17.9)	(27.2)	(27.7)	(100)	(9.5)	(11.0)	(29.1)	(50.4)

Table 13.3 (continued)

	Urban					Rural				
Republic	Total	ED4	ED3	ED2	ED1	Total	ED4	ED3	ED2	ED1
Tadzhikistan	227.2	51.0	53.0	61.0	82.2	280.6	7.2	24.4	85.1	163.9
	(100)	(22.5)	(14.5)	(26.9)	(36.2)	(100)	(2.6)	(8.7)	(30.3)	(58.4)
Armenia	333.5	89.3	108.2	65.2	70.8	174.3	13.6	27.0	48.8	84.9
	(100)	(26.8)	(32.4)	(19.6)	(21.2)	(100)	(7.8)	(15.5)	(28.0)	(48.7)
Turkmenia	212.2	46.5	30.8	64.8	70.1	173.8	5.7	20.6	72.5	75.0
	(100)	(21.9)	(14.5)	(30.5)	(33.0)	(100)	(3.3)	(11.9)	(41.7)	(43.2)
Estonia	242.5	64.4	51.9	70.4	55.8	101.6	16.2	8.8	28.1	48.5
	(100)	(26.6)	(21.4)	(29.0)	(23.0)	(100)	(15.9)	(8.7)	(27.7)	(47.7)
Totals	35,787.3	9,427.3	6,806.0	10,677.2	8,876.8	22,262.6	2,265.0	1,845.0	6,008.3	12,083.5
	(100)	(26.3)	(19.0)	(29.8)	(24.8)	(100)	(10.2)	(8.3)	(27.0)	(54.3)

Source: TsSU, *Itogy . . . 1970 goda*, vol. 3, table 1.
Note: Percentages given in parentheses.

The numbers of women aged 20 to 54 provide only a rough approximation of the numbers of mothers, but they are useful for orders of magnitude. Russian-republic women predominate, and the two largest republics account for 80.1 and 70.8 percent of all urban and rural women aged 20 to 54. Somewhat surprising is the large proportion of women in the highest-education category, ED4. However, because of the negative relation between education and fertility, the proportion of mothers with ED4 is probably smaller than the proportion of women with ED4. Moreover the ED4 category includes not only graduates of higher-education institutions but also those who completed more than half of a higher-education program, as well as a large group of graduates of specialized secondary schools. If the fertility and economic behavior of those three subgroups of women differs, as it well may, we are unfortunately not able to capture the difference in our analysis. The lowest-education level (ED1) is similarly heterogeneous, ranging from women with virtually no schooling at all up to women who were one year short of completing middle school. The Moslem republics generally have smaller percentages than the average in the urban and higher-education categories.

As a measure of reproductive behavior the number of children per thousand mothers is deficient for our purposes in several important respects. First, it does not represent completed fertility, since the average age of the mothers varies among the 120 groups. To control for differences in average age, we estimated the probable completed fertility of the mothers in each of the groups and ran a number of the regressions using the estimated data. The results, however, did not differ in any substantial respects from the regressions based on the census data. Second, the data exclude women with no children, both married and unmarried. Third, children aged sixteen and over are excluded. Finally, fourth, children who had died are not accounted for.

The effect of the last three deficiencies is to understate the magnitude of fertility differences among republics; in table 13.1 the mean total fertility rate is 3.41 children per woman (column 1) while the mean child/mother ratio is 2.417 children per mother (column 3). The corresponding coefficients of variation are 0.44 and 0.29. Nevertheless, the two measures move very closely together. The correlation coefficient is 0.92, and the rank order of the republics is highly similar.[3] The results reported here ought therefore to be broadly consistent with what we might find had a more suitable measure of fertility been available.

13.2 Aggregate Effects of Education, Residence, and Republic

The 1970 census data broadly follow the expected patterns. Rural fertility uniformly exceeds urban fertility in all republics and education levels. Fertility generally declines with increasing education, although there are some exceptions. The ranking of republics by fertility is for the most part the same for the eight education/residence groups.

Although all three variables influence fertility systematically if not uniformly, the interesting question is the relative influence of the three. The question may be posed in the following way: To what extent is the difference in the mean fertility of these 120 groups of mothers due to differences in their education level and their place of residence, rather than to the different characteristics of the republic in which they reside? To provide a basis for answering that question, the fertility data were regressed on those variables.[4] Each of the three is represented as a dummy variable; two levels for residence—urban (URB) and rural (RUR); four levels for education; and fifteen levels for republic.[5] The results are presented in table 13.4.

The regression coefficients in column 1 are to be read as fertility differences between a given observation group and the group that was arbitrarily selected as the base, namely, the group of rural women in the Russian republic with elementary education or less. The regression constant, 2,375.5, is the estimate of the fertility (average number of childen per thousand mothers) in that base group. The coefficients in column 1 are the amounts by which fertility increases or decreases for mothers in the 119 other groups. Thus a mother who had completed higher education (ED4) and lived in a city (URB) in the Georgian republic had an estimated fertility of 2,375.5 − 635.2 (for ED4) − 602.8 (for URB) + 365.1 (for Georgia) = 1,502.6; R^2 is 0.895 signifying that 89.5 percent of the variation in the census fertility data is explained statistically by the three variables.[6]

The figures in column 3 and 4 represent the percentages of the total variation in fertility accounted for by each of the variables in the order in which they enter the equation. ED4 alone accounts for 6.7 percent of the variation, and the education variable overall accounts for 13.1 percent. Urban residence accounts for 16.5 percent, and the republic variable overall accounts for about 60 percent.[7]

Education and residence reflect the influence of social structure, in the sense that people who share the same culture may be expected to behave differently according to whether they live in a city or a village or have more or less education. In those terms these two variables of social structure account for about 30 percent of the variation in the fertility means of the 120

Table 13.4
Aggregate effects of education, residence, and republic on fertility

Dependent variable: fertility (mean = 2,268.1)[a]
Intercept: 2,375.5

Independent variables	Coefficient	*t*-ratio	Percentage of total variation explained[b]		
			Type I SS		Type IV SS
	(1)	(2)	(3)	(4)	(5)
Education					
ED4	−635.2	(−9.3)	6.7		9.1
ED3	−496.5	(−7.3)	6.3		5.6
ED2	−76.5	(−1.1)	0.1		0.1
Subtotal				13.1	
Residence					
URB	−602.8	(−12.6)	16.5	16.5	16.5
Republic					
Ukraine	−119.5	(−0.9)	4.9		0.1
Belorussia	69.5	(0.5)	2.9		—
Uzbekistan	1,179.8	(9.0)	4.8		8.4
Kazakhstan	588.6	(4.5)	0.1		2.1
Georgia	365.1	(2.8)	0.3		0.8
Azerbaidzhan	1,348.6	(10.3)	8.9		11.0
Lithuania	−35.1	(−0.3)	3.1		—
Moldavia	86.8	(0.7)	2.4		0.1
Latvia	−217.5	(−1.7)	8.6		0.3
Kirghizia	788.1	(6.0)	0.1		3.7
Tadzhikistan	1,158.0	(8.8)	3.5		8.1
Armenia	1,117.9	(8.5)	5.1		7.5
Turkmenia	1,281.6	(9.7)	15.0		9.9
Estonia	−171.0	(−1.3)	0.2		0.2
Subtotal				59.9	
Total explained variation			89.5	89.5	

[a] Number of children per thousand mothers.
[b] Type I SS refers to the incremental sum of squares; the amount by which the explained variation increases as each variable is added in the order in which it appears in the table. Type IV SS measures the amount by which the explained sum of squares increases if that variable enters last.

groups of mothers. It is very likely, however, that some portion of the 60 percent accounted for by republic is due to other variables of social structure and the remainder by nationality-based differences in culture. As a preliminary statement we may regard the figure of 60 percent as the upper limit of the influence of culture operating through values.[8]

The effect of education is concentrated at the two upper education levels. The fertility behavior of women with incomplete secondary education (ED2) differs very little from that of women with primary education or less; the coefficient of −76.5 is not statistically significant. The big impact comes with completed general secondary education (ED3). Movement to this educational level reduces the number of children per thousand women by 496.5; the coefficient is statistically significant. Movement to the highest-education level (ED4) reduces the number of children by an additional 138.7, to 635.2 fewer than the low-education women; this coefficient is also highly significant. The apparent insensitivity of fertility to increased education below the level of completed secondary education is spurious, however. Among rural mothers in some cases the fertility of ED2 groups exceeds that of ED1 groups, and in other cases it declines (see table 13.2). The small value of the ED2 coefficient is the consequence of these offsetting tendencies.

A thousand urban mothers have 602.8 fewer children than a thousand rural mothers; the coefficient is highly significant. The difference between the fertility of urban and rural mothers exceeds that between ED3 and ED1, but it is less than that between ED4 and ED1.

If the women in the 120 groups were homogeneous in all respects other than these three variables, the results would suggest that social structure, conveyed through the influence of residence and education, has a very large impact on fertility relative to that of republic. Rural mothers in Azerbaidzhan with low education (ED1) have 1,348.6 more children than mothers in Russia with the same two social characteristics. But with higher education and urban residence the fertility of mothers in Azerbaidzhan would be reduced by 1,238 (that is, −635.2 and −602.8), to a level only slightly above that of low-education rural mothers in Russia. In fact the actual mean fertility of urban high-education mothers in all the Moslem republics ranges between 2,064 (Azerbaidzhan) and 1,670 (Kazakhstan), in all cases lower than that of the level of 2,269 for rural low-education mothers in Russia (table 13.1, columns 4 and 5). Social structural influences appear to be as powerful as the influence of republic in those republics in which the latter influence is greatest (Azerbaidzhan) and more powerful in those republics in which it is weaker.

Since a relatively large proportion of the urban high-education mothers in the Moslem republics are not Moslems, these results reflect both cultural and social structural differences, but the latter clearly exert a strong influence on fertility.

13.3 Macro Residence and Income

Of the total variation in the fertility of the observation groups, we have found that 30 percent is explained by differences in the two variables of social structure—mother's residence and education. Republic differences account for twice that amount, or about 60 percent. Why is it that women who live in different republics have different numbers of children, even after residence and education are controlled for?

Part of the answer is surely to be found in the cultural differences among republics. But the question is, How much? Can the full 60 percent be explained by cultural differences? Or is part of the 60 percent due to features of social structure other than residence and education?

In this section we test for two additional features of social structure that may account for part of the variation among republics. But it is appropriate at this point to elaborate on the distinction drawn here between culture and social structure. The distinction is not a sharp one. As used here, the term "culture" applies to values, and corresponds to what are referred to as tastes in economic analysis. They may be thought of as psychological properties, like consciousness or preferences. Social structure refers to circumstances external to an individual that influence behavior, like living in a city, or having a high income. The concept of an "income constraint" in economic analysis is a characteristic of social structure. The general paradigm is that people who hold the same cultural values are constrained to behave differently if they are married or unmarried, or if they have high or low incomes.

As applied to the subject of this chapter, the difference between culture and social structure is blurred because the position a person occupies in the social structure is not completely independent of his values. Participating in the labor force constrains the fertility of mothers in certain ways, and, if more non-Moslem than Moslem women participate in the labor force, one may assert that to a certain extent nationality differences in fertility are due to differences in social structure rather than culture. The difficulty, however, is that cultural values are involved in the decision on whether to participate in the labor force. Nevertheless, the difference between cultural values (tastes) as internal properties and social structure (constraints) as external properties is worth preserving. In the discussion to follow, variation in fertility due to such variables as mother's education will be regarded as evidence of the influence of social structure, even though the prior decision to attain that level of education was partially influenced by culture. That is to say, when culture influences fertility behavior indirectly through its effect on a person's location in "social space," the behavior will be regarded as a response to social structure. Culture, or "pure" culture, will be regarded as influencing fertility behavior only when that influence is direct.

In this section we test the effect on fertility of two social variables, each of them based on a hypothesis regarding its effect on fertility. The first is rurality of the republic. The census variable URB identifies the group of mothers as living in cities or urban-type settlements. The population of the latter can be as small as 3,000. A variable that broad is unlikely to discriminate very finely among the ways in which urban residence influences fertility behavior.

Why should living in a city cause women to have fewer children than living in a village? Presumably the answer has something to do with the differences between the costs of having children in the two kinds of residence. Residence is thus a proxy for a whole set of factors that influence fertility decisions.

We would expect that those factors operate with different force in cities of different sizes, as the published data indeed show.[9] Ideally, we would like to decompose the variable URB into several levels by size of urban residence, like the education variable in the census data, but the data are not available. We can, however, test a somewhat different effect of urban residence. Kharchev and Matskovskii (1978, p. 184) remark that in small cities and even in villages located near large administrative centers, reproductive behavior and the social conditions that influence it are similar to those in the administrativu centers. Pursuing that point, we may expect that the social conditions of women classified as rural differ according to what may be called the "rurality" of their social environment. There is a sense in which a rural woman in a rural republic like Uzbekistan is more "rural" than a rural woman in an urbanized republic like Latvia. Specifically, the costs of children relative to other goods for a Latvian rural woman are likely to be more similar to those confronting an urban woman than would be the case for an Uzbek rural woman. Or otherwise put, the more urbanized a republic becomes, the more the fertility of its rural women approaches that of its urban women. To test this proposition, we introduced a measure (A70) of the percentage of the employed population engaged in agriculture in the republic in 1970.[10] We expect the sign of the coefficient to be positive.

The relationship of A70 to URB may be thought of as that between macro and micro residence. URB reflects the social conditions of the immediate neighborhood—the micro residence—which ranges from a small village to a large city. A70 reflects the social conditions of the republic—or macro residence—in which the city or village is located. Hence we expect, for example, that if two groups of mothers lived in urban micro residences, other things equal, their fertility should be the same. But if the first micro residence were situated in a highly rural macro residence while the second were in a highly urban one, we would expect the fertility to be higher in the first. Thus A70 should compensate in part for the deficiencies of the dichotomous variable URB as a measure of the relative costs of children insofar as these costs are influenced by place of residence.

The republics differ, second, in respect to levels of family income. Were the data available, one would wish to distinguish fathers' from mothers' income. In accordance with the usual assumption that children are a normal good, republics with higher male wage rates should show higher fertility. High-male-wage republics, however, are likely to be high-female-wage republics as well, which should depress fertility, for in most industrial countries the negative substitution effect of high women's wage rates on fertility tends to exceed the positive income effect. Since wives' income is a larger share of family income in the U.S.S.R. than in western countries, we should expect the substitution effect to be relatively larger in the U.S.S.R.

Unfortunately, sex differences in wage rates are not published in the U.S.S.R., nor are republic differences available. Some western scholars, however, have developed estimates of republic per capita income (Gillula 1979, p. 627) and republic per capita consumption (MacAuley 1979, p. 109). The two sets of estimates are highly correlated ($r = 0.97$); in the absence of extensive opportunities for private investment in capital one would expect the correlation to be high. We tested both sets of estimates in the regressions, and, since the consumption estimates yielded the higher R^2, we use it in the analysis that follows as a proxy for income.

For the present purpose, however, it is inappropriate to define the income variable in per capita terms, for per capita income is inversely related to the dependent variable, number of children per thousand mothers.[11] We have used instead a measure of income per adult (YADULT) which consists of the MacAuley estimates of consumption per capita, adjusted by removing from the denominator the number of children aged 0 to 14 in each republic. The data are reported in table 13.5. The effect of the adjustment is to increase the relative income measure of the high-fertility republics like Tadzhikistan and to reduce that of the low-fertility republics like Latvia.

Table 13.5
Agricultural employment and consumption by republic

Republic	Percentage of employed population engaged in agriculture, 1970 (A70)	Consumption per capita, 1966 (U.S.S.R. = 100)	Consumption per adult, 1966 (U.S.S.R. = 100) (YADULT)
	(1)	(2)	(3)
Russia	18.9	107.9	104.3
Ukraine	30.8	95.9	90.8
Belorussia	35.2	94.4	94.5
Uzbekistan	44.4	79.2	102.3
Kazakhstan	27.0	91.2	103.7
Georgia	37.2	89.7	91.8
Azerbaidzhan	34.6	70.5	89.6
Lithuania	31.3	116.0	112.9
Moldavia	53.6	87.8	91.9
Latvia	19.1	122.6	111.2
Kirghizia	35.6	76.9	93.7
Tadzhikistan	46.4	68.5	91.0
Armenia	27.4	89.9	105.0
Turkmenia	37.8	83.3	107.2
Estonia	17.3	131.3	119.7

Sources: Column 1 from TsSU, *Itogy . . . 1970 goda*, vol. 5, p. 295; column 2, MacAuley (1979), p. 114; column 3 calculated from column 2, less number of children 0–14 in each republic, as reported in *Itogy*, vol. 2 table 3.

The results of the regressions are reported in table 13.6. Education and residence alone (model I) account for 30 percent of the variation, as reported earlier. The addition of the republic percentage engaged in agriculture (A70) adds 11.8 percentage points to the explained variation, raising R^2 to 0.414.[12] The coefficient is positive and significant; a 1 percent increase in the percentage of the republic labor force engaged in agriculture increases the number of children per thousand mothers in that republic by 25.5, or by about 1 percent of the mean. Hence the result sustains the hypothesis that the more rural the macro residence, the higher the fertility of mothers in the same micro residential circumstances. The effect of urbanization on fertility is greater than that captured by the narrower Soviet definition of urban/rural residence.

Republic income per adult (YADULT) has about half the explanatory power of A70, accounting for 5.4 percent of the variation in fertility (model II). The coefficient is statistically significant, and its sign is negative, con-

Table 13.6
Sources of variation in fertility

Variables	Model I	Model II	Model III	Model IV	Model V	Model VI	Model VII	Model VIII	Correlation matrix FERT	A70	YADULT	FLFPR
A. Percentage of variation explained												
ED4	6.7	6.7	6.7	6.7	6.7	6.7	6.7					
ED3	6.3	6.3	6.3	6.3	6.3	6.3	6.3					
ED2	0.1*	0.1*	0.1*	0.1*	0.1*	0.1*	0.1*					
All ED	13.1	13.1	13.1	13.1	13.1	13.1	13.1					
URB	16.5	16.5	16.5	16.5	16.5	16.5	16.5					
A70	11.8		11.8	11.8			11.8		0.34			
YADULT		5.4	0 *						−0.23	−0.64		
FLFPR						22.9	15.9		−0.30	−0.21	0.25	
MOSPCT				40.2	51.7		28.2		0.82	0.39	−0.23	−0.25
Total	41.4	35.2	41.4	81.6	81.3	52.5	85.5					
B. Coefficients												
ED4	−635.2	−635.2	−635.2	−470.7	−465.3	−547.2	−449.1	−443.7				
ED3	−496.5	−496.5	−496.5	−434.8	−432.8	−978.2	−663.0	−692.0				
ED2	−76.5*	−76.5*	−76.5*	−33.1*	−31.7*	−720.7	−333.8	−372.6*				
URB	−602.8	−602.8	−602.8	−348.9	−340.7	−850.1	−491.5	−506.3				
A70	25.5		24.5	4.4*			2.1*					
YADULT		−18.7	−1.6*									

Table 13.6 (continued)

Variables	Model I	Model II	Model III	Model IV	Model V	Model VI	Model VII	Model VIII	Correlation matrix FERT	A70	YADULT	FLFPR
FLFPR						−41.3	−18.8	−21.4				
MOSPCT				15.7	16.5		14.2	14.2				
C. Standardized coefficients (β)												
A70	0.34		0.33	0.06*			0.03*					
YADULT		−0.23	−0.02									
FLFPR						−0.66	−0.30					
MOSPCT				0.72	0.74		0.64					
INTERCEPT	2028.6	4757.8	2219.1	2633.7	2248.0	6719.5	3940.6	4334.5				
R^2	0.41	0.35	0.41	0.82	0.81	0.53	0.86					

Note: All estimates are significant at the 0.01 level when followed by an asterisk.

sistent with the hypothesis that the substitution effect of higher women's wage rates is large and negative. But when YADULT is added after A70 (model III), it loses all explanatory power. The coefficient becomes very small and is not statistically significant. The explanation is in the high degree of correlation between A70 and YADULT ($r = 0.64$; see correlation matrix section of table 13.6). Since the more industrialized republics tend to have higher incomes, A70 picks up most of the effect of income on fertility.

If better income data were available, there is reason to believe that income would prove to have a larger influence on fertility than has been detected here. First, male and female wage rates have different effects on fertility, which are not captured by so crude a measure as income per adult. Second, the YADULT data, like the A70 data, are deficient because they refer to the republic as a whole: the families in the eight education-residence groups in each repulic are all regarded as having the same income per adult, that of the republic average. Hence the variable YADULT is unable to capture whatever influence income may have on fertility variation with republics. Interrepublic variation is also distorted because, for example, low-income rural mothers in Russia are regarded as having a higher per adult income (104.3; U.S.S.R. = 100) than high-education urban mothers in Georgia (91.8; U.S.S.R. = 100). Reference to Georgia reminds one of the third deficiency in the YADULT variable—the uncertainty of all estimates of the distribution of income and consumption in the U.S.S.R. because of the difficulty of taking account of incomes earned in the second economy. Hence the weakness of YADULT as an explanatory variable does not preclude the possibility that income, properly measured, may exert a significant influence on fertility.

The three variables of social structure in model I account for 41.4 percent of the variation in the fertility means. That compares with the 89.5 percent that is explained when the identity of the republics is known (table 13.4). The two figures testify to the substantial influence of social structure in the explanation of fertility. Without knowing the republic or the nationality of the homogeneous groups of mothers, but knowing only one characteristic of the social structure of their republics—percentage engaged in agriculture—we can explain almost half the variation that could be explained if we knew the identity of the republics. Had we better income data, it is safe to say that the explanatory power of social structure would be considerably higher.

13.4 Nationality and Female Labor Participation

The cultural difference that dominates Soviet society is that between Moslems and non-Moslems.[13] The general view is that Moslems place a higher value on large numbers of children than non-Moslems. Presumably that view must carry the ceteris paribus proviso. In terms of our data it should mean that the larger the percentage of Moslems within each of our observation groups, the larger the number of children that group of women will have. In this case residence and education are equal because of the way the mothers are initially classified; and macro residence and republic income are controlled for by virtue of the data we have added. What is required is a set of measures of the percentage of Moslems.

Our estimates are presented in table 13.7. They are derived from census tabulations of the ethnic composition of the republics and the educational distribution of ethnic groups. However, complete data on all the smaller ethnic groups are not available in all cases, and a variety of approximations had to be made. Moreover, since there were no data on mothers, we again had to resort to the data on women; and since the educational distribution data referred to women over 11, our estimates also apply to all women over 11. Thus the estimates are in error to the extent that the educational and residential distribution of mothers differs from that of women over 11. Nevertheless, they can serve to correct to some extent for the relatively large numbers of non-Moslem women among the higher-education and urban groups in the Moslem republics.

The addition of the percentage-of-Moslems variable (MOSPCT) to the regression equation (model IV) adds 40.2 percent to the explained variation, raising the R^2 to 0.816. This compares with the R^2 of 0.895 in table 13.4. Thus the two variables A70 and MOSPCT carry an explanatory power almost equal to that of the identity of the republics in which the mothers reside (the effect of YADULT is negligible). Or otherwise put, the two variables provide virtually the full explanation of that portion of the variation in fertility that is due to republic of residence.

To the extent that MOSPCT conveys the direct effect of culture on fertility, the results imply that it is substantial. It explains 40.2 percent of the variation in fertility, almost as much as the other three variables combined (ED, URB, A70). That result, however, reflects not only the impact of culture—Moslem-ness—on fertility but also the large variance of MOSPCT. The coefficient of variation of MOSPCT is 131 percent; that is, the standard deviation exceeds the mean by 31 percent. In contrast, the coefficients of variation of A70 and YADULT are only 30 percent and 9 percent, respectively. Hence the large explanatory power of MOSPCT relative to A70 and YADULT reflects primarily the large variance of MOSPCT among our 120 groups of mothers, and less the size of the impact that culture makes on fertility.

Table 13.7
Moslem women over 11 as a percentage of all women over 11 in the U.S.S.R., by republic, education, and residence, 1970.

	Urban					Rural				
Republic	Total	ED4	ED3	ED2	ED1	Total	ED4	ED3	ED2	ED1
Russia	3.4	2.0	3.1	3.7	3.8	8.6	5.3	9.1	9.2	8.7
Ukraine	0.3	0.2	0.2	0.3	0	0	0	0	0.1	0
Belorussia	0.2	0.1	0.1	0.2	0.2	0	0	0	0	0
Uzbekistan	57.0	38.3	55.5	54.9	64.5	95.7	81.3	95.9	95.9	96.2
Kazakhstan	21.6	16.2	24.4	18.2	24.3	53.9	38.1	61.7	49.1	55.8
Georgia	2.6	0.7	1.2	2.8	4.9	7.2	1.6	1.9	5.2	9.8
Azerbaidzhan	59.5	51.4	52.2	54.1	66.8	87.2	78.8	80.8	88.0	87.8
Lithuania	0.1	0.1	0.1	0.2	0.1	0.1	0.1	0.1	0.1	0.1
Moldavia	0.1	0.1	0.1	0.1	0.1	0	0	0	0	0
Latvia	0.1	0.1	0.1	0.2	0.2	0	0	0	0	0
Kirghizia	34.8	22.2	10.7	52.7	39.1	75.8	48.4	78.8	73.9	78.0
Tadzhikistan	55.8	28.3	48.9	50.2	67.0	97.9	65.3	96.2	98.0	98.7
Armenia	1.3	0.3	0.5	1.2	2.3	16.3	4.5	6.3	16.3	18.5
Turkmenia	60.0	27.7	53.6	60.1	69.8	98.2	75.5	98.1	99.2	98.4
Estonia	0.2	0.1	0.2	0.3	0.2	0	0	0	0	0

Source: TsSU, *Itogy . . . 1970 goda*, vol. 4, tables 2–29 and 37–53. Where the data in these tables were incomplete, estimates were made on the basis of other census data, such as those in vol. 3, table 1.
Note: Zero used where less than 0.05 percent.

The impact of Moslem-ness on fertility is better conveyed through the size of the regression coefficients. A 1 percent difference in the percentage of Moslems in a group of mothers is equivalent to a difference of 16 children per thousand mothers. It would therefore require a 21.8 percent difference in MOSPCT to equal the impact of urban/rural residence (348.9) and a 29.4 percent difference in MOSPCT to equal the impact of a technical or higher education (470.7). Viewed in these terms the direct impact of culture is not as large as the analysis of variance suggests.

In addition to its direct impact, however, culture exerts an indirect influence on fertility, as discussed earlier. That indirect influence is suggested by the correlation of 0.39 between MOSPCT and macro residence (A70) and of −0.23 between MOSPCT and income per adult (YADULT). Because of its large variance MOSPCT picks up in model IV much of the variation that is conveyed through the coefficient of A70 in model III. Hence, when MOSPCT appears in the equation (model IV), the coefficient of A70 becomes very small and is no longer statistically significant. Indeed if we exclude A70 and YADULT from the regression (as in model V) the influence of MOSPCT rises further, accounting for 51.7 percent of the variation in fertility. This compares with the 59.9 percent that is explained by republic of residence in table 13.4. If we know only the percentage of Moslems among the 120 groups of mothers but not their republic of residence, we could explain almost as much of the fertility variation (81.3 percent) as if we knew their republics. Additional information about their macro residence and the per adult income of their republic would add virtually nothing to the explanation of fertility variation.

The indirect influence of culture, however, is conveyed not only through macro residence and income. To the extent that culture also influences the choice of mother's attained education level and the decision to live in a city or a village, some portion of the variation in fertility accounted for by ED and URB also represents the indirect effect of culture. Indeed the correlation between FERT (fertility) and MOSPCT is 0.82, implying that 67 percent of the variation in fertility is accounted for by MOSPCT alone.

Finally, notice must be taken of the influence of the female labor force participation rate (FLFPR) on fertility. Some analysts exclude FLFPR as an independent variable because, it is argued, the choice of whether or not to participate in the labor force is part of the same decision-making process as the choice of whether or not to have a child; to choose to have a child is to choose to withdraw from the labor force. If that indeed is the behavior to be modeled, then FLFPR should not be regarded as a variable independent of fertility.

Many analysts, however, regard the two decisions as being much less interdependent than portrayed above. While they are related to some degree, each one is influenced by a variety of other factors, such as the woman's wage rate, the husband's income, and so forth. Hence FLFPR should be included in the fertility equation. The question of the direction of causation is also a point of dispute. In the Soviet case it can be argued that the decision runs primarily from the fertility choice to the labor participation choice. That is to say, women normally expect to be in the labor force, but they drop out for a time after having decided to have a child. Nevertheless, there are contexts in which the causation runs the other way. The relative unavailability of "women's jobs" in some regions of the country leads to a lower rate of female labor participation in those regions, which in turn decreases the cost of having a child. In this context the fertility decision is dependent on labor force participation. In any case the correlation between fertility and female labor participation is −0.30, smaller than that between fertility and all the other variables we have added to the original data. That relatively low correlation suggests that, in the Soviet context at least, fertility and labor force participation are only moderately interdependent and both are heavily influenced by other factors.

The female labor participation rate data were developed from the census data on (1) the number of women engaged in social production and (2) the number of women in the able-bodied ages 16 to 54 as shown in table 13.8. Since the participation rates of all women 16 to 54 are higher than those of mothers, the data are deficient for our purposes. However, the groups with high participation rates for all women (Estonian urban high-education women) are likely also to have high participation rates for the mothers in those groups, and similarly for groups with low participation rates. Hence, although the absolute levels of the participation rates of women are higher than those for mothers, the data may, nevertheless, serve as a reasonable proxy for the relative participation rates of mothers.

When FLFPR is the only variable added to the equation (model VI), it accounts for 22.9 percent of the variation. This compares with the 51.7 percent accounted for by MOSPCT when it serves as the only variable added (model V). Part of that difference is due to the smaller variance of FLFPR, which is a consequence of the generally high labor participation of Soviet women. Its coefficient of variation is only 14 percent, compared to 131 percent for MOSPCT. Given that relatively small variance, the fact that its explanatory power is almost half that of MOSPCT testifies to the heavy influence it exerts on fertility. In the full equation (model VII) the explanatory power of FLFPR declines to 15.9 percent. But when FLFPR is

Table 13.8
Female labor force participation rate in the U.S.S.R., by republic, education, and residence, 1970

	Urban				Rural			
Republic	ED4	ED3	ED2	ED1	ED4	ED3	ED2	ED1
Russia	93.3	81.3	82.9	98.0	97.1	81.7	79.1	89.6
Ukraine	91.7	81.5	75.8	90.0	95.6	86.5	83.4	95.7
Belorussia	90.8	80.1	80.1	99.0	95.5	80.9	75.7	101.0
Uzbekistan	86.6	66.9	66.0	75.3	93.1	89.0	81.8	90.0
Kazakhstan	88.8	72.8	74.6	84.0	95.5	80.0	71.3	80.5
Georgia	84.0	75.8	57.5	83.4	92.5	80.8	72.6	105.4
Azerbaidzhan	83.2	61.3	54.6	66.2	91.6	69.9	68.7	80.8
Lithuania	92.2	78.4	76.7	96.8	96.3	78.5	65.9	94.7
Moldavia	90.9	77.9	77.0	91.4	96.6	86.1	87.1	108.6
Latvia	93.8	90.6	86.3	113.5	97.3	90.7	81.6	98.7
Kirghizia	88.9	68.3	70.4	81.0	96.2	84.5	92.7	89.4
Tadzhikistan	91.9	67.8	67.0	70.4	93.9	80.6	69.6	75.4
Armenia	82.9	66.2	58.5	79.0	94.5	64.7	72.7	92.4
Turkmenia	91.5	68.6	63.2	73.0	93.8	91.3	81.9	87.8
Estonia	95.0	92.9	85.3	115.9	96.9	91.9	79.5	101.0
Unweighted means	89.7	74.7	71.7	87.8	95.1	82.5	77.6	92.7

Source: TsSu, *Itogy . . . 1970 goda*, vol. 5, tables 7 and 11 for number of women in social production. *Itogy*, vol. 3, table 1, for number of able-bodied women.
Note: The female labor force participation rate is calculated as the ratio of number of women in social production to number of able-bodied women. The percentage can exceed 100 percent because there are women in the labor force who are older (and perhaps younger) than the age interval 16 to 54 that defines the term "able-bodied."

accounted for, the explanatory power of the culture variable MOSPCT declines considerably, from 40.2 percent when FLFPR is ignored (model IV) to 28.2 percent when FLFPR is accounted for.

In the full equation the coefficient of FLFPR declines from −41.3 (model IV) to −18.8 (model VII). It remains, nevertheless, fairly large, larger indeed than that of MOSPCT. A 1 percent increase in FLFPR decreases the number of children per thousand by 18.8 percent, while a 1 percent increase in MOSPCT increases fertility by 14.2 percent. Because of its greater variance MOSPCT shows a larger impact in standard units; the beta coefficient is 0.64, compared to −0.30 for FLFPR. That result is of some interest for the interpretation of fertility variation but not for policy analysis. One can readily imagine policies that might alter women's labor force participation rates, but it is difficult to imagine policies that would change fertility by altering the percentage of Moslems in the population.

Perhaps the most interesting effect of the introduction of FLFPR, however, is the changes that occur in the coefficients of the other variables, changes that offer an important insight into fertility behavior. In models I to V the regression coefficient of ED4 is larger than that of ED3, and the coefficient of ED2 is small and not statistically significant. With FLFPR in the model, however, the coefficient of ED4 becomes much smaller than that of ED3.[14] The meaning of that result is that, when labor force participation is held constant, ED4 mothers (with specialized secondary and higher education) actually have more children (the coefficient is less negative) than ED3 mothers (with general secondary education). The interpretation is that the reason ED4 mothers in fact have fewer children than ED3 mothers is not that they love children less but that they love work more: they participate more fully in the labor force. That inversion occurs even when the percentage of Moslems is held constant (model VII).

In a similar vein, in all the models that ignore FLFPR (models I to V) the coefficient of ED2 is small and not statistically significant. It appears that a few years of education beyond the primary level has no significant effect on fertility, that the negative relation between fertility and women's education applies only to women who have at least completed secondary education. But when labor force participation is controlled for (models VI and VII) the coefficient of ED2 becomes quite large and statistically significant. What that result says is that, while ED2 mothers have about the same number of children as ED1 mothers, they participate in the labor force to a much smaller degree (table 13.8). When labor participation is held constant, those extra years of education prove to have a significant negative effect on fertility. It is evident that the factors that influence the differential labor participation of women have an important effect on differential fertility.

Model VII was estimated by the method of ordinary least squares, as were all the preceding models. In view of the possibility of simultaneous equation bias, model VIII was estimated using two-stage least squares. The coefficient of FLFPR is slightly larger (21.4), but it is not statistically significant (Prob value = 0.08). The other coefficients are not greatly changed. In the FLFPR regression moreover the coefficient of FERT is extremely small while the education coefficients are large.[15] The results suggest that in the U.S.S.R. the decision regarding a mother's labor force participation is made primarily on the basis of her education level, with number of children playing a very small part. The decision regarding the number of children to bear, however, is significantly influenced by the prior decision regarding her labor force participation.

13.5 Concluding Remarks

If one were to rank the characteristics of a society in the order in which they bear the stamp of culture, the language that people speak would top the list. Family organization, however, would not be far behind. One would expect therefore that societies with diverse cultures would diverge particularly in family organization.

Soviet family organization follows that pattern. With respect to one of the major features of family organization—numbers of children—the fifteen republics vary greatly. Taking the percentage of Moslems as the measure of the major cultural difference among groups of Soviet mothers, the correlation between that percentage and the measure of fertility in the data studied in this chapter is 0.82.

But culture does not uniquely determine behavior. It may be thought of as a schedule, prescribing the different forms of behavior that are appropriate under specified conditions. With respect to family behavior the influence of culture is conveyed through the shape of the preference system for children relative to other valued things. People who share the same culture and therefore have similar preference systems may, nevertheless, behave differently if they confront different conditions. From this perspective fertility variation in the U.S.S.R. reflects not only the differences in culturally based preference systems but also in the constraints on the behavior of different groups of persons.

The original data consist of the mean fertility of 120 groups of mothers who are homogeneous with respect to republic, education, and urban/rural residence. We have regarded those three characteristics as bundles of various kinds of constraints that affect the cost, material and psychic, of having children relative to other valued things. Thus we interpret the lower fertility of urban mothers as signifying that the cost of having children is higher and the cost of other things lower in urban families than in rural. We assume, in other words, that urban families have the same preferences as rural families of the same culture and, if they lived in rural areas, they would have the same number of children as rural families do.

Those bundles of constraints that determine relative costs are generated by the ways in which the society organizes its social and economic activities. The ways in which one earns an income, cares for children, organizes recreation, and so forth, differ according to one's location in "social space," according to one's particular set of socially salient characteristics: being female or male, being child or adult, having a high or low education, living in a city or a village, having a high or low income, being a writer or machinist. We refer to these characteristics as features of the social structure. People who share the same culture but occupy different positions in the social structure face different bundles of constraints. Hence their culture-based preferences are the same, but they behave differently.

Proceeding from this paradigm, we have sought to distill from the data the relative importance of culture and social structure in determining fertility in the U.S.S.R. The two, however, are not statistically independent, for culture also influences social structure. The choice of whether to move to the city or whether to acquire a few more years of education is also influenced by culture-based preferences. Hence we found it useful to distinguish two effects of culture on fertility: the direct effect, reflecting culture-based preferences for children, and the indirect effect, reflecting culture-based preferences for certain positions in social structure, which in turn influence the costs of children.

Our findings regarding the relative influence of culture and social structure are summarized in figure 13.1. If we knew nothing about the 120 observation groups except the percentage of Moslems in each group, we could account for 67 percent of the variation in their mean fertility (bar I in figure 13.1).[16] That percentage may be taken as the total effect of culture. Four variables of social structure, however, account for 57.3 percent of the variation (bar II). When they are controlled for, the explanatory power of the culture variable drops to 28.2 percent. That percentage may be taken as the measure of the direct effect of culture on fertility. Thus the effect of social structure on fertility, as conveyed by those four variables, is about twice as large as the direct effect of culture on fertility. Some portion of the effect of

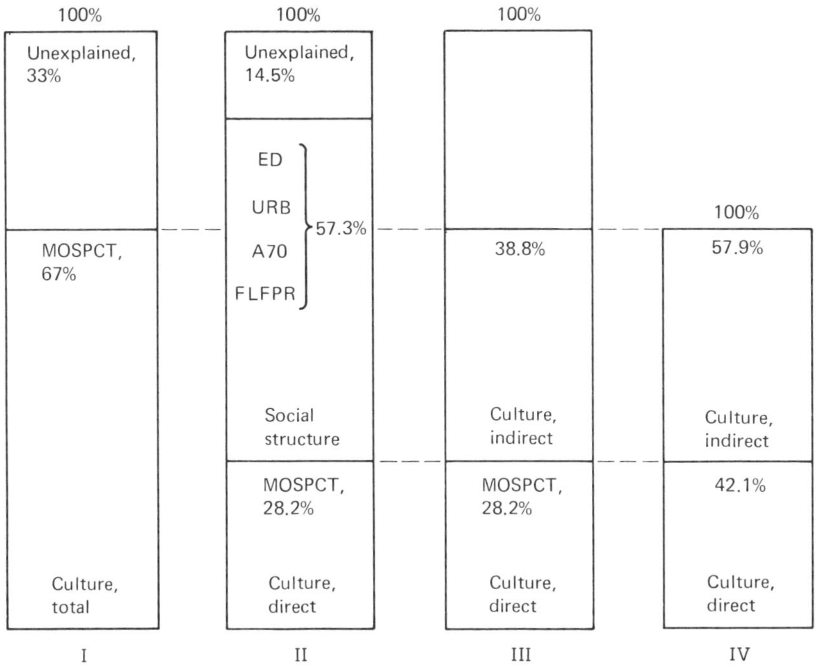

Figure 13.1

social structure, however, may be regarded as the indirect effect of culture, operating through cultural preferences regarding women's education, urbanization, and so forth. We take that portion to be 38.8 percent (bar III)—the difference between the total and direct effects of culture.

Were the data available, we might expect the foregoing findings to be modified in various ways. If data were available on individuals rather than on group means, for example, we would expect the explanatory power of such social structural variables as female labor participation to be larger and the direct influence of culture correspondingly smaller. If data were available on male and female wage rates, we would expect income to exert a larger influence on fertility, adding to the explanatory power of social structure. With better and more complete data we expect that the influence of social structure, relative to culture, would be larger than we have found here, and the indirect influence of culture larger, relative to the direct, than we have found here. Our conclusion then is that culture exerts a dominating influence on fertility, but much of that influence, and possibly most of it, is indirect, operating through the choices people make that define their positions in the social structure.

Notes

The research was supported by the National Council for Soviet and East European Research. I am grateful to Barney K. Schwalberg and Martin C. Spechler for their advice and criticism.

1. That is the definition given by the Central Statistical Administration in other of its statistical compilations, such as *Zhenshchiny v SSSR*, p. 92 and *Dety v SSSR*, p. 9.

2. Before 1962 it was called a "seven-year school" (*semiletka*). Afterward it was extended to an eighth year (*vos'miletka*).

3. In no case does the rank order of a republic in column 3 differ by more than 2 from its rank order in column 1. Most differ by 1 or zero.

4. The data could be used for an analysis of the fertility of Soviet mothers by weighting the observations. However, weighting could cause the Russian republic to dominate the results so heavily as to swamp the other republics. Moreover our interest here is in understanding the variation among the observation groups and not in projecting back to the Soviet population.

5. All regressions were run using the Statistical Analysis System package, particularly procedures GLM, STEPWISE, and SYSREG.

6. It should be noted that the R^2 applies not to the variation in fertility among Soviet mothers in general but to the variation among the means of the fertility rates of the 120 groups; that is to say, the regression equation in table 13.4 provides a basis for predicting only the mean fertility of a sample of a thousand women randomly selected from a population of all Soviet women who share the same characteristics of republic, residence and education. The variance among the women in the sample is not known. The R^2 in table 13.4 is therefore not comparable to the R^2 normally found in cross-section data in which the dependent variable refers to individuals rather than to the means of groups of individuals; in the case of individual data the R^2 is normally much smaller than the value of 0.895 in table 13.4.

7. When the variables are entered last in the equations (column 5), the explanatory power of the various levels within each variable changes, but the variation accounted for by each of the three variables does not change greatly. The measures in column 5 are not additive, however.

8. The effect of the multinational composition of the republics is to understate the influence of culture in republic-based data. This tends to offset the overstatement referred to here, but by an amount that is likely to be small relative to the degree of overstatement due to the omission of other social structure variables.

9. Urban women born during 1920 to 1924 had an average of 2.08 children. But those of them who lived in Moscow, Leningrad, and Kiev had an average of 1.68 children (Sifman 1974, p. 51).

10. Data from the 1970 census, vol. 5, p. 295. We tested two other measures of rurality: (1) percentage of employed population engaged in agriculture in 1959, on the assumption that the number of children per mother in 1970 reflects the social

structure of an earlier year, and (2) percentage of the republic's population living in rural settlements in 1970, from Feshbach and Rapawy (1976, p. 127). A70 had the largest explanatory power.

11. I am grateful to the anonymous reader for directing my attention to this point and for other valuable comments as well.

12. The variables that we added (A70, YADULT, MOSPCT, and FLFPR) are mean values for each group of mothers. They may therefore understate the influence of those variables on fertility. For example, if two republics have the same mean values of A70 but different fertility rates, it would appear that A70 cannot explain the fertility difference. It is possible, nevertheless, that within each republic fertility may vary greatly with A70. Our added variables, however, do reveal a considerable range of variation among observation groups. Hence the appearance of a statistically significant relation between them and fertility creates a presumption that the relation also describes the behavior of individuals. I am grateful to Barney Schwalberg and F. Trenery Dolbear for their advice on this issue.

13. There are also cultural differences among Moslems and non-Moslems that must influence tastes regarding children. But those differences are minor, compared to that which distinguishes Moslems from all others.

14. In model VI the coefficient of ED4 is smaller than ED2 as well, but that may reflect the absence of the MOSPCT variable.

15. $$\begin{aligned} \text{FLFPR} = \underset{(0.55)}{12.2} &+ \underset{(2.5)}{11.3\text{ED4}} - \underset{(-0.61)}{2.7\text{ED3}} - \underset{(-4.6)}{15.2\text{ED2}} \\ &+ \underset{(2.7)}{0.36\text{YADULT}} - \underset{(-3.5)}{0.44\text{MOSPCT}} + \underset{(3.1)}{0.02\ \text{FERT}}. \end{aligned}$$

16. The simple correlation (r) between FERT and MOSPCT is 0.82. Hence r^2 is 0.67.

References

Belova, V. A., et al., 1977. *Skol'ko detei budet v sovetskoi sem'e*. Moscow: *Statistika*.

Feshbach, M., and S. Rapawy, 1976. Soviet population and manpower trends. In U.S. Joint Economic Committee, *Soviet Economy in a New Perspective*. Washington, GPO, October 14, 1976, pp. 113–154.

Gillula, J. W., 1979. The economic interdependence of Soviet republics. In U.S. Joint Economic Committee, *Soviet Economy in a Time of Change*. Washington: GPO, Oct. 10, 1979, vol. 1, pp. 618–655.

Kharchev, A. G., and M. S. Matskovskii, 1978. *Sovremennaia sem'ia i ee problemy*. Moscow: *Statistika*.

MacAuley, A., 1979. *Economic Welfare in the USSR*. Madison: University of Wisconsin Press.

Naselenie SSSR—spravochnik. Moscow: *Politizdat*.

Sifman, R. I., 1974. *Dinamika rozhdaemosti v SSSR*. Moscow: *Statistika*.

TsSU, 1979. *Deti v SSSR*. Moscow: *Statistika*.

TsSU, 1972–74. *Itogy vsesoiuznoi perepisi naseleniia 1970 goda*. Vols. 1–7. Moscow: *Statistika*.

TsSU, 1975. *Zhenshchiny v SSSR*. Moscow: *Statistika*.

14 Energy Prices and Decisions on Energy Use in the U.S.S.R.

Robert W. Campbell

The Soviet economy is a voracious consumer of energy, largely because, as in the United States, energy has been easily available and relatively cheap. There is a great deal of evidence suggesting that in many respects the U.S.S.R. is very wasteful of energy. With an industrial output no more than three-fourths as big as that of the United States in 1975, Soviet industry used almost as much energy as did U.S. industry. In the same year, despite an agricultural output no more than 80 to 85 percent of the U.S. level, Soviet agriculture used appreciably more energy than U.S. agriculture. (Campbell 1978, pp. 20, 23.) Soviet automotive equipment has long had compression ratios and hence fuel efficiency considerably inferior to western equipment and to what Soviet research institutions calculate as economically optimal, even before the rapid rise of energy costs in the 1970s. The Soviet Union today faces rapidly rising real costs of energy, however, and one of the crucial goals of energy policy should be conservation. There is some dispute as to how important prices are in influencing decisions about resource use in the U.S.S.R., but I believe energy prices have a role to play in any Soviet effort to reduce energy consumption. The question naturally arises of how adequately energy prices in the Soviet economy signal to decision-makers the national-economic cost of their choices concerning energy use.

Because of the importance of spatial and transport considerations, because of the many stages in the process of production, transformation, and consumption, and because the price system is used to redistribute rents, the system of energy prices in the U.S.S.R. is very complex. Because it is a multistage industry, there is an elaborate set of prices on intermediate products that influences such decisions internal to the energy sector itself as location, output mix, and choice among competing technologies. Some of these problems have been explored in earlier publications by the author (Campbell 1970), but in the present study the concern is a rather narrow one, how adequately the system of energy prices conveys the true cost of energy to energy consumers, as a way of guiding their decisions about demand. In general, I am interested in *final* users, such as the steel industry, though, in view of the importance of conversion to electric power in the U.S.S.R., I also want to consider the fuel consumption decisions internal to the electric power sector and the decisions of the firms who are the final users of the electric power and heat it produces.

One of the distinctive features of the Soviet energy price system is that in addition to the system of actual transactions prices the energy sector has a fairly long tradition of using various forms of "planning prices" that differ significantly from transactions prices. For each of these kinds of prices there is a sphere of economic decisions in which they influence energy use, and it is necessary to assess the adequacy of each. A second distinction is that between several major energy forms, for each of which the Soviet price-setting approach is different. In the following discussion we consider in turn three main groups of energy products; boiler and furnace fuel, fuel for internal combustion engines, and the fuel that is converted to electric power and then consumed in that form. This covers the bulk of energy consumption in the U.S.S.R., as shown in the following tabulation of energy use in 1975, in million tons of standard fuel (Campbell 1978, pp. 8, 98.):

Total primary energy consumption	1,482.4
Boiler and furnace fuel	1,066.0
Power stations	486.7
Other	579.3
Motor Fuels	166.6
Other (losses, used as raw materials, lubricants, etc.)	249.8

This division is motivated by a fairly strong separation of pricing and by rather distinctive concerns and methodologies in price setting in these three divisions.

14.1 Pricing of Boiler and Furnace Fuels

In the U.S.S.R. decisions about energy use take place in two rather distinct spheres of economic decision making, each with its own set of energy prices. The first is what I call project-making decisions—choices about such matters as technology, location, and capital intensity for new production capacities. The second sphere is *khozraschet* decision making, decisions mostly about current input mixes that are within the competence of the decision-makers at the level of operating firms and involve rather short-term adjustments within the constraints of existing technologies and equipment. The prices relevant to the latter tend generally to be transactions prices, via their influence on such managerial desiderata as cost minimization. The decision-makers in the other sphere, however, have a different set of objectives and are supposed to use not transactions prices but a separate set of valuations created in a centralized way and intended to reflect better than transactions prices the actual national economic costs of energy. The first task is to describe briefly each of these kinds of prices.

Planning Prices

An early example of the energy prices used by project makers is the set of "indicators of current and capital costs" of different kinds of fuel delivered to the various regions, produced by SOPS for the Gosplan (Probst 1964).[1] Cost in this study embraced both current production cost and capital cost, though at that time it was still not quite acceptable to combine these as *privedennye zatraty*, by summing current cost and an interest charge on capital. Also the generation of those cost figures did not involve a prior or simultaneous set of decisions about what fuels would be supplied to each region, and consequently provided cost estimates for producing and delivering various plausible kinds of fuel to each region. That particular study marked a systematization of existing practice, its main goal being to replace the many separate cost calculations put out by various producing and using ministries with a regionally complete set of costs figured according to a standardized and economically justified methodology for all the different kinds of fuel.

Zamykaiushchie Zatraty

More recently, Soviet planning practice has institutionalized the calculation and official use in the fuel sector of so-called *zamykaiushchie zatraty*, (ZZ hereafter), intended to convey the national economic cost of various kinds of boiler and furnace fuel in each of the main economic regions. ZZ can variously be thought of as marginal costs, opportunity cost valuations, or the shadow prices from a linear programming approach, though the exact meaning in any given discussion is highly variable, depending on the structure of the linear programming model used or the kind of opportunity cost calculation that was made to generate them. The ZZ most likely to be encountered in this literature seem to have been created in the following way.[2] A linear programming problem is formulated in which the constraints are aggregate demand for boiler and furnace fuel in each region, and capacity levels for various sources, specified both by location and type of fuel. Some sources are left unconstrained. The capacity of some specific transport links may also be set as constraints. Also given are the capital and operating costs of producing the various energy sources and capital and operating costs of transportation. The objective function in the problem is to minimize *privedennye zatraty* for satisfying the specified aggregate demand. From such a linear programming problem there emerges a shadow price for boiler and furnace fuel in each region, an allocation of each kind of fuel to each region, a transport plan, and output levels for each of the sources (some of these being determined by the constraints mentioned here.) Associated with this solution is the identification of the "closing fuel or fuels of the country," the cheapest among those sources whose output levels in the solution have not come up against an output constraint.

Differential prices for specific kinds of fuel in any given region are then generated by a separate opportunity cost calculation. For the closing fuel this would simply be its delivered cost in the given region. For a constrained fuel, however, it would involve calculating the opportunity cost of making available an additional unit of that fuel in the given region. This would usually be accomplished by diverting it from some other user in the same region, though it may sometimes be from another region (Makarov 1979, p. 230). To identify the user from whom a diversion would be made, it is necessary to specify the "marginal use" of the fuel in question, the use where its differential advantage compared to the replacement fuel is the smallest. To be concrete, the ZZ for gas in a given region is the cost associated with replacing it with the closing fuel of the region, probably coal, in the last intramarginal use of gas in that region. The ZZ for the fuel in question differs from the regional general figure then by the differential advantage the fuel in question enjoys over the closing fuel in the last intramarginal use. This differential advantage will consist of both any *fuel* economies the more advantageous fuel may possess and economies in the other cost elements involved in the use of the two fuels. (All this is clearly spelled out in Makarov 1979, pp. 225ff.) There is one slight failure of closure here, in that it is supposed that the BTUs required to meet a given demand vary somewhat from fuel to fuel, and it is never made clear how it is possible to specify aggregate regional demand before the composition of supply by fuel has been determined.

Because there are some uncertainties about the cost data assumed, and about the output constraints, computations of ZZ have usually been made on the basis of several sets of assumptions about those magnitudes, and the final ZZ are expressed in terms of a range rather than a single figure. They have also been computed for different forecast periods. Two sets, officially approved by the Gosplan for planning calculations, were intended to be applied in calculations for 1975 to 1980, and beyond 1980, respectively. (ANSSSR 1973). As an example of what the ZZ look like, see those for the 1975 to 1980 period shown in table 14.1. A final twist in the determination of ZZ has been the inclusion of prices differentiated seasonally.

Transactions Prices

Despite the official promulgation of ZZ to be used by planners, they are not used as the prices at which fuel and energy forms are actually bought and sold. In preparation for what follows, it may be helpful to describe briefly here some of the peculiarities of transaction prices for boiler and furnace fuels in the U.S.S.R. The main fuels with which we are concerned in this section are steam coal, residual fuel oil (*mazut*), and natural gas. (Peat and oil shale are also used to some degree for these purposes but only on a local basis). Coal is priced FOB, basin of origin, with quite a bit of regional variation depending on quality and on cost of production at any given site. The delivered price to a user in a given regional market thus depends on the quality mix and the source or sources from which the coal has come. To get a figure for the transactions price of coal in any given region, we have to find some representative user, such as power stations, and simply take the average cost for the kind of purchases they actually make. There is some expectation that an attempt will be made to choose sourcing to minimize delivered cost because of the cost-minimizing motives of the purchasers.

Gas is priced more simply, FOB at the delivery point of the pipeline, and these delivered prices are differentiated by zones in a fairly simple way. There are some special prices for different categories of users, but the bulk of gas for boiler and furnace use is paid for at the standard regional price.

Mazut is also priced FOB delivery terminal, and the price is differentiated only among three zones. The first is the whole European territory of the U.S.S.R. plus Central Asia; the second is Siberia; the third is the Far East.

In reality the situation is somewhat more complicated than described here. For coal there are price variations for ash content, and for sorted as opposed to run-of-mill coal. For *mazut* there are price variations for viscosity and sulfur content.

With this background established, we can now proceed to deal with two concerns. The first is how well transactions prices correspond to the ZZ for boiler and furnace fuels. The second is adequacy of the ZZ themselves as measures of the real opportunity cost of boiler and furnace fuels in the various regions.

Table 14.1
Comparison of ZZ and transactions prices, 1975 to 1980

	Coal		Gas		*Mazut*	
Regions	ZZ	Actual	ZZ	Actual	ZZ	Actual
Northwest	22–24	26.9	23–26	20.5	22–25	16.70
Murmansk oblast'	23–26		—	—	26–28	16.70
Komi ASSR	14–16		17–20		16–19	16.70
Center	21–23	21.1	23–26	17.9–18.8	22–25	16.70
Central Blackearth	20–22	20.9	22–25	—	21–24	16.70
North Caucasus	20–22	18.7	21–23	12 –12.8	20–22	16.70
Middle Volga	19–21	18.6	21–23	16.2	20–22	16.70
Lower Volga	20–22	18.6	22–24	16.2	21–23	16.70
North Ural	15–18	16.1	19–21	9.4–14.5	18–20	16.70
South Ural	15–17 (13–16)	16.1	19–21	13.7	17–20	16.70
Kemerovo oblast' & Altai Krai	9–11	10.3	—		15–17	18.9
Novosibirsk & Tomsk oblast'	10–13	10.3	15–18		14–17	18.9
Omsk oblast'	12–15 (10–13)	10.3	—		14–17	18.9
Krasnoiarsk Krai	10–12	9.0	—		15–17	18.9
Irkutsk oblast'	9–12	9.0	—		14–16	18.9
Transbaikal	11–12	9.0	—		15–17	18.9
Amursk oblast'	11–13	19.4	—		17–19	21.7
Khabarovsk Krai	12–14	19.4	17–20		16–17	21.7

Table 14.1 (continued)

Regions	Coal		Gas		*Mazut*	
	ZZ	Actual	ZZ	Actual	ZZ	Actual
Primorsk Krai	16–18	19.4	—		19–21	21.7
East Ukraine & Rostov oblast'	19–21	17.6	22–24	13.7–15.4	21–23	16.70
West Ukraine & Moldavia	21–23	20.4	23–26	16.2	22–25	16.70
Belorussia & Lithuania	22–24	21.1	24–27	17.9–18.8	23–26	16.70
Latvia & Estonia	23–25	23.9	25–27	20.5	24–26	16.70
Georgia	21–23	27.8	21–24	12.8	20–23	16.70
Armenia & Azerbaidzhan	22–24	27.8	20–24	18.8	19–23	16.70
Turkmenistan	—	19.6	14–16	11.1	13–15	16.70
Uzbekistan	14–16	19.6	15–17	9.4	14–16	16.70
Tadzhikistan	—	19.6	15–18	11.1	14–17	16.70
Kirgiziia	13–15	19.6	16–19		15–18	16.70
West Kazakhstan	18–20	19.6	17–19		16–18	16.70
Northeast Kazahkstan	10–13 (8–10)	13.9 13.9	—		15–18	16.70
South Kazakhstan	13–15 (10–13)	13.9	18–20	11.4	17–19	16.70

Sources: The ZZ are taken from ANSSSR (1973, p. 12). In the case of coal they refer to run-of-mine steam coal. For coal, transactions prices are taken from Torbin (1974, p. 175), except for Northwest which is from Torbin (1974, p. 172). For gas, transactions prices are from Avrukh (1970, pp. 131–132). Avrukh reports them by regional energy system, but the correspondence with the regional breakdown used for ZZ is very close. For *mazut*, transactions prices are taken from Avrukh (1970, pp. 133–135), and Torbin (1974, p. 175), and Shkatov and Suponitskii (1969, pp. 67–69). Mazut prices are differentiated by sulfur content and viscosity, and the prices here are for grade 40, sulfurous (0.5 to 2 percent sulfur) *mazut*.

Note: All figures are shown as rubles per ton of standard fuel. Alternative figures in parentheses assume that Ekibastuz coal could be used in the given region.

Comparison of ZZ and Transactions Prices

Table 14.1 compares the ZZ published by the Gosplan for economic calculations to be made in the 1975 to 1980 period with a representative transaction price in the same region.[3] In line with the explanation here, the ZZ are given for several different boiler and furnace fuels. Note that with a few exceptions the difference between the ZZ for coal and that for each of the other fuels is about the same absolute amount in every region, since the difference is determined by the differential advantage in use for the marginal user. In those regions where the difference for a given fuel is appreciably smaller than in other regions, the explanation is that its differential advantage is reduced either because gas is relatively freely available so that it has pushed its way into the less advantageous uses or the demand structure is peculiar in that the most advantageous uses are unimportant in the mix. Industrial furnaces are usually the most advantageous users, and the western Ukraine and Moldavia, to take one example, have little such demand so that gas use spills over to less advantageous uses. Where the gas-coal ZZ gap is large, the opposite is the case, as illustrated by northeast Kazahkstan, a metallurgical center with very limited access to gas. The differential advantage for *mazut* as figured by the opportunity cost calculation described earlier is generally much less than for gas since *mazut* is much more expensive to use than gas in terms of storage, handling, boiler conversion, and so on.

The important fact revealed by the table is that the transactions prices are relatively close to the ZZ for coal but tend to be appreciably below the ZZ for *mazut* and gas. It is not easy for me to understand what the Soviet energy planners were trying to accomplish by this policy—it was *not* motivated by a desire to encourage the substitution of gas and *mazut* for coal, since most such substitution would take place in new facilities, and the project makers who design new facilities are explicitly enjoined to base their decisions on ZZ rather than actual prices. I suspect that one of the main reasons is that the price setters still operate with a cost-of-production bias and would have been uncomfortable with the profits that would be generated for the oil and gas industry by transactions prices closer to the ZZ. It may also be that the transactions prices, set in 1967, were based on earlier, and more optimistic views of cost than emerged by the time the ZZ were calculated (in the early 1970s).

Additional corroboration of the significant underpricing of gas in transactions prices compared to its opportunity cost value is found in a very interesting and informative calculation of the savings from substituting gas for other fuel in various regions. (I'lina and Utkina 1978.) This book presents the results of a detailed study of the savings achievable by substituting gas for other fuels, calculated in a much more disaggregated way than was used for the ZZ, taking account of the concrete locational and demand structural features within each region. Its purpose is basically to determine a "scale of effectiveness" of gas utilization, comparative gains in different uses from substituting it for other fuels, to help guide decisions about the allocation of fuel within regions. One feature of the study holds implications about the relation of actual prices for gas to its opportunity cost. The calculation of economic effects in the study is carried out in two forms. One figures the economic advantage of gas compared to other fuels, costing both gas and the alternative at actual prices; the other is the same except that it costs the alternative fuel at ZZ. Consistently in these calculations, the economic advantage of gas is significantly larger compared to other fuels when fuel costs are figured at transactions prices, than when they are figured at ZZ. It seems warranted to conclude therefore that the differential advantages of gas must be less fully reflected in transaction prices than in ZZ.

The study corroborates the validity of the official ZZ in showing that when both gas and coal are valued at ZZ, there is almost zero additional economic effect for substituting gas for coal in power stations. The advantage is already fully reflected in the ZZ differential. What it does not answer, however, is to what extent the calculations underlying the ZZ are correct in their assumption that power stations are the marginal user of gas in all regions. That is an assumption that I believe might well not hold up when the gas available to each region is allocated among users according to the "scale of effectiveness."

There is a similar implication in the study that the relative transaction prices for gas and *mazut* do not fully reflect the differential advantage of gas. The results of the study show a significant economic effect in substituting gas for *mazut* in industrial boilers when the cost of the two energy sources is figured in transactions prices.

Relation of ZZ to Actual Costs

My second point is that I believe the ZZ themselves understate real costs. The ZZ shown in table 14.1 for 1975 to 1980 are well below opportunity cost as a result of being based on overoptimistic estimates of domestic costs of production and transport. This is suggested by anomalies in the table itself—if Minenergo in Leningrad had to pay 26.9 rubles/ton of standard fuel for coal, that casts doubt on the production and transport cost coefficients which went into a linear programming problem that concluded additional coal could have been supplied to the region at 22 to 24 rubles per ton of standard fuel.

There is also a lot of evidence that costs in the energy-producing sectors have risen in the seventies far more than anyone anticipated—the ZZ were based on expectations of costs in the seventies that have proved false. In the oil industry the finding charges introduced in 1976 have turned out to be far less than actual finding costs. One source says that in oil and gas they cover only about one-fourth of the actual finding costs (*Finansy SSSR* 1979:8, p. 19). The pricing system introduced for oil in 1976 involved partial acceptance of the principle of marginal cost pricing and collected rent through a centralized charge. But average costs rose enough that from 1979 centrally collected rent charges were dropped altogether, and rent was redistributed within the branch to cover high cost producers (*Ekonomicheskaia Gazeta* 1980:17, p. 10). To offset rising costs further, in the same year the fixed capital charge for oil producers was dropped from the economywide 6 percent to 3.9 percent (*Ekonomika neftianoi promyshlennosti*, 1980:8, p. 2). In the 1979 plan coal-mining enterprises were scheduled to make a loss of 1 BR (billion rubles), and in order to cover this and certain outlays that should be considered costs (though they are covered out of profits in Soviet accounting such as certain incentive funds), the total subsidy to coal-mining enterprises was to be 2.2 BR (*Finansy SSSR* 1979:8, p. 20). I have seen less discussion of these issues for gas, but the situation there must be about the same. As new versions of the ZZ have been produced since the early seventies, the level of ZZ has consistently been corrected in an upward direction. For example, there exist two sets of ZZ for the period after 1980, the set published at the same time as the 1975 to 1980 set and one published more recently (in Makarov 1979, p. 240). The latter tends to be almost double the earlier projection.

It also appears that ZZ have been figured in a context that considers only domestic demand. It will be remembered that in my earlier description of how ZZ are calculated nothing was said about export as one of the demand constraints to be met. It may still be that some planned amount of export requirements are figured in as one of the demand constraints in the linear programming problem and that the sources simply omit to mention that. But quite clearly the price obtainable on the world market has not been considered in the opportunity cost calculation. As a relatively small contributor to international trade in energy products the U.S.S.R. is a price taker, and the real cost of oil to Soviet users is the world market price. In a period when world market prices have been rising rapidly, the ZZ would have to be much higher if they really were to reflect the opportunity cost of using in the domestic economy energy products that could be exported.

Most Soviet energy policy-makers are reluctant to accept the world market price as the opportunity cost of oil for domestic calculations. Makarov mentions the question of export prices explicitly:

In forming the ZZ for fuel, a certain role could be played in some cases by fuel export. In the situation which has developed after the energy crisis in the capitalist countries of the West, when the capacity of the external market has significantly exceeded export, and the export effectiveness for certain kinds of fuel is extremely high, theoretically export can sometimes fulfill the function of the marginal user. ZZ for the corresponding kinds of fuel (oil, for example) can in principle be determined taking account of foreign market prices. (Makarov 1979, p. 231).

He asserts that considering the potential gain from export would *not* change the valuations as he has calculated them. What is implied here is that the opportunity cost of replacing high quality fuel with the closing fuel is as high as the opportunity cost of foregoing exports (p. 232). This argument, however is difficult to accept.

Other sources either imply or assert that considering export value *would* make a big difference. For example, there has long been a controversy as to the proper valuation for gas permanently invested in an artificial underground storage reservoir, in the calculations the project makers make concerning the design of the reservoir (see, for example, *Gazovaia promyshlennost'* 1979:6, pp. 22–24). For a storage reservoir of given active capacity and daily productivity, the amount of gas that must be left permanently in the reservoir can be varied, depending on the amount of compressor capacity, the number of wells, and other variables chosen in the design. Gosstroi SSSR has issued an instruction to the effect that in design decisions for these reservoirs, the gas permanently invested in the reservoir should be valued at the ZZ approved for the 1975 to 1980 period corrected by a coefficient of 2 to take account of the difference between domestic prices and world market prices (*Ekonomika gazovoi promyshlennost*, 1979, vol. 9, p. 25. This instruction was issued January 11, 1979). As another example of the disjunction between ZZ and transactions prices, in actually costing the investment in gas once the design is chosen, however, the gas will be valued at 6 rubles per thousand cubic meters or about 5 rubles per ton of standard fuel, though the ZZ for gas in the European U.S.S.R. is about 22 to 25 rubles per ton of standard fuel.

In constrast to the oil industry within the gas industry there seems to be a well-established view that domestic uses of oil and gas conflict with export potential and that the export price rather than the cost of replacing gas with coal should be used as the relevant opportunity cost in setting the ZZ. This view has been especially strongly set forth in two places—Vainshtein et al. (1978a, pp. 19–27) and Vainshtein et al. (1978b). The latter is most interesting

Table 14.2
Revisions of ZZ for post-1980 period

	Coal		Gas		*Mazut*	
	Original	Revised	Original	Revised	Original	Revised
Northwest	19–22	35–37	22–24	41–43	21–23	46.2–47.6
Murmansk Oblast'	21–23	36–38	25–28	44–46	24–26	na
Komi ASSR	12–14	24–26	15–18	32–34	14–17	na
Center	18–21	34–36	22–24	40–42	21–23	46.2–47.6
Central Blackearth	19–21	33–35	22–24	41–43	21–24	46.2–47.6
North Caucasus	20–22	32–34	21–23	41–43	20–22	46.8–48.9
Middle Volga	17–19	30–32	20–22	37–39	18–21	44.8–46.9
Lower Volga	18–20	32–34	20–23	38–40	20–22	44.8–46.9
North Ural	14–16	25–28	18–20	34–36	17–19	44.8–46.9
South Ural	13–16 (12–14)	25–27 (23–26)	18–20	35–37	17–19	44.8–46.9
Kemerovo Oblast' & Altai Krai	8–10	15–17	14–17	25–27	14–16	44.8–46.9
Novosibirsk & Tomsk oblast'	9–12	17–19	14–17	25–28	13–16	44.8–46.9
Omsk Oblast'	11–14 (10–12)	20–22 (13–15)	14–17	27–30	13–16	44.8–46.9
Krasnoiarsk Krai	9–11	13–15	14–17	27–29	13–16	44.8–46.9
Irkutsk Oblast'	7–9	14–16	12–15	21–24	11–13	44.8–46.9
Transbaikal	9–10	10–18	—	—	13–14	na
Amursk Oblast'	11–13	18–20	—	—	17–19	48.3–49.6
Khabarovsk Krai	12–14	20–22	17–20	27–29	16–18	48.3–49.6

Table 14.2 (continued)

	Coal		Gas		*Mazut*	
	Original	Revised	Original	Revised	Original	Revised
Primorsk Krai	16–18	18–20	—	30–33	19–21	48.3–49.6
East Ukraine & Rostov oblast'	19–21	31–33	22–24	40–43	21–23	46.8–48.3
West Ukraine & Moldavia	20–23	33–35	24–26	43–45	23–25	46.8–48.3
Belorussia & Lithuania	20–23	35–37	23–25	43–45	22–25	(29–33)
Latvia & Estonia	21–23	36–38	24–26	43–45	23–26	(30–34)
Georgia	21–24	33–35	21–24	43–45	20–23	46.8–48.3
Armenia & Azerbaidzhan	21–24	35–37	20–23	42–44	20–22	46.8–48.3
Turkmenistan	14–16	22–24	14–17	28–30	14–16	46.8–48.3
Uzebekistan	14–16	20–22	15–17	29–32	15–17	46.8–48.3
Tadzhikistan	14–16	23–25	15–18	31–33	15–18	46.8–48.3
Kirgiziia	13–15	24–26	16–18	30–32	15–17	46.8–48.3
West Kazakhstan	—	29–31	16–19	33–35	16–18	44.8–46.2
Northeast Kazakhstan	9–12 (7–10)	16–18 (10–12)	19–22	30–33	18–21	44.8–46.2
South Kazakhstan	12–14 (9–12)	18–20 (13–15)	18–21	31–33	18–20	44.8–46.2

Sources: Original figures from ANSSSR (1973, p. 13). Revised figures for coal and gas from Makarov (1979, p. 240). Revised figures for *mazut* from Makarov (1979, p. 240), except those in parentheses, which are from the same source, p. 241.
Note: Alternative figures in parentheses assume that Ekibastuz coal could be used in the given region.

because it is accompanied by an extensive discussion that provides some clues as to how well Soviet economists understand the issue. At the time the authors wrote, the world market price for oil was $11.50 per barrel, or $80.50 per ton. (They also looked at export prices for gas but their premises on that matter are less fully explored.) They assert that these world market prices imply an opportunity cost and hence a ZZ of 100 to 135 rubles per ton of standard fuel for oil and gas used domestically (compared to the official ZZ of 20 to 25 rubles per ton). The translation into rubles of the opportunity cost of foregoing exports is figured by means of what the Russians call the "import equivalent," a ruble/dollar conversion ratio conceptualized as the number of rubles of domestic outlays saved by a dollar's worth of imports. Unfortunately, I know of no discussions stating clearly what the value of the import equivalent is currently considered to be, nor do I know whether it is calculated as a marginal concept or as an average concept. But the values quoted imply that these authors consider the value of the import equivalent to be in the range 1.78 to 2.42, which is consistent with the conversion coefficient used in the Gosstroi instruction.

Given what has happened to world market prices since the time of the study by Vainshtein et al., it is clear that the current level of ZZ for oil are many times below the real opportunity cost of oil where the world market is considered. In view of the fact that there is now talk of importing oil, it is even harder than before to find any justification for not considering foreign trade in energy as an aspect of optimizing the fuel and energy balance. As a corollary, if the ZZ now being published for the post-1980 period (see table 14.2) are at all reasonably close to the domestic marginal cost of production of the closing fuels, then oil and gas are being badly misallocated, and the production mix is a long way from optimum. That is, if the ZZ for coal in a given region is in fact reasonably close to the cost of producing and shipping coal to that region from a source whose output could be expanded, oil being used in that region should be exported and replaced with gas or even coal. Table 14.2 indicates ZZ for coal in the European part of the U.S.S.R. at about 50 rubles per natural ton compared to an opportunity cost of foregoing oil exports of something in the range of 200 to 300 rubles per natural ton (if the world price is $30 per barrel and the import equivalent is 1 to 1.5).

There is some recognition of the desirability of internal substitution to free oil for export in a statement by Academician Styrikovich (*EKO* 1979:11, p. 87). He says that, given the disparity between world price ratios and the domestic opportunity cost as expressed by ZZ, the U.S.S.R. should maintain oil exports by substituting coal and gas in domestic uses. Of course that shift can be made only over a fairly lengthy period of time, but, given that the ZZ are explicitly intended for investment decisions, it is precisely through them these scarcity relationships should be communicated.

The discussion of the Vainshtein proposal in the Khachaturov series (1978b) is especially interesting as a test of how Soviet planners react to the suggestion that world market prices should influence domestic calculations. Some of the group who commented on the proposal can accept it (A. A. Beschinskii and some of the other energy economists, for example) but others are very dubious. One of the Gosplan representatives, for example, cannot quite accept the logic that the world market price should determine the extensive and intensive margin in oil development, and that this would require new ZZs and prices for coal and all other energy resources, which would then force still more cost and price changes throughout the whole economy (pp. 94–95). The basic sticking point of course is a reluctance to let the world price structure affect domestic decisions. As V. P. Krasovskii says, the authors' proposal to push out both the intensive and extensive margins of oil output on the basis of world market prices "is justified, in relation to export. . . . But the extension of this practice outside the framework of export markets and its transfer to internal markets is unacceptable" (Vainshtein 1978b, p. 97). Makarov and Melent'ev, in a recent statement (*Planovoe Khoziaistvo* 1980:4, p. 89) take this same position, saying that high world market prices for oil "raise the economic attraction of fuel export, though conditions on the world market cannot, in our view, directly influence the development of our energy policy."

As another suggestion that the planners who established the ZZs have overoptimistic perspectives on energy costs, they originally expected that energy costs would fall between the tenth FYP and the eleventh, and hence the ZZs originally forecast in the early seventies for 1981 to 1985, and included in the official Gosplan directives for using ZZs in planning, were appreciably below those approved for 1975 to 1980. Since then, however, the ZZs projected for the period after 1980 were raised sharply. The differences are shown in table 14.2—note that the new ZZs are above the old generally by about 75 percent for coal and by as much as three and four times for gas and *mazut* in some regions.

Makarov suggests that there were two reasons for this adjustment. The first was the rise in the cost of producing and transporting coal, which in its role as the closing fuel basically determined the ZZs. There have supposedly been big increases in labor costs in coal mining in the late 1970s because of special incentives offered to miners, increases in equipment costs, the introduction of practices to reduce environmental externalities (Makarov 1979, p. 238). There is abundant evidence in other sources as well that coal-mining costs have risen rapidly since the 1967 price reform. The prices were set in 1967 to generate significant profits for coal. Yet by 1976 coal industry profit had dropped to zero, and in the Ukraine there were significant losses (Guren 1976, p. 78).

The second was the growing relative scarcity of *mazut*, which meant that it would increasingly have to be reserved for the highest priority applications (basically to cover peak load needs in power generation) where its advantage over coal (the closing fuel) was greater than in the closing uses originally envisaged and underlying the 1975 to 1980 ZZ values (base-load condensing stations).

What is puzzling, however, is that, in the recalculation and upward adjustment of the 1981 to 1985 ZZs compared to those published earlier, the valuations for gas seem to have been raised slightly more than those for coal (what is relevant here is the absolute gap which measures the relative advantage). Since the gas situation is likely to be somewhat less tight than the coal situation, I would think that gas will, if anything, be making its way into uses where its relative advantage over coal is less than it was previously. Another interesting sidelight on the changing situation is that with the shift in the regional distribution of gas production and the rise in transport cost, the *privedennye zatraty* for gas, in most regions based on the directions of flow that seem optimal, are now about as high as the current ZZs (see Furman 1978, pp. 22–30). That would imply that gas no longer is earning a significant differential rent compared with the other closing fuel, coal. Of course, as I explained earlier, even the revised ZZs are well below the correct opportunity cost valuation considering world prices, and gas production surely still earns very large rents.

14.2 Motor Fuels

Apparently very little effort has ever been made by Soviet energy policymakers to consider explicitly the link between prices for boiler and furnace fuel and prices for motor fuel. There are no official ZZ for motor fuel, and so far as I can tell, none are estimated even unofficially for any of the motor fuels. As one small exception, Makarov provides ZZ for various refinery fractions—gasoline, diesel, and heavy (Makarov 1979, p. 342), presumably for after 1980. He says the ZZ for light fractions are the costs of getting additional products of this kind by using secondary refining processes to shift the refinery mix away from *mazut* to lighter products. Presumably in this calculation he uses the new ZZs in figuring the cost in *mazut*. His figures show ZZ well above the current gasoline prices—for example, 103 to 107 rubles per ton in the European U.S.S.R. verous the 78 rubles per ton that was the transaction price for gasoline of grade A-66 up to 1982 (Campbell 1976, p. 71). He gives 94 to 97 rubles per ton for diesel fuel, compared to the 66 rubles per ton set in 1967, though this disparity was somewhat eased when diesel fuel prices were raised in 1970 (Belousov 1971, p. 42—unfortunately I don't know how *much* they were raised).

Consistently, with the lack of any interest in ZZs for motor fuel, the interrelated questions of total crude oil output, the refinery split between motor fuel and *mazut*, and the mix between *mazut* and other boiler and furnace fuels are not explicitly considered in any of this literature. What economic rationality calls for is determination of the optimal output of oil. The optimal amount is that which, when refined into the two main classes in the proper proportions, will equate the marginal cost of *mazut* with alternatives in the boiler and furnace fuel market and the marginal cost of motor fuel, either with its marginal productivity or the cost of such alternatives as electric power for railroad traction. In general, achieving this equilibrium should require adjusting both the output level of crude oil and the refinery split between motor fuel and *mazut*. (This description of the problem would be slightly modified if we introduce the possibility of exporting crude oil or products as well as using them domestically.) My impression is that in Soviet practice the refinery split is taken as more or less given by tradition or by the capacities of current refinery equipment and enough crude oil is produced to generate the amount of motor fuel considered necessary, given the customary split. In this situation the supply of *mazut* then emerges as an afterthought. The kind of test of the outcome that the fuel planners ought to be making, especially today when they are losing their ability to control the level of crude oil output, is whether the value of refined products that could be produced by reducing the output of residual fuel oil from the current volume of refinery runs by one ton, corrected for processing cost, is more or less than the ZZ for a ton of *mazut*. A comparison of the value of refinery products with the cost of crude oil is often suggested in Soviet discussions about whether it is profitable to produce an additional ton of crude oil in some marginal fashion. That is, proposals for intensifying production at the internal margin are often tested by asking whether the value of extra products thus made available, less processing costs, is more or less than the cost of the marginal output of crude oil. For example, a recent article (*Ekonomika neftianoi promyshlennosti* 1980:2, pp. 6–9) chooses among alternative variants for tertiary recovery by this approach. A novel feature of the example cited is the use of wholesale prices for light products but ZZ for *mazut*. Nevertheless, despite the relatively common use of this kind of a test for measures proposed to increase output of crude oil, I have seen only one case applying the same reasoning to refining, in which the depth of refining and the opportunity cost of residual fuel oil was brought into the discussion.

14.3 Electric Power Production and Use

Electric power stations transform various forms of fuel into electric power. In the U.S.S.R. where cogeneration (what the Russians call *teplofikatsia*) is extensively used to capture by-product heat from power generation, hot-water and low potential steam are an important secondary output of the electric power sector. In thinking about the effect of price on economic decisions in this area, we should consider two stages. First, we consider the reactions of the electric power industry as we would any other final user. That is, we wonder whether the pricing of alternative fuels is such as to lead to the right fuel mix in power generation and whether the price of fuel in general is set at the correct level to induce optimal efforts toward reducing the heat rate. (We leave aside here the more complicated issues of the role nuclear and hydro generation might play as alternative to fossil fired power and heat generation.) Second, we consider how the outputs of this process are priced—are heat and electric power properly priced so that, when decision-makers face the alternative of meeting some need either by using electric power or by direct fuel use, prices offer the appropriate guidance, and similarly, when they are faced with meeting some need for low potential heat either by using by-product heat from cogeneration plants or from direct fuel use, will they be able to make the right choice?

Electric power is a high-quality energy form, produced from other forms at a large energy loss, and it is sometimes possible to obtain very large energy savings by using the primary form rather than electricity. The classic example of a wasteful chain is burning gas in a power station to produce electric power for residential space heating, as opposed to using gas directly for space heating. The big issue here is whether the prices of electricity and heat are high enough to convey to users the energy loss inherent in the conversion in power stations.

This is a very complicated set of issues, and I want to deal with only some aspects of it, and in a somewhat summary way. There *are* numerous innovations that could be made to reduce the heat rate in Soviet fossil-fired power stations. My thesis, however, is that there are already strong forces leading to conservation of energy in electric power stations and that pricing is not the main force underlying this decision. Soviet power industry decision-makers seem to have achieved an impressively low heat rate, largely because of two

Table 14.3
ZZ for electric power, 1975 to 1980 (rubles per megawatt hour, or kopecks per 10 kilowatt hours)

	Baseload supply[a]			Peakload supply[b]
	Total	Fuel cost	Other	
Center	12–13	7.5–8	4.5–5	33–37
Middle Volga	11–12	7–7.5	4–4.5	32–35
South	12–13	6.5–7.5	5.5	34–37
Northwest	12–13	7–8	5	34–38
Ural	11.5–12	4.5–5.5	7–6.5	32–36
North Caucasus	11–12	6.5–7.5	4.5	34–37
Transcaucasia	11–12	6.5–7.5	4.5	33–37
Siberia	7.5–8	1	6.5–7	12–13
North Kazakhstan	10–11	2.5–3.5	7.5	18–19
Central Asia	10.5–11.5	5–6	5.5	21–23
Far East	12–14	5–6	7–8	23–24

Source: These ZZ are available in ANSSSR (1973, p. 19), except for the breakdown into fuel cost and other which is from Makarov (1973, p. 111).
[a] 7,000 hours per year.
[b] 1,000 hours per year.

main technical policies that have been followed in system design—cogeneration and the introduction of supercritical temperatures and pressures. My suspicion is that in both these areas decisions have probably been biased toward excessive substitution of capital for energy inputs rather than the opposite. Very large investments have been made to effect cogeneration, and, if cogeneration heat rates are compared with those in the best condensing stations, one wonders if it is really economical. It is also relatively easy to show that they have paid very high capital costs (in rubles per kilowatt) in new units to get very little improvement in heat rate. (For documentation of these points see Cambell 1980, chap. 4).

The ZZ system includes prices for electric power, though as shown in table 14.3, electric power ZZ are specified for a much smaller number of regions than is the case for boiler and furnace fuels. These ZZs are said to have been developed by recalculating the cost of power in various regional systems through pricing fuel inputs at the ZZ for the closing fuel in the region.

It is difficult to check how these electric power ZZs compare with the actual charges for power in the various regions, because power is charged for through a multipart rate structure. Industrial consumers with loads below 100 kva, the railroads, agricultural enterprises, and urban transport are charged on the basis of a single-part tariff, while others are billed via a two-part tariff, separately for a measure of load and for actual power consumption. A description of the rate structure used in figuring electricity charges is available in Chernukin (1975, p. 204).

We can, however, compare ZZ with actual rates for some illustrative cases as follows. In the 1975 to 1980 period an industrial user in Moscow who used power in some more or less continuous use, such as electric furnaces, say, would pay 43.10 rubles per kw of installed capacity per year, plus 7.7 kopecks per 10 kwh. Assuming more or less continuous use (7,000 out of the possible maximum 8,760 hours in a year), the charge for the amount consumed by each kilowatt of load would be 53.9 rubles, and the total bill 97 rubles. That would work out at 1.39 kopecks per kwh. This is about the same as the ZZ for the center region in which Moscow is located—12 to 13 kopecks per 10 kwh. At the other extreme a peak user (who used his equipment only 1,000 hours per year) would pay 43.10 rubles per kw of installed capacity plus a consumption charge of 1,000 × 7.7 kopecks per 10 kwh or 7.70 rubles for a total of 50.80 rubles for the 1,000 kwh he had used. That would be 5.1 kopecks per kwh which is well above the ZZ for peak use. Makarov (1979, p. 243) shows some ZZ for customers with 3,000 to 4,000 hours of annual use, and calculations of total charges per kilowatt-hour to customers with this use pattern would be above those ZZs. The lowest single-part tariff in Moscow for the various users, as shown by the following tabulation (kopecks per 10 kwh), are well above the ZZ of 12 to 13 kopecks per 10 kwh, except for agricultural enterprises:

Industry	25
Railroad transport	15
Urban transport	14.5
Agriculture	10

Similar calculations carried out for each of the nine energy systems for which rate structures are given in Chernukhin (1975, p. 204) show the same pattern. Overall it seems warranted to conclude that electric power tends to be priced above the ZZ, rather than below it as we found for gas and *mazut*.

There is some corroboration of this finding in the I'lina-Utkina study. Their tables of economic effectiveness include a few cases in which gas would replace electric power, and these show that, when gas is substituted for electric power (in heat treating furnaces, for example), there is a considerable saving.

This is a significant and somewhat surprising conclusion—it would seem to bias decisions against electric power variants and toward direct-fuel variants in such energy-using processes as furnaces and heat treating, a strange behavior in a society where verbally, at least, the prejudice seems generally to be in favor of electrification! One of the quantitatively most important uses where there is a direct-fuel rather than electric power choice is in the railroads, but, as explained earlier, we do not know the price/ZZ relationship for diesel fuel to compare with that for electric power.

I have never seen any officially approved ZZs for cogenerated heat from power stations, though one source (Beschinskii 1976, p. 93) indicates that they *are* used in various kinds of planning and are calculated by costing the energy in the heat delivered at the cost of the relevant closing fuel in the region concerned. The efficiency of boilers in heat and power combines has averaged about 80 percent in the seventies (Campbell 1979, p. 20). In combination with the data of table 14.1 this would suggest ZZs for the fuel input alone as shown in the following tabulation for a number of representative locations (in rubles per gigacalorie):

Leningrad	3.8–4.2
Moscow	3.7–4.0
Eastern Ukraine	3.3–3.7
Southern Urals	3.0–3.5

It should be emphasized that these would be the ZZ for the fuel component only in the heat, without consideration of the rather considerable outlays on capturing the heat in the power station and delivering it to the customer. I have been unable to find much information on the cost structure of cogeneration heating operations; but an illustrative calculation in Chernukhin (1975, pp. 168–169) shows that nonfuel costs are about one-third the fuel costs. If that is generally the case, the figures listed here would be raised to 4.5 to 5+ rubles per gigacalorie.

The rate structure for cogenerated heat from power stations is a complex one—there is differentiation among the various regional power systems, and variation by characteristics of the heat supplied and by class of customer. But it has been reported in one source that the *average* price for cogenerated steam under the rate structure in effect since 1967 would be about 4.07 rubles per gigacalorie for industrial consumers and 2.85 rubles per gigacalorie for residential housing. Shkatov and Suponitskii (1969, p. 79) and another source shows that for Moscow the range would be from 4.39 to 5.08 rubles per gigacalorie (Chernukhin 1975, p. 205). Considering our estimate of handling here costs, there is an implication that prices for cogenerated heat are fairly closely in line with the corresponding ZZs.

14.4 The Price Reform of 1982

Soviet planners have been aware for several years that transactions prices for energy are well below any concept of cost of either the Marxian or a more sophisticated variety, and at a time when there is a strong campaign for conservation, it was well understood that prices should be raised. An opportunity to do so came with the general reform of prices of January 1, 1982. Some information on the new prices for energy has been released, though not yet enough to present a complete picture of the post-1982 transactions prices. Nevertheless, it is perfectly clear, from both the discussion before the reform and sketchy published information, that the new prices for fuels are still well below the opportunity costs.

The price reform raised coal prices considerably. The new price system for coal is quite complicated, having introduced an elaborate set of discounts and premiums for quality, though it simplified somewhat the zonal system. According to one source the all-industry average of 9.52 rubles per ton under the old prices will rise to 13.48 rubles under the new for a 42 percent increase (*EKO* 1981:6, p. 149). Corrected for heat content, the new average price is about 20 rubles per ton of standard fuel. Since the 20 ruble figure is based on FOB mine prices, it is almost impossible to judge how consistent the new coal prices are with the ZZs for the post-1980 period. To check the correspondence of the ZZ in any given region with the actual delivered price of coal to that region, it would be necessary to have a great deal more information than is available on FOB mine prices, sources for each consuming region, and transportation costs. It seems likely that both the price reform and the calculation of the ZZs were based on essentially the same information regarding coal production costs at the various sources, and in the absence of evidence to the contrary, it is my presumption that transaction prices for coal are not now appreciably out of line with ZZs.

For gas and oil, however, the ZZs include a significant rent element, and we can compare the new prices with ZZs to see how well that rent has been allowed for.

The most detailed information available on the post-1982 prices is for gas. In the "majority of economic regions of the R.S.F.S.R., the Ukraine, and the Baltic Republics" the new price for industrial consumers is 28 rubles per 1,000 cubic metres (about 23.5 rubles per ton of standard fuel) compared to the ZZs of 40 to 46 rubles per ton of standard fuel shown in table 14.2 (*Ekonomika gazovoi promyshlennosti* 1981:12, pp. 15–10). The price in the North Caucasus and in the Transcaucasia will be 25 rubles per ton of standard fuel, compared to ZZs of 40–45 rubles per ton. The same disparity continues across all the regions for which information is given, and in some extreme cases the new prices are less than half the post-1980 ZZs. For example, in Uzbekistan and Turkmenistan the transactions price is 13 rubles compared to a ZZ of 28 to 30 rubles per ton of standard fuel. It is stated that at the old prices the 1980 output had an average price of 17.85 rubles per thousand cubic meters but would have been worth 25.88 rubles per thousand cubic meters at the new prices. It seems very likely that the main consideration of the price setters was to adjust for cost changes rather than to bring prices into line with opportunity costs. Most of the increase of 8 rubles per thousand cubic meters was to cover increases in production and transport costs, reintroduction of the finding charge, and restoration of regular payments of interest on the capital invested in the industry. Of the 10 to 11 billion rubles which the 1980 output would be worth at the new prices, only about 500 million rubles would be paid into the state budget as rent charges.

We also have the word of gas industry economists that these prices reflect inadequately the advantage of gas over coal. As one source says, "Despite repeated proposals by Mingazprom to take account in prices of the effectiveness of using gas compared to coal, and the necessity of seasonal price differentiation, these questions were not solved in the price revisions" (*Ekonomika gazovoi promyshlennosti* 1981 : 12, p. 17).

Very little information has appeared so far on the new prices for residual fuel oil. But all the indications are that they were not raised to anywhere near the level of the ZZs. We know, for instance, that the new price at which crude oil will be sold to refineries, or delivered to export organizations, is a countrywide uniform 30 rubles per ton, or 21 rubles per ton of standard fuel (*EKO* 1981 : 6, p. 150). Given the usual way of costing the joint products that come out of refineries, the *mazut* FOB refinery price is unlikely to be much different from that. One discussion before new prices were actually settled mentioned several alternative price schedules for *mazut* (*Khimiia i tekhnologiia topliv i masel* 1979 : 7, p. 25). Those projected prices are all well below the new post-1980 ZZs shown in table 14.2. For example, table 14.2 shows 42.6 to 47.2 rubles per ton of standard fuel for *mazut* in the northwest, while the new price proposed in the article was 36 rubles per ton. The new price proposed for the central region was only 28.50 rubles per ton of standard fuel compared to a ZZ of 46.2 to 47.6 rubles. There is additional evidence that the new prices on petroleum products are to be kept well below marginal cost, by squeezing out rent in the pricing of crude oil. An interesting and informative article in *Ekonomika neftianoi promyshlennosti* (1980 : 8, pp. 2–4) says that, to adjust to the cost increases that have occurred since 1967, the overall level of crude oil prices had to be raised by 2.3 times. Since that would not be high enough to cover production cost at the margin, however, a notional price five times the current level was also established for use in calculating the effectiveness of investment in new measures to increase petroleum production. The author says explicitly that this notional price is based on *privedennye zatraty* in the highest cost fields to be used in the new Five-Year Plan. (A fuller description of how that cost, described as a *special normativ*, has been calculated is given in *Ekonomika neftianoi promyshlennosti*, 1981:2, pp. 10–12.) Thus someone has calculated that it is justified at the margin to produce oil at a cost 5 times its present level, but the price at which oil goes to refineries will be only 2.3 times the present level. Since in the Soviet cost-based system for setting transaction prices, *mazut* gets priced at approximately the cost of crude oil to refineries, its price will be 2.2 times less than the marginal cost of crude oil. In short, I think that the new prices must still be communicating to Soviet decision-makers signals that will cause them to greatly underestimate the cost and value of energy and especially the cost of petroleum products. The article cited earlier in *Ekonomika neftianoi promyshlennosti* (1980:8) is quite clear on this point. The author (S. M. Levin, who is deputy chief of the economic planning department of the Ministry of the Oil Industry) is dissatisfied with the new system primarily because it fails to signal a price for oil suitable for guiding project makers on the production side to know how far out to push the margin. But he is also aware that the level of price increases now being considered will not communicate to the users the real domestic opportunity cost of *mazut* and other petroleum products and will be inadequate to hasten their replacement with cheaper substitutes.

I am not so sure we have enough evidence to substantiate a judgment that the ZZs are themselves below the true opportunity cost. They may not be much out of line with marginal costs when supply and demand are considered solely in the domestic context. On the other hand, it is almost certain that they are too low in the light of export opportunities and that they will not provide nearly enough encouragement for the project makers in the Soviet system to make the capital investments that will permit conservation of oil and substitution of other energy forms for oil to permit the optimum level of petroleum exports. This should not perhaps be considered a defect of pricing policy per se—pricing policy simply derives from a more fundamental policy decision, not to let the tail of export possibilities wag the domestic energy policy dog. Whether or not that is rational gets us into a broad range of concerns that it would be inappropriate to discuss here. But what comes out the study of the pricing controversies is some direct evidence as to what concept of cost the ZZs *are* communicating. In a recent paper Arthur Wright has provided a useful demonstration that, whether we are talking about Soviet oil exports, or the division of exports between East and West, or the possibility of imports, the important fact is that for the U.S.S.R. the relevant benchmark for the cost and value of oil is the world market price. What the analysis of the ZZ system in this chapter suggests, however, is that the Soviet decision-makers do not necessarily accept that definition of rationality, nor act according to it.

Notes

1. SOPS is the Council for the Study of Productive Forces, under the Gosplan, charged among other things with study of issues of regional differentiation and development.

2. For explanations of the concept of ZZ, and for a history of its development and application, three helpful sources are Makarov and Vigdorchik (1979), Makarov and Melent'ev (1973), and ANSSSR (1973).

3. As indicated in the preceding section, there is a considerable variation in actual transactions prices in any given region depending on source in the case of coal and on quality indicators. In deciding what to use as transactions price in table 14.1, I take what seem to be the most representative sources and quality grades.

References

Books

ANSSSR (Akademiia Nauk SSSR), 1973. Otdelenie fiziko-tekhnicheskikh problem energetiki. *Rukovodiashchie ukazaniia k ispol' zovaniiu zamykaiushchikh zatrat na toplivo i elektricheskuiu energiiu* ("*Instructions for Using Marginal Costs of Fuel and Electric Energy*"). Moscow.

Avrukh, A. Ia., 1970. *Problemy sebestoimosti i tsenoobrazovaniia v energetike* ("*Problems of Cost and Price Formation in Electric Power*"). Moscow.

Belousov, P. A., 1971. *Planirovanie perspektivnykh optovykh tsen* ("*Planning Future Wholesale Prices*"). Moscow.

Beschinskii, A. A., 1976. *Ekonomicheskie problemy elektrifikatsii* ("*Economic Problems of Electrification*"). Moscow.

Campbell, Robert W., 1970. Price, rent, and decision making: The economic reform in Soviet oil and gas production. In H. W. Gottinger (ed.), *Jahrbuch der Wirtschaft Osteuropas*. Munich: Gunter Olzog Verlag.

Campbell, Robert W., 1976. *Trends in the Soviet Oil and Gas Industry*. Baltimore, Md.: Johns Hopkins University Press.

Campbell, Robert W., 1978. *Soviet Energy Balances*, The Rand Corporation R-2257-DOE, December.

Campbell, Robert W., 1979. *Basic Data on Soviet Energy Branches*, The Rand Corporation N-1332-DOE, December.

Campbell, Robert W., 1980. *Soviet Energy Technologies; Planning, Policy, Research and Development.* Bloomington: Indiana University Press.

Furman, I. Ia., 1978. *Ekonomika magistral'nogo transporta gaza* ("*Economics of Gas Transmission*"). Moscow.

Chernukhin, A. A., and Iu. N. Flakserman, 1975. *Ekonomika energetiki SSSR.* ("*Economics of Electric Power in the U.S.S.R.*"). Moscow.

Guren, M. M., 1976. *Voprosy tsenoobrazovaniia* ("*Questions of Price Formation*"). Issue 6. Moscow.

I'lina, E. N., and L. D. Utkina, 1978. *Ekonomicheskaia effektivnost' ispol'zovaniia prirodnogo gaza* ("*Economic Effectiveness of Use of Natural Gas*"). Moscow.

Makarov, A. A., and L. A. Melent'ev, 1973. *Metody issledovanii i optimizatsii energeticheskogo khoziaistva* ("*Methods of Studying and Optimizing the Energy Sector*"). Novosibirsk.

Makarov, A. A., and A. G. Vigdorchik, 1979. *Toplivno-energeticheskii kompleks* ("*The Fuel and Energy Complex*"). Moscow.

Probst, A. E., et al., 1978. *Sravnitel'nye tekhniko-ekonomicheskie pokazateli po dobyche i transportu topliva po raionam SSSR* ("*Comparative Technical-Economic Indicators for Production and Transport of Fuel by Regions of the U.S.S.R.*"). Moscow.

Ryps, G. S., 1979. *Ekonomicheskie problemy raspredeleniia gaza* ("*Economic Problems of Allocating Gas*"). Leningrad.

Shkatov, V. K., and B. S. Suponitskii, 1969. *Optovye tseny na produktsiiu tiazheloi promyshlennosti* ("*Wholesale Prices on the Output of Heavy Industry*"). Moscow.

Torbin, V. I., 1974. *Territorial'naia differentsiatsiia tsen v tiazheloi promyshlennosti* ("*Territorial Differentiation of Prices in Heavy Industry*"). Moscow.

Vainshtein, B. S., A. D. Khaitun and N. M. Sokolov, 1978a. Effektivnost' neftegazovogo kompleksa Zapadnoi Sibiri, ("Effectiveness of the oil and gas complex of western Siberia"). *Voprosy ekonomiki* 10: pp. 19–27.

Vainshtein, B. S., N. M. Sokolov, and A. D. Khaitun, 1978. Ob effektivnosti mezhotraslevykh narodno-khoziaistvennykh kompleksov ("On the effectiveness of Interbranch National-Economic complexes"). In ANSSSR, *Metody i praktika opredeleniia effektivnosti kapital'nykh vlozhenii i novoi tekhniki,* ("*Methods and Practice in Determining the Effectiveness of Capital Investment and New Technology*"). Issue 29. Moscow.

Periodicals

EKO, Ekonomika i organizatsiia promyshlennogo proizvodstva ("*Economics and Organization of Industrial Production*").

Ekonomika gazovoi promyshlennosti ("*Economics of the Gas Industry*").

Ekonomika neftianoi promyshlennosti ("*Economics of the Oil Industry*").

Gazovaia promyshlennost' ("*The Gas Industry*").

Voprosy ekonomiki ("*Questions of Economics*").

Index